Read What People Are Saying About Kevin Trudeau:

Kevin Trudeau gives the best information about everything in life that I will ever need. **He has changed my life to become the best, forever.** *My wishes are coming true and are truly at my command.* Rich Hayden, Palm Springs, California.

I am attracting success based on these time-tested, proven principles. I am taking control of my life. And **I am able to manifest any wish or desire** *in my personal and professional life. This program is an absolute must-have. It has absolutely improved my life in every area, and I would recommend it to everyone without reservation. Absolutely fantastic.* Loren P., Monterey, California.

When I started the **Your Wish is Your Command** *program, I was earning $85,000 a year. Now, three years later,* **I'm earning over $1 million a year.** *This works.*

---

*I was in prison when I learned the "***Your Wish is Your Command***" method. I came out of prison without a penny. Using Kevin's method, I have made over $5 million since leaving prison. I have a company that does over $150 million in annual sales. This works like magic.*

I use the **Your Wish is Your Command** *method to manifest the relationship of my dreams. This is the best thing I've ever done.*

I read The Secret, Think and Grow Rich, Ask and It Is Given, and studied the Law of Attraction and Manifesting Methods for years without getting any results. The **Your Wish is Your Command** *program taught me the secret behind the secret. Within six months after listening to Kevin's program,* **I made more money than I had in the previous six years.** *This is by far the best manifesting course ever created. Kevin teaches things that no one knows, and those missing keys make all the difference.*

In one session with Kevin, I felt layers shed off my body. I walked out of the room feeling lighter, **with complete freedom, and a feeling of overwhelming love and light.**

*Kevin is the greatest and best teacher of this material. He makes everything so clear and easy to apply. After going through the **Your Wish is Your Command** course, I finally had the step-by-step recipe to make my dreams come true. **I manifested a new BMW, a new house, a major promotion with increased income, and I am now debt-free.***

---

*I just had a one-on-one with Kevin. The energy is still bubbling up. It's almost like as if I was a soda that Kevin shook up and then opened. The bubbles are fizzing up and popping. I felt it during the session, and I feel it now. I finally understand the idea of allowing emotions to come up and be released. **This is awesome! I am free.** I feel physically lighter. My digestion has improved. I have so much more energy. I'm not tired when I get home from work. And I only need six hours sleep instead of needing ten.*

---

*The week I spent with Kevin was off the charts, incredible, and amazing. **The best, most impactful event I've ever attended!***

***My life has improved so much** through applying your teachings. It's more than I could have ever dreamed of. Thank you, thank you, thank you.*

---

*Since joining GIN, my life has changed in spectacular ways. I've received everything from a job that has **tripled my yearly income**, happy daily living, negativity immunity, and a beautiful Mercedes, 100% paid for, title in hand. I'm trying to wrap my head around all this, but one thing I know for sure is that it's all because of you and your training and the Global Information Network.*

---

*Since becoming a Partner with Kevin, I feel light and free. I am sleeping better than ever. I feel like being a partner with Kevin is like being **protected by his love and energy**. I am feeling joy like never before.*

---

*I would consider you, Kevin, **a modern Guru and the world's best mentor**. What I have learned from you and applied has created. Tremendous and overwhelming success in my life. I will be your student forever.*

KEVIN TRUDEAU

YOUR WISH IS YOUR COMMAND

HOW TO MANIFEST YOUR DESIRES

THE MISSING SECRETS

Hopefully, the discussion in this book will stimulate reflection and encourage readers to find their own way. Please note, however, the observations and suggestions in this book are made with the understanding that individual circumstances vary, and what works for one person may not be suitable for another. Your journey is uniquely your own, and any transformation or growth you experience is based on your own choices and efforts. Readers are therefore encouraged to use their personal judgment and discretion when applying any of the suggestions or concepts discussed in this book. By reading this book, you acknowledge that you are solely responsible for your well-being and that any actions you take are at your own discretion. **Please take time to read the important statement immediately below**:

THE CONTENTS OF THIS BOOK ARE FOR INFORMATIONAL PURPOSES ONLY. THE AUTHOR AND PUBLISHER DISCLAIM ANY RESPONSIBILITY FOR ANY OUTCOMES, ACTIONS, OR DECISIONS TAKEN AS A RESULT OF READING THIS BOOK. THE INFORMATION CONTAINED IN THIS BOOK IS PROVIDED ON AN "AS IS" BASIS, WITHOUT ANY WARRANTY, EXPRESS OR IMPLIED. IF YOU ARE EXPERIENCING PERSONAL CHALLENGES THAT REQUIRE PROFESSIONAL ASSISTANCE, PLEASE SEEK THE APPROPRIATE SUPPORT FROM A QUALIFIED EXPERT. AND OF COURSE, DO NOT HESITATE TO SEEK EMERGENCY ASSISTANCE WHERE CIRCUMSTANCES WARRANT. NOTHING CONTAINED IN THIS BOOK IS OR SHOULD BE CONSIDERED OR USED AS A SUBSTITUTE FOR PROFESSIONAL ADVICE BY AN APPROPRIATELY CREDENTIALED AND QUALIFIED PROFESSIONAL.

Copy Editing by: Eric Hubler
Page Design by: emcbookdesign.com

Printed in: United States of America

Table of Contents

LESSON 1

You Were Born to Win but Conditioned to Lose

Today is the first day of the rest of your life. You are about to learn secrets to manifesting your desires that up until now have not been made available to the general public. They have been kept as closely guarded secrets of the privileged elite class.

These are secrets I learned as a member of a "secret society" called the Brotherhood. As one of the highest-ranking members of that organization, I had access to members in other secret societies, including Yale University's Skull and Bones, the Bilderberg Group, and Bohemian Grove.

The global privileged elite class, such as royal families, have learned these "secrets to manifesting" and teach them to their children. I have actually been in many palaces around the world actually teaching the children of the rich and powerful these methods of how to use their mind to create their reality.

This is one of the reasons that the rich get richer and the poor get poorer.

The rich KNOW HOW to use their minds to create their reality and manifest their dreams.

Broke people simply do not know HOW to use the power of their mind to manifest goals, dreams, and desires.

That is NOW about to change for YOU.

1

I'd like to personally congratulate you on getting this book, *Your Wish Is Your Command: How to Manifest Your Desires*.

This is a very special book.

You are not reading this by accident.

This book, if you read the entire book, and DO all I tell you to DO, can help you make all of your dreams come true.

This book contains a revolutionary breakthrough in "manifesting methods" that can help you become virtually a success magnet, a money magnet.

If you read the entire book, and if you do what I suggest you do, then you virtually can have your own personal Genie granting you your every wish.

Your dreams can come true.

You can learn how to manifest your desires.

You can learn how to make what you want to happen actually happen in your life.

But there is a reason that up until now, you have not manifested your goals and dreams.

You were actually BORN to succeed. You are a creative being. You are powerful beyond your understanding. You can virtually COMMAND your wishes to manifest. This is not theory. This is science. Quantum physics has now proven this is true.

But you have been CONDITIONED to fail.

First, your DNA contains all the negative COUNTER-SUCCESS INTENTIONS from your ancestors. Science has proven that your DNA does, in fact, contain "energy" from your ancestors. Postulates, affirmations, declarations, decisions, and beliefs that LIMIT and STOP you from succeeding in life and manifesting your dreams are encoded in your DNA.

Reading this book WILL start to deprogram your DNA and start to reduce or eliminate those counter-intentions that are preventing and stopping success from becoming your reality.

In addition to your DNA programming, your MIND has been programmed for failure from the moment you were conceived in the womb. Throughout your life, you have been told things like:
  – You are not good enough.
  – You are not smart enough.
  – You are a loser.
  – Stop being a dreamer.
  – You can't do that.
And many more.

As you read this book, you will be DEPROGRAMMED from these FAILURE programs. These will start to be reduced and eliminated.

This book could produce miraculous results for you. It is unlike any book you have ever read on success.

It comes directly from the live training I gave to a group of about 100 people many years ago.

We were in the Swiss Alps, in between Switzerland, Bavaria, and Austria, at a private luxury compound, people paid $50,000 to come for a weekend and learn this information from me.

I recorded all of the sessions.

I then went into the studio, edited those sessions, and created an audio series. Originally, it was on CDs.

Today, people from all over the world have purchased this audio series and have paid up to $1,000.

The results reported from those who listened to the audios or attended the live event are nothing more than spectacular and amazing.

THOUSANDS of people from around the world have listened to that audio series and reported that their entire lives have improved in major ways. People have reported making more money, thinking about what they want and having it manifest, finding love, losing weight—virtually having their own personal Genie that is granting their every wish.

Now you have in your hand the book version of this material.

This book is already being called the *Think and Grow Rich* of our time.

This book will provide you with information on how to manifest your dreams, how to make your dreams come true, and how to help you get what you want in life.

The first four Lessons cover basic, foundational information.

As you're reading Lessons 1, 2, 3, and 4, you may think, "Wow, we're spending a lot of time on some foundational material."

There's a reason why.

Unless you have a strong foundation on some very key, specific, basic information, you will never be able to get full benefit from the program.

So as you're reading the first four Lessons, understand that these basics, these foundational principles, are virtually a very vital and overlooked key to your success.

I'm going to give you a couple helpful hints.

If you want to get the most benefit out of this program, read this entire book as fast as possible.

You want to complete this book in at least fourteen days or sooner, if possible.

The faster you read the book, the more intensively you read and concentrate on the book, the more benefits you will get.

This program is not only going to give you information and teach you some techniques on how to manifest your dreams, goals, and desires.

It's going to virtually reprogram you for success.

It's going to turn you into a success magnet.

It's going to make you a money magnet.

It's going to change your vibration or your frequency, so you start attracting good things in your life.

Some of you reading this book may feel like you have a black cloud over your head or you're unlucky. Things don't go your way. You have a hard time holding onto money. Your health is always challenged. You always have little catastrophes going on in your life. You never seem to make any progress. You're struggling to make your dreams come true. You don't see a way out.

This book is going to change that for you.

Read this book as fast as possible. Finish it in at least fourteen days.

When you do, things are going to change in your life.

Your luck is going to radically change. You are going to become luckier just by reading this book.

This is because the words in this book are infused with energy. The ways the words are phrased are done in such a way that they will subconsciously "reprogram" your brain for success. This will happen automatically as you read the book.

The method includes patterns of phrases that "reprogram your subconscious" and bypass your analytical mind. The word patterns in the book include hypnotic language patterns that bypass the analytical mind that resists change. There are embedded commands that "tell" your subconscious to release your success potential.

This powerful technique is not in any other success book you may have read. Reading this book will reduce, and in some cases, fully eliminate, the counter-intentions that are in your DNA and mind that are preventing you from manifesting your goals and dreams.

Engrams, or energetic imprints, called samskaras in the East, CONTROL your thoughts, actions, and words. They control you with uncontrollable and sometimes irrational emotions, thoughts, and actions that self-sabotage your success.

These act as COUNTER-INTENTIONS to your CURRENT intention to manifest your goals and dreams.

Words, phrases, and concepts are repeated in this book using a method known as "spaced repetition."

As you read the book, without any effort on your part, your vibration or frequency will change. This is because your subconscious mind starts to change. Your "programming" starts to change.

The vibration of your DNA starts to change. This means you start to become a success "attractor field" that virtually ATTRACTS what you want into your life.

Your "attractor field" will change in a positive way so that you will start attracting into your life more of what you want!

I'm going to reprogram you for success just by you reading this powerful, life-changing book.

People who have gone through this program have seen amazing results.

As I mentioned, tens of thousands of people all around the world have purchased the audio version of this program and paid as much as $1,000.

The people who were in the live event in the Alps paid $50,000 to attend.

And every one of those people's lives today is radically changed.

Many of them have become millionaires.

If you want more money. If you want to be luckier.

If you want to win at gambling.

If you want to bring in the love of your life and have a passionate, romantic, loving relationship.

If you want to have power and control in your life.

If you want to feel secure and confident and have an amazing sense of certainty.

If you want to have more courage.

If you want to have better health and more dynamic energy.

If you want to make more money.

If you want to have money come to you, as if by magic …

Read this book as fast as possible.

It is being called the *Think and Grow Rich* of our time.

It is a revolutionary breakthrough in success development.

I want you to know that your dreams and goals can come true.

Napoleon Hill said it best:

"Whatever the mind of man can conceive and bring itself to believe, it can achieve."

Whatever dreams you have, you can make them come true.

This program is going to start helping you achieve all of your goals and dreams.

Henry Ford made a very powerful statement. He said,

"If you think you can or if you think you can't, either way, you're right. It's the thinking that makes it so."

Some of you who are reading this right now may not even finish the entire book.

You are a quitter. Winners NEVER quit. And quitters NEVER win.

If you are a quitter, it is odd that you wonder why you don't have your dreams and goals in your life.

You wonder why you're struggling financially.

Successful people are always willing to do what the other guys are NOT willing to do.

Successful people are always DOING what the other guys are still talking about.

You have in your hands exactly what you have been asking for! Your WISH HAS BEEN GRANTED.

DON'T BLOW IT!

Your ship has finally come in.

Take advantage of what you have in your hands.

Some of you realize that you're not reading this by accident. Some of you know that you're at the right place at the right time.

Some of you have been praying and hoping for an opportunity, and realize this book could be it.

Do your best to read at least one or two Lessons every single day until you finish the book. You WILL see amazing results in your life.

And you will start feeling different.

You'll start becoming luckier.

Your eyes will be open to the possibilities.

And in a few short months or a few short years, your life will be radically changed.

Then you'll be one of the thousands and thousands and thousands of people that have already written me, telling me their amazing success stories because they went through the material in this book and applied the information.

So the bottom line is this.

READ THIS BOOK NOW!

Read it QUICKLY.

Finish the book in at least fourteen days, sooner if possible.

Just by reading this book, your life will be improved.

If you apply the information in this book, you can virtually make any dream you want become a reality. It's happening for people all over the world.

Why not you? And why not right now?

I want you to really integrate this material into your life and see spectacular results for yourself.

I want you to make all your dreams come true.

I want you to get the desires of your heart. So I want to help you.

After you finish reading this book, you will qualify for an ALL-EXPENSE paid luxury five-day cruise with ME. This is where you can meet me personally and thousands of other people just like you who have read this book and want more out of life.

This cruise would normally cost over $10,000 per person, but YOU can get it 100% FREE.

The reason I am offering you this gift is because I want to personally mentor people who are serious about making their goals and dreams come true. I want to help WINNERS get more out of life.

But you MUST read this entire book first.

Sound too good to be true? Well, it is true.

See, just by getting this book, your luck has already changed! Good things are ALREADY starting to happen in your life.

At the end of this book, you will learn more.

This book will change your life if you engage.

Enjoy *Your Wish Is Your Command.*

Remember, *all of your dreams can come true.*

Just *don't let anyone steal your dreams.*

LESSON 2

WHO Do You LISTEN To?

Today, we're going to be talking about how to make all your dreams come true—how to manifest whatever desire that you have.

And make those desires actually happen in your life.

And most importantly, make those desires happen incredibly fast.

Today, we're going to be talking about how all of you can have your own Aladdin's Lamp. And how all of you, at any time you want in your life, can call forth your own Genie who can grant you your every wish.

Now, that sounds like a tall order, I know, but it's true.

The fact is that SOME people around the world HAVE manifested their goals and dreams in record time with what appears to be little or no effort.

There are millions of people around the world that live in multi-million-dollar homes, drive cars like Rolls-Royces or Mercedes, and make millions a year in income.

What one person has done, YOU can do also. These other people are not "special." They are not smarter than you. They are not more talented. They used their MIND to create their physical reality, either by deliberate conscious intent, or unknowingly.

By the end of this book, you will KNOW exactly HOW to, by DELIBERATE INTENT, create your reality and manifest your goals and dreams.

As you read this book, you might start to have questions. Write your questions down. You will find that as you continue to read the book, your questions will be answered.

Now let's talk about how to manifest your desires, how to make whatever desire you want happen, and happen fast, with incredible speed.

One of your desires may be to have a lot of money.

Or to have nicer cars, to have a nicer home.

Many people who were at the live event where I taught this material were blown away by the people I introduced them to, such as members of royal families, billionaires, and major international celebrities.

Many in attendance were blown away by the luxurious opulence of the location, the castle, and the hundreds of millions in antiques and artwork.

They were like, "I want this!"

"I want the castle."

"I want the Rolls-Royces. I want the Ferraris."

"And I want the helicopters."

"And I want the luxury cuisine. And the private chefs and the butlers."

"And I want the clothes and the jewelry."

"And oh, my God!"

"I want the lifestyle. I want the freedom."

"I want to not have to go to work every day."

Every one of you reading this has different desires and dreams in terms of monetary things, material things. Obviously, with money, you can do a lot of things.

I am going to be talking about how to achieve your desires, and one of those desires may be money or some material things. Other desires might be better health, a romantic relationship, happiness or inner joy, or spiritual freedom.

I am going to teach you the steps so that you can get whatever you desire and want in life, and to make that happen fast.

There are many people teaching "how to manifest" or things like the "Law of Attraction."

With all the success gurus out there, WHO SHOULD YOU LISTEN TO?

This is the NUMBER ONE most important concept when it comes to making your dreams come true.

If you listen to the wrong person, you could get the "wrong directions" and NEVER get to your destination.

If you listen to the wrong person, you may never get the correct "recipe" or "formula" for success and thus NEVER MANIFEST YOUR DREAMS.

If you go to the library or go online and Google search "How to manifest" or something similar, there are virtually thousands of books on the subject. Not just in English, but in hundreds of languages.

In fact, in every language, there are thousands of books available on "manifesting," or the Law of Attraction, or how to be successful, or how to set and achieve goals.

Many authors from around the world have written books on these "success" subjects. Many of them were translated into English, but thousands were not.

So there are books written in the Russian language about "how to manifest." There are books in Chinese. There are books written in Japanese, Hindi, Spanish, and German.

There are THOUSANDS of books written on the subjects of "how to manifest," "the Law of Attraction," "how to be successful," "how to make money," "how to get what you want," and other such subjects in EVERY language, all around the world.

The point is there are THOUSANDS of authors who speak English as their first language that have written books on this subject, but there are thousands MORE authors that have written books on this subject in languages other than English that English-speaking people will never know about.

The bottom line is, there's a lot of information out there that's been published in books about this subject of manifesting.

There's also a huge amount of information that has been recorded in audios, videos, and home-study courses.

And there's a lot of information presented in live lectures, workshops, or seminars by various people on how to make your dreams come true.

I was just listening recently to an audio series available as a digital download on the internet, produced by a very well-known group. I'm not going to mention their name. I don't want to down anybody in particular, but this was a multi-hour audio series.

They sold it for $5,000.

The goofy thing is, and I say this with all due respect, you listen to various people talking about how to make your dreams come true, how to manifest your desires, how to make your wishes, your hopes, actually manifest in the physical universe right before your eyes, how to make whatever you want to have happen, happen.

When you read these books or listen to these people, a lot of the stuff actually sounds pretty good. A lot of it is amazingly logical, and it sounds good.

The problem is, you begin to believe what you're hearing.

Now, here's the challenge.

If that stuff really worked that those people are teaching, has it worked for *them*?

Do they have their desires?

Do they have, in their life, what they want?

Do they have Aladdin's **Lamp**?

Do they have their **Genie** that they can ask whatever they want and it magically happens in their life?

Does what they want actually occur in their life?

And the answer is amazingly, overwhelmingly, with rare exception, NO!

The people that are teaching you are teaching you theory.

They're not giving you information that really works in real life. They are not teaching things that really work in real life because, quite frankly, they don't know. They got almost all their information from simply reading other people's books, and they are just repeating what others wrote before.

They are not teaching from personal experience. They have not made millions FIRST BEFORE they teach YOU how to make money.

They have not had decades of successfully manifesting their goals and dreams BEFORE they wrote a book on manifesting.

They don't have the evidence themselves that what they're teaching actually works.

When I taught this live in the Alps to a hundred people who paid $50,000 each to attend, the wealth and opulence were beyond anyone's imagination.

They were just blown away. The opulence, the Alps, the luxury accommodations.

The facility we were in is not available to the public.

You know that that kind of luxury, wealth, and opulence is something that the public never really sees.

Cameras are not allowed. The media is not allowed.

You're not going to see that kind of location and those facilities on *Lifestyles of the Rich and Famous* because we don't give access. It's almost too opulent.

Now, when you think about that, what those people were looking at and personally experiencing is the real physical manifestation of various people's hopes, dreams, and desires that have actually been created in real life.

They were seeing it with their own eyes and touching it with their own hands.

It's easier for them to have a high level of belief and confidence that this stuff really works because they were seeing that these "manifesting" methods WORKED and actually produced REAL RESULTS. This was NOT theory.

Those in attendance also met a bunch of the billionaires, members of royal families, and celebrities that came to the event because they were friends of mine and they wanted to "sharpen their axe" and get a refresher on the "manifesting techniques." They also were there to be in my presence.

The most important FIRST question you must ask is, **"Who do you listen to and why should you listen to me, and why should you believe what I'm going to be sharing with you in this book?"**

As you read this book, you are going to be exposed to information that is going to be different and unique than what you maybe learned or experienced before regarding this subject.

You may begin to question what I am sharing. You may ask, "Is this really true? Does this really work? Should I really listen to this guy?"

You were not at the live event where I first taught this and on which this book is based. If you were there, it would be easy to see that what I am going to teach you works. It is the real thing. It is not theory.

Now, I have thousands of letters and emails from people all over the world who have listened to the audio version of *Your Wish Is Your Command*, all sharing how, by using the techniques and methods that you will soon learn, they manifested all their goals and dreams.

THIS WORKS, IF YOU WORK IT.

This works amazingly well. And it works for everyone who applies it.

You will find it is easy to apply.

It's easy to learn.

Will you apply it?

I do not know.

That's going to be your choice.

We will talk about why you may not apply it. And how to correct that problem.

Because a lot of people that go to seminars, a lot of people that listen to audios on how to achieve success or riches, how to make money or how to be happy, how to have more confidence, how to make their dreams come true in real life, how to get whatever they want, how to make whatever they want happen in real life — any type of book that you read about this — many people have blocks and stoppages that allow them to only go to a certain level and then stop.

And they don't go any further.

So we'll talk about how to overcome that and why that occurs.

But, the question remains, Who Do You Listen To?

When we talk about money, the question is, Who Do You Listen To? when you want to learn how to make money?

If you look at every course, read every book on how to get rich, you will find that 99 percent of the books written on how to get rich, and the courses taught on how to get rich and the seminars and lectures and workshops taught, and the audios or video home study courses that you can buy on how to get rich, 99.9 percent of them are produced by people who've never made any real money.

Now that's really important, because if what they were teaching works so well, why aren't they super rich?

Again, Who Do You Listen To?

Now, some people say, well, there are books written by Donald Trump. He's a multi-billionaire.

There are books written by Warren Buffett. He's one of the richest men in the world.

That's true.

They actually have achieved super wealth BEFORE THEY WROTE A BOOK ABOUT HOW TO ACHIEVE SUCCESS. Right?

So then the question is this, and this is a very important question that most people never discuss or talk about:

If somebody is super-wealthy and they actually write a book on how to get rich, did you know that they themselves probably did not write that book?

This is really important.

Warren Buffett never wrote a book.

Donald Trump never wrote a book.

Now, I respect both of those guys incredibly well, but they've never written a book.

What they do is they sit down with a ghostwriter. The ghostwriter asks them a bunch of questions and interviews them a little bit. And the ghostwriter writes the book.

That's the first problem.

So you're not getting the true information. It's not BAD information, but much of it is simply NOT what Trump or Buffett actually know to be true.

This happened to me. One of my publishers wanted me to write a new book. I was too busy. They said they would get a ghostwriter. I was interviewed for many hours. The ghostwriter sent me a draft of the first chapter.

IT WAS ALL WRONG! It was filled with total BS! The writer put down what he THOUGHT was correct based on HIS theories and opinions.

I canceled the project.

I am writing this book MYSELF. So everything you are getting here is DIRECTLY FROM ME.

Warren Buffett, Bill Gates, almost all successful people who've "authored" books on success did NOT write their books.

They've probably never even read the book they were supposed to have written.

They probably don't even know what's in their books.

So you're not really getting their information.

The other thing that's really important for you to understand is something that you will have a hard time believing is true.

The super-wealthy, with rare exception, do NOT want to share their secrets to success. They do NOT want YOU to know HOW to use your mind to manifest your desires.

Andrew Carnegie, by the way, was one of the rare exceptions.

Andrew Carnegie started U.S. Steel at the turn of the twentieth century. He was the richest man on planet Earth. He was an exception to this rule. There were several others that were exceptions as well.

Generally, the super-wealthy, absolutely, categorically, do not want anyone else to know their secrets of success.

They do not want competition.

As a matter of fact, the super-wealthy, overwhelmingly, categorically throughout history, always believed that wealth is genetic.

That you have to have a certain genetic makeup, a certain DNA structure, a certain DNA vibration, in order to be wealthy.

And if you don't fall into that category, you're not entitled to wealth.

You're not entitled to know the secrets.

And even if you did learn the secrets, they believe you wouldn't be able to apply them correctly anyway.

This is because they believe your genetics aren't programmed for success.

Some of you may have a hard time believing that, but that throughout history has been true.

Donald Trump said this. When he was asked "What is a key to success?" President Trump has said in the past, **genetics**. He actually said **"genetics," that it is IN THE GENES, that YOU HAVE TO HAVE A BRAIN.**

In other words, you're born with it.

Henry Ford said this as well.

Go back and look at the movie *Titanic*. At the turn of the twentieth century, you had the first-class cabin, and then you had the second-class and third-class people. They never dined together. They never socialized together.

Listen to some of those conversations from that movie, and you will see what people actually believed and said publicly. This is the same as in other countries, such as India, when they had the caste system.

If you read books back in the 1800s, 1700s, or even the turn of the twentieth century, and you listen to wealthy people like Henry Ford, they always believed that privilege and wealth was specifically designed and meant to be exclusive to the elite class of people.

And that's why they never married outside of their class—the "class" meaning they had to be wealthy. If you had a daughter, your daughter had to marry somebody who was from a wealthy family, someone who had the proper genetics.

In England, they call it blue bloods.

Throughout history, the idea of genetics was a major key.

The point I'm trying to make is this: the super-wealthy around the world will never tell you this publicly, but they believe that the secrets of success, the knowledge that they have, should be kept exclusively within their groups.

And that's why secret societies were put together.

There are many secret societies that aren't so secret.

The Freemasons were one of the most prevalent throughout history.

And you can go to virtually any city around the world, specifically in America, and you see Masonic lodges. They're huge.

Many Masonic lodges were massive, beautiful structures, where Masons would gather and share their secrets.

There are thirty-three degrees, or levels, in the Masons.

Some of you are familiar with the phrase, "You're giving the guy the **third degree.**"

Well, that comes from the Freemasons, because when you got to the third degree, you had a series of questions asked to you. You were drilled with questions. That's one of the procedures done at the third degree.

The highest level in the Masons is the thirty-third degree.

But most people don't know that some who reach the thirty-third degree level are "tapped on the shoulder" and brought into the "inner sanctum" of Freemasonry. This is the ULTRA secret part of the Masons.

Some of the people that were at the live event met several of my friends who were thirty-third-degree Masons AND part of the Masons' "inner sanctum." They came forth to share their knowledge and give knowledge and information from the **Masonic Lodge** about "how to manipulate energy" that never had been before released.

I share this now so that you know the information you're getting in this book is from the real high-level people, the "global elites" that the attendees at the live event actually met.

Secret societies were put together where the elite class could meet with one another, share and teach their secrets to one another, and keep those secrets within and amongst their families.

Secondly, they could share and keep those secrets amongst their peers, people within their, quote, **genetic pool**.

That's the history. This is not "racism" as we know and define it today, but it IS in fact a form of racism defined as believing that certain people with a certain "bloodline" are "superior" to others.

I'm not suggesting that what many of the "elites" believe is true or not true.

I'm just giving you kind of a history lesson here.

So Who Do You Listen To?

Well, you can't listen to most of the people who write the books on "success" or "manifesting." They just don't KNOW how to manifest. They only KNOW ABOUT how to manifest.

You can't listen to most of the people who teach the seminars on "manifesting," because 99 percent of them really don't know this information. They only KNOW ABOUT how to manifest.

It may surprise you that much of the information in those books and seminars is just made up! Much of it is 100 percent NOT TRUE. Much of it is FICTION and "sound good theory."

I know many of these "success gurus." Most are very well-intentioned people. Many really do believe that what they're saying is true and useful, but they're teaching you theory.

Most of those theories really don't work most of the time.

In their own personal lives, they haven't proved or shown by example that they work.

Most don't have the results to show that they themselves actually CAN manifest what they want. They teach mostly theory.

You really can't listen to most of the people who are writing books on how to get rich because 99 percent of them, number **one**, aren't rich.

Those that do have some money don't have hundreds of millions of dollars.

So they're not super rich, and they're teaching you how to get rich.

But when you ask them, how did they make the money that they have? They tell you they made most of their money selling books and courses on "how to make money"!

They may make a million dollars a year or **half** a million dollars a year or $300,000 a year, which a lot of you think is huge money. I have to tell you, that's not huge money.

Remember, most of them were broke when they first started selling books or courses on "how to make money" or how to manifest. In fact, most of them FAILED at various businesses before they decided to teach others "how to manifest and make money," even though this is a subject that they do not KNOW from personal successful experience.

Most of these people are really just good salesmen.

They're selling books, tapes and seminars. They've never really done anything in real life at all in terms of starting a business that became successful.

There's a book I was reading that's written in the Russian language. It's not translated into English.

This book is in a series of books by this Russian author. The last book in the series is a book on money … how to make money.

In the book about money, the author said,

"I wrote this book about money years ago. And I decided not to publish it until I became super-wealthy. Because if this information in this book is true, then I should be able to use it myself and make huge amounts of money. Then, only after I used my own information and the information I learned from others to make huge money, would I publish the book. If I used my information and made huge money, then I could write and sell this book and would not need any royalties from the book because I would already be rich. I could give all my royalties away! I am happy to share with you that I AM super rich using these methods, and I am giving all my royalties away from the sale of this book!"

He DID become super-wealthy, using the methods he shared, which are what you will learn in THIS book. Only THEN did he publish his "money book." THIS makes a lot of sense.

This is the same with THIS book, *Your Wish Is Your Command*. I used these methods to make billions. I taught this to hundreds of my friends and business associates, most of whom today are multi-millionaires.

So Who Do You Listen To?

You can't listen to most of the people who write books on how to make dreams and desires come true, or produce home study courses on audios and videos, or teach seminars, because 99 percent of them have no proven track record of success. Their "theories" have not been proven to work in real life.

You really can't listen to most of the people who teach you how to make money in books and seminars. Now, not that all of them are bad. In this book, I am actually going to give you a suggested reading list of books that ARE GOOD and WILL be helpful!

Just don't waste your time on the junk.

Remember, most of the people who write or teach on the subject of manifesting or how to make money are NOT rich. They haven't made hundreds of millions of dollars.

What they teach has NOT worked for them.

Remember, most of them made all their money teaching others how to make money.

In many cases, they're giving you really bad information that will cost you time and money.

And you really can't read books by the super-wealthy like the Warren Buffetts of the world or the Donald Trumps or the Bill Gateses, because, number one, most do NOT write their own books.

They don't even know the information that's in the books they allegedly wrote.

In those books, you're not getting information directly from the source.

Number two, remember this truth. And know that they will never tell you this truth. They'll deny it, but it's absolutely true. **They do not want you to know the true secrets of manifesting and making money because they do not want competition.**

As a matter of fact—and this will scare you, but it's true—what they will categorically do is they will give you **wrong** information so that you will achieve a little bit of success, but not that much success.

Isn't that interesting?

They'll let you have a little bit of success, but not that much success.

So they'll give you wrong information on purpose to virtually sabotage your ultimate success to keep you as a worker instead of teaching you the REAL secrets that will give you the opportunity to manifest HUNDREDS of millions, if that is something you desire.

So Who Do You Listen To?

Some of you might be thinking, "Kevin, I get it, you want me to listen to YOU."

Yes, I am a MESSENGER of these secrets. They are NOT MY secret methods.

I didn't invent any of this information.

I was TAUGHT all the information in this book by BILLION-AIRES and my mentors in the Brotherhood. I also share my personal experience and the experience I have observed from OTHERS who have manifested their own goals and dreams with ease and in record time.

I'm just the messenger of these secrets. I'm just the teacher.

I learned this information from SOURCE. None of it's mine.

I've learned it, I've applied it, and I've taught it.

Where did I get this information from?

Where did the information that you're going to be receiving in this book come from?

I mentioned secret societies. There is nothing to be scared about when we talk about secret societies. No conspiracy theories, no mystical stuff, no Satan worshiping, nothing like that.

Secret societies are basically just a group of people that would get together and basically share information with other members, people who were within the correct "gene pool." That's really what it comes down to. This is a historical fact.

The elite class set up societies where they could work together and benefit one another as a group. They believed that wealth—and the knowledge to attain it—should be kept amongst themselves. They believed that "success" was "in the genes."

Thus, they set up various secret societies.

Freemasons, as I mentioned, were one.

A very famous one is at Yale University. This very famous American university has a secret society called Skull and Bones.

Skull and Bones has a building on the Yale campus. You can see it. Members go in and out of the building, and they also meet with other members at various other locations and venues, but all in secret. They even have their own island. I have been there.

This is all common knowledge. Skull and Bones is not a secret. But what goes on between members IS a secret.

If you're a member of the Skull and Bones, you don't hide that fact. You're proud of that membership.

U.S. President George H.W. Bush, U.S. President George W. Bush, former Secretary of State John Kerry, as well as many politicians, Supreme Court justices, and billionaire businessmen, were all Skull and Bones members.

As a matter of fact, the American CIA was started by the Skull and Bones. There's a great movie with Matt Damon about that called

The Good Shepherd. Watch it. You can see a little bit about the Skull and Bones.

The movie is not a great movie, but it does talk a little bit about Skull and Bones and gives you some inside information on how the meetings work and how the networking works amongst members.

There are lots of secret societies all around the world. The Illuminati is another. Bohemian Grove is another. Many U.S. Presidents and other global leaders were part of the Bohemian Grove organization.

One of the most powerful secret societies, which is actually at the pinnacle, or highest level of secret societies, is called the Brotherhood.

The Brotherhood is a unique society because it keeps its membership very secret. It also keeps its very existence secret.

Many members of Skull and Bones are also members of the Brotherhood.

Many members of Freemasons, when they reach the thirty-third degree and are invited into the "inner sanctum," become members of the Brotherhood.

Certain members of the Illuminati and various other organizations around the world become members of the Brotherhood.

The Brotherhood takes people who are "special" or "gifted" in various areas. They could have an exceptionally high IQ or have some extrasensory perception abilities. The organization trains its members and "makes them better and more powerful." The group teaches its members how to use their mind to manipulate energy and manifest things in the material world.

The group teaches its members knowledge of how the universe works, how this planet works, and how, as a human being, you can be happy and healthy, and make your desires come true.

The group releases abilities in its members so they can go through this life in an exciting, joyous, adventurous, fulfilling way based on each person's individual desires and wishes.

That's key.

It's YOUR desires and YOUR wishes that are important, not other people's.

Every person on the planet has different desires, different dreams, and different wishes.

Some of you think that whatever dream you have, everyone shares the same dream.

That's not true.

Some of you think that every desire that you have is a desire that everyone else should have. You think that others must have the same desires as you. And that's not true.

When I taught this live, some of the people in attendance were looking around the luxurious and opulent castle and saying, "I want this!"

Yet others were saying that the place was too big. They did not want 200 staff members working for them.

So each person will always have a different desire.

Some of you might desire to have a log cabin. That's where you want to live with a little garden out in the back.

Some of you have a desire to just have a nice, small, little home with a brand-new car. That's your desire, that's your dream, that's your wish, and that's what you want to have.

Some of you have dreams of being the best parent in the world.

Some of you have a dream of being the best policeman in the world.

Some of you have a dream of being a happy, wonderful fireman.

Some of you want to be a doctor or a nurse or a teacher or a pharmacist or a surgeon.

You all have different goals, desires, and dreams.

Some of you want to be a great cook.

There is no reason to think that every person has a dream or goal of being a billionaire. There's nothing wrong with not wanting to be a billionaire, but very few people actually have that desire.

What I am going to be sharing with you in this book is how to make whatever *your* desire and *your* dream is, come true.

Remember, the members of these various societies got together and shared the information that is in the book, so that people could follow their bliss, follow their motivation, follow their heart.

So that this training could help them make whatever dreams they had for their own life come true.

That's why this information was shared.

Much of this information goes back thousands of years.

Some of the manuscripts that I've actually read as part of the group were on yellowing paper, hundreds and hundreds of years old. Some of it was translated from manuscripts that were over a thousand years old, originally written in ancient languages.

Most of the original manuscripts that I learned this information from, as a member of the Brotherhood, were VERY old and originally written in languages other than English.

There are manuscripts I read in the Brotherhood that were originally written in German, Russian, Hebrew, Arabic, Greek, or Latin.

What you are learning in this book is really the secret secrets of the ancients. Yet all of this is now proven by modern science and physics.

This training on "how to manifest" that you are being taught has been used by the privileged elite class throughout history. It works, and works 100 percent of the time … IF you work it.

Over time, this information has been codified, it has been simplified, and it has been put in easier-to-understand formats.

That always happens with information over time. It becomes simpler, and simpler, and simpler. It becomes easier to understand and apply.

As I have said, the information you're going to get in this book is not mine. It comes from many people and "higher beings." It has been collected, used, and tested for thousands of years. And up until now, it has ONLY been available to the privileged elite class and those in certain secret societies such as the Brotherhood.

Where does this material actually originate from? Aliens? "God"? I'm not going to get into that today. That is something we can discuss after you finish the book. That data is perhaps over a lot of your heads and your level of belief or understanding.

The bottom line is the information and training you are getting in this book is used today by an incredibly small group of very wealthy and powerful people.

When you compare the number of people that have been trained in this information on "manifesting" to the eight-plus billion people on planet Earth today, it is true to say that a very small group of people have had access to this information that YOU are now getting access to. You should feel VERY privileged and lucky. Quite frankly, your wish has been granted.

You are at the right place at the right time. You are NOT reading this by accident. Your life is about to get better in every area.

Those of you reading this **do** have access to this "secret" information. If you **use and apply** this information, you can have an amazing life.

And it's not just about manifesting money or material things. You can "have it all." You can have wealth, health, and happiness. You can have inner peace, fulfillment, and satisfaction. You can feel that you have purpose in your life. You can have amazing relationships. You can have spiritual freedom and liberation.

You can wake up full of wonder of the planet that we live on. You can feel excited, motivated, and inspired. You can have tons of energy and enthusiasm.

You can be happy, and enjoy and experience exhilaration, fulfillment, and ultimate joy and bliss.

And for some of you, being rich—having millions in the bank, or having your own private jet, is your bliss.

For some of you, a private jet does not excite or interest you at all.

Maybe for you, your bliss is being able to fly first class once in a while, and that's perfectly fine.

There's no right and wrong when it comes to desires. Whatever your desire is, is your desire.

So Who Do You Listen To?

This is the FIRST most important "secret success principle." Most people listen to the wrong people. Most of you listen to your family, spouse, friends, neighbors, and work associates. Many of you listen to and FOLLOW various internet podcasters or various people on YouTube. You "listen" to everything you read on the internet.

Continuing to do this will keep you a failure.

It is critical that you don't allow "garbage" to fill your mind. Garbage in, garbage out.

Most of you are listening to people that DO NOT KNOW THE TRUE AND CORRECT METHODS OF MANIFESTING AND ACHIEVING SUCCESS.

I would suggest that you **listen to people who have what you want.**

Listen to people who have what **YOU** want.

AND, **listen to people that not only have what you want, but have been where you are!**

Read that a hundred times!

Remember, the information in this book comes from people who HAVE WHAT YOU WANT.

They have superior health; amazing relationships with friends; loving, exciting romantic relationships; massive amounts of money and material things; power; control; feelings of certainty; confidence; joy; happiness; feeling "connected" to GOD and the universe … basically, they HAVE IT ALL.

Is that what YOU want?

LISTEN TO THEM!

Most importantly, many of us have been where you are now. We have faced adversity. Many of us were born poor. Some of us had learning disabilities. We experienced lost love, deaths of people close to us, lawsuits, and depression.

Successful people are not people without problems; they are people who have learned how to OVERCOME their problems.

We know what you have gone through. We know where you are in life. We have been there. We also KNOW the road to paradise. We can show you how to get to where you want to be.

The material in this book, the methods and techniques presented, are proven to work 100 percent of the time when applied properly. This "success and manifesting system" has passed the test of time.

It works.

It works better and faster than anything else out there.

This is the first time in history where this information is being revealed and released on a large-scale basis. I can tell you there's only a very small number of people, very few, who are excited to have this information out to the general public.

One of the first people in known history that felt that this information should be let out to the general public and not remain a closely guarded secret reserved for the privileged elite class was Andrew Carnegie, the richest man in the world.

Mr. Carnegie, who had full knowledge of this information, was also a member of the Brotherhood.

Andrew Carnegie started U.S. Steel. He sold U.S. Steel to the JP Morgan group for over 700 billion dollars when you adjust for inflation. That was in CASH. Carnegie had more CASH than any person who ever lived.

Carnegie gave all his money away before he died. He wanted everyone to have access to the same "secrets of success" that he used to make his fortune.

But Henry Ford, who was also one of the richest men in the world at the time, and many other Brotherhood members, did NOT want this information released to the general public. Ford was very vocal about keeping these "success secrets" a secret only available to the privileged few.

Ford was against Andrew Carnegie, or anyone, sharing this information with people outside of the elite class and with people who were not members of the various societies. Ford won. This information was NOT released in full.

Carnegie DID give Napoleon Hill information about success, but never the entire formula.

When I decided to leave the Brotherhood and share this information, I was met by violent opposition. The powerful and connected Brotherhood members who controlled the mainstream media and many agencies in government engaged in extreme negative opposition. I will explain the reasons for this massive opposition later.

However, several very high-level members of the Brotherhood and other societies DID want me to teach to the masses the secrets to manifesting goals, dreams, and desires. These people believed that the world would be a better place if more people knew exactly how the universe really works and how they can use the power of their minds to create their own reality.

When I recorded the live training event at the castle in the Alps, there were several people, including members of royal families, inner-sanctum thirty-third-degree members of the Masons, Skull and Bones members, and of course high-level Brotherhood members, one of whom was the owner of the palatial castle where the event was held.

There were two members of the Illuminati that had come out and introduced themselves to the group and engaged in a long question-and-answer session, explaining in detail HOW they used this material to "see" energy and "move" energy, thus being able to manifest and create in life what they desired.

These people have all come out publicly to back me up and show their support. Because they know the information that I am teaching, they want to validate and verify that this information is true and accurate, and that it works.

They came to the event so people could see firsthand the results that this training produces in real life. People could see their lifestyles, what they **have**, what they've achieved, their state of health and happiness, and their state of being.

The people could see firsthand that this training is the real deal. It isn't smoke and mirrors or fantasy. People could see real examples, beyond just me, that this works 100 percent, better than anything else out there from any other audio, video, seminar, book, or teacher, or guru, or whatever.

The people in attendance could see with their own eyes that this material is the real deal on a scale that they have never imagined before.

Those in attendance were meeting and talking with members of royal families, the richest people on the planet, the people that control the flow of oil, people that control the flow of information to the media, control food—virtually the people that control the planet.

That's who they had a chance to meet: the individual people and their families.

I share this so that you understand what you have in your hands. I hope that you can see that what you are about to learn is truly something special.

So, Who Do You Listen To?

I would suggest that the information you're going to get is going to be mind-blowing, eye-opening, and ridiculously simplistic to the point of surprise for many of you.

You will probably say to yourself, "I can't believe it's so easy."

Yes, but there are a lot of nuances that make *it* work.

But *it* is easy to learn, and incredibly easy to apply.

The results should happen for you faster than you could ever dream possible.

Let's talk about a few things first.

First, you're going to learn a lot of information in this book.

The information that I'm going to be sharing with you in this book is just a thumbnail sketch, kind of a bird's-eye view, of the entire "success system that never fails." But this book just scratches, the scratch of the surface of what I KNOW. Yet it is really all you need to make all your dreams come true.

I can't give you everything I know and have learned over the last forty-five years in this book.

I went through thousands, and thousands, and thousands, and thousands, and thousands of hours of training.

When you are in societies, the training is actually given to one another. It's actually not done in classrooms very often. I did receive some training in workshops, such as the various live training sessions I deliver. The training is also done in seminars and lectures.

Most of the training, however, is taught to members via books, where members actually have to read things. Many of the books and manuscripts are very old and not available to the general public. They are "secret" manuscripts exclusively available to Brotherhood members only. Many of them are available only to the highest-ranking members.

The reason I point that out is that today, very few people read.

One of the interesting decisions made by society members—and this has been throughout history, by the way, is to keep the information exclusive to members. When you have the elite class having exclusive access to vital information that allows them to create and maintain power, wealth, and control, they want to keep that information and knowledge to themselves so that they do not have competition.

Throughout the history of the world, the ruling classes, the elite class of people that had this knowledge, wanted to keep the knowledge to themselves so they didn't have competition. They wanted to keep power, wealth, and control for their own "group."

The way to do that was, first and foremost, to keep the masses illiterate.

If we can keep the masses unable to read, then they will not be able to read the "holy books" or read the manuscripts that contain the secrets of the universe. The masses will have to bow down and "worship" those who CAN read and who DO have access to the secret knowledge.

This is one of the reasons why in schools around the world, reading levels are continuing to go down.

Throughout history, the majority of the population was always illiterate.

In today's society, we have schools and education, and we think, "Oh, everybody can read and write."

It's not really true.

In America, for example, phonics, which was taught in all schools, was taken out of the schools and replaced with a method called the "look see" method.

This was a conscious action step taken by the U.S. Government to make sure kids can't really read. It was done to "dumb down" the children.

Putting fluoride in drinking water reduces IQ. Fact. Proven. Documented. This is being done on purpose to "dumb down" the population.

The amount of reading that people engage in is diminishing. Fewer and fewer people actually read. The ability to concentrate is diminishing greatly. People can't focus.

In the societies, members learn much of this information and knowledge from reading.

Reading is something that is really overlooked and undervalued.

Knowledge that comes through reading is quite different than from any other method.

Leaders are always readers.

If you look at the leaders of countries around the world, if you look at the billionaires around the world, if you look at the captains of industry around the world, you will find that they are always massive readers.

They read, read, read all the time.

Now think about that.

I mentioned to you that I learned much of this information from reading, and information is shared to members within societies primarily through reading. So, when you see somebody who is a ferocious reader, ask yourself, "I wonder if he's a society member?"

That person might actually be a member of a secret society because reading is one of the things that we're taught to do.

One of the things that we are trained to do very early on is to read and gather information through reading.

Reading is a vitally important method that members use to get and learn this information.

The societies, as I mentioned, are known, but it's really what goes on inside the societies that has always been kept a secret.

People who are members gladly state that they are a member of some "secret" society.

"Hey, I'm John, former Secretary of State John Kerry, and I'm a member of Skull and Bones."

Okay, John, what goes on inside Skull and Bones?

"Well, I can't tell you, it's a secret."

"Hi, I am Joe. I'm a thirty-third-degree member of the Freemasons. I am proud of that."

Great. Tell me, what goes on inside Freemasonry at the highest levels?

"Oh, that is a secret."

Benjamin Franklin was a member of the Freemasons, a thirty-third-degree member. Most of America's Founding Fathers were Masons including George Washington. Washington, DC, was built BY Masons using Masonic symbolism and sacred geometry.

Throughout history, many of America's most powerful people and leaders were Masons.

They were proud of that membership. They used to wear their Masonic garb in public.

But when you ask them what went on inside, what did you learn? That's when they stopped talking.

"No, no, no. I'll let you know that I'm a member, but not what I learned as a member."

I am coming forward as a former member of the Brotherhood, not just myself, but the friends that I brought along with me to the event. It was almost a "coming out party."

We are now sharing with you this powerful and life-changing information and knowledge.

I mentioned a little bit earlier about how this information was taught to us.

A little bit through lectures, workshops, or seminars; primarily through reading.

The third method in which this information is shared is via one another. One-on-one communication with other members. Information is shared between one member to another member. Much of this was done one-on-one, face-to-face.

There are lines of communication just like it has been done throughout history, where information has been passed down verbally, one person to another person, face-to-face. In many cases, information is passed down verbally verbatim, although most of it is backed up in written form.

But it is passed down verbally verbatim, which is really interesting.

You start sitting down with somebody over a cup of coffee. Many of these society meetings aren't so secret. In recent times, it's very common for us to sit down at a coffee shop and have a cup of coffee and share information.

If you recorded that twenty-minute conversation, the information that went back and forth may go over the heads of 90 percent of the people. But the information shared between the society members, because we know what we're talking about—and it's not in code, but we know what we're talking about—it makes sense to us. We understand what is being said. It resonates perfectly. We get so much information that we can use in our real lives.

So we first learn much of this knowledge by some workshop or group lecture.

Secondly, mostly by reading, and reading "secret" manuscripts that are not available to non-members.

Thirdly, by one-on-one communication.

The last method of learning is something that we don't do today very often. We don't even use the words very often, although Donald Trump brought it out with his TV show *The Apprentice.*

How many times have you heard "apprentice" in today's society?

"What are you doing?" "Well, I'm an apprentice."

How many people say, "I'm an apprentice?"

That's how we learned almost everything throughout history.

You got an apprenticeship.

You wanted to be a plumber; you became an apprentice.

You found a master plumber, you became his apprentice, and you learned from the master plumber.

Go back and look at martial arts. A kung fu master would take a "student" or apprentice.

Yogis would take a student, "initiate," or "apprentice."

Go look at the *Star Wars* movies. You had the Jedi Knight. The Master Jedi Knight always had an apprentice.

And it was a one-on-one training. You could call it "Fly on The Wall Training." You OBSERVED the Master. You "mimicked and modeled" successful actions, thoughts, and words.

Sometimes we call the Master a "mentor."

This is the fourth method in which the societies share information; through a virtual apprenticeship program.

It's something that we just do not do today outside societies in the general population. When you're in a society, you actually get a mentor and you become an apprentice, and you learn directly from one person.

That's how you're trained, and the training is a lifelong experience.

In the Brotherhood, your mentor is called your "uncle" if he is a man, or your "aunt" if your mentor is a woman.

You always have a mentor. For life, you will always have a "Master," an uncle or aunt. Even when you are a mentor (an uncle or aunt to another member) and you have an apprentice, you still always are an apprentice.

With that in mind, I want to talk about the first, most important thing that we're taught based on this concept of how to learn.

How did we learn this information, whether it's in the Masons, whether it's in the Brotherhood, whether it's in the Illuminati, whether it's in the Skull and Bones, or any of the other hundreds of secret societies? How did we learn this information?

First, we are taught to **LISTEN TO PEOPLE THAT HAVE WHAT WE WANT AND HAVE BEEN WHERE WE ARE.**

We have to make sure we are listening to the RIGHT PEOPLE; therefore, we will get the RIGHT formulas that WORK and have been proven by the test of time.

Later, we learn to LISTEN TO OUR INNER VOICE. That comes later.

Lastly on this first subject of Who Do You Listen To, remember that YOU LEARN FROM EVERYONE.

The wise man learns from the FOOL, but the fool does not learn from the wise man.

Think about this.

You are reading this book. You are listening to the right person. In fact, I am just a messenger. As you read this book, know that you are listening to the right PEOPLE.

Who do YOU listen to? Who HAVE you listened to in the past? Choose WISELY.

LESSON 3

The Teachability Index

In the Brotherhood, we are taught that we have to be teachable.

We have to be coachable.

This is the first thing that we're trained on.

Actually, before you are even let in as a member, you are tested to see if you are teachable and coachable. Sometimes it can take years before a person is allowed in as a member.

Some groups, like the Masons, allow people to become members very easily, but you don't learn anything, really, until you get way up to the top. Even though you're in, you're not getting anything of great value. The "secrets" are not revealed to you. You're just kind of going through an almost an interview process. This is because if you join the Freemasons, very few people reach the thirty-third degree level.

That's because most Masons don't qualify for the higher levels.

What's the qualification for being a member of the Brotherhood and getting to the highest levels and learning all the information?

In addition to having certain "abilities" in your DNA and your mind, you have to be teachable and coachable.

This is the key, by the way, to achieving great success. You have to be OPEN to learning. You have to be HUMBLE. You have to submit and be an empty vessel. There are many people that are members but very few reach the highest levels.

What is the number one, the first and foremost qualification?

That KEY qualification is ... are you teachable?

If you're not teachable, if you're not coachable, you then disqualify yourself.

So the first thing we're taught to question is are we great teachers. It is not are we great people. It is not are we so smart. But actually, do we know how dumb we are! Do we understand that we don't know what we don't know.

Do we know that "I don't know what I don't know?"

Think about that statement. Ask yourself: Do YOU know that you don't know what you don't know?

Are you at a point of humility where you can say, "I know nothing"?

We were tested to find out if we could say, "I'm going to listen to everything and I'm not going to challenge it by disagreeing, yet at the same time I'm also not going to blindly follow or believe everything I hear." There is a beautiful balance between self-determinism and being teachable.

We had to say, "I am going to believe what you're saying must be true, but I am going to question it, yet not resist it, until I understand why it's true."

You must be teachable. This is the first most important thing for you to understand.

Today and tomorrow and throughout your life, understand this concept.

If you get nothing else from this book but this one concept I'm going to teach you right now, you will be better off, happier, and much more successful in your life.

You will achieve greater things faster than you could ever dream possible by learning this one simple concept.

And that is, you must be teachable.

You must be coachable.

How do you determine that?

There's an index.

There's a Teachability Index which will determine how teachable you are.

And you must consider this all the time. Every day.

This is a concept that takes five minutes to learn, but a lifetime to master.

You can't learn this concept right now and say, "I got it."

No, you're never going to "get it." It will always be a work in progress.

You're always getting it.

Do you understand that?

You're always getting it.

How teachable are you?

How coachable are you?

So what's your Teachability Index?

There are two variables when it comes to your Teachability Index.

The first variable is, What is your willingness to learn on a scale of 1 to 10.

Ask yourself, on a scale of 1 to 10, how high is your willingness to learn this information and change your life for the better?

Now this Teachability Index is applied in life and every area of study.

Let's say you want to learn a foreign language.

You have to ask yourself, if you're going to succeed in learning a foreign language, you must be teachable. You must have a high Teachability Index. Otherwise, you're wasting your time.

If you want to learn this information and all the other information that I will provide to you, you must be teachable.

Some people in the societies may have a high Teachability Index in the beginning, but later on, they think they know everything. They stop being teachable.

I've had apprentices who stopped being teachable.

I had one guy, for example, who maxed out his income, which is what you can quantify.

His income was about a million dollars a year, and then he stopped being teachable. He was still my apprentice, but I stopped teaching him because I'm waiting for him to become teachable again.

I have nothing more to teach him, nothing more to give him, because it's going in one ear and out the other.

So on a scale of 1 to 10, what's your willingness to learn this information?

Again, if this was a language course, I'd say, What's your willingness to learn this language?

The question is regarding *Your Wish Is Your Command: How to Manifest Your Desires*, which I am teaching you in this book, along with how anyone can make millions with the moneymaking secrets they don't want you to know about. What is your willingness to learn this information, on a scale of 1 to 10?

Obviously, the people who came to the live event and spent $50,000—spent money on travel, some coming from halfway around the world—had no idea who they were meeting or where they were going.

They weren't blindfolded, of course, but they came on just complete faith.

When they arrived and saw the castle and met some of the richest, most powerful people in the world, they were all blown away. Many I know were doing backflips from what they had seen.

Most, if not all, of the people who were in the room probably had a high willingness to learn because they have proven it by their actions.

Faith without actions is dead.

You are reading this book. You didn't invest that much money. Most of you probably won't even read this entire book.

You'll throw it under the bed or on the shelf like every other course on success you bought.

So, I ask you again. What is your willingness to learn? On a scale of 1 to 10?

What are you willing to do?

Successful people are always willing to do what the other guys are not willing to do.

Successful people are always too busy DOING what the other guys are still talking about.

Successful people are willing to sacrifice. They are willing to give something up. They are willing to give up something GOOD to get something GREAT.

Successful people always engage in delayed gratification. They understand they have to PUT IN FIRST, before they can TAKE OUT.

How much time are you willing to really invest to learn this and be able to have your wish be your command?

How much money are you willing to invest so that you can manifest your desires and make all your dreams come true?

How much effort are you willing to put in so that you can have total financial and time FREEDOM?

What is your willingness to learn?

Some of you think, "I'm a 10! I'm a 10! I have a 10 willingness to learn, but I have to go right now because there's a movie I want to see, and I have to check my social media accounts."

Okay. Yeah, sure. You have a high willingness to learn. NOT!

You don't have a high willingness to learn if you are not willing to shut off the TV for a week and focus on reading this book. THINK ABOUT THAT.

Some of you are thinking, "I didn't know this was going to be that hard."

What is your willingness to learn?

This may change from time to time, but think about it.

On a scale of 1 to 10, what is your willingness to learn?

Ten is the highest. One is the lowest.

Generally speaking, people think they have a high willingness to learn, but they don't.

The real question is, "What are you willing to give up to learn this?"

"What's your favorite thing to do?"

"Is it going to the movies?"

"Is it to go bowling?"

"Is it eating in nice restaurants?"

"Is it poker night?"

"Is it watching TV?"

"Is it surfing the web, or checking social media?"

"What is your favorite thing to do? Is it playing with your kids?"

What is your favorite thing to do?

Are you willing to give that up for a week or a month, or dramatically reduce that?

Golfing. Some of you like golfing.

Are you willing to put the golf clubs away for a year?

"Oh, my God, I didn't know it was going to be that hard," you might be thinking.

What is your willingness to learn? If you don't have a high Teachability Index ... success will not be yours.

You're all apprentices to me right now, but I'm going to tell you, you're not all going to be Jedi Knights.

You're not all going to be masters unless you have a high willingness to learn.

And the willingness to learn scale is really the question, "What are you willing to give up?"

So, rate yourself right now on a scale of 1 to 10.

Now, the next variable, and this is even tougher than the first one.

What is your willingness to accept change?

I'm going to tell you something.

If you're not happy with where you're at right now, you have patterns. You have done things a certain way. You have, most importantly, *thought* a certain way. The way you have been THINKING has to change. The way you have been SPEAKING has to change. The way you ACT has to change.

What is your willingness to change the way you think, the way you feel about things, the way you think about things, the patterns of speech and the words you say, and some of the things you do?

What is your willingness to change?

If you eat at McDonald's three times a week, what if I said, "You're going to have to change that, you can't eat at McDonald's anymore"? You can still eat food!

What if I said that? And you love McDonald's?

What is your willingness to accept change?

Some of you think, well, I'm a 10 on a willingness to learn.

I'm going to learn this. But change?

No, I don't want to change anything in my life.

If you want things in your life to change, you will have to change things in your life!

If your willingness to learn is a 10, but your willingness to accept change is a zero, then 10 times zero is zero. So you have a **zero** Teachability Index. You are NOT teachable. You will NOT learn this. You will NOT see results.

You have to have a high willingness to learn and a high willingness to accept change, to have a high Teachability Index.

Those who have the highest Teachability Index basically say, "I'll do whatever it takes to learn this. Whatever you say, I'll do. I'll give up anything, no problem. I have a high willingness to learn. This is my obsession, to learn this. This is my number one priority, to learn this."

If you are this person, then you are teachable! The world will be yours. Your dreams WILL come true. You are humble and open to receiving. CONGRATULATIONS.

I hope you have a 10 willingness to learn, and you say, "I will change anything in my life and change any way of thinking."

I hope you have a 10 willingness to accept change.

Ten times ten is 100.

You are the perfect student.

You are my apprentice. Follow me.

In a short period of time, every desire in your life will manifest, because you'll learn this better than anyone.

And I have to tell you, I had a 10 and a 10 when I started, which is why I learned this so quickly. I was committed to being the BEST student. I was a SERVANT to my "uncle."

I came from nothing. Yet I understood a basic concept when I was very young.

A guy told me this early on in my training.

He said something very profound.

He said, "Kevin, are you happy with where you're at?"

I said, "I want more. I'm angry, I'm frustrated, I'm overweight, I'm just not comfortable in my skin."

"I'm struggling with finances."

"I want a different life. I want to wake up happy."

"I want to go to bed with a big smile on my face."

"I want to sleep beautifully all night long."

"I want to wake up excited for my life."

"I want to accept the challenges that are presented to me with gusto and enthusiasm and vigor and adventure."

"I want things to go smoothly, and when they don't, I want to laugh at them."

"I want to just feel great no matter what the situation is."

"I want to have a healthy body and strong body."

"I want to be flexible, and I never want to get sick."

"I want to be able to go anywhere, do anything I want."

"I want to be fulfilled."

"I want to add value to society."

"I want to feel like I have a purpose in life."

"I want to be excited when I look at a tree or a mountain or a stream."

"I want to enjoy experiences."

"I want to do things."

Those were my desires. Yours may be different.

He said to me, "So, Kevin, you want things to be different in your life?"

I said, "Yes. I want things to be different."

He told me, "Kevin, if you want things in your life to change, you're going to have to change things in your life."

Think about that. It was, at the time, the most profound statement I had ever heard.

If you want things in your life to change, you're going to have to change things in your life.

"What do you mean?" I asked.

He tells me, "Kevin, you're going to have to **do** things differently than you have in the past. You can't do the same actions as you did in the past. If you do the same thing over and over again and expect a different result, you're an insane person. That's just not going to happen."

Think about that.

If you want things in your life to change.

If you want your circumstances to change.

If you want everything to change and be better and different, then you're going to have to do things differently.

You're going to have to change things in your life.

You're going to have to change the things you're doing, the actions.

You have to change the words you use and the way you speak.

But most importantly, you're going to have to change the way you think.

Think about the Teachability Index.

How teachable are you?

You're all becoming apprentices.

You're all getting a mentor, and it's not me.

I'm just the messenger of the information. Not an individual mentor to you.

Later, I will share with you how you can get your own personal "mentor" and be an apprentice to somebody who is a master, one-on-one.

But that's not going to be available to everybody reading this book, because not everybody qualifies. Not everyone reading this book has a high Teachability Index.

We go up and down in our Teachability Index because we're like a sponge. We get a lot of information, and when our sponge gets full, we can't take any more in, and we stop being teachable.

Do you understand that?

So even if you have a super high Teachability Index right now, in three hours, your Teachability Index may go down because you may be overwhelmed. Which is why I'm putting this information and knowledge in this book.

This way you can read it over and over again.

You have to be able to absorb information. You have to have room in your vessel for more information. If your vessel is full, then no more liquid can fit in it. If you have a full glass and I pour water into it, it just overflows and spills on the floor.

When you're overwhelmed, you are FULL. When you are full, and you are processing or digesting all this new data, and then you stop being teachable.

So, willingness to learn.

What is your willingness to learn, and what is your willingness to accept change?

I remember one time when I started, I was super high in both of those categories.

After a while, I was absorbing, absorbing, absorbing. But I wasn't using the information, and therefore I couldn't take any more in. I had not fully digested everything. I was FULL. I had no more room for anything more.

I remember I was sitting there in a room full of people. It was a lecture. I was there to learn.

The instructor said, "I'm going to teach a two-day seminar where I will go in-depth on all this information." That sounded good to me. I wanted to learn MORE.

The lecture was in Boston, Massachusetts, where I was living,

He said he was going to teach us how to make a million dollars a year without ever leaving the house. I'm sitting there and I'm thinking, "I'm definitely going to that seminar. I want that!"

Then he says, "The seminar is going to be in Los Angeles, California."

And I said to myself, "I'm **not** going to that seminar."

And then he said, "The seminar is $5,000."

This is back in the '80s. That was A LOT of money.

And I said to myself, "I'm **definitely** not going to that seminar."

Then this wise man said, "Now, for some of you in the room, going to Los Angeles is too far, and $5,000 is too much money. So you won't go to the seminar. And that's why you'll always be a loser. You know the price of everything by the value of nothing."

That just hit me like a ton of bricks.

I thought to myself, "Wow, my willingness to learn must be very low. I wasn't willing to invest the time, travel that distance, and invest that type of money to learn this information."

My willingness to learn must be low.

I had been slapped across the face by my uncle a million times about the Teachability Index; I knew that my Teachability Index was low, and I was stuck.

If you aren't teachable, you are not growing. If you aren't growing, you're dying. You never stay at the place you're at. You are always going forward OR backward.

I thought, "I'm not teachable." So I MADE myself say, "I'm going. The moment I made that decision, I changed instantly. My willingness to learn went up. I went back up to a 10 and I focused on my Teachability Index so that my willingness to learn was a 10, which means I was willing to invest, give up things, and invest time and money IN MYSELF.

My willingness to learn and my willingness to accept change went up. My Teachability Index went up. This meant I was willing to listen and change and do things differently.

With the information I learned in that seminar, I DID make lots of money. But I didn't make a million dollars the next year as he said. I made two and a half million dollars the next year—and actually in only eight months after the seminar.

I made that money without ever leaving my house, using the information I learned at that seminar.

By the way, I wasn't the top earner from that seminar. That really annoyed me. There were other people that attended that left and made MORE money. I thought I was the person with the highest Teachability Index. I thought I was going to be the best student.

But obviously there were some other people that had an even higher Teachability Index than me.

So, what's your Teachability Index?

What's your willingness to learn on a scale of 1 to 10?

What's your willingness to accept change on a scale of 1 to 10?

What are you willing to give up?

How much money are you willing to invest in yourself? How much time are you willing to invest in yourself and your own personal growth and development?

And what is your willingness to accept change?

Are you willing to do things differently?

Are you willing to think differently?

Are you willing to speak differently?

That's the question.

Have a HIGH Teachability Index and you are on your way to making all your dreams come true.

LESSON 4

❧

The Training Balance Scale

Remember Lesson 2, WHO Do You Listen TO?

So, Who Do You Listen To?

I would suggest the information you are going to get in this book is more than just valuable. It is INVALUABLE.

Why?

Because it is not coming from me, an individual success or manifesting guru.

It is coming from the collective amount of information that has been taught in the secret societies for over 1,000 years.

At the live event where I taught this information, and from which this book comes from, we had in attendance other members of several of those societies, including thirty-third-degree members of the Freemasons, as well as members of the Masonic inner sanctum.

We had members of the Skull and Bones that have come forward.

It was the first time ever in history that members of these secret societies have come forth, revealed themselves, and shared what went on "behind the curtain."

Obviously, they are not making themselves known to the public. But it was the first time these people have ever come forward, and released this information, and shared their personal experiences USING this information.

They are backing me up on releasing this information. They are behind this book. They want YOU to have access to this knowledge so you can better your life.

This information, I think, is the purest information you will get on the subject of manifesting and making money. It comes directly from the source. The proven results speak for themselves.

How do you know this is true? Look at the evidence.

Obviously, those who were in attendance could see the physical, material evidence of massive success. They MET the people and me personally.

This information obviously works. It has worked better and faster than anything else, has the longest track record, and the most amount of history.

Most importantly, the evidence is real. They could see it and touch it. Later, those people EXPERIENCED for themselves that this knowledge WORKS and works fast.

It is not myth. It is not fantasy.

So, Who Do You Listen To? If you want to learn how to manifest your dreams and "attract" money into your life? You should know the answer now.

How teachable are you?

What is your willingness to learn, on a scale of 1 to 10?

And what is your willingness to accept change, on a scale of 1 to 10?

At the live event, a question was asked about other books written on the subjects of success, manifesting, and making money. The question was specifically about some of the great books out there that give stories of successful people.

That may be the person who wrote the book isn't super-wealthy. They don't claim to be, but they claim to be a teacher. And are those books good?

Maybe the authors of those books don't have the desire to become billionaires. Therefore, if they don't have that desire, there is nothing wrong with the fact that they aren't billionaires.

The question basically was, "Can't we listen to what they are saying, because the information in those books sounds really good and it makes sense?"

That is a very good question, and here is the answer.

When you read books such as *The Celestine Prophecy* or *The Alchemist,* you are reading books of FICTION. They are not REAL stories of REAL people.

These books tell stories that never happened, about people that never existed. These books give you a myth. They are books that tell a fable. They are stories about a nonexistent person, in a nonexistent place, where nonexistent things happen.

These are not biographies; these are not autobiographies. These are made-up stories, and there is no secret that they are made up.

The authors have some convoluted, whacked-out theory of how success works, how the physical universe works, how Earth works, how energy works, how happiness works, and how manifesting dreams and desires works.

They have this theory of how these things work. And it is ONLY a theory.

They can't prove their theory is true by their own personal results USING that theory. Nor can they find anyone in real life who used that theory and created massive results.

So what they say is, "I don't want success. I have no desires. Don't look at me. I have all the desires of my life."

Maybe that is true. Maybe they do have all the desires of their life, which is fine.

All of these authors have very small desires, though. They all have small dreams, which I think is a little bit interesting.

Sometimes there is something called justification.

"I don't want a big house; I like my small house."

"I don't want a new car; I like my fifteen-year-old car."

Sometimes we justify that we don't want something when, in fact, it is because we believe we can't get it.

These people have all these ideas and theories about how manifesting works, and in order to teach it, they have to make up a story.

They create a fictional story about a person, and how this person goes through their made-up life, and how things happen in their made-up life which proves this author's theory is true.

Then we read this book. Maybe it is really well-written, and we like the book, and it is a great book, and we enjoy it.

The problem is, it never happened. The story you are reading about is made up. And again, it is no secret that it is made up. It is listed as a work of fiction. They are not trying to convince you that it is real. It is a fable. It is a myth. It is a made-up story.

They say, "Well, I am using this as an example."

It can't be an example, because it never happened.

If their theory of how things happen is true, why do they have to make up a story?

Why can't they just point to a real person and share with you a real person's story?

Why can't they give a real-life example of their theory working in real life, producing real results?

The answer is, because there isn't a real person who ever achieved their desires in the manner in which these books are presenting.

The information in the books is fake. It is FALSE DATA.

The success recipe is fake. It is an UNWORKABLE, FALSE recipe that does NOT work in real life.

The recipe for success they share doesn't work, because if it did work, they would have a real-life example to share. And if it REALLY was true, they would have HUNDREDS of real-life examples that it works—like WE DO.

Does that make sense?

That is why I brought the attendees to the castle owned by someone who used THIS SYSTEM, so they could SEE the results. That is why I brought my rich and powerful friends to the event, so the attendees could meet real people who USED this system and created MASSIVE results in REAL LIFE.

This book on manifesting is not theory.

We are going to be sharing with you many real experiences, in the real world, from real people who have used this system and generated virtually their own personal Genie to grant them their every wish.

This can happen to you as well.

Everything in this book, all the examples given, comes from real people.

Not a myth, not a fantasy.

That is the big difference.

Another question that came up in the live event was about the Teachability Index.

The question was, "How do you know that you have a high Teachability Index? How can you know that you have a high willingness to learn? And, how can you know that you have a high willingness to accept change?"

Maybe you think you have a high willingness to learn, but you really don't.

There are two answers to that question.

What are you willing to give up? What is your favorite thing?

This is a simple test.

If one of your favorite things is golfing, are you willing to put the golf clubs away for a year?

If your favorite thing is watching TV, are you willing to not watch TV for a week?

Or, if you watch a certain show or podcast a number of hours a night, are you willing to cut down to one hour a night? Or half an hour a night?

What is your favorite TV show, or podcast, or streaming show? Now, let's be really specific here. What is your favorite show that you have to watch all the time?

Are you willing not to watch it for a year?

That will tell you what your willingness to learn is.

What is your favorite thing? Are you willing to give it up?

That will really tell you what your willingness to learn is.

Now the question is, "What if I want a high willingness to learn, but I just can't seem to motivate myself, to give up the things I love the most? Can I still have a high willingness to learn?"

The answer is yes.

First, you have to determine where your Teachability Index is right now.

If it is not 10 and 10—10, willingness to learn, and 10, willingness to accept change—it doesn't mean you go home. It doesn't mean you stop reading this book and say, "Forget it. I can't learn this. I don't have a high willingness to learn."

It just means that you have to acknowledge that "I don't have a high willingness to learn, YET."

Let's say that you want to play golf, and you have never golfed before. Well, that means you are starting at a very bad place. You have never played golf before, so you want to play a round of golf. You want to enjoy yourself, but you have never played golf before.

So, if you go on a golf course and try to golf, you are going to be hacking up the course. You are probably going to be miserable.

Your goal is to have a great time playing golf.

That is okay, because, you know, "I am just a beginner."

So, the key element is what your goal is.

This is important that you understand this.

Your goal is always the first thing in front of you.

Some of you think your goal is to manifest your desires.

Some of you think your goal is to learn this information.

Some of you think your goal is to make a million dollars.

No, that's not true.

Everyone's goal, everyone's first objective, is different. The goal is the first thing in front of you.

Which means, if you are at 10 and 10 on the Teachability Index, your goal is not to get a 100% Teachability Index. You're there.

So your goal is going to be the next step FROM WHERE YOU CURRENTLY ARE.

But if you are sitting over here and you acknowledge that your Teachability Index is 3 and 2, meaning only 25%, then your goal is to get to a 50% Teachability Index.

That is your objective.

Your goal should not be to go from a 25% Teachability Index to 100%. GO AT A GRADIENT that is reasonable. Trying to move from 25% to 100% is TOO STEEP A GRADIENT.

If your maximum bench press is 200 pounds, you don't set a goal to hit 500 pounds. That is TOO STEEP A GRADIENT.

If you can run one mile before you have to stop, you don't set a goal to run ten miles. That is TOO STEEP A GRADIENT.

Do you understand that?

Key point: Your objective, your goal, what you focus on, is always what is in front of you, what the next step is. And it has to be REASONABLE. It has to be something you KNOW you COULD achieve.

So the first step is, you need to decide who should you listen to when it comes to success, manifesting, and making money?

You can listen to the gurus who write the books, that make up stories, because they can't find a real person on planet Earth that actually did what they think is the secret to success.

Remember, if their secret to success is so true, let's find one person that did it.

I read this one book. This author had a theory about the secret to his success:

"The way to be successful, to make money, is that you MUST breathe properly with intention several times a day, and you have to meditate two times a day, THEN you don't have to do anything, you just let what you want come to you."

"Let it come to you. Sit and let it come to you."

And he gave all these stories of these people throughout history that he made up. These are all fables.

Well, guess what I said? "If that is true, let's talk to some REAL people who have made hundreds of millions and ask them if that is what THEY did." There were a bunch of billionaires around at the live event. It was funny when I asked if any of them sat in his room, and went "Um, Om" and meditated all day, and his billions just magically came to him.

There wasn't a single one. They laughed at the idea. FALSE DATA.

Those people worked their ass off. They worked hard. They put in a massive amount of hours WORKING and MAKING THINGS HAPPEN.

They were obsessed with making money, and they put a lot of effort into it and a lot of focus.

They didn't sit around meditating all day saying, "The universe is going to give me the stuff."

I am not going to fluff this or give you "sound good" information. Your time is too valuable. I do not want to do you a disservice.

I am just going to tell you how it is, even if I step on some toes and offend some people.

So the first thing is: Who Do You Listen To?

You have to listen to people who have done it in real life.

This shows that it works.

It's proven to work.

It's not theory.

That is the first step.

Always ask yourself:

"Is this information from a source that I feel comfortable with?"

If you say YES, then continue. If you say NO, then you can't go any further.

So you have to get to step one.

If you are there, then your next step is,

"I need to be as teachable as I can be."

"I need to acknowledge what my Teachability Index is."

And you need to get your Teachability Index up.

Your goal is getting your Teachability Index up.

So then the question is, "Well, how do I have confidence that the information in this book is coming from the right source? How do I get to a high level of belief or confidence in the material in this book?"

And the next question is, "How do I get my Teachability Index up? How do I do that?"

Here is the answer.

The reason we put this in a book is, if you go back to what I said earlier about how we were taught this in the societies, it was in stages and at levels.

I mentioned this was taught a little bit through workshops and lectures, but more through the books, through one-on-one communication, and through mentoring—having a mentor or being an apprentice.

The key is that when we are learning this from a person one-on-one, that person can see where we are at. They can see what the next logical step is for US.

The mentor is not going to take us further than where we are at.

So if we are stuck on the Teachability Index, for some people, the mentor or the teacher would work with the apprentice only on the Teachability Index until the person was ready to go to the next level of training.

Sometimes it was for weeks, months, or years before they got to a level where they can teach them something beyond that.

And they would teach them something, knowing that they were going to teach them something that the student can learn, based on their Teachability Index.

Because if their Teachability Index was so low, no one could teach them a high-level piece of knowledge because they wouldn't learn it. They would not be READY to receive it.

Only when the student is READY will the teacher appear.

So I would teach them a very simple piece of knowledge, so that they would learn it at their current Teachability Index.

Does this make sense?

How do you get the Teachability Index up?

Generally speaking, the person has to make these decisions on their own and choose on their own.

The student has to make their own decisions and take their own responsibility.

The way to help them is by teaching them a little something that they can learn, based on their current Teachability Index level.

And when they learn it, and the student sees that this works, that this is good, and they like it, THEN their Teachability Index will then go up.

Their belief in it will go up. Their confidence in the system and me goes up.

Their confidence that they can do it can go up.

Therefore their willingness to learn will go up, and their willingness to accept change will go up.

That is the first method you can use to get your Teachability Index up.

The second method is by exposing the student to other people that have what they want. By seeing and meeting real people who have what you want, your desire will go up, and your confidence that you can achieve greatness, as well, will go up.

When your desire goes up, when your confidence in yourself goes up, your willingness to learn and your willingness to accept change will go up.

Does this make sense?

The question is what the best method for YOU is to get your Teachability Index up. Every person is different. Only you can know what is best for you.

I can say with 100 percent confidence that MOST of you reading this book have a much lower Teachability Index than you realize. Think about that.

You may be wondering, "How do I get my Teachability Index up based on where I am at, and with the tools I have available?"

The answer is: Read this book all the way through. Get the audios of the live event from which this book is derived. Read and listen to this material. OVER AND OVER again.

I have received thousands of emails and letters from people all over the world who said they listened to the audios dozens of times and in some cases over a hundred times BEFORE it finally CLICKED for them.

When it CLICKED, within months, weeks, or days, they started manifesting what they wanted as if by magic. Their WISH virtually was at their command.

Read this book all the way through with an open mind. Try as best you can to be an empty vessel willing and ready to receive.

As you read this for the very first time, some of you will have a very low willingness to learn and a low willingness to accept change.

But after you read it once, go back and read it again, or get the audios of my live lecture that I gave to the people at the castle.

The second time you read it, your willingness to learn will be higher. Your willingness to accept change will be higher.

Then read it again, and then read it again.

At the end of this book, I'm going to give you additional materials and resources, which I'm going to encourage you to get—audios, as well as books. Some of it is free.

You also have the option of coming to a live event and meeting me in person. At a live event, you will meet real people who are using this material and living their dreams. You will SEE the results firsthand.

Increasing your willingness to learn and willingness to accept change is an ongoing process.

Each one of the steps that I am describing in this book ideally should be mastered by you at as high a level as you can get to before you try to master the next step. Each step builds on the previous. You can only go as high as your foundation is deep.

But you don't have that luxury, and you don't have that amount of time. So, as best you can, try to understand, comprehend, and internalize each step in this system. It will serve you well and give you the best results.

If you are at a low level right now, in terms of willingness to learn and willingness to accept change, just acknowledge it. And just know, "I am probably not that teachable RIGHT NOW."

That doesn't mean you are completely unteachable. It just means you can get better.

Every day in every way, you are getting better, better, and better.

You *are* going to learn some of this stuff. And as you learn some of it, your Teachability Index should go up.

With one exception.

Let's say you have a super high willingness to learn right now, and a high willingness to accept change. Let's say you are close to 100% teachable on the Teachability Index scale.

You are absorbing all this in so fast that your sponge is going to get full quickly. Maybe a few hours from now, that may dramatically shift. You might take a ton in, and it may take you only a few hours to "digest" it. Then you are ready for more.

That is why reading this book or listening to the audios over, and over, and over, and over, and over, and over, and over again, is really your mission.

"How much should I read or listen to each day?" you may ask.

I designed the original lecture with breaks approximately every hour. So, reading or listening for an hour and then taking a short break is a good way to give you a chance to digest what you read or listened to. Then go on and read more. Everyone of you will be different. But reading EVERY day is important, even if it's only for ten minutes. Putting a little in each day or a lot each day is fine, but every day would be helpful and better for you.

I will give you another little trick. If you read or listen to the audios in twenty-minute intervals, with a five-to-ten-minute break, this method is ideal.

This means you read or listen for twenty minutes, then stop. Take a five-to-ten-minute break. Go get a glass of water. Go for a walk. Go have some lunch.

Then, read or listen for another twenty minutes. Then take another break for five, or ten, or fifteen minutes, or an hour or two. Then listen to another twenty minutes.

That is really the ideal way for you to be able to completely absorb all this information.

But reading or listening for three hours straight every day also works!

Some of you reading this are VERY serious and VERY committed to yourself and your success. You will say, "I am going to start at nine o'clock in the morning and read all day until five. And then I will read all day on the next day." And you will do this until you complete the book.

That's fine as well.

But just read this book and listen to the audios over and over and over and over again because there is so much information packed in this book that when you read it a second time you will read things that you will swear were NOT there the first time you read it!

I would also suggest that you buy some baroque classical music, and play that softly in the background as you read the book.

Baroque classical music will actually lower your resting heart rate, reduce your blood pressure, and synchronize the left and right brain hemispheres. It will actually put you in what is called an Alpha state. This is the ideal state of the brain for learning new information, because it will be synchronized into both hemispheres of the brain and allow the information to bypass the analytical mind. That is where your resistance is! The good news is, because of the hypnotic language patterns the text is written in as well as the embedded commands and energy transference, resistance is futile. You WILL eliminate your failure programming, and you WILL replace that with SUCCESS programming. Your subconscious will be working twenty-four hours a day, seven days a week to make your dreams come true.

If listening to that music while you are reading is irritating or distracting, then don't have the music playing. That is a concentration and focus issue you need to address. In terms of how to focus, and what causes you not to be able to focus or be able to control your mind so that it can be in two different places, I will address that later.

So we talked about two basic things.

The first two steps.

Who Do You Listen To?

You should be listening to people who have the results to prove what they say is true. And ideally, people who were at where you are.

But remember, you LEARN from EVERYONE. There is a DIFFERENCE between who you LEARN from and who you LISTEN to. Think about that.

Second, what is your Teachability Index?

You may notice I am hammering the Teachability Index.

Why?

Because, if you ain't teachable, then everything goes in one ear and out the other.

You have to focus on the Teachability Index every day. Because your teachability changes every day. Some days you are very teachable. Other days you are arrogant and think you know everything. You can't say, "Oh, I am teachable" and expect to just be that way forever and never change.

Even in a day, you can be teachable in the morning and not teachable in the afternoon.

You have to constantly consider your own Teachability Index. Think about that.

Now the third step.

The third step is called **The Training Balance Scale.**

I learned this at the home of one of my mentors in the society, in Memphis, Tennessee.

He was one of the wealthiest guys in Tennessee. I was there for an entire day for one-on-one mentoring. We spent eight hours working on this one concept.

Think about working eight hours on just ONE concept. Think about that. When I taught the live seminar on this subject, it was two full days, about eight hours a day. In those two days and in this entire book, I cover LOTS of material. I could easily write an entire thousand-page book on just ONE of these concepts.

I am jamming in so much material in this relatively small book. I am really just scratching the surface of what is available in terms of knowledge. I am giving you, in this book, kind of a thumbnail sketch, a bird's-eye view, of the material and secret knowledge that I have been trained in. This is just the tip of the iceberg.

The good news is even with just a "taste," you can STILL learn how to manifest your goals and dreams faster and easier than ever before. When you finish reading this book, you WILL have all you need to make your dreams come true. Thousands of other people have proven that to be true. JUST with the information in this book, and NOTHING else, THOUSANDS of people report manifesting money, relationships, and material things faster and easier than they ever had and in MUCH larger and better amounts.

In the Brotherhood, each one of these subjects, such as the Teachability Index, could take hundreds of hours to learn fully and then years to FULLY integrate to the level of MASTER.

When I learned this next concept that I am teaching you now, it took me an entire eight-hour day to just get the BASICS. After that day, I was blown away with what I learned, yet I felt like I didn't get anywhere close to learning all the information on this subject. I was very teachable. I knew I did not know what I did not know.

And it was true.

This concept is called **The Training Balance Scale.**

I am going to give you a short overview of this vitally important concept. If I were to focus on this one topic, it would take an entire book.

Someone reading this will think, "Is this concept really THAT valuable and important? Is that really needed, to spend all that time on something like Teachability Index, or 'Who Do you Listen To?', or Training Balance Scale?"

The answer is, "Yeah, it is, IF you want to be able to command your wishes into existence and manifest all your goals and dreams faster and easier than ever before."

But maybe you really aren't ready. Maybe you really don't have a burning desire for success but only a weak and pitiful "wish" to be successful.

The good news is you DON'T have to be THAT committed right now. Even if you have a mild desire to improve the conditions of your life, you are in good shape. The fact that you are reading this shows me that you ARE ready ENOUGH to begin making your dreams a reality.

See, you eat an elephant one bite at a time.

If we are going to teach you mathematics, think of all the information that can be taught on the subject of mathematics. If you have never learned anything about mathematics, and this is the first lesson on mathematics, you would start learning mathematics at the beginning and increase on an easy gradient.

First, I would have to teach you what the numbers are—zero through nine.

You don't even know how to make a number 3 or what a number 3 is. You don't know what a 3 represents. You don't know what a 5 represents. So I have to teach you the numbers first, and explain that this squiggly line, which we call a three, means three "things." I would have to show you three oranges and three other things, so you get what 3 means, and what 2 means, and what 5 means, and so forth.

I'd have to teach it to you by throwing three paper clips down, and saying, "That's three." And then I'd show you five paper clips and go, "That's five." And I'd start showing you what these numbers represent by giving you something in the physical universe, something with mass that you could see, touch, and feel.

You have to start there, first.

Then I'd have to teach you addition, then subtraction, then multiplication, then division. Think about when we learned all this stuff. How many years did it take to learn just basic math?

Remember long division? How to carry numbers? Then we have to teach fractions.

Wow!

How do you multiply fractions—and decimals? Then what about geometry, algebra, calculus, trigonometry?

Do you understand that?

The same principle applies here.

When you look at a concept like the Teachability Index, think of it as mathematics. You may think you know everything already about the Teachability Index. Remember what I said in the beginning of this book?

You don't know what you don't know.

I laugh because I am holding back.

There is so much knowledge and information, for example about the Teachability Index, that I have NOT told you. In fact, there is

MUCH more about the Teachability Index that I have NOT told you—much more than I DID tell you in this book.

I just scratched the scratch of the scratch of the surface.

I am just giving you a little bit, enough, just what you need right now, so that your eyes don't roll in the back of your head, and you get so overwhelmed and feel like you are drinking water from a firehose!

I DO go into each one of these subjects, or concepts, or principles, in great depth if you are interested in expanding your knowledge of the subject and becoming even more of an expert or master at manifesting.

This book is what we call the basic book, the foundational book, the FIRST step toward total personal mastery. It really is the first group of lessons in the Success Mastery Course, a powerful training that I offer.

This book gives you the basic information. It is just giving you the scratch of the scratch of the scratch of the surface of each one of the concepts, yet that is enough for you to start manifesting things in your life FAST.

You can later take each of the concepts and go through additional training where it is all broken down even more. This gives you major new cognitions. This increases your awareness, understanding, and consciousness toward HOW manifesting works and WHY YOU can become a powerful creative force that has your abilities to manifest fully released.

You could spend thirty or more hours studying each concept. But that is advanced material, which goes way beyond what is in this book.

You may ask, "Do I need all that advanced training?"

The answer is, "No."

Everything you need is in this book.

You don't need to be a black belt in martial arts to be able to fully protect yourself.

You don't need to go to the music conservatory for ten years to be able to play an instrument beautifully and enjoy yourself doing it.

You don't **need** advanced training on this material because you have one lifetime here.

Keep this in mind: You have one lifetime here. You are starting from zero.

If you were born into an elite family, by the time you are twenty or thirty years old, you are not at point zero. Some of you reading this are thirty, forty, fifty years old.

Guess what?

If you were born into an elite family, you would have had that much time to learn all this stuff and more.

You don't need to learn everything on the subject of manifesting or making money. You just need to know enough. This book is MORE than enough.

You can take this information and create so much in your life, it is going to blow you away, like it already has for thousands of people just like you all around the world.

Most of the time, people relish and enjoy the ACT of creating more so than enjoying WHAT they create. This new knowledge and new power that will be yours when you finish this book will release your ability to CREATE whatever you desire.

After many of you finish this book, you may not want to do anything more other than just enjoy using your new powers. You don't have to go any further.

But some of you may choose to take yourself to another level of mastery and excellence … of SUPERPOWER.

That information will be available to you, but it is not a requirement.

My gosh, the information you are going to have access to in this book will allow you to create more than you could ever dream possible. And only when you actually start HAVING, attaining, and experiencing your dreams, will you be able to dream bigger.

Dream BIG. And don't let anyone steal your dreams.

So let's talk about the Training Balance Scale. Here is a visualization of the Training Balance Scale to help you as we discuss it. You may want to come back and refer to this image as you read a paragraph to help make a cognitive connection.

The Training Balance Scale

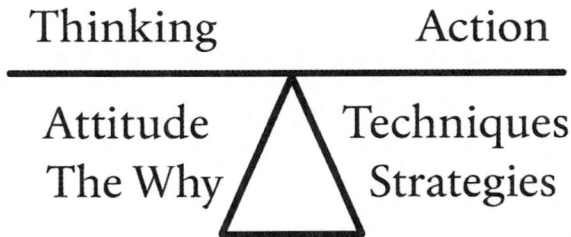

Thinking	Action
Attitude	Techniques
The Why	Strategies

Again, I learned this for the first time when I was in Memphis, many years ago. This was a profound learning experience for me.

The Training Balance Scale is a scale. On one side of the scale is what is called thinking.

You could also call it …

– Thoughts.
– Desires.
– Dreams.
– Goals.
– Attitude.
– Mental processes.
– Objectives.

This side of the scale deals with thoughts. It deals with your mind—what goes on inside your mind, how you think. It is NOT how you feel. Thoughts CREATE feelings. Actions create feelings as well. Feelings FUEL thoughts and actions, but do not create thoughts or actions. THIS UNDERSTANDING IS CRITICAL.

You can also put down a word called vibration. Intention. Energy.

This side of the Training Balance Scale DOES, however, include feelings, but only AFTER those feelings are created by either your thoughts or actions.

Your emotions and feelings do go on this side of the scale.

So, this side of the Training Balance Scale, if you were to break it down, deals with your thoughts and your emotions. How you think and how you feel.

The second side of the Training Balance Scale is action.

— Physical movements.
— What you do.
— Techniques.
— Strategies.
— Action steps.
— Plans.
— Activities.

This side of the Training Balance Scale is the physical actions that you do.

It is the acting out, the DOING.

So the difference is:

"I am thinking of calling my brother." That is on the thought side of the Training Balance Scale. Physically picking up the phone and dialing is on the action side.

The thought part is, "I am thinking of a battle plan, a plan of attack. I am thinking of putting a project into motion." That's my thought.

Physically putting that into motion, such as buying a filing cabinet, getting a desk, setting up a corporation, writing a business plan—those things are on the action side of the scale. The actual doing is on the action side of the scale.

Another way of describing the thought side of the scale is to call it the WHY.

The action side of the Training Balance Scale is the HOW.

The reason this is called the Training Balance Scale is when you are learning information, the theory is that there should be a balance between these two.

There should be a balance between dreams, goals, attitude, motivation, and inspiration on the THOUGHT side of the scale, and learning the HOW to do things and actually DOING things to make your dreams come true on the other/action side.

If you are going to train someone, you want to motivate them and get them excited, so you talk about their dreams and their goals, and how they are going to feel when they are successful, when they achieve and attain their desires.

But there should be a balance between doing that and also teaching them techniques.

Specifically, how do they make a phone call? How do they set up the corporation? How do they do this? How do they do that?

There should be a balance between teaching the real techniques that you apply in real life, the how, and motivating or working on a person's goals, dreams and attitude.

You must teach them how they are going to feel when they achieve this success.

But there should be a balance between attitude and thoughts on the one side, with technique on the other side.

The theory is—I am using the word theory on purpose—if you work only on motivation, then you wind up with a motivated idiot.

If you go to sales training seminars, or you go to a lot of these guru seminars on how to be successful, you may walk on fire and do all kinds of different things. You probably get motivated. But you leave not knowing what to DO.

They work on motivation, motivation, motivation. They work on your attitude. That is good. But without knowing what to actually DO, what action steps to actually take, you will not succeed. You will only end up frustrated.

The other side of the coin is you go to some of these boring, boring seminars where they teach you technique, technique, technique, technique, technique, skills, skills, skills, skills, skills.

The how, the how, the how, the procedure, the method, the system.

They work on only the action side of the Training Balance Scale.

That person leaves the seminar and does nothing, because he is not motivated. And even if they DO something, they do not get results because correct actions without the right ATTITUDE and VIBRATION does NOT produce results.

So the theory is, when you train somebody, you have to have a balance between working on their motivation, attitude, dreams, goals, thoughts on the one side, and the HOW on the other side.

You must be trained in both. You NEED both. You NEED techniques, skills, methods, procedures.

You NEED to know the how.

You have to work on the why **and** the how when you are training someone.

Well, none of you are training anybody right now.

You are being trained.

So the reason we bring this up is that you need to understand both sides of the Training Balance Scale and the importance of BOTH.

So, as you are learning new information, you should work on both sides of the Training Balance Scale.

Always first work on YOU. WHY?

You should be working on your goals, your dreams, your wants, your desires, your thoughts, your attitude, and your motivation.

And you should also be working on the how.

Learn the skills, the techniques, the methods, the actions you will need to take to make your dreams come true.

Learn exactly how to do the actions.

You must spend time on BOTH sides of the scale.

But the theory is that the balance should be that you learn equal amounts of both. The theory is the scale should be balanced.

And this, my friends, is the great myth that will keep you broke and prevent you from attaining your desires.

It is a myth, purposely put on you by the elite class.

There are actually two groups of the elite class out there. This is one of the reasons why I left the Brotherhood.

You have the elite class group that is benefiting society. These are the "good guys."

And then there is what is called the parasitical elite class, which lives off of society. This group is the "bad guys."

The parasitical elite class, unfortunately, is the majority. They live off your labor.

That is the reason why they want to stay in the position of power and control.

But they want you to *believe* you have opportunity. That there is free enterprise. That you have freedom.

Let me tell you something.

When you go to a job and you work for fifty years, you bring home your paycheck, and you are just barely making ends meet. You are SLOWLY paying off the mortgage. You live most of your life in debt. You work simply to pay your bills and exist.

You are not free. You are a slave. You think you're free. You think you're part of the free enterprise system, but you're not. You are a slave.

I don't have time to get into all the details about this issue, but the way the interest rates and fees are set up on mortgages, loans, and credit cards, and the way taxes are set up, you are part of a slavery system.

This is why 97 percent of people in America die with less than $1,000 cash in the bank. It is worse in other countries. They have been slaves their whole lives.

People have basically worked their whole lives making other people wealthy and allowing other people to live their dreams. Statistics vary, but it is said that 99 percent of people die with most of their desires unfulfilled.

How sad.

So this is a myth: that you have to have a balance on the scale.

What the truth is, is that the thought side of the Training Balance Scale, the thinking, your ATTITUDE, is 90 percent of success.

Your thinking, your thoughts, YOUR VIBRATION are ultimately more important than the how, or the techniques, or the skills when it comes to you creating things in your life, and making your desires come true.

When you are making your wishes manifest right before your eyes and you are making millions or earning whatever amount you want, when you are making your desires happen, the most important ingredient for this success to happen is your thoughts… YOUR VIBRATION.

I was sitting in a guy's house in Charlotte, North Carolina, many years ago. An incredibly wealthy guy. MUCH wealthier than I was at the time. I remember I was listening to him, and he made what I thought was the stupidest statement of all time.

And I remember thinking it was the stupidest statement of all time the moment I heard it. I resisted what he said. I disagreed with it.

The statement was, "When your attitude's right, the facts don't count."

I thought, how stupid; facts DO count.

Your thinking or your attitude is not going to change the facts. And so later, I challenged him. But at this moment in time, I was very fortunate, because the Teachability Index is always at the forefront of my thought. Every day, I ask myself, How teachable am I? How teachable am I? How teachable am I? How teachable am I?

What is my willingness to learn?

What is my willingness to accept change?

How teachable am I?

And when he made that statement, the first thing that popped into my head was: This is a stupid and naive statement.

BUT the second thing that popped into my head was: How teachable am I?

I thought, "high willingness to learn, high willingness to accept change."

If I think this is a stupid statement, I am willing to change that if I can get some more information, because clearly I don't understand it completely.

The reason we say NO to things is because we don't KNOW enough.

So later we were sitting at his home and I challenged him, and asked, "Explain this statement to me. I am confused because it doesn't make any sense to me."

With a big smile on his face, he just simply said this:

"When your attitude's right, the facts don't count, first and foremost because what you think are facts ain't facts anyway. They are usually just people's opinions."

I thought, "Huh?"

He went on, "Look, what you think are facts aren't facts. They are mostly people's opinions. When your attitude is right, facts don't count, because what you think are facts are mostly opinions."

He continued, "Just let me give you a couple examples. After the Second World War, there was a glut of ships in the world because the war was over. There were tons of ships everywhere, and none of them were being used. The war had ended. All the massive construction of shipping that was done because of the needs of the war created the largest excess glut of ships in history. You couldn't give ships away; because it would just cost you money to get rid of ships because you had to haul the ships away. And you couldn't sell them for scrap metal, because it cost too much to get the ship to a scrap metal facility.

"It was just a disaster. There were just ships blocking up ports and harbors. They were everywhere. You couldn't give them away. And if you were stuck with ships, it was a disaster just having them. It costs money just to hold onto ships."

"And everyone knew that this was a fact, and everyone knew that anybody in shipping was basically screwed. They just were losing money hand over fist."

"These were the facts."

"But there was one guy, by the name of Aristotle Onassis, who happened to be a member of the Brotherhood. He understood that what most people think are facts are nothing but opinions."

"At a coffee shop, on a napkin, he just did some basic mathematical calculations using information that was available to everyone."

"He realized that the reason there was a glut of ships was because of the war. International commercial shipping had ceased. Nobody was shipping things because of the war. They did not want to get torpedoed. Plus, there were shortages of everything. There was a war going on, a world war."

"Onassis realized that if shipping went back to just the same levels it was before the war, there ain't enough ships in the world that were seaworthy to handle that demand."

"Onassis also came to a simple conclusion. Because of the war, the world had become internationalized. Americans were now eating pizza, which they never heard of before the war."

"But now the American GIs were coming back from Italy, talking about, hey, we got pizza. So Americans wanted Italian products."

"Germans wanted American products. Japanese needed products because of the war. All of Europe and Russia needed products from America because America was the only major country that did not get its manufacturing destroyed by the war."

"The world had become internationalized."

"So Onassis said, if shipping goes back to just the levels it was before the war, there aren't enough ships right now."

"But because of the war shipping will increase, faster than ever."

"And so Onassis went out and got every ship he could. Within three years, he was the richest man in the world, based on shipping. Because he discerned fact from opinion."

The key here is the how is not so important as the thought process and your attitude.

This next concept that you need to understand—basic foundational KEY critical concept number three—is that you have to understand thoughts and what your thoughts are. Thoughts are THINGS. They have physical MASS.

And you also have to understand the how, the action steps, what you are physically doing, and the techniques.

But you should focus MOST of your attention on the thoughts.

Work on the thought process. Work on the thinking process. Do not worry about the how.

When you get your thinking and attitude right, the HOW WILL PRESENT ITSELF. The HOW will SHOW UP in your life as if by magic.

I am going to write more about this later.

The key that you need to understand is that your thinking—your thoughts, your dreams, how you feel, are 90 percent of importance to make success work.

Most people fail because they are always concerned about the how. They're concerned about, "How am I going to get the money to do that business? How can that happen? I don't understand how that is going to happen. I don't have the skills. I don't have the knowledge. I don't have the techniques. I don't have the know-how."

None of that matters.

When your thinking is right, when your thoughts are correct, the how doesn't matter.

I am going to explain more about how this works later. But you just need to understand, at this point, the basics of the Training Balance Scale: that you have a thought process, and you have a how process. You have both.

But most important is your thinking, thinking, thinking.

It is all about your thoughts.

LESSON 5

The Four Magic Steps

The next concept I want to talk about, major concept number four, is the four steps that you go through when processing information.

There are Four Basic steps the mind goes through when it is processing new information.

First is what is called "**unconscious incompetence.**"

This is when you don't know that you don't know.

Next is called "**conscious incompetence.**"

This is when you know that you don't know.

Next is called "**conscious competence.**"

This is when you know that you know.

And last is called "**unconscious competence.**"

This is when you *know*, and it happens automatically.

It is called autopilot.

You need to understand these four areas of the brain (actually the mind), the thought process, and the learning process.

Because your objective is to get the unconscious competence when it comes to this information, the system the book is teaching you.

This is when this information that you are learning is part of you and is happening automatically.

It just naturally occurs. You don't "think" about it anymore. You are not consciously applying this data. It is a knowing, like how you KNOW your own name.

What is your name?

Boom. You know your own name. You don't have to think about it. You are unconsciously competent. You know that you know. It's autopilot.

If I say, Can you tie your shoes?

"Yeah."

You'd bend over and you'd tie your shoe.

Well, think about the very first time you needed to tie a shoelace. You didn't even know that you didn't know; you were unconsciously incompetent.

Then someone showed you how to tie a shoelace. You couldn't do it. As soon as you knew you could NOT tie your shoe, that you did to know HOW, you become consciously incompetent.

You knew you didn't know.

Then you were **taught** how to tie your shoe.

And every time you tied the shoelace, it took you a few seconds. You had to think about it.

You would think, "How do I do it? Left over right. Where … ?"

And you thought through the process.

You became consciously competent.

After a while, you did not have to think about how to tie the shoelace. You just tied the shoelace.

You became unconsciously competent.

Think about driving home. Some people drive home from work, you get home, and you think, "Boy, I don't even remember how I got here. My mind was someplace else."

You got home safely because you are unconsciously competent regarding driving and how to get home. When it comes to driving home, you know exactly how to drive home. You don't think about it anymore. It is out of the conscious state. It is unconscious. You just know it. It is in the knowledge bank.

This information you are learning in this book must become a part of you, virtually part of your DNA. That is one of the reasons why you want to read this book over and over and over and over again. And/or listen to the audios over and over again.

This method will DEPROGRAM your FAILURE PROGRAMS and get this information in you at the unconscious competence level.

So, for example, if I were to ask you, "What was the first concept we talked about?" some of you don't INSTANTLY know the answer. You have to think about it or check through your notes.

Well, you should know the first concept as well as you know your own name. That FIRST concept is Who Do You Listen To.

And you should be able to understand Who Do You Listen To and why you listen to certain people and not others.

If I say, "What was the second concept we talked about?"

Again, some of you don't know. It is the Teachability Index.

What is the Teachability Index? Can you explain it? You should instantly know, without even thinking about it, that there are two variables: Willingness to learn and willingness to accept change.

If you need to think about that, you are not unconsciously competent yet.

No problem.

But the point is, all of these concepts, when they become unconsciously knowledge, they become part of your knowledge bank.

When you become unconsciously competent in all these areas, and all the material in this book, THAT is when the magic will start. That is when, without even doing anything, all these things will begin to work.

When I say work, what are we talking about specifically?

We are talking about manifesting your desires in record time. And have it happen as if by magic.

Have it happen easily and effortlessly. That is what we are talking about.

Believe and you receive; doubt and go without.

Work on getting all this knowledge into your DNA. Make it a part of you. It is not when you get this book, but rather when this book gets IN YOU!

LESSON 6

To Be a Master, You Must Master the Basics

The first Four Basic Concepts we covered are:
- Who Do You Listen To?
- The Teachability Index.
- The Training Balance Scale.
- The Four Magic Steps that you go through when learning information.

A question that comes up is, how do you get to unconscious competence? How do you get to that level of mastery? The answer is actually very simple.

All of you start at the bottom, and when you're learning information, you get to conscious competence quickly. That's when you know the information, but you have to consciously apply that information. You have to think about it. You have to think about HOW to apply it.

The only way you can get to unconscious competence is by utilizing one of two methods.

Number one, by doing that action over and over and over at the conscious competence level.

The example is tying the shoelace. Over time, you will get to unconscious competence.

How did you get to unconscious competence when tying the shoelace? How did you get to unconscious competence by knowing your way from work to home?

The answer is by doing it over and over and over and over and over and over and over again at the conscious competence level. You do it over and over and over again, and all of a sudden, you become unconsciously competent.

The question is, how actually does that work?

What's the mechanism in which to get to unconscious competence?

Another way of defining unconscious competence is calling it the knowledge bank, knowingness … Where it's completely internalized. It's part of you. You don't have to think about it anymore.

When you actually do something over and over and over and over again, you're actually creating neural pathways in the brain. These are biological connections between cells—dendrites—that connect and actually grow in size.

These neural pathways are actually energy and electrical channels where information or energy is transmitted through the brain. They're actual patterns that develop in the brain.

So, by getting to the unconscious competence level, the first way you do that is by doing it over and over and over and over again, creating that neural pathway.

There is a second method to getting to the unconscious competence level.

It's very interesting and extremely powerful.

The second method is by observing someone else actually doing the thing you want to be able to do at the unconscious competence level.

One of the advantages of having a mentor, one of the advantages of being an apprentice, one of the advantages of being a "Fly on The Wall" is you get to observe someone else effortlessly operating on autopilot and DOING what you also want to be able to do effortlessly on autopilot.

This is the reason why associating with people who have what you want is so important.

Your income will be the average of your five best friends', the five people you spend the most time with.

This is one of the major benefits of the societies like the Brotherhood.

Not only did we get the knowledge, but we got to observe people *using* the knowledge in real life. By that attentive and focused observation, it was like monkey see, monkey do.

This is a major advantage. When you can join a club and associate with winners and successful people who are already using these techniques at the unconscious competence level, you learn via osmosis. It gives you virtually an UNFAIR advantage over others. Your success potential goes up 100 times!

If you're learning from or observing somebody who's doing it wrong, you're going to do it wrong as well.

That's why if you want to be a great chef and you happen to be the apprentice of a spectacular chef, there's a good chance you're going to become a spectacular chef.

If you want to be a spectacular musician and you get to work with and be an apprentice of a spectacular musician, then you get that advantage. You will become a spectacular musician.

When you start associating with and observing people who are brilliant or a success in any profession, you get to see what they do, see how they act, hear how they talk, and learn how they think. You then become like them.

My mom always said, "If you hang around those people long enough, you will turn out just like them!" Lucky for me, I was hanging around the happiest, most successful people in the world.

Success does breed success.

Success does rub off.

Having a mentor, associating with people that have what you want, and in this case, utilizing this information with successful results, will help you do it, too.

Being able to witness them, watch them, and observe them does create neural pathways in the brain as well and gets you to autopilot faster, where you KNOW this information because it is a part of you. It is WHO YOU ARE.

Which method to get to unconscious competence is more important, or which is better?

Both are important. Both work. You should be doing BOTH. There is a synergistic effect that happens when you employ BOTH methods to get to unconscious competence. I would suggest to you that unless you are observing and associating with successful people on a regular basis—unless you are listening to them, watching them, mimicking their actions, speech pattern, and ways of thinking, and modeling their behavior—your level of proficiency, your level of success, is not going to be as good as it could be.

You actually may become unconsciously competent in doing the system incorrectly because you may be doing it wrong all the time.

Practice does not make perfect. PERFECT practice makes perfect.

So learning this information from those who have achieved successful results with it and use it professionally, perfectly, and to a very high level, is something that you have to do.

It isn't a one-time thing. It's an ongoing process.

The way you get to unconscious competence is by observing those people who are doing it CORRECTLY and getting RESULTS.

Now, from a practical standpoint, how are you going to do this? Because none of you reading this book have that physical mentor that you can watch, observe, and learn from.

You don't have a super-successful person that can make you their apprentice.

The answer is, you do the best you can with what you have and where you are.

We didn't have physical mentors that we were around every single day either. But we were around them once in a while. And when we were around them, we took full advantage of that situation and, by PAYING ATTENTION with FOCUS, we observed them in action, and then kept that picture in our mind. We kept that meeting in our mind, and then mimicked their actions, thoughts, and words thereafter.

So, what do you do?

You are going to have some advantages that other folks won't have because you are reading this book. The fact that you are reading this book tells me you are special. You are ready. Your ship has come in.

At the end of this book, you will be given the opportunity to have a plethora of audio and written material being made available to you, some of which is free. You will also be given the opportunity to join my private global club where you CAN have a personal mentor and where you CAN meet, associate, and become friends with people from all around the world who are using this material and getting spectacular results.

You could even be a "Fly on The Wall" at one of my homes where you can observe me in action and learn directly from a master.

Remember, information is not coming from me, the guru. I did not invent or "discover" this.

I just happen to be the selected teacher and messenger of this information. The information is information that I learned from my association and involvement with the Brotherhood. I reached the highest level in that organization.

This training also comes from many of the other people that were at the live training event that I recorded. These were members of the Freemasons' inner sanctum, above the thirty-third-degree level, the Illuminati, Skull and Bones, royal family members, and many other folks from the other societies as well.

So we are a group of people that learned this information from the various societies we were a part of, and who were all members of the elite class. We have the physical evidence in our lives that it works.

Those who were in the live audience could see the results with their own eyes and meet the people personally.

I am now presenting it to you in this book, in what we believe to be a very easy-to-digest format, so that you can apply it and see speedy, spectacular results yourself.

We have actually tested this with many others first, people who were "outside of this group."

The results have been nothing more than spectacular. Those people have said to us that

learning this information and applying it has just been mind-blowing. The speed in which their dreams and desires are coming into physical reality has shattered their beliefs about being able to attain goals and dreams.

Whatever you want in life, you can have. You can virtually Be, Do, and Have whatever you desire.

An important key is getting to that unconscious competence level.

Doing "it" correctly over and over again at the conscious competence level will get you to unconscious competence. And observing others who are already at the unconscious competence level will help you get there as well. Doing both is best.

Do the right things, long enough, consistently.

That's why everything here in this book is in a very particular order of teaching.

That's why you must have a high willingness to learn and a high willingness to accept change.

You have to be high on the Teachability Index.

What is the number one reason that people just don't succeed? Is it lack of knowledge?"

And the answer is actually no.

The answer is either they may be listening to the wrong people, or they have a low Teachability Index.

If you want to be a great chef and you're listening to a guy who's a short-order cook, who's never made a soufflé in his life … Guess what? You're never going to learn how to make a soufflé.

If you want to be a world-class chef and learn how to cook spectacular food, and you're learning from a guy who fries eggs … well, you get the idea.

You are not learning how to create spectacular cuisine because you're learning from somebody who doesn't know how to create spectacular cuisine.

To be the best, you must learn from the best.

If you want to be a great piano player and you listen to somebody who's maybe a very good honky-tonk piano player, but certainly not a concert pianist, you're never going to be a spectacular pianist. You're never going to be a great musician because you're not learning from the best.

Same thing here … If you want to create things in your life, if you want to have happiness, you need to learn from the best.

So the first reason people fail is they don't learn from the right people, which means they're not getting the right information. But if you find the right people, you do get the right information.

Somebody would say, "Well, up until now, this information has been secret. There was no way I could learn from the best."

That's absolutely true.

However, there IS *enough* information out there from the right people that, if you use discernment to find the RIGHT information and then USE it, you could get results.

True, not all the material has been released to the public until this book. But a lot of this stuff is available if you look hard enough. When the student is ready, the teacher WILL appear.

True, the **key** elements have never been available, but some of the information has been available, and enough has been available so that you can apply it and reach spectacular results. Others have to some degree.

True, the first reason that people fail is they don't have the right teachers. They're not learning from the right people. They're not listening to the right people. They are getting FALSE DATA. This means they're getting the wrong information.

The second reason people fail is they have a low Teachability Index. They just refuse to be willing to give up things, to be obsessed with learning. They have a low willingness to learn.

And even if they do have a high willingness to learn, they have a low willingness to accept change. They keep doing the same thing over and over and over again, and they just refuse to change their patterns. Yet they expect a different result. Insane.

Those wrong patterns are in effect neural pathways, which is why willingness to accept change is critical. You have to understand the reason why you may have a hard time with willingness to change. The reason it may be hard for you to be really willing to change is because you've done the same thing for so long. You've established very, very, very strong, embedded, ingrained, large neural pathways in your brain.

You can't just eliminate a failure habit. You must REPLACE it with a SUCCESS habit.

New neural pathways have to be developed, which creates new patterns. So a low Teachability Index is a major thing.

The next reason people fail is they spend too much time on the how. Remember the Training Balance Scale? People who fail also spend too much time on the technique or the skill, thinking that's the key.

People have too many excuses, such as, "Well, I don't know how to do that. I don't know how to raise the money for that business. I don't know how in the world I could have enough money to pay off all my bills. I don't have any idea how in the world I could be able to take a one-month holiday to Europe."

Failures are always good at one thing: making excuses.

They think of their desire, something they want, their dream. And then what they do is they come up with all the reasons why it won't happen in their life. Here are some of the excuses:

- Because they don't know the technique, they don't know the how.
- They don't know where the money is coming from.
- They get stuck on the HOW side of the Training Balance Scale.

That's a key. Keep your eye on the DREAM. And don't let anyone steal your dream.

What one person has done, you can do also. If you think you can or think you can't, either way you are RIGHT; it is the THINKING that makes it true. Nothing is impossible for those who BELIEVE.

The fourth reason people fail is they don't spend enough time at the conscious competence level to develop new neural pathways so that they get to the unconscious competence level, where new patterns have been established—new habits, new neural pathways—and the information becomes a part of you, where you are operating on autopilot. Where your subconscious takes over and virtually is working on your success twenty-four hours a day, seven days a week.

Proper successful actions, words, and thoughts then happen instinctively, instantaneously, effortlessly, easily, thus creating successful results as if by magic, and as if by doing nothing.

Now all of this knowledge is beginning to make sense to you.

I'm touching on a few things so you have a general understanding, so as we go further, it'll all start falling into place. I am planting seeds in your subconscious that will create success for you.

The Four Basic Concepts that we discussed must be reviewed.

You must *know* them, not just *know about* them.

They are the foundation from which all the information in the rest of the book will be built.

Remember, you can only build as high up as your foundation is deep.

At this point in the live event, many people said to me, "You know, we're spending a lot of time here on what I would classify as some very simplistic, very basic information. When are you going to get to the real meat?" Some of you may be thinking the same thing. You may be saying, "Kevin, I know this stuff already."

Well, to KNOW and not to DO, is NOT to know.

Let me tell you the news:

These Four Basic Concepts, *this is the real meat ...*

The rest of the information is actually easy and simple. But none of it will stick. None of it will take root unless you have a fertile environment for the rest of the information to grab, grow, take hold, and develop.

It's like if you're going to plant seeds, you need to prepare the soil first. If you don't prepare the soil, if the soil isn't fertile, you can plant seed, and you can water it all you want, and get all the sunlight on it you want, but the seed will never take root and grow. The soil has to be prepared.

If you're going to build a skyscraper, you must build a foundation. And that foundation has to be strong; it has to be deep. Without that foundation, nothing will happen.

And what are we looking to achieve here?

You know, this book is entitled, *Your Wish Is Your Command: How to Manifest Your Desires.* This means whatever you want in life, you can call it forth.

Whatever you desire. Whatever you want.

You can virtually give the command and manifest it in your physical experience.

Whatever your heart desires.

Whatever you want to see in front of you.

Whatever you want to be, do, or have.

All you have to do is give the command, and it's there.

You have Aladdin's Lamp.

The Genie is at your command.

Give the command, and it will come forth with amazing speed.

Whether that be happiness.

Whether that be money.

Whether that be a bigger house or something material, like a car.

Whether that be something internal, a feeling, happiness, joy, or glee.

Whether it be a relationship.

Whether it be a better relationship with the person you're with.

Whether it be happiness in your home.

Whether it be a better relationship with your friends, coworkers, children, or family members.

Whether it be learning a foreign language or learning to play a musical instrument.

Or whether it means traveling.

Or whether it means doing something where you're praised and you're given accolades for.

Whether it be growing in your career and hitting levels of appreciation in your life from the people around you, that you've always desired.

Whether it be getting your physical body to a place where you feel fantastic in your skin.

Whether it's physical health.

Whatever it is you want, this book is designed to give you the tools so that all you have to do, in effect, is give the command.

Your Wish Is Your Command.

Whatever you command, it can come forth. That's what we're achieving.

Later in the book, we will be focusing strictly on money.

Today, we're laying all the foundation for everything.

That's the objective.

And somebody always says, "But I know this stuff. This stuff sounds something like I've heard before."

Really? You know this stuff? You know it? Do you know it? You know it?

"To know and not to do is not to know."

I had a friend of mine; he was giving a lecture. He was talking about being positive. I was at this lecture. He was talking about how most people aren't really positive, enthusiastic, and happy.

This woman raises her hand, and she says, "I don't understand. I'm happy all the time."

And my friend looked at her and said, "Really? You should tell your face."

Everyone cracked up laughing because she had this scowl on her face, which certainly didn't make it appear that she was happy. She **thought** she was happy, but she certainly wasn't emanating that feeling. She was DELUSIONAL.

So if you think you know this information, but you don't have the results to show it, I can categorically tell you, you don't know it. You're doing something wrong.

Maybe you know ABOUT this information, but you do not KNOW it.

Think about it. You know how to do this? Really? Okay.

You know how to make a soufflé? Really? How come you can't make one?

Obviously, you don't know. You think you know, but you don't. Your Teachability Index is zero.

Do you understand this?

I keep going back to these four concepts, the foundational concepts.

Who Do You Listen To, the Teachability Index, the Training Balance Scale, and the Four Magic Steps, getting to unconscious competence.

Now, these are four concepts that you should know, know, know, know, and know, just like your own name.

So if I were to ask you, who do you listen to and why? You should be able to explain it to me clearly, concisely, and with brevity.

Who Do You Listen To?

Someone may ask, "Well, how would you explain that concisely, Kevin?" I would say, "Listen to people that have what you want, that have the physical evidence that it works, and have been where you are. But learn from everyone. The rich man learns from the fool, but the fool does not learn from the rich man."

That's it. That makes sense.

Teachability Index.

Can you explain that to me? Yeah. There are two variables.

One, what is your willingness to learn?

Next, what is your willingness to accept change?

You have to be high in both of those concepts. You have to be very high. You have to have a high willingness to learn. Well, how do you determine if you have a high willingness to learn?

What are you willing to give up? Are you willing to give up your favorite thing to learn?

What is your willingness to accept change? Are you willing to do something completely different? You need to be teachable.

Training Balance Scale. Can you explain that? Yeah.

There are two sides of the Training Balance Scale. One is the thoughts; one is the actions.

One is the attitude, the motivation, the why, the dream, the thinking.

And the other side is the how, the techniques, the skills, the action steps, the doing part.

Which is more important? The thoughts are 90 percent of this process. Makes sense.

Next, the fourth basic concept … What are the four levels of learning or the Four Magic Steps?

You should instantly tell me, not by looking at your notes:

– unconscious incompetence,
– conscious incompetence,
– conscious competence,
– and unconscious competence.

And if I were to say, well, how do you get to unconscious competence?

Well, there are two ways. By doing it yourself over and over and over and over again at the conscious competence level, to develop new neural pathways, new patterns, new habits. Perfect practice makes perfect. And by observing and associating with people that are doing it correctly … Observing, observing, observing, watching, mimicking them and modeling yourself after them, because they already have established neural pathways. This way you're seeing firsthand exactly how it works.

That's the key.

Vitally important.

Now why are we spending so much time on the basics?

Because, as I mentioned, this is the foundation. We need to have a fertile environment for everything else to grow. Otherwise, nothing else will stick.

If you were my apprentice, I would focus on these Four Basic Concepts, getting you primed and ready to learn. This is how I was taught as an apprentice. I would follow my master, in effect.

Now, it's not like a Shaolin monk following his master, or a disciple following a spiritual guru. We're not walking around in robes, not like a Jedi Knight in *Star Wars*, where Anakin Skywalker was following around Obi-Wan Kenobi, or Obi-Wan Kenobi was following around his master, Yoda.

No. ***But yes.***

In my case, and all the other people who were at the live event that the attendees met, we could all be classified as "masters" because we have had apprentices.

But guess what?

We still have mentors. We are all still apprentices, even though we've had many, many, many apprentices ourselves, and who we have been teachers to. To be a MASTER, you must always be a great student. You must always be growing. You are either growing or dying.

A man told me he had twenty years of business experience. After we talked for a while, I realized it actually had ONE year of business experience REPEATED TWENTY times. HE STOPPED GROWING. He stopped learning. He "knew it all." ZERO TEACHABILITY.

But how does it work in real life in the societies? The training, as I mentioned, was occasionally in a seminar or workshop, sitting in groups. Here, we would observe the other masters who were also still learning.

Much of the training was given one-on-one, speaking one-on-one over coffee or discussing on the phone one-on-one. In these settings, we would observe our "uncle," master, teacher, and mentor.

Books … Someone says, How can you be an apprentice and observe from a book?

Well, think about this concept. Did you ever read a novel, a really good novel? And you read this novel, and you're sitting there, and you're reading the novel, and the novel is talking about the hero, and the hero is in the Amazon jungle. And he has his machete and he's wearing a ripped T-shirt because his body is perspiring so much and there's bugs all over his body. There was a slight rain earlier, so the jungle is moist and humid, and it's hot, and he has shorts on and hiking boots.

He has this large machete, and he has a bandana around his head, and he's going through the jungle in search of the villain.

And you're reading this novel as it describes the green foliage that he's going through and the types of plants, and the sounds he's hearing, and the bugs he's seeing, and the feel that his feet are experiencing when they moosh into the moist earth, and the color of the earth and the smells that he's having, and how he's breathing because of the heat, and the humidity, and he's tired and how his muscles are beginning to ache and his arm is beginning to get weary from the heavy machete chopping into the foliage as he's going through the bush.

And as you're reading this, it's enthralling, it's very well written. And you're reading this novel, and somebody walks in the room and says to you, "Hey, Charlie!"

And you continue to read the novel, oblivious to your friend who's walked in, calling your name.

And the person says, "Charlie! Charlie! Earth to Charlie!"

And finally, you look up, not hearing a word, and you say, "Did you say something to me?"

That's happened to all of us. Or you know exactly what I'm talking about.

You're so engrossed in this novel that you're not even in the room anymore, because you are in the Amazon. You have become oblivious to your friend two feet away from you, yelling your name.

That's how … Now listen carefully.

That is how you associate, you mimic, you observe successful people who are using this information in their real life. That's how books work.

The books that we read, that we were given, use these techniques. They're not manuals per se, but they're stories of real people, members of the societies, with real, accurate descriptions of their daily life and them acting out these principles and techniques in their daily life.

Does this make sense?

This is why I tell you: The first concept was, Who Do You Listen To?

When you start reading books about mythical characters, you're screwing yourself up, because now you're mimicking and modeling yourself after the short-order cook, when you want to learn how to cook a soufflé, because these are not real people.

If there was a simple thing for you to do, if you wanted to be outrageously successful, you'd go and get autobiographies and biographies of people who have what you want.

If you want to be a chef, read the autobiographies and biographies of great chefs.

If you want to be a musician, read the biographies and autobiographies of great musicians, because that's who you have to mimic and model yourself after.

These are the people that have developed the habits and neural pathways in their brain, who've reached levels of unconscious competence that you should be modeling yourself after.

And since you can't meet them because they're dead, you can still associate with them.

Now pay attention.

Read carefully what I'm saying.

You can still associate with them, even though they're dead ... through books.

Leaders are always readers.

Books are magic.

Books are powerful.

Books allow our brains and our imaginations to be utilized to create images, sights, sounds, smells through the power of our imagination in our brain, which creates neural pathways even faster than physical observation with our eyes.

Isn't this interesting?

And some of you wonder why we had to read books when we were kids. And some of you wonder why books are being pushed away by the powerful, parasitical elite class ...

Because the power of books is known.

So we associate and observe.

You're here and getting to the unconscious competence level, utilizing the fundamentals, the Four Basics.

Who Do You Listen To?

Teachability Index.

Training Balance Scale.

And the Four Magic Steps of learning information.

This is the foundation.

When we worked with our mentors, as I mentioned, in some cases, our mentors would give us books where we would begin to learn these concepts. And the books that we were given had emphasis on one of these four characteristics.

I had to figure out what the emphasis of the story was; were the observations I was getting from the book focusing me on the Teachability Index, or the Training Balance Scale, or the Four Magic Steps, or Who Do I Listen To?

I was given books to read so that I would continue to focus on these four fundamentals. And obviously, I was given books because there are thousands and thousands and thousands of these books. We were given books based on our need and our weakness. It was as if we were being PRESCRIBED a book to handle our "issues" and needs.

But every book always covered all of the basics, with emphasis on one over the other.

At the end of this book, you're going to be given a list of books, not from the societies, because they are unavailable to you for multiple reasons. Our books were in society libraries, in members' homes.

We couldn't grab them from the libraries and take them with us. The libraries are in people's homes. They're not in the Skull and Bones building. They're not in the Illuminati building. They're not in the Brotherhood building. They're not in the Freemason buildings.

No. This information, as I mentioned, is passed on through generations, through families, through people, and these books and libraries are actually physically in homes around the world.

That's where the information is, and that's why it can't be taken out.

So you're going to get the second best. You're going to get a list of other books which my colleagues and I have read, and come close, come close to the secret manuscripts we had access to.

So we learned this information from, I mentioned, some lectures, some one-on-one conversations, books, and again, by physically observing.

So how would we do it in real life? The books were probably the main focus because that was something that we could do on our own.

And then the physical observation, because we knew what members of society were members of *our* societies. We could observe them, and we were given access, although in many cases, not direct access; in some cases, only indirect access through our mentors, our teachers, our sponsors. Every group called these individuals different things.

Sometimes one society calls your teacher The Man, which is interesting because a lot of minorities in America use that in a very defamatory way.

And that's really where it came from, from the secret societies, as the person who has power over you, in effect.

But we observed. We looked. We were taught that we had to observe.

And how were we trained? When I was with my mentor, or if I was observing another member of the society, I would also LISTEN and PAY ATTENTION to EVERY DETAIL. The way you do ANYTHING is the way you do EVERYTHING. Think about that.

Sometimes I would get a phone call at two o'clock in the morning.
"Hello?"

"Hey, did you see so-and-so today do his such-and-such thing?"
"Yeah. "

"What did you observe?"

Two o'clock in the morning, I'm getting a phone call.

This was part of the training. This was part of the teaching. That's a little bit of the advantage of having that one-on-one person.

But for you, you have this book. You also have the audios of the live event. So you have an advantage that we didn't have.

My colleagues and I have put together this book for you and the audios because when you finish, I know you're not going to get it all.

You can read it over and over or listen to the audios over and over, which will be incredibly powerful at helping you learn this information, integrating it into your DNA, and getting to unconscious competence.

But why do I spend so much time again on this foundational material?

I was with a Shaolin monk. Some people may have watched the TV series called *Kung Fu* back in the '70s, with David Carradine. *Kung Fu* was about a Shaolin monk from the Shaolin temple in China, which is a real place, thousands of years old.

This particular TV series starred David Carradine … His character was named Kwai Chang Caine. He was a Shaolin monk. A Shaolin monk, at the time, was a Buddhist monk who was trained in the martial arts of kung fu, tai chi, and qigong.

The Shaolin Temple was actually the birthplace of all martial arts in the world.

The Shaolin monks, before they were martial artists, were peaceful, meditating monks. Unfortunately, because they were peaceful, meditating monks, bandits would come in, beat up the monks, kill the monks, and steal from the monks.

The monks got a little tired of this, so they decided to go out and find some warriors that they could hire to protect them. So they sent out monks east, west, north, and south to find warriors who could defend the Shaolin temple.

When the monks returned, they brought back warriors from the east, west, north, and south, as far as India, Japan, and different provinces in China.

Before this time, the warriors or the fighters around the world only were trained and were taught and knew of the fighting techniques of their particular region. So each one of these warriors that returned to the Shaolin temple, each had a unique and quite different fighting style.

This was the first time in history where all these fighting styles, experts in these various fighting styles, got together and met each other. They began to share their techniques with one another.

Over the years, these monks began to integrate all the various styles together into one style, which became known as kung fu. The monks also did something else that was unique.

They observed animals like the tiger, the crane, the snake, and the praying mantis.

And they watched how these animals fought in the wild. And they took all of this knowledge, and over the years developed a style of fighting which became the most feared, awesome, and overpowering fighting style on the planet, the Shaolin Kung Fu.

These styles were put together in forms or routines so that the monks could practice their martial arts, so they could defend themselves, but at the same time, meditate. They developed forms, which were moving meditation.

This TV series about Kwai Chang Caine was about a monk who left the temple and traveled throughout America, got into a bunch of fights, protected people, and showed off his kung fu.

The Shaolin temple is a real place, and I've always been intrigued by the Shaolin monks and their incredible ability.

A few years ago, for the first time in history, the Chinese government allowed 35 of the monks to leave the temple and do a worldwide tour showing the world the abilities of the Shaolin fighting monks. Up until this time, no one really saw the Shaolin monks in action. It was all stories. It was all legend as to what these monks could do.

Well, when the monks traveled, the legends were nothing compared to just how awesome these monks' abilities actually were. The monks amazed everyone with their ability to move their chi energy and do phenomenal feats with their physical bodies that were mind-blowing to all who saw them.

On the last day of the tour, the lead monk, Shi Yan Ming, decided to leave the temple—or actually not return to the temple, but leave the hotel—because he was defecting and he wanted to teach the world these secrets for the first time in history.

For years, he was on the run from the Chinese government. He was on the run from the immigration authorities in America.

Well, I met this monk. I brought him to my home. He lived with me for a while. When I first met him, his English was not very good. So I had my Chinese kung fu teacher, Grand Master Tsai, with me to help interpret.

So my first day, I said to my Chinese kung fu teacher friend, who spoke English, "Tell the monk that I want to learn the secrets of the Shaolin temple. I want to learn the advanced stuff, and make sure you let the monk know that I have studied the martial arts for years and years, and I am very proficient in the martial arts, so I don't want to learn any basic things. I want to learn the advanced, secret stuff taught at the Shaolin temple."

So my good friend and teacher, Grand Master Tsai, talked Chinese to the monk, and he turned to me and he said, "Well, the monk says he wants to teach you how to throw a punch."

I said, "No, no, no, no. Tell the monk I know how to throw punches. You have been training me for yours. You are a Grand Master. I KNOW how to throw punches. I want to learn the advanced stuff. I want the real meat. I want the secrets."

They chatted again.

Grand Master Tsai turned to me and said, "Well, the monk says he really wants to teach you how to throw a punch."

I said, "No, no, no. Tell him I know how to throw a punch. I don't need to learn how to throw just a basic punch. I want to learn the real advanced stuff."

They chatted again and Grand Master Tsai said, with a smirky smile on his face, "Well, he say he really want to teach you how to throw a punch. He say he want to see your punch first, and he want to see how good you are."

So, they set up a candle, lit the candle flame, and said, "He wants you to throw your punch as hard as you can, and stop one inch before candle flame."

I said, "Fine." I thought he probably wants to see how much I can control, you know, a powerful punch.

So I asked him, "What type of punches does he want? Does he want a cutting punch? Does he want a side punch? Does he want a spinning backfist punch?"

"No, no, just any punch."

So I throw a Shaolin cutting punch at the candle flame, and I stop exactly one inch from the candle flame with perfect control.

Quite frankly, I was pretty impressed with my own punch.

They talked in Chinese, and Grand Master Tsai said, "The monk says he's very impressed with your punch. He say he now want to show you his punch."

So, sure, I wanted to see the monk's punch. I mean, it couldn't be any better than mine.

So the monk gets up there, looks at the candle flame, looks at me, and smiles, and throws his very short punch. And he stops about a foot and a half from the candle flame, and the candle flame went out!

He stopped his hand a foot and a half from the flame, with a fist, with this very short punch, and the candle flame went out!

My eyes got as big as saucers, and I said, "Oh my God, tell him I want to learn how to do that!"

And he said, "That's what he been trying to tell you. He wants to show you how to throw a *punch*."

And the reason why I tell you this story is that sometimes we think, "I don't want to learn the basics. I want to learn the advanced stuff."

And this Shaolin master said to me, very simply, "If you want to be a master, you have to be a master of the basics."

And what I learned, and what you should understand, is that these Four Basic Principles—

   – Who Do You Listen To,

   – Teachability Index,

   – Training Balance Scale, and

   – The Four Magic Steps—

are not as simple as you think.

Some people think they're just a punch.

No.

If you really focus in on the Training Balance Scale, after you finish this book, you'll be amazed at how different you'll be at learning all the in-depth knowledge in this information. You will see how profound the Four Basic Concepts are and how significant they are.

The Shaolin monk was going to teach me for the next six weeks how to throw a punch … because the secret of the Shaolin temple is being able to throw one strike.

Remember his secret … If you want to be a master, you must be a master of the basics.

He taught me this other very important principle. And these are the same principles from the societies, by the way.

He told me this. I want you to pay attention to this very carefully, because this is brilliant.

He said, "How many different strikes can you throw?" And I started rattling off all these different punches, all these different kicks, all these different elbow strikes, all these different knee strikes, rattling off one after the other, after the other, after the other.

These were all the different strikes that I knew. I knew MANY different strikes, and I knew them really well.

He listened and then said this brilliant statement: "At the Shaolin temple, we say, 'I am not afraid of the ten thousand strikes, you know that you've practiced only once. I am deathly afraid of the one strike you know that you've practiced ten thousand times."

Think about that.

I am not afraid of the ten thousand strikes you know you've practiced once.

I am deathly afraid of the one strike, you know that you've practiced ten thousand times.

Key principle.

Master the basics.

This is a key principle.

And by definition, "Master the basics" is "Focus on the fundamentals." And there are not a lot of fundamentals. This is a secret. The secret is that most people think there are all these secrets. Therefore, they think they can't be successful because they don't know all of the secrets.

The biggest secret of the societies is that there are only a few basic concepts, but the key is mastering them to a level that nobody could imagine.

Just like a punch. A simple punch is NOT just a simple punch.

The reason the Shaolin monk could stop his punch (or his fist) a foot and a half before the candle flame and blow the candle flame out was, he learned how to throw a punch and actually throw his, what's called chi energy, through his body, through the fist. The chi energy would actually leave the physical body and go out into the flame, causing the flame to go out.

Now, when he would hit you—if he was going to hit somebody with that same punch—it would virtually throw you across the room. Because he focused on something as simple as a simple punch, but learned how to make it much more than a punch.

That's why he said, "It's not a punch. It's a PUNCH."

There's a big difference.

Some of you are just thinking, Who Do You Listen To? All right, I got that.

Teachability Index? I got it.

Training Balance Scale? I know that. Understood. Next!

The Four Magic Steps? Got it. Now get to the real stuff.

Well, first off, if you've got that attitude, guess what? Your Teachability Index is zero. You haven't gotten it yet. Do you understand?

You've got to keep saying, teach me more about Who Do I Listen To?

Teach me more about the Teachability Index.

Teach me more about the Training Balance Scale.

Teach me more.

Years ago, I was at one of our private Brotherhood meetings with a few other members at a super highly trained member's home in Barbados. I was sitting there in awe. It was about a $35 million house, this magnificent structure.

We flew in on the private planes, and I was thinking how very fortunate I was to be with my teachers. Every time I'm with my teachers, I do very little talking. Every time I'm with my teachers, I do very little talking. I ask questions but mostly I observe and listen.

The reason I'm telling you this is because you should feel the same way right now.

I'm trying to get you to understand this concept of humility and being an empty vessel ready to receive.

One of my early teachers said, "God gave you two ears and one mouth. Use them proportionately."

Think about that.

So we were sitting there in Barbados, chatting about different concepts, and I asked, "At what point can you stop learning about the basics? At what point can you say, I think I really got the basics?"

He said to me and all of us there … I thought this was brilliant … "When you want to learn just a little more, and you love the idea of learning and being educated on the basics, you don't have to learn any more."

But at that point, you can't STOP learning the basics and digging deeper into their secrets.

It's like a drug.

You love learning about the basics. You love focusing on the fundamentals. You love tweaking them and integrating them just a little bit more.

You love it so much that that you can't not learn. You can't not ask. You can't not get another example, another observation to build another neural pathway. Because what's occurring is when you start getting to unconscious competence and those neural pathways get bigger and bigger and bigger, you're actually getting a chemical rush, biologically in the body, from learning more about that thing.

Do you understand? This is why willingness to accept change is hard, because you've developed big neural pathways that locked in your failure habits.

Those neural pathways for the failure habits that you've developed over time are making you crave to continue doing that failure habit because you're feeding that neural pathway.

And when you stop doing that failure habit, you're not feeding that neural pathway, but it's craving for more. So you have conflict. You struggle. You have a counter-intention stopping you from succeeding.

You're just starting to establish a brand-new neural pathway as you read this book. But you have a big old neural pathway craving for attention and craving for you to do that same thing and focus on that failure thing, and do that old habit, that old pattern.

Here you are establishing a new neural pathway, which right now is very small. It doesn't have that cravingness yet. It is not powerful enough yet. You are still ADDICTED to your old failure habits.

That's why it's hard to have a high willingness to accept change. Change creates anxiety, just like stopping any addiction.

Does this make sense?

This is why understanding these basic concepts is so vitally important.

We had an advantage being society members, because we were around this material twenty-four hours a day, seven days a week. We had our phone calls. We had our coffees. We had our book meetings. We knew we were going to get tested and challenged on this stuff. We knew we were going to get the phone call. We knew we were going to meet somebody.

And we knew that if we failed, that if somebody came up to us that we knew was a society member, and they knew I was the apprentice, and they asked me a question about what did I observe from that guy, and I didn't really give a good answer, or if they sensed and they knew that my willingness to learn or my willingness to accept change was low—guess what? I wasn't moving on to the next level.

They were not going to teach me anything new because there was nothing for me to learn or be exposed to, because I hadn't learned my lesson yet. I had not MASTERED the basics, at least to some level. So I would not qualify to go on to the next level.

If you can't add, we're not going to move on to subtraction. If you can't add, subtract, multiply, and divide, we're not doing algebra. Sorry.

We can't go there until you are proficient and an expert in addition, subtraction, multiplication, and division. You have to be an expert in those before we get to algebra.

So in our lives as society members, we had not a fear, but a strong motivation to really master these basics.

Who Do You Listen To, Teachability Index, Training Balance Scale, and the Four Magic Steps.

We had to master them. Otherwise, we weren't moving on. Our membership in the society was potentially at risk. We weren't going to get kicked out, but we were treated like the lowest privates in the Army, and were probably going to be a lowly private in the Army our whole life.

We were never going to get to general.

The highest level in the Army is a five-star general. The highest level in the Masons is a thirty-third degree who is also in the inner sanctum. There aren't that many five-star generals. There aren't that many thirty-third-degree Masons who are also in the inner sanctum. We actually had a couple at the live event.

There aren't that many top people in the Brotherhood. Besides myself, we also had a couple at the live event.

There are not many at the HIGHEST levels, masters, gurus. For those who reach those levels, you had to do something special, and you got information, knowledge, and experience that other people just didn't have access to if they were a lowly private, even though they're still part of the Army.

Does this make sense?

"To know and not to do is not to know." You have to **know** this stuff. The basics. You have to focus on the fundamentals. The Four Basic Fundamentals.

Who Do You Listen To, Teachability Index, Training Balance Scale, and the Four Magic Steps that you go through when you learn information.

These are the foundational Basics. Review them in your mind. Think about them over and over again.

Now, someone always asks, "How do I learn this again? What is the best way to learn this and internalize it so it becomes a part of me?"

You learn it by observing other people, and by doing it over and over again at the conscious competence level.

But you must be observing people. Who do you observe? You observe the people that are experts in it, who are doing it.

Some of you are thinking, "I don't know any experts."

Guess what? You're reading material from one. And I say that humbly.

That's why you read this book or listen to the audios over and over and over and over and over again. At the end of this book, we're going to give you the list of recommended books and audios for you to consider.

That's going to be your method.

We also offer to you some live events where you can meet me and others like me. You can join my private club and have access to all that I did in the Brotherhood.

You can have a mentor. You can get phone calls. You can have one-on-one meetings.

But you have to qualify. And how do you qualify? Just like we qualified. We had to prove that we were willing to do what the other guys were not willing to do. We had to show we were serious about success.

If we didn't have high willingness to learn and high willingness to accept change, if we were not reading books, then we did not get to meet people in person and we were not invited to the higher levels.

So you're going to be given that same opportunity.

We're trying to basically duplicate our method of learning, the way we got this stuff in the societies, with you.

And right now, your method is by reading this book and some of the other books on the recommended list, as well as listening to some of the suggested audios.

And for those of you who really get it, you'll be available to join my private club and attend the workshops and the live events. And you'll be able to get personal mentors and be an apprentice to learn this information, if you choose to.

Some of you are just going to get this information and basically go, "Oh, my God, this is amazing," and start applying it and start becoming, doing, and having more than you could ever imagine and be happier than ever, and you're going to be at the level you wanted to be.

And you're going to say, "I'm done! Ahhh! This is fantastic!"

That's great! Some of you are thinking, "Hey, I'm making plenty of money, I am super happy and fulfilled, who needs millions? I'm making a couple of hundred grand. You know, I manifested my dreams. My body looks great. My health is great. What else do I need? I hit a home run with this book! I hit the lottery!"

Listen, I applaud you, because it's your desires you're going after, not mine. So whatever desires you have, achieve them, put a big smile on your face, and feel great. And whatever your dream is, it is.

You don't have to be a billionaire. There's no right and wrong here. All that is important is that you feel fulfilled, and you feel happy, and you feel great, and you feel you're achieving your goals and desires, and you feel fantastic and better than ever.

That's what it comes down to. This book, *Your Wish Is Your Command*, is for YOU.

What wish do you have? What dream do you have? What desire do you have?

Think about it.

What desires do you have in your life? STOP. Answer the question. OUT LOUD.

What wishes do you have in your life, in any area of your life? STOP. Answer the question. OUT LOUD.

What wish do you have? What desire do you have?

What do you want? What do you want? What do you want?

Guess what?

You're going to be taught in this book how to make a command and make it happen.

Some of you will read this book and want to go further. Fine. Some of you are going to be so happy with what you got out of this book that you don't want any more. That's great too.

Your wish can be your command. You can be, do, and have whatever you desire. Whatever the mind can conceive and bring itself to believe, it can achieve.

This isn't made up. This isn't theory. Those in attendance at the live event were seeing it physically, touching it, and eating it. They were meeting the people, real flesh-and-blood people.

Your dreams can become reality.

Your wishes can happen.

What you want ... What you desire ... You can have.

What you want, WANTS YOU. You can make your dreams a reality and have it happen in record time.

Focus on the fundamentals.

Master the basics.

Build the foundation, and you'll be able to build your whole life.

And the foundation is:

Who Do You Listen To?

Teachability Index.

Training Balance Scale.

And the Four Magic Steps, leading to unconscious competence.

LESSON 7

How to Be, Do, and Have Whatever You Desire

At the live event, during the breaks, many people would come up to me and ask questions. I also listened to the attendees talking with one another and the other high-ranking members of various societies.

It was just great to listen to them talk to one another about how basic, simplistic, yet unbelievably eye-opening this information is. They understood just how profound, how deep, and how powerful these simple concepts are.

One question that came up is, "Do we learn more by teaching?"

I talked about the ways that we, as members of the societies, learned this information. I mentioned that there were on some occasions "workshops or seminars" that we participated in, in groups. I mentioned that we learned a lot of this information via reading books.

And I explained the reason we learned it from the books. They weren't manuals with instructions, but they were generally around 80 percent, stories of PEOPLE applying the system.

These stories were about real people. And some of these manuscripts, by the way, are actually over a thousand years old. Many of them were obviously not originals. Rather, many of them were passed down verbally, verbatim, and later put on paper.

Now they are housed in society members' homes in manuscript form. Some of them have been reprinted, and reprinted, and reprinted over the millennia.

We were given access to these books. And we learned by reading the books, by using our *imagination*. Your imagination is POWERFUL. The ability to SEE an image in your mind and attach emotion to it is POWERFUL. Reading stories helps release your ability to use your imagination. It TRAINS your mind.

We also actually observed real people in real life. And by observing, we developed those neural pathways in our mind. That is how we learned the basics.

We also learned it by observing our teachers. Our "mentors," the people that we were assigned to, that were effectively our personal coaches.

We also observed other people who were in the societies and observed them.

And we were always kind of "on call" for being questioned on what our observations and cognitions were, because observations and cognitions were very powerful and life-changing.

Obviously, doing it ourselves, over and over, at the conscious competence level, also got this information in our brain, created new success habits, and the data got "in us" and became a part of us.

But there was also another method. However, this method was used later, once we had achieved some level of expertise and mastery. This method of getting the information IN US and PART OF US is: Teaching the information.

This is overdone in today's society. Everybody wants to be a teacher. Everybody wants to teach a seminar or write a book before they know anything and before they have achieved any real results.

It is really unbelievable to me to see who is teaching on the subject of manifesting.

Why don't they learn it first before teaching it?

There is an old saying: "Those you can't do, TEACH."

Then someone says, "Well, you learn it best by teaching."

Well, you can't learn anything that you don't know by teaching it.

Do you understand? You are just teaching wrong stuff. You are adding all of your old habits, all of your old patterns, into the new material that you KNOW ABOUT, and when you turn around and try to teach it, you muddle up the whole water by adding in all your theories and beliefs that are FALSE DATA.

I will give you a perfect example of this. We used to play a game when we were kids called "telephone." We would get five or six people in a circle, and have someone whisper a short story to the first person in his ear so no one else could hear it. It would be only one or two minutes long.

That person would turn around and whisper it to the next person, who would then turn around and whisper it to the next person, who would whisper it to the next person, who would whisper it to the next person.

And that person would get up and tell the story.

And it was nothing like the story that the first person started with.

Do you know what I'm talking about here?

That is how the teaching method works today, with all of these people trying to teach what they heard or read about in a book. They don't KNOW the information, they only KNOW ABOUT the information.

So the problem here is: when I teach you, and then you turn around and teach another guy before you know it, you are adding all your own garbage, and you are changing the recipe.

And that is why the guy fourth down the chain is not learning the truth. He is getting all wrong information. He is getting FALSE DATA.

This is the method of teaching today. That is why when you read most books on success or manifesting, you are listening to the wrong person.

Who Do You Listen To? The person who wrote the book or is teaching the seminar or made the YouTube video? This great teacher of wisdom and knowledge, who got it from four mentors, who got it from their mentors, who got it from some books they read, who got it from some other books that they read or some seminars they went to?

All of these people started teaching manifesting to people they really learned it, before they really knew it, before they had proven by personal experience and doing, that it really works.

And it gets muddled up all the way down the track.

And that is why 90 percent of the books, seminars, videos, and workshops on success or manifesting are not only a waste of time, but detrimental. They are HURTING your chance of success. They are sending you down a path that leads to nowhere. This is because they are giving you wrong information. FALSE DATA.

In most cases, they are not giving you that wrong information, that FALSE DATA, on purpose.

They mostly are very well-intentioned people. But you are not getting the true information directly from SOURCE.

Yes, we get to the level of superior expertise, or superior proficiency in this data, when we start teaching it.

The axiom is true: Learn this well enough to teach it. And you learn it well enough to teach it, by TEACHING it.

But you teach it TO YOURSELF FIRST and get RESULTS BEFORE you teach it to others. You TALK to yourself AS IF you were teaching yourself. You explain it to yourself. You coach yourself.

I can tell you, as you are my apprentice, you are learning until the day you die. You have to have that spirit of always being a student. Work on always being the BEST student.

You have to have a high Teachability Index till the day you die. You are always learning from somebody.

But you should not be teaching this stuff to others until you have really mastered it and produced tangible results. We, as society members, never started teaching it until the mastery, the proficiency of the data, was evidenced by the physical manifestations in the real physical universe.

In other words, we could make the soufflé.

Does this make sense?

I kicked butt making that soufflé thousands of times before I taught anybody else how to make a soufflé.

Do you understand that?

So, some of you are already itching to teach this stuff.

Slow down, calm down.

Because right now, you still have a mind full of junk and counter-intentions. You have wrong neural pathways, failure habits, and screwed-up knowledge. So you are adding this garbage into anything you try to teach.

You can't teach this to others just yet. You need to master it yourself first, by using the methods I taught you.

So again, how are you going to learn this information … the basics?

First, for you, it is this book. Read it over, and over, and over, and over again. Listen to the audios over and over again. You can read this book or listen to the audios one hundred times, and on the hundredth time, you will read something or hear something that you will SWEAR was NOT there the other ninety-nine times!

Why?

The reason you read this book or listen to the audios over and over again, the reason you read any book more than one time or over, and over, and over, and over again, is because every time you do—or any time you observe a master doing something, or anytime you apply this and observe yourself and your results—*you are at a new place. You are a different person.*

You have a different set of neural pathways, at different sizes and strengths, that are vibrating and attracting different things.

You are a new person tomorrow, compared to today.

If you were to re-read this book tomorrow, starting from the beginning up to this point, it would be like a brand-new experience; you would think you were reading a NEW, different book. This is because you are ALREADY a different person compared to the person who started reading this book.

You are going to be receiving all this information differently, and you will be picking up different things and understanding things in different ways.

So the way that you learn this data is to read this book or listen to the audios, over and over and over and over.

This is the key.

I am hammering this point because MOST people miss *this critical point.*

I love it when people say, "I listened to an audio once and loved it. Why do I have to listen again?" Well, you ate once. Why do you have to eat again? You breathed ONCE, why take another breath? You watched your favorite movie once, why did you have to watch it fifty times? You listened to your favorite song ONCE, why listen again?

There are a couple of great books out there. One is by Dale Carnegie: *How to Win Friends and Influence People.* It teaches specifically some great techniques.

I go to people, "Have you read the Dale Carnegie book?"

"Oh, yeah, I read that."

"So you know it?"

"Yeah, I know it all, *I read it.*"

"When did you read it?"

"I read that ... hmmmmm, I read that about twenty-five years ago."

And I say, "You know, they redid the whole book, you should read it again."

Of course, they did NOT rewrite the book. It's the same book.

But this guy goes and reads it in this new unit of time, and says, "Oh, my God, yeah, they redid the whole book, it is like a brand-new book. It is totally different than what it was when I first read it."

"It is the same book, Charlie; *you* are different."

You eat every day. You feed your body every day.

You have got to feed your mind every day because **your mind is** growing. Your mind is growing just like your body. It needs positive information every day, even if it is the same information you fed it yesterday. This is called spaced repetition.

The material becomes new every time you listen to it, read it, observe it, or do it.

You make the soufflé a thousand times. Every time you make it, it is a new experience, and you are learning something new every time you do it.

Every time you throw a punch, the monk taught me, it is a new experience. You are learning something new every single time. You are adding to what you knew. You are adding something new, because you are a new person.

So read this book and listen to the audios over and over again, constantly. Feed your mind every day.

You can master the basics. And master all the material.

When you get to a certain level of mastery, we will know when you are there because there are a series of methods that we will employ to "test you" and your new powerful abilities.

We can know which people are truly engaging and participating in the process of "becoming a better you," of internalizing this knowledge and learning experience.

We will know which ones of you are ready for the next level. And the next level is, you can participate in some live training and meet me and others at my level in person.

Now, by the way, all of you reading this: Don't expect that you will automatically be invited to a live training event. Some of you are like, "Huh? What do you mean? Don't I automatically get to go to live events and meet you if I join your private club?"

Yes, you get to go to SOME live events. But to get to the higher levels, you do have to qualify, just like I had to qualify to move up within the Brotherhood.

Just like a military person has to qualify to become an officer and then move all his way up to general, and then up to two-star, three-star, four-star, and five-star general.

Just like you had to qualify in the Masons to get up to the thirty-third degree, and only a small number were allowed to be in the inner sanctum.

Every person who passed the third degree didn't automatically make it to the fourth.

Every person who was at the twentieth degree didn't automatically make it to the twenty-first.

Some didn't get accepted. They didn't qualify. Why? Because they stopped understanding who they should listen to. Their Teachability Index was low. They were out of whack on the Training Balance Scale, and they weren't unconsciously competent on the information that they already learned.

See, if you have learned a certain amount of data, you SHOULD be able to DO it and see results.

Let's say we taught you how to make five dishes. Well, if you're not a master at making those five dishes, we're not going to teach you how to make a sixth dish here at the cooking school.

Does this make sense?

So, for you, if you focus and really LEARN the information in this book, and continue to listen to the audios, then if you qualify, you will be invited to come to some live training with me personally or people that are at my level.

And then, if you qualify, by becoming unconsciously competent in the material you are being exposed to, then you will qualify to have a personal mentor.

I can see some of you right now thinking, "I want that!"

And some of you don't even care.

Somebody may not want to have a personal mentor, be able to go to live events, and be personally exposed to high-ranking society members, because after reading this book and applying the material, you will be so successful, having so many wonderful things happen in your life, you won't even care about more.

That is perfectly fine. In fact, that is great.

Because you will be following your heart's desire, your bliss, your happiness, and attaining your dreams.

There is no right and wrong here. Nobody's better just because they have gotten to the thirty-third degree in the Masons and are in the inner sanctum. That is not for everyone.

No one is better because they have gotten to be a certain level in a certain group or my private club. We just have more knowledge, which makes us available and a resource for those who want more knowledge. It does not make us better.

So some of you will be allowed to have personal mentors, if you qualify and if you want one.

And then you will be able to get one-on-one training and observe your mentor and other members personally. And by that personal observation, you will go to another level of manifesting power and success.

You should always, throughout this entire process, be applying this material yourself.

You are developing neural pathways by doing it.

Which means you are being taught how to make the dish. You are being taught how to make the soufflé. That means you should actually go and make some soufflés. You have to physically do it. When you go and actually APPLY and DO what you are learning, you then REALLY learn it by your own personal experience.

I love people who follow the gurus, the seminar teachers, the lecturers. The guys who do all the big fancy seminars and all the stuff. And I pop in once in a while, and I talk to people. It goes like this:

"Oh, do you like this particular teacher?"

"Oh, I go to all of his seminars. I love him. He's the best."

"Oh, really? You go to all of them?"

"I have gone for years."

"Yeah?"

"Never miss one."

"Oh, good. So you must be applying this in your life?"

"Well, you know, I am still learning."

"Still learning."

See, they missed the point.

Because one of the most powerful ways to learn this stuff really is not by teaching it to others, it is teaching it to yourself and DOING IT. Getting out there and APPLYING it. Make some mistakes, LEARN from your personal experience.

See, this person wants to be a teacher. It's like you are in cooking school. You have learned how to make a soufflé. You have come to all the classes. So it is now time to go and cook a meal. TRY to apply it. It is okay if you "fail."

Trust me, when you go into the kitchen and ATTEMPT to cook on your own, you are going to learn more than you have in the last five years going to those seminars.

So you need to apply the stuff in your own life. Then you will have COGNITIONS. You will have EXPERIENCE and the physical evidence that you know it works, because you have made it work.

And in that process of doing it, and teaching yourself as you go—you will learn more.

So for you, listening to the audios, reading this book, doing it, teaching yourself as you go, making it work, manifesting the things you want in your life, is the process.

Then you can get a mentor, learn more by observation, attend seminars, and weekend events. Your power, knowledge, and deep understanding will grow. And then, only then, will you be at the point where you qualify to potentially teach this, and BE a mentor to someone else.

Now, some people say, "Well, I don't want to be a one-on-one mentor. I want to teach the big seminars and write a book."

Okay. But there is a reason why we don't teach this in big seminars. We DO have LARGE EVENTS. But they are not really "seminars."

As I mentioned, the way we learned this in the societies was not through big seminars. The guys who teach the big seminars make their money teaching seminars.

I know most of the people who teach the seminars personally, by the way. Most are great people who are very well-intentioned. I have spoken on the stages. I have gotten paid a million dollars to speak, to stand up on the stage.

But almost all the guys and ladies that do the seminars, do so because of their ego. I am not saying this in a judgmental or critical way. They are following their bliss. They get so much pleasure out of teaching. They love being on stage, like being a rock star. And there is nothing wrong with that.

But in terms of your benefit, you are not going to get that much LASTING benefit. Your ability to manifest is not going to go up THAT much.

Someone says, "Well, my *desire* is to teach big seminars."

Well, that is fine. Nothing wrong with that at all.

But if you really want to learn this material and become a magnificent manifester, it isn't by teaching it at this point. You will need to fine-tune your knowledge through personal experience and personal results. You have to get better than you are right now.

By doing it yourself and teaching YOURSELF as you go, you will learn more than by trying to teach it to others.

Believe me, as you start going through this, your ego will get out of the way. This book is designed to dissolve your ego, to make you humbler and an empty vessel.

Some of you have this big dream of teaching big seminars or writing books or doing a podcast or YouTube videos. If that is your goal and dream, it will probably fade away because you will see that it is just such a short-term, ego-driven goal anyway.

Other desires will start springing forth within you. REAL desires that are in alignment with who you really are.

But I have to be careful here, because if it is your dream and desire to someday be on stage and teach people, then I embrace that. I support that.

Whatever your dream and goal is, whatever will make you happier, is what I support.

So let's just make sure we've got the five basics down.

Then we are going to go on.

The five basics …

"But oh, there are Four Basics," you say.

Some of you weren't paying attention.

The first one is, Who Do You Listen To?

The second one is the Teachability Index.

The third is the Training Balance Scale.

The fourth is the Four Magic Steps leading up to unconscious competence.

What is the fifth one?

The fifth one is, master the first four.

The fifth basic is ALSO a basic.

The fifth one is the most important of the basics: Master the basics. Focus on the fundamentals.

That is the Fifth Basic. That is the most important.

If you spend much of your time and effort on the Four Basics, magical things will happen in your life.

Why?

Recall the phrase: 'When the student is ready, the teacher will appear."

What does that mean?

By the way, it's true.

Being 'ready' means:

You are 100 percent teachable—you have a 10 willingness to learn, and a 10 willingness to accept change.

You are not focused on the how, but you are focused on your dream. You have embraced the Training Balance Scale and spend 90 percent of your time on thinking and attitude. Remember, it is your attitude (thinking), not your aptitude (skills), that determines your altitude (success) in life.

And you are focusing on getting this knowledge to the unconscious competence level.

It is as the Shaolin monk said. Focus on that one strike ten thousand times. A master is someone who has mastered the basics.

Remember the phrase, "I am not afraid of the ten thousand strikes you know that you have practiced once. I am deathly afraid of the one strike you have practiced ten thousand times."

See, I am not impressed with the people who KNOW ABOUT all this information that I am teaching you in this book.

I am impressed with the person who has focused on and mastered the Four Basics, and *knows* them better than anybody, because that is the person that will GET RESULTS.

That is the person who is going to create more.

If someone really KNOWS the Four Basics, and focuses on them and understands how in depth each one of them is, and how complex they can be, and how much meat you can delve into, how much minutia is in each one of those, that is when magic happens in his life.

The person who KNOWS ABOUT all this stuff hasn't focused on any of it to get to a high level of proficiency.

It's like the person who knows ten thousand strikes, but he gets killed in a fight.

You should be afraid of the one person who knows one strike that he has practiced ten thousand times.

That was Bruce Lee.

Some of you may not remember his story, which I won't go into at length. But he revolutionized martial arts, because up until that point, all the martial artists knew so much material that they would get into fights for hours with one another.

Bruce Lee would get into the ring with these masters, and he would end the fight within a minute, because he only focused on a couple of strikes.

Boom boom, it was over because he understood this concept of true mastery.

So the Five Basics:

Who Do You Listen To, Teachability Index, Training Balance Scale, Four Magic Steps, and the Fifth Basic, which is the most important, is Master the Basics.

Focus on the fundamentals.

Spend much of your time and effort going back to those Four Basics, over and over, and over and over, and over again.

Focusing, learning, putting effort, developing neural pathways, developing new habits, new patterns, changing your DNA.

You change your thoughts and behavior by focusing on those Four Basics.

Every time you focus on the basics and apply them and do something in your life with a proper thought process, you change the way you do things and think.

You are developing bigger, new, success-oriented neural pathways, and that is when miracles appear in your life, as if by magic.

Because it is magic.

When you get to the unconscious competence level of this material, all of a sudden, everything starts happening in your life, by magic.

So where are we at now?

You KNOW ABOUT the basics. You don't have them down yet, because we haven't focused on them. I am giving you the thumbnail sketch. I am giving you the bird's-eye view. I am giving you the overview here.

Now, I could, like I said, take each one of these basics, and lecture you for hours on each one.

I could "DRILL" you on these. There ARE powerful "DRILLS" that will help you MASTER those basics.

They will increase your knowledge, proficiency, depth of knowledge, and your depth of understanding on every concept presented in this book. Those are available to members of my private club.

These drills will basically get you doing something, physically and mentally. They drill a concept so that you experience *knowing* this material. It is a powerful learning tool. And as you do a drill, someone observes you, correcting your "out points," like a coach.

Remember, it is stupid to practice something over and over and over again if you are doing it wrong. Practice does NOT make perfect. PERFECT PRACTICE makes perfect.

Does that make sense?

You have to practice the right way. These drills will help you practice things the right way.

You will experience a new level of understanding by doing it and having somebody correct you.

Then you get to unconscious competence much faster. You get to the point where you are tying the shoe without thinking. And you are a genius at tying your shoelace. You are on autopilot.

That is when you will be able to throw that punch and stop a foot and a half before the candle flame, and the candle flame will go out.

Because the punch, to anybody else, is just a punch.

But to you, the punch is a PUNCH.

See, to anybody else, the Training Balance Scale is just a Training Balance Scale.

To anybody else, the Teachability Index is just a Teachability Index.

"I get it. I have to be teachable. I have to be coachable. I got it. I got it."

"You don't get it!"

Because the fact that you are not listening to me, you THINK you KNOW it all already, and you want me to get to the MEAT, that you are cutting me off, and you don't want to learn anything more about the basics, means you don't GET the Teachability Index.

Does this make sense?

You just showed me you don't *know* it.

Some of you are thinking, "Ah, ah, ah, say that again."

I love it when I am talking about a concept, and they quickly stop me and say, "I got it."

I smile and say, "No. The fact that you just told me you got it tells me you don't get it."

Because you, at that moment, stopped being teachable.

And unless you are high in the Teachability Index, your ability to achieve success will be limited. I don't care if you are 85 years old and you are worth $100 billion. You STILL have to have a high Teachability Index.

Guess what?

Those guys, and I know many of them, are still teachable. They are always CURIOUS. They are always asking questions and listening.

As a matter of fact, they are usually the most teachable because they are the true Masters at manifesting. They know that they don't know.

They DO know that they know a lot. But even though they KNOW that they KNOW certain things, they still KNOW that they don't KNOW what they don't know.

We don't know what we don't know. Think about that. There is still so much we don't know.

Truly successful people become more teachable in time.

And those who become less teachable over time because they think they know it all, they never move up and get any more knowledge. They stop learning, they stop growing. And generally, they start going backwards, because if you are not growing, you are dying.

So let's talk about what is NEXT after the basics.

Now we have our foundation, and we are going to start planting some seeds.

Let's start talking about specifically how you can be, do, or have anything you want in life.

How you can make whatever you desire happen in your life, for real, and happen fast.

Let's talk about the power.

Let's talk about the button you can push to manifest whatever you want into your physical experience.

Let's talk about how to get Aladdin's Lamp and have your own personal Genie that will grant your every wish.

We are going to continue to go back to and reference the five Basics, over and over and over and over again.

The Fifth Basic is Master the Basics.

We will keep going back to them because without them as your base, you are not going to learn any of this stuff. You are not going to get to unconscious competence and change your DNA vibration. You are not going to manifest your desires in life. Aladdin's Lamp, your own personal Genie, will continue to be elusive.

Do you want a personal Genie? Do you want him today?

"Today?" Yeah. Right now.

You don't have to wait five years.

Your Genie is going to be given to you today, and he will be at your beck and call today.

You will be able to tell him whatever you want. And your Genie will make any wish you want come true fast.

In the 1960s, there was a man by the name of Earl Nightingale. Some of you know about him or heard his name. Earl Nightingale, in the '60s, made an LP, a record album. This was before cassettes, CDs, or digital downloads. They were called vinyl records.

His LP was entitled *The Strangest Secret*. It became one of the best-selling personal development recordings of all time.

Earl Nightingale popularized a little-known secret concept that was rarely discussed or written about up until that point.

In Earl Nightingale's recording, *The Strangest Secret*, he coined the definition of what he called The Strangest Secret. He said, "On planet Earth, all across the globe, there is a secret of success. It is The Strangest Secret."

The secret was,

"You become what you think about most of the time."

The Strangest Secret, according to Earl Nightingale, was:

"You become what you think about most of the time."

Think about that.

According to scientists and quantum physics, THOUGHTS ARE THINGS. Science has now proven that thoughts have physical MASS. And thoughts have a VIBRATION that either ATTRACTS or REPELS matter in the universe.

The first time in the twentieth century this powerful truth about how the mind works and the TRUE proven method of manifesting was popularized was back in the '20s and '30s by a man by the name of Napoleon Hill.

Napoleon Hill wrote several books on success. His first book, which was actually a series of small books, is something most people have never heard of: *The Law of Success in Sixteen Lessons.*

Napoleon Hill's story is quite unique. At the turn of the twentieth century, the richest man on planet Earth was Andrew Carnegie. Andrew Carnegie's steel company would become U.S. Steel. He was a Scotsman. He lived before TVs, telephones, and transatlantic air travel.

It was a much slower time. He became the richest man in the world, making his money in the steel business. He didn't invent the steel business, by the way. Andrew Carnegie understood a basic principle, which is, "Pioneering don't pay." This is an interesting principle.

Carnegie became the richest man in the world AND was a member of the Brotherhood. He knew the powerful secret techniques to manifest, and he utilized them.

He did the unthinkable at the time. Carnegie decided to reveal to the world some of these manifesting techniques. He hired a man by the name of Napoleon Hill. He told Hill, "I am going to teach you some of these manifesting and moneymaking techniques. But more importantly, I want you to observe myself and others so you can see how they are applied in real life."

Carnegie was clear that these techniques are not his invention or creation but, rather are used by all of the richest people in the world.

Carnegie introduced Hill to Henry Ford—one of the richest, most successful people in the world—Thomas Edison, Harvey Firestone—who owned Firestone Tire Company—and a lot of other extremely wealthy people whose names you wouldn't even recognize. But at the time, they were the richest people in the world.

Carnegie told Hill, "I am going to introduce you to these people. They are not going to know what you are doing. But you are going to observe them."

Key. He had Napoleon Hill observe. It is the same technique that I was taught. You take an apprentice and you have them observe a master. And then you query them. You ask them questions such as, "What did you observe?" And you point out things that they didn't observe. That is how we learned. That is how *you* learn.

He gave Napoleon Hill books. Napoleon Hill was not a member of the Brotherhood. But Carnegie took him on, as an apprentice in effect, and taught him the same material.

Carnegie told Hill, "I want you to learn this material over the next twenty years. Then, I want you to write a manuscript describing the principles of manifesting. But I want this manuscript to be focused on money."

Thus, in 1926, Hill published a series of books called *The Law of Success in Sixteen Lessons.*

Napoleon Hill was amazed at what he was taught by Andrew Carnegie and what he observed from Henry Ford and many of the others.

Again, these were the richest, most successful, and powerful people in the world. Never before in history had somebody done this, and never since, *until now.*

Hill was taught the same way we were taught. We were introduced to the richest, most successful, and powerful people in the world, and they became our mentors. We observed them and how they applied these principles and methods of manifesting, but not just from a manifesting money standpoint.

When I say the word rich, yes, most were the financially richest people, people who have the most money. But more importantly, these were people who were rich in terms of happiness and living with a sense of purpose. They were fulfilled and satisfied. They loved living. They loved life.

They were people who were really making *their* dreams and desires come true.

I want you to understand, this is not all about money.

Yes, we are going to talk about money.

But I am not really talking about rich or successful from a monetary standpoint. I am talking about making YOUR dreams come true, WHATEVER THOSE DREAMS ARE. It does NOT have to be about money.

Rich or successful is really defined by how blissfully happy you are.

Now, it is probably hard to be blissfully happy if you can't pay your bills, if you are massively in debt, or if creditors and bill collectors are hounding you. It is probably hard to be blissfully happy, although not impossible, if you are constantly under financial pressure.

So being blissfully happy is really the objective here. There is nothing wrong with having lots of money. But money will NOT give you deep inner peace, happiness, and joy. Money is a tool. You should LOVE people and USE money. Unfortunately, many rich people LOVE money and USE people. Getting your thinking right about money will serve you well.

Napoleon Hill learned many manifesting principles and put them forth in the book *The Law of Success in Sixteen Lessons.*

Interestingly, when he published the book, members of the societies got together. Keep in mind that most of these society members controlled the media, publishing houses, manufacturing, and so forth. That is just how the world works.

When you are in the societies and learn these principles, you can easily become one of the captains of industry.

So when Hill published this book, a group of society members, led by Henry Ford, opposed Hill revealing some of these secrets. They actually were successful in getting the book suppressed; they got it off the market and had it edited down dramatically.

It basically just vanished from public access.

In 1937, Napoleon Hill published a watered-down version called *Think and Grow Rich.*

Yet the same thing happened with this version. It was pulled off the market and watered down dramatically. Most of the key elements were taken out. Again, this was spearheaded by Henry Ford.

Still, both of Hill's books are very good.

In the book, Napoleon Hill made a statement he learned from Carnegie and from observing Ford and others. That statement is powerful, and I want to focus on it.

Napoleon Hill stated, "Whatever the mind of man can conceive, and bring itself to believe, it can achieve." Think about that statement. Read it again.

Now, combine that with Earl Nightingale's definition of The Strangest Secret, which is,

"You become what you think about most of the time."

With those two statements in mind, let me talk specifically about how to manifest your desire, and exactly how the METHOD actually works.

A book came out years ago which became very popular, called *The Secret.* It is a wonderful, wonderful book, and I encourage everyone to read it. It is a great book.

In *The Secret*, the book describes something called the Law of Attraction. It is really the first book to popularize on a mass scale the concept of the Law of Attraction. It is not the first time the Law of Attraction has been talked about in a book. There are many books written at the turn of the twentieth century that discuss the Law of Attraction and how you can use it to "attract" what you want in your life.

The Secret became hot for a while, but it quickly began to fade away for a lot of reasons. Most people today have not even heard of it. The biggest reason why the book lost popularity is that many millions of copies of *The Secret* that were sold worldwide, and then hundreds of other Law of Attraction books were written and sold.

It is estimated that somewhere around fifty million books teaching or exposing the Law of Attraction have been sold in just the last few years. But why has the Law of Attraction dramatically begun to fade away? Why has there been so much negative publicity about the Law of Attraction being a complete scam?

Here is why.

Because when people read the book *The Secret* or any of the similar books teaching The Law of Attraction, people would start applying the Law of Attraction technique in their life, AS IT WAS EXPLAINED IN THE BOOK. MOST people did NOT see any results.

Yes, some people would see some results, but the vast majority, an estimated 95 percent, saw no results. Thus, they said, "It was a scam."

This happened to Napoleon Hill back in the '20s and '30s with his books *The Law of Success in Sixteen Lessons* and *Think and Grow Rich*.

Because the original versions were pulled and the key elements stripped away, the majority of people read watered-down versions, with key ingredients missing. Thus, when they applied it, some people saw some results, but 95 percent of those who read Napoleon Hill's works saw no results.

Thus, people said the techniques must be a scam. It wasn't that it was a scam, but rather there were KEY MISSING INGREDIENTS to the success recipe.

Let's say there was a man who made a delicious chocolate cake. He had the recipe. If you followed it exactly, you got a delicious chocolate cake. But the man with the "secret" recipe didn't want other people to make the same delicious chocolate cake he made. So he never shared the REAL recipe. He shared a "changed version" of the recipe. He took out some key ingredients of that recipe and maybe even changed some of the others.

You then got a different recipe from the original that produced a delicious chocolate cake. When you followed the recipe you received, you did not know that there were some missing ingredients or ingredients were changed. Even if you followed THAT altered recipe exactly, you would NOT get the same delicious chocolate cake.

But maybe you did get a delicious chocolate cake because you were a buffoon, and actually didn't follow the recipe exactly.

You got the altered recipe, but you screwed up the altered recipe, and by accident, you actually made a good recipe and you got delicious chocolate cake. You got a good result BY ACCIDENT.

Does this make sense?

So this is what happened over the years with the Law of Attraction and Napoleon Hill's works.

I am here to tell you, and my colleagues are telling you as well, that there IS a magical recipe for success. Those in attendance said that the evidence of that success was right before their eyes. They said firsthand that the magical formula, the TRUE Law of Attraction formula, does work.

I am telling you that the Law of Attraction is categorically true, IF YOU HAVE ALL THE INGREDIENTS AND FOLLOW THE FORMULA.

Whatever the mind of man—which means your mind—can conceive—which means whatever YOU can conceive in your mind, whatever you can DREAM or wish for, whatever you want to be, do, or have—as long as you believe it will happen—which means you have 100 percent CONFIDENCE that it WILL happen—then IT WILL HAPPEN.

In the words of Earl Nightingale, "Whatever you think about, whatever you want that you think about, that is what you get."

Is it that easy? No, quite frankly. There are a lot of little key elements that have to be used. You will learn those in this book. You will learn the recipe, the formula, and the steps that produce results. You will learn the success system that never fails.

When you learn all the key elements and you know them at the unconscious competence level, then it does become incredibly easy.

So here is how it works.

First, I am going to give you the thumbnail sketch.

Then you will take a break. Then we will actually put this into action. And your Genie, in the next couple of hours, is going to be given commands from you. Some of you tonight, before you go to bed, will start seeing physical manifestations of what you want actually happen.

It might blow your mind.

You are about to learn the real recipe, unaltered, without the missing ingredients, without the changes, without people's opinions or ideas of how this works.

You are about to get the real secret recipe, in total, that has never been released to the public before.

So here is how it works. Here is the overview first.

You have a brain within your skull. Outside of your skull is something else. It is called the mind.

You have a brain AND you have a MIND. They are NOT the same thing.

In every continent and culture, there are different words for the mind.

We all know and can concur and agree that we have a brain in our skull.

Whether you believe or disbelieve that there is some type of energetic field outside your body, that surrounds your body, called the mind, is irrelevant.

The reason why it doesn't matter if you believe this or not is because what I am going to tell you is a physiological—not a mystical, not a spiritual—but a physiological, scientifically proven fact today.

Just like you have blood in your veins, that is proven.

Just like you have a brain in your skull, that is proven.

Just like you have a heart in your chest that pumps blood, that is proven.

Just like you have hormones in your body, that is proven.

What I am going to share with you is physiologically, scientifically proven, quantifiable, and measurable.

Whether you believe it or not is irrelevant.

I remember, I was chatting with a guy one time, and I asked, "Well, don't you have to believe this to make it work?"

He said, "*No. Because some things don't require belief.*"

I asked, "What do you mean?"

He said to me, "Think of the Law of Gravity. Whether you believe in the Law of Gravity or not, it is always a constant, because it is a Law of Gravity, not a belief of gravity."

He went on, "If you walk to the top of a roof, whether you believe in the Law of Gravity or not, if you walk off the edge, you are going to go down."

I challenged him, "But wait a minute. I read a lot of these mystical, esoterical, spiritual books that say if I just have enough BELIEF, I can defy the Law of Gravity."

He replied, "Guess what, maybe that is true. So let's see if it is or not. Show me somebody, just ONE person, that will walk off this building and float. If you can't show me at least ONE person, then maybe it isn't true, or at least it is not true for YOU.

But BELIEVING you can overcome the Law of Gravity is TOO far of a stretch for you right now. So who cares whether being able to overcome the Law of Gravity is true or not? The fact is, 99.9 percent of the people will go down if they walk off the top of the building."

Does this make sense?

So let's just deal with the fact that 99.9 percent of the people WILL go DOWN. MAYBE that one person that may exist on planet Earth can defy the Law of Gravity. Although there are eight billion people on the planet—and I don't know how many billions, and billions, and billions over the last couple of hundred years have lived—if there is no picture, no evidence, no recording of somebody walking off a building and floating in midair, then it probably is just a myth and legend.

So whether a hundred years from now somebody will develop the belief or power where they can defy gravity, that is fine.

But let's deal with our reality today.

Look, you are thirty, forty, fifty years old; what do you have, forty, fifty, sixty years left here?

In your lifetime, you are not going to walk off the top of a building and float. You are not "Superman." And guess what, even if you could, how is that going to benefit your life anyway?

So stop thinking in THEORY and MAYBES.

Let's just deal with the facts and reality as we know them. That reality and truth is that the Law of Gravity is a constant, whether you believe in it or not. You cannot overcome it. The Law of Gravity will always work.

So let's just deal with these laws on how the body works, how the mind works, how the brain works, and how the physical universe works as we know them today. Let's just deal with the accepted laws for now.

Read carefully and pay attention, and you will be able to create anything you want in your life, just like MILLIONS of others have who used this system that you are learning in this book.

Forget the theory, let's just deal with the accepted reality. Because even dealing with this limited, accepted reality, you can still create and manifest anything you want.

You don't have to be so esoteric, and mystical, or meditate for eight hours a day, thinking that that is going to give you nirvana.

And by the way, if you are reading this and you are thinking, "I love meditating," I embrace and support that. I am not downing meditating. I am trying to make a point.

Whatever you want to do is fine, provided that you don't whine and complain that you are not getting what you want when you use *your* manifesting technique instead of this ***proven technique***.

Does this make sense?

Imagine saying to me, "I am not going to make a soufflé the way you said, because I think I can do it this other way and make it better."

Good, then how come you can't make an excellent soufflé like I do?

When all these other people and I are making soufflés (soufflé is the metaphor for manifesting what we want) every day, we think, "This is like a no-brainer. We make soufflés." Why don't you just do what we're doing? We are making soufflés. Why do you have to come up with some other theory that has never been proven?

You are going to live your whole life and then die having never really been good at manifesting your dreams. And even if you do, why do you want to do it the hard way and struggle your whole life going down some other track?

So let's just deal with the simple, basic fundamentals of how this works.

Then we are going to do it together.

The point is you have a brain, and you *potentially* have a mind.

Right now, some of you have already crashed on the basic: Who Are You Going to Listen To?

When I mention that the MIND is NOT the brain, that they are two separate entities, some of you are already going … "Huh?" Some of you already shifted on who you are going to listen to.

You are thinking about, "Well, wait a minute, I am a Christian. Is that going to be in conflict with my religious beliefs?" You are already resisting instead of being an empty vessel. Your Teachability Index might be low right now.

Or you might be thinking, "I am a Hindu, or I am a Jew, or I am an atheist. How is this going to conflict with that?" Some of you are thinking about, "Wait a minute, I went to a so-and-so seminar, and he said something different."

So you are already not very teachable.

That is why you have to always focus on the basics. You might already be challenging 'Who are you going to listen to? And the Teachability Index. Some of you have crashed on the Teachability Index, the "willingness to learn" part. You are thinking, "Wait a minute."

Can you see that you have crashed on "willingness to accept change"?

You might be thinking, But that is not how I think. That is not what I believe."

If you continue to think like you have always thought, you will continue to get what you have always got.

If you want things in your life to change, you are going to have to change things in your life.

Understand?

Some of you already shifted on the Training Balance Scale. You are thinking about the 'doing' part, "But I need to know HOW to do this. **What** to do. How am I going to do that?"

You are focusing on the side of the Training Balance Scale that you don't need to focus on right now, because 90 percent of this is thoughts. Are you with me so far?

PAY ATTENTION.

FOCUS.

CONCENTRATE.

That is why the Basics are what you should always be thinking about in the back of your mind.

So, you DO have a brain. You may or may not have a mind. But you can agree that you have a brain, and you *potentially* have something else outside the body. Whether it is called a field, an electromagnetic energy field, an aura, or the mind, whatever you want to call it, it doesn't really matter; consider that it MIGHT be there.

But you KNOW and agree that you have a brain for sure.

Thomas Edison—the guy who invented the lightbulb—Edison holds more patents than anybody else in history. Although I think Tesla comes close.

Thomas Edison was a genius. He was special.

Genius Albert Einstein; you know him: $E = mc^2$, the theory of relativity—sometimes referred to as the smartest man who have ever lived.

Both of these people said the same thing. They scientifically proved, at the turn of the twentieth century, that *the brain is a transmitter and receiver of vibrational frequency.*

Thomas Edison was not an idiot. Albert Einstein was not a moron. These men were geniuses. Early in the 1900s, they both concurred that every cell in the human body emits a different frequency. Everything on planet Earth and in the universe is made up of energy.

Everything emits a frequency or vibration, whether it is a rock, an apple, a piece of wood, a plant, or an inanimate object like a television or a carpet.

Everything on planet Earth and in the universe emits a different frequency.

A frequency is also called a vibration.

And it's sometimes called energy.

It is quantifiable, and it is measurable.

Your DNA emits a unique frequency and vibration. Every atom emits a frequency. The terms energy, frequency, and vibration, although technically different, are really the same, so here the terms will be used interchangeably.

Radio waves or cell phone signals are frequencies. Frequencies pass through all known matter.

Example: If you are in a house, and you get an old transistor radio with an antenna, and you turn it on, music magically appears from your transistor radio. The antenna in your house picked up radio frequencies that are broadcast from either a satellite or a transmitter.

Cell phones pick up frequencies that are broadcast from the cell phone towers.

A transmitter puts out a frequency which instantly is picked up by your receiver, IF YOUR RECEIVER IS DIALED INTO THE SAME FREQUENCY. That frequency bypasses space and time. The frequency from the radio or cell phone transmitter travels across the ether, and it passes through steel, brick, mortar, concrete, glass, or wood.

It passes right through it, as if by magic.

Scientists today cannot explain how a radio or cell phone transmission (frequency) passes through solid steel, or glass, or bricks, or mortar, or stone.

All that scientists know is that it does.

The reason why radio or cell phone frequencies pass through SOLID matter like steel is because frequencies are at a quantum physics level. They are smaller than an atom, smaller than an electron. Frequencies are smaller than the smallest known particle.

They are frequencies.

Frequencies or "vibrations" obviously exist. They are real. They are scientifically proven.

The human brain, according to Thomas Edison and Albert Einstein, is both a transmitter and a receiver of frequency or vibration.

The genius Edison, the inventor of the lightbulb, the creator of all types of inventions, was arguably the greatest inventor of all time. He, along with the mathematician genius, Albert Einstein, said that the human brain emits frequencies, which, when focused, are picked up by other human brains. And, they said that the frequencies that the brain emits pass through the ether and affect other physical matter.

THEY said that your brain puts out a frequency, which is picked up by other brains, and it also affects matter in the physical universe.

The frequencies that your brain emits actually pass through the ether, which means they can pass through solid matter like steel.

Your brain broadcasts basically the same type of frequency that a radio or cell phone transmitter puts out. Therefore, it can pass through solid matter in the same way that radio or cell phone frequencies can.

Your brain puts out frequencies on five different bands: Gamma, Beta, Alpha, Theta, and Delta.

The beta band is the SLAVE or poverty band. The Theta band is the WEALTH band. Actually, the most powerful is right in between Alpha and Theta. If you broadcast on THIS wavelength, you can manifest anything you desire because it affects matter and other brains in the most effective and powerful way.

Additionally, according to Edison and Einstein, the frequency that you are transmitting from your brain is smaller than radio or cell phone frequencies and has a unique characteristic.

Unlike radio or cell phone frequencies, the frequency that your brain transmits travels via the zero-point field, and thus travels instantaneously. It does not travel from one place to another just faster than the speed of light, but *instantaneously*.

If you transmitted a thought this moment, it can be picked up in the exact same moment by another human brain on the opposite side of the planet.

A radio or cell phone transmission of frequency can only travel in a straight line, which is why if you're broadcasting from a satellite, you need other satellites to bounce off of, to get the transmission to the other part of the globe.

But the unique ability that your transmitter (your brain) has is that YOUR broadcast is INSTANTANEOUSLY at ALL PLACES IN THE UNIVERSE the moment you broadcast it.

Radio or cell phone waves also lose power. This is why there are many cell phone towers, so that you are always close to a tower. Otherwise the cell phone frequency will lose its power and intensity. It gets weaker over a distance.

But the frequencies your brain broadcasts have the unique ability to bypass space and time. This is proven by quantum physics. It is science, not magic.

When you think a thought, you emit a frequency. Instantaneously, without any time lag, that frequency is everywhere in the universe. It affects all matter in the universe. It is also picked up by and affects all other human brains, everywhere on the planet, at the same instantaneous moment, and with the same amount of energy, power, and intensity.

This is science.

In the early 1900s, when Napoleon Hill wrote his books, he was taught this directly by the richest man in the world. He was told this fact about thoughts, frequency, and vibration by Andrew Carnegie. Hill verified this when he talked with Henry Ford, and all the wealthy people Hill observed and interviewed as he did his research.

This is one of the secrets that all the super-rich know.

This is the secret that I was taught. This is the secret that all my colleagues know.

You have in your head the most powerful transmitter and receiver of frequency, or energy, or vibration, on the planet. It is one of a kind. No machine can duplicate what your brain does in terms of being able to broadcast a frequency in the quantum zero-point field.

Your brain is a receiver and a transmitter of frequency.

That is the first concept.

The second concept is the Law of Attraction.

The definition of this law is: Whatever frequency your brain emits, that exact same frequency is attracted to you. Like attracts like.

You create a magnetic pull with the frequencies of vibrations you emit. You create an attractor field that "attracts" from the entire universe the same vibrations you emit.

Therefore, whatever frequency you emit, that exact same frequency is drawn to you magnetically.

Beyond being science (actually quantum physics), this is a scriptural and spiritual principle. For those of you who are Christians or Jews who follow the Torah, or the Bible; for those of you who are Muslims and follow the Qur'an; for members of the Hindu faith, who believe in the Vedas; for people who believe in Confucianism or Buddhism, this concept is NOT in conflict with any spiritual or religious tradition.

All these spiritual books, including the Zohar, teach very similar concepts.

What you sow, also you reap. The concept of karma. What goes around comes around.

But from a purely scientific, quantum physics standpoint, we are talking about when you emit a frequency, that frequency comes back. This means that the universe will have to manifest in your life situations, events, circumstances, situations, people, and things that MATCH the frequency you are emitting from your brain!

This effectively means you have always had a Genie that will grant you your every wish. You have always had your own Aladdin's Lamp. That Genie IS YOUR BRAIN. The Genie is *you.*

That is why this book is called *Your Wish Is **Your** Command*, not *Your Wish Is **My** Command.*

You get to command whatever you want to have happen or manifest in your life.

When you put out a frequency, the Law of Attraction says it must manifest.

The Law of Attraction is actually a *senior* law to the Law of Gravity.

Let me explain that briefly.

Oops, let's go back to the Four Basics first and check in to see how you are doing.

Who should you listen to? The guru? The guy who wrote some book on success? Your mother, your sister, your friend? Your relative? Me?

How about listening to Thomas Edison? How about Albert Einstein? How about the richest man in the world, Andrew Carnegie? Don't look at me. I am just the messenger.

What's your Teachability Index right now? What is your willingness to learn? For some of you, it went up because all of a sudden, as you read the last few pages, you started to think, "Uh? Wow!"

And some of you are thinking about me, and my friends and colleagues that were at the live event, imagining the opulent place where the event was held and all the wealth that surrounded those people, and you are thinking, "What Kevin is saying is real. This is not fantasy land. Kevin and his wealthy, powerful friends are real people, who really believe this, who really do what Kevin is telling me to do, who really do what Kevin is telling me to do—and they have the results!"

Test yourself right now. Where are you on the Teachability Index? What is your willingness to learn? And because I am throwing out some unique, controversial concepts that may challenge what you previously believed to be true, what is your willingness to accept change?

Remember, you are not only going to be changing some of your behaviors, patterns, and the way you previously did actions, but also changing the way you think.

So, let's go back. Spaced repetition. Remember, I told you this book would be different. This book WILL change you and reprogram you; just relax and be in a state of allowing. Be an open, empty vessel.

Your brain puts out frequencies; it broadcasts "vibrations."

The Law of Attraction says that this creates a magnetic pull; thus, you start "attracting" into your life things that have the exact same frequency.

Here is the bottom line. What I am going to teach you is **how** to put out the frequency of what you want, ON THE RIGHT FREQUENCY WAVE, for maximum results.

If you broadcast a frequency on the Beta wave, as 90 percent of normal people do, you will NOT get results. The BETA wave is the SLAVE wave; it is the poverty wave.

The ALPHA/THETA wave is the billionaire brain wave.

ALL wealthy people, all people who manifest easily and effortlessly, broadcast their desires on the Alpha/Theta wave, NOT the Beta wave.

That is the first key. How to put out the frequency of what you want ON THE RIGHT WAVE and how to make that frequency intense and powerful enough to have a strong enough magnetic pull, to PULL or attract into your physical universe, into your own existence, right before your eyes, that which you want.

I am going to teach you **how** to use your transmitter and receiver, and use the Law of Attraction to make what you want happen fast.

Now, I mentioned that the Law of Attraction is senior to the Law of Gravity. Some of you think, "Wait a minute, I thought the Law of Gravity was a law!"

Yes, it is a physical law. But then there is a quantum law which goes beyond physical laws. You can have a physical law, but sometimes there is a quantum law that is senior to that physical law. The quantum law is superior and will always take precedence.

Some of you just frowned and put your hands on your hips, questioning what you just read. Your Teachability Index just went down. Willingness to accept change went down.

Think about this.

There is a Law of Gravity. I mentioned whether you believe in the Law of Gravity or not, it's still true; it is still a LAW. If you walk off the top of the building, you will fall and go straight down.

The Law of Gravity works. Period. It is a law, period.

But wait, look up in the sky and sometimes you see an airplane or a bird. How does an airplane or a bird fly? If there is a Law of Gravity, how do they defy the Law of Gravity?

The answer is, there is a physical law that is senior to the Law of Gravity.

It is called the Law of Lift.

The Law of Lift takes precedence over, and is senior to, the Law of Gravity.

So, we have physical laws in this universe, and then we have senior laws to the known physical laws. The most senior law, a quantum law, is the Law of Attraction.

This law is based above the physical realm, in the quantum realm. It goes beyond physical. It is based on the fact that EVERYTHING in the universe has a frequency or vibration. Thus, whatever vibration or frequency you broadcast, that your brain puts out, will attract into your life something in the universe or CREATE something in the universe that matches that frequency. It will APPEAR to defy physical laws.

Read that paragraph again.

This is why the Training Balance Scale is so important. When you understand that powerful concept, that TRUTH, you should have a cognition, you should have a breakthrough from your previous, limiting beliefs.

When you understand this concept, you now understand why the HOW is not so important at the beginning of the process of manifesting. The UNIVERSE will figure out the HOW for you and present it to you.

"But HOW am I going to get the money, Kevin?"

The HOW doesn't matter right now, because you are using the Law of Attraction to get the UNIVERSE to figure out the HOW and present it to you.

The HOW doesn't matter at this point because when you use your thoughts and the Law of Attraction, the how becomes irrelevant. The HOW will present itself. The universe will present to you the how because by LAW it MUST manifest or create in your life a THING that matches the frequency you are broadcasting.

Now you might understand what my friend said: "When your attitude is right, the facts don't count."

Now that statement makes sense, because most of what you THINK are facts are almost always just opinion. And things that ARE facts are physical facts or laws, which are superseded by the Law of Attraction. The Law of Attraction OVERRIDES FACTS. It makes FACTS irrelevant.

The Law of Attraction supersedes and overrides facts in the same way that the Law of Lift supersedes the Law of Gravity.

The bottom line is this:

You can be, do, or have anything you want by using the most powerful, fastest transmitter and receiver of frequency, vibration, and energy, called your brain. But you must use your brain with DELIBERATE INTENT and broadcast those frequencies on the right wave band.

The fact that the Law of Attraction exists in the universe means YOU have the power to have a desire and COMMAND IT INTO EXISTENCE.

This means that whatever you THINK ABOUT, you are transmitting its frequency. Thus, you are automatically attracting it into your physical existence. The entire universe is WORKING FOR YOU to manifest your desire FOR YOU. Even if the universe has to SUPERSEDE physical laws to make it happen.

This is why when you see someone do this—think about what they desire and broadcast that THOUGHT, that frequency or vibration, on the right WAVE BAND, and manifest it in their life—it looks like magic, or luck, or serendipity, or coincidence. It is NOT coincidence or luck. That person manifested their desire by DELIBERATE INTENT.

But most people look at that person and say, "Oh, you are the luckiest guy in the world. I can't believe that just happened. How could that happen? Boy, that is a miracle."

Yes, miracle, luck, serendipity, coincidence, strange circumstances, phenomena beyond our understanding. That is what it LOOKS like. But now you know manifesting is actually a DELIBERATE CREATION done by a PERSON using these techniques with DELIBERATE INTENT.

The Law of Attraction is a senior law to physical laws. When you are using your transmitter, the brain, to broadcast a frequency on the Alpha/Theta wave into the ether, you are activating this Law of Attraction, and thus you can virtually override physical laws and manifest things as if by magic. To others, it might seem like you are able to perform miracles. But they are NOT miracles, they just APPEAR to be miracles. You are simply using a quantum law of physics.

Just remember, you can be, do, and have virtually anything you want.

Before you read the next chapter, go back and think about the Four Basics. Most importantly, make sure you have a high Teachability Index.

Now you might understand more the statement, "Whatever the mind can conceive and bring itself to believe, it can achieve."

Do you understand this statement now: "You were BORN to win. You were designed for accomplishment. You were engineered for success. And you were endowed with the seeds of greatness."

LESSON 8

The Brain:
A Transmitter and Receiver of Frequency

A good question that comes up is, are we talking about the same Law of Attraction as described in the book *The Secret,* or the Teachings of Abraham in the book *Ask and It Is Given*, or other such books?

The Law of Attraction is a law. It was popularized in the book *The Secret.* The Law of Attraction that I am talking about here is the same law described in that book.

However, as you will see by reading the rest of this book, *how* to apply the Law of Attraction is different. This book does not contain THEORY. It contains the TRUTH from REAL people who, over centuries, have APPLIED the CORRECT formula that makes the Law of Attraction work, and work fast.

The Law of Attraction is, by definition, what it is. However, I think you are going to see, as you continue to read this book, some very clear distinctions on how we as society or ex-society members have been taught HOW the Law of Attraction works in real life.

Those distinctions, those nuances, I know are going to be the huge difference for you. Because it is those DISTINCTIONS that will produce results for you in your life. They are absolutely enormous, distinctive differences from what you might be familiar with or read about from people who do not KNOW but only KNOW ABOUT the Law of Attraction and manifesting.

Another question I get often is about when I talked about the brain, and Einstein, as well as Thomas Edison, and that in the early 1900s it became scientifically proven that the human brain actually does, in fact, transmit vibration, or frequency, or energy, and that it can be measured.

And the question is, how come we are not hearing more about that today in the mainstream media when you consider all the advancements in scientific research and equipment that we have now compared to then?

That is actually a very big question that goes directly toward the explanation of the globalists and the "parasitical elite class," and their agenda and plan for global control.

I will be brief and just give you the gist of it here because it is an important thing to know that will ultimately help you manifest your dreams.

Society members, the elite class, throughout history, believed that they were genetically programmed to be, in fact, the ruling class. They believed their genes were superior.

I am not saying this is true… I am simply reporting the historical facts. From a historical perspective, throughout history, the elite class of society, the ruling classes, were primarily the royal families.

The kings and the royal families were the rulers of entire countries and all the people. This was one "class" or "caste."

Then there were the elite class of industry leaders, those who controlled the monopolies of the world's necessities, the things everyone used and needed, such as water, food, fuel, banking, and trade routes.

So there were two basic ruling classes. It is essentially the same today; we just call them different things. First are the rulers of countries, the rulers of the people, royal families, or today, the politicians. Then, secondly, those who control the monopolies of the necessities people need based on the time period. Throughout history, those monopolies were different.

For many centuries, a major necessity was salt. Those who controlled the salt and had a monopoly on salt had awesome power and control over the people.

In American history, necessities included the railroads, communications like the telegraph and telephone, and banking.

Most people had to bank, and if you had to travel or move your products, you had to use the railroads; there was no option. So if you controlled those necessities and had a monopoly, meaning you had little or no competition, you had awesome power and control over society.

Obviously today one necessity is oil. Whether the price of oil is fifty dollars a barrel or two hundred dollars a barrel, people and industry still NEED to use oil.

Food, throughout history, has always been a necessity. Those who control food and the distribution of food have awesome control and power.

Today, as I write this book, there are many other necessities such as social media, the internet, electric power, cell phones, and service, and many more.

The elite class controls these industries. Members of the elite class always believed that they were genetically programmed to be superior. They believe that they have smarter thinking, and are genetically programmed to rule over the vast majority of people, who have a different genetic model.

These genetic models that they were referring to were vibrational; it was in the DNA. Throughout history, the DNA of "blue bloods," the DNA of the ruling class, the DNA of the elite class, was kept "pure" by only marrying other members of the same class.

This is historical. I am just giving historical facts.

They believed that their DNA actually vibrated at different frequencies than the DNA of, let's say, the working class, which vibrated at a lower frequency." They believed that intelligence, or personality traits such as criminality, were IN THE GENES.

Throughout history, the ruling class has always wanted to make sure that the workers kept their vibration at a much lower frequency and stayed broadcasting from their brain on the BETA wave: the SLAVE wave, the POVERTY wave.

In China, for example, the rulers made sure that they controlled the drug opium. They also made sure that the majority of Chinese workers were taking opium on a daily, regular basis. This is one way they controlled the people and kept themselves in power and control.

That drug keeps the vibrational frequency of a person's DNA and mind very low. It makes sure that desires don't spring up. It keeps a person's brain broadcasting on the Beta wave, the slave wave.

Therefore, these people were kept docile. They had no hopes, desires, or dreams. They had little motivation, enthusiasm, drive, or initiative. They never wanted to do anything substantial in their life.

Adding fluoride in the water supply and getting people to drink and bathe in that fluoridated water has a similar effect on people.

This helps the rulers remain the rulers, and the workers remain the workers.

Throughout history, the concept that the brain actually emits and transmits vibration, frequency, or energy, and receives vibration, frequency, or energy, has been known but kept a secret, exclusively for the privileged elite class.

The understanding that thoughts are things and that the brain broadcasts frequencies is a factual, biological, quantifiable, scientifically proven and documented concept.

It is not fantasy, not mysticism, not spirituality. Therefore, I am not saying you have to believe this and take it on faith. This data is quantifiable.

The knowledge of how the brain works is something that the elite class and most members of the various global societies, still to this day, want to keep secret. They want to keep that knowledge for themselves.

It is not the Law of Attraction that they are focused on keeping a secret. It is the fact that your brain transmits frequencies, and if you broadcast that frequency on the Alpha/Theta WEALTH wave, you can ATTRACT into your life what you are thinking about.

This is the concept that "they" are desperate to keep secret.

Today, just like throughout history, the rulers around the world of the various countries are mostly members of secret societies. President Bush was a well-known, documented member of Skull and Bones. The highest-ranking members of Skull and Bones founded the CIA.

Well-known members of the Skull and Bones, Yale's secret society, include former Secretary of State John Kerry. Many senators, many U.S. Supreme Court justices, the people who control the World Bank, the International Monetary Fund, and many of the world's largest corporations, are members of secret societies.

Actually, ALL of today's billionaires are members of secret societies.

America's founding fathers were high-ranking members of the Masons. It was not secret.

So all the people that control the governments, all the people that control today's monopolies, are secret society members.

The people that control these monopolies do not want you to know the truth about your own amazing ability and power.

What we are talking about here, and what Einstein talked about, and what Thomas Edison documented, is this scientific fact: Your brain emits frequency, vibration, or energy. A frequency, when broadcast on the Alpha/Theta wave, is so powerful it affects matter and other brains. And your brain also receives frequencies emitted from other people and from everything in the universe.

The reason why you haven't heard more about it is because the people that control the flow of information globally do not want you to know it. Because if you do know about this life-changing concept, then you will realize just how much power you have right now. You will be fully aware that you, in fact, have Aladdin's Lamp and your own personal Genie, which can make anything you want actually happen and manifest.

With this knowledge, and how to use this knowledge, you can be, do, and have anything you want. You have the power.

Those who were at the live event had an advantage to some degree over those of you reading this book. Those who were physically sitting there were seeing not only the opulent place we were in, but also, knowing it was not open to the public, were quite frankly in awe.

Being able to see the physical manifestations that this really works in real life helped their "belief" that I was someone they SHOULD absolutely listen to.

Being able to meet real people, my friends and colleagues, many of whom were not only wealthy and powerful, but in some cases famous or celebrities, added much credibility to the material I was presenting.

Those in attendance realized that I am talking factually, not going rah-rah on a stage, jumping up and down, with music and dancers, and giving a motivational speech.

But rather just talking to them factually helped them absolutely know that this is 100 percent real and true and has produced real tangible results for real people in real life. Their level of excitement and confidence that they would be able to apply this and get results was just going through the roof.

Those of you reading this book have one disadvantage compared to those who were in attendance. They had the ability to see not just myself, but my colleagues live and in the flesh. Many of my colleagues who were in the room are some of the richest people in the world.

Some of these people are very well known, have been on television and written in magazines and newspapers. And to have these people come forth and basically reveal that they have been members of secret societies was in some cases unprecedented.

Members of Skull and Bones, the Illuminati, the Masons, the Brotherhood, and Bohemian Grove were there. To be blessed to have those people in the room with me, validating and verifying that, yes, this is how it works, this is the secret, this is what goes on behind the curtain, behind closed doors, this is what the majority of the population around the world will never know, never hear about, and never be exposed to—and yes, what Kevin is saying is all true—made an impression for all those in attendance.

When those special high-level people said, "This 'system' that you are learning now is how the magic works on planet Earth, and this is what we've been able to manifest using it, and what Kevin is teaching is what we've been taught," the attendees paid attention. They were VERY teachable.

Imagine having all those people with enormous wealth say, "This is how we have been taught. This is how we have applied this, and these are the results. And the results that you are seeing is not just wealth—even though you are seeing that obviously, we have been able to manifest wealth beyond your wildest imaginations, like nothing you have ever seen, even on *Lifestyles of the Rich and Famous*—but more importantly, we have used these techniques to manifest health, happiness, and great relationships."

The kind of wealth and opulence and money that the attendees were exposed to is something that most people just don't even know exists.

They were seeing this firsthand, and that was awe-inspiring. Obviously, seeing it firsthand raises your level of belief and confidence that this really works.

The attendees were also meeting and talking with people that were just at a different level, a "higher level," than people they had talked to before in their lives. The attendees were exposed to the "inner circle" of powerful people from around the world.

They got a glimpse of the secrets that go on in that inner sanctum, or inner circle. You are seeing how and why it always goes back to: Who Do You Listen To?

We have talked about the five basics. I have emphasized the importance of always focusing on the fundamentals and mastering the basics and always going back to those basics.

I talked about the importance of Who Do You Listen To. To really focus on that. I talked about your Teachability Index. How teachable are you?

It's funny, because during several of the breaks at the live event, several people would come up to me smiling, saying, "I get it. I really get it." Some of you might be thinking that too right now.

Let me point something out to you. Let me talk about the Teachability Index. Hopefully, you can see why I could speak on this one subject for hours, in terms of all the nuances and ways to really be perfect on this.

When you say, "I get it," your Teachability Index goes down. You instantly become less teachable. You think you know it all. Your willingness to learn and to accept change goes lower. Because you think you know it all, you are no longer an empty vessel. You are less teachable.

When you "know it all"—when you say, "I know that; I get that"—when you think you know it all, you've become less teachable. It's important to grasp a concept, but also to know that you don't know what you don't know. You need to know you never get it perfectly. You can ALWAYS learn more and get better.

The way to really be perfectly teachable is when you are listening to a concept, to have something click, to have a cognition, to feel like you DO understand it. You can't be confused throughout your whole life. That's not what I'm suggesting.

But what you should say is, "Wow, I get it so far. I think I understand it. But I know there is so much more I need to learn. And I know there is so much more I don't even know. But I think I am grasping and getting the concept to some degree."

Don't think that you fully get it, but rather, "I'm getting what he's presenting. I can use this. I'm understanding it. Wow. How much more is there? There must be so much more. And boy, I don't know what I don't know."

You have to have that balance. Again, complete willingness to learn and a complete willingness to accept change.

The Training Balance Scale emphasizes that the thought process is the majority of what we need to be focused on. Your THOUGHTS and FEELINGS put out a vibration. This is a KEY.

And the skills, the techniques, and the how are what most people focus on, which is why they fail.

When you understand the importance of the Training Balance Scale, you will always be able to catch yourself when you are focusing on, "How are we going to do that?"

Let's talk about relationships. If a person wants to have a romantic relationship, they always say, "You know, I don't know how I am going to meet my mate. I don't know what I should do and how I should do it."

And the answer is, the how is irrelevant in the beginning. Focusing on the HOW is NOT the first step to manifesting a relationship. The HOW initially is completely irrelevant. You don't have to know how. Get your THINKING right, your thoughts right, the vibration and frequency you are broadcasting right, and THEN the HOW will present itself. And with the right THINKING, when you DO the action steps, they will produce results.

The Training Balance Scale suggests that the techniques and the skills are not that important. But society emphasizes to you that it *is* important and that you should focus on the HOW.

When you focus on the HOW, you will always believe you are not capable of achieving what you want. Getting you to focus on the HOW is one of the techniques that is being used globally to keep people in a state of never achieving.

Remember, that is the goal of the "elites."

One of the goals of the elite class is to make sure that they remain in the elite class, and that everybody else remains virtually slaves. They don't want an uprising. They do not want a large group of people realizing that they have power and rising to their level.

That creates competition, and that reduces the power, control, and the financial resources of the current elite class.

Then, of course, are the Four Magic Steps, ending with unconscious competence, where you are doing this "system of manifesting" automatically. You are not thinking about it anymore. It just happens automatically, and you live your life like a magician. Everything just happens perfectly.

And of course, there is the Fifth Basic which is to master the Basics—focus on the fundamentals.

Then we talked about the two powerful concepts.

One is that your brain is both a transmitter and receiver of frequency, vibration, or energy. The words are synonymous as they are used here. Pick the word that you feel comfortable with.

Your brain broadcasts a signal that is similar to, but actually more powerful and at a higher frequency than, a radio or cell phone frequency.

The second concept is the Law of Attraction.

The definition of this law is: Whatever frequency your brain emits, that exact same frequency is attracted to you. Like attracts like.

You now have a couple of concepts that you have to grasp first before I teach you how to apply them and produce results with them. Here are basic concepts that you should grasp to some degree and understand at least a little before we can go on.

First new concept.

Everything on Earth is made of atoms. We all know that. We went to school so we should know that everything is made of atoms.

You also have to understand that throughout history, science has created technology and instruments that can see smaller and smaller particles. When atoms were first discovered, scientists proclaimed, with their arrogance, that the atom was the smallest particle in the universe.

Scientists are always arrogant. They always think they know everything. All they could see was the atom.

Their instrument could only see that far, or that close up, or amplify that much. So they could see an atom. Therefore, they determined, since that is all they could see, the atom must be the smallest particle on the planet.

Well, years later, when they developed a new instrument that could actually magnify even more powerfully, they found out that the atom is not a whole particle. They discovered that the atom actually consists of electrons, circulating around a nucleus, which contains protons and neutrons. (See image next page.)

Atom Structure

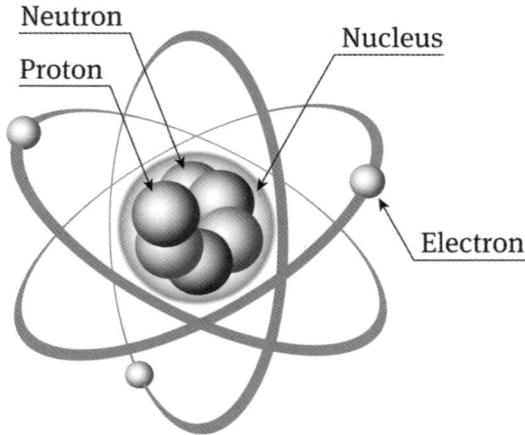

And then they said, again with complete arrogance, "Oh my, this electron is smaller than an atom. Therefore, the electron is the smallest particle in the universe."

What they should have said is, "Look, with the instrument that we have right now, the smallest particle we can see is the electron. But obviously, there must be something probably smaller that we can't see yet."

It would be decades later before they would discover what WE in the societies always knew, that the electron is BOTH a particle AND a wave. It only becomes a particle when it is observed. More on this and how this is important to manifesting later.

You know what an atom looks like. It has a nucleus in the middle and then circulating around it is an electron or electrons, depending on what element it is.

When you observe it, the electron as a particle rotates around the nucleus in a virtual orbit.

Here's the question. What holds the electron in orbit around the nucleus? Gravity? NO. The answer is energy, or a vibration, or a frequency, is holding it in orbit. The nucleus has a vibration that REPELS and ATTRACTS the electron. It is NOT gravity.

And the BIGGER question is, what is the SPACE BETWEEN the electron and nucleus? There is NOTHING THERE, according to scientists. THIS IS THE ZERO-POINT FIELD. This is where THOUGHTS are!

Scientists now have instruments that can actually see smaller than the electron. They see that the electron is a WAVE of energy and HAS a vibration or frequency. The electron is ENERGY.

The electron is NOT solid. It is actually full of holes. Nothing in the universe is solid. EVERYTHING vibrates and emits a frequency. Everything has a unique vibration.

Scientists today still do not completely understand how a transmitted radio wave or cell phone signal travels through "solid matter." The answer is, NOTHING is SOLID. There is SPACE BETWEEN the electron and nucleus. AND there is space WITHIN the electron.

Think about it. How does your cell phone pick up a signal when you are in an elevator in a building? The signal is a frequency. It is energy. It is a vibration. That frequency is traveling, not in one little beam, but everywhere in all directions all at once.

Think about this. This is awesome when you think about it.

You could be virtually anywhere and pick up a signal. This means that frequency is permeating all space. If you are in a room, and you walk anywhere in the room, your cell phone is still picking up the signal. Therefore, the signal is not directly in a line. The signal is almost like a gaseous thing, which is permeating the whole room with a vibration.

This is hard for a lot of people to completely comprehend, but that's what frequency or vibration is.

Scientists don't fully understand, nor can they explain, how a signal can be broadcast from a radio transmitter, or a satellite, or one of these cell towers, and how it can travel for miles and virtually permeate every bit of space, almost instantly, traveling at the speed of light.

These signals pass through trees, and buildings, and glass, and steel, and brick, and mortar. When you go into a subway, you can still pick up a signal in many cases. Isn't that amazing? The cell phone or radio signals are everywhere, like this invisible gas that fills up everything and passes through almost everything.

It's almost like magic. You might be thinking, "Wow, I never really thought about that."

It is almost like science fiction, but it's factual. It's actually physical. It's quantum physics. Just because you can't see it with your eyes, doesn't mean it is not physical. It is part of the physical universe. Everything is, at its core, energy, frequency, and vibration. We just can't see it with our physical eyes.

The KEY concept you have to understand is that vibration, frequency, and energy exist. Everything on the planet is made up of atoms, which are made up of electrons, protons, and neutrons. These are nothing more than energy, vibration, or frequency.

Therefore, everything on the planet, every single thing, at the end of the day, *is the same.*

Scientists as well as spiritual masters **have** actually said this for hundreds of years. They have said that everything is made up of the same material. Now we know that everything on the planet is made up of the same atoms. It is just the combinations of atoms that are different.

Everything is made up of the exact same material: atoms. You and I are made up of the exact same material: atoms. And they are all the SAME atoms as everything else as they constantly move from one "thing" to another. The atoms that you are made of at one time were the atoms that someone else or something else was made of.

The desk here is made up of the same material that you and I are made up of: atoms. Water is made up of the same material: atoms.

Flowers and trees are made up of the same material: atoms. Everything is made up of the same material: atoms.

Those atoms are made up of the exact same things: electrons, protons, and neutrons.

The electrons, protons, and neutrons ARE the same thing at their core: vibration, frequency, energy.

There is only one reason why everything looks, smells, sounds, and feels different, with different colors, shapes, sizes, textures, and so forth.

There is one reason why we have gold, and why we have silver, and why we have wood, and why we have iron, and why we have steel, and why we have rock, and why we have this flower, and a virtually infinite number of apparently different flowers: because each has its own unique frequency or vibration.

There are virtually an infinite number of potential combinations of frequencies. When you take one frequency and mix it with another, you have a new, different frequency. The change may be slight, but it is still different.

The potential number of frequency combinations is virtually endless. It's infinite. Everything you are seeing, smelling, tasting, hearing, or touching is made up of the same thing.

The only difference is the vibrational frequency of that thing.

That's what makes this flower look different than that flower. Both are made up of the exact same atoms, the exact same material. The only difference is that the combination and the ratios of atoms to one another are different. Therefore, the vibration is different.

Therefore, the result of what you see in the physical universe is different.

So, the concept that you have to grasp and understand—and if you don't fully comprehend it, it is still okay—is that everything on the planet is made up of atoms.

We can all concur on that. We know that. It is FACT, TRUTH. It is not me saying this.

Einstein said this, and every scientist on the planet agrees. Everything is made up of atoms.

Nothing has been found YET that is not made up of atoms.

Even moon rocks and meteors from outside of our solar system are made up of the *same* atoms. And atoms are all made up of the same thing. And the electrons, protons, and neutrons are simply made up of vibration.

Therefore, everything you see is made up of vibration. Another way of saying it is: everything you see is basically a combination of different frequencies producing its own unique frequency.

Yet another way of saying it is: everything you see is nothing but "energy."

Everything is *vibrating*. Everything has a *frequency*. Everything is just pure *energy*.

Do your best to understand and comprehend this concept or reality.

The next important concept to grasp is that your brain is a transmitter of frequency and a receiver of frequency.

Now, let me take this concept one step further.

You—and I'm not going to talk about who you REALLY are in this book; that is higher-level training and not needed at this stage.

But *you* have the power and ability to create any frequency you want, and use your brain to transmit that frequency on the WEALTH or MANIFESTING wave right between Alpha and Theta.

Let me say that again, to make sure you understand this.

The first concept is that everything *is* a frequency, or a vibration, or energy. Everything on the planet is *vibrating*.

Just imagine that everything you are seeing is vibrating at a unique, different frequency.

This table is vibrating at a different frequency. This lamp is vibrating at a different frequency.

Every one of these flowers is vibrating at a different frequency. The chocolates are vibrating at a different frequency, and every chocolate in the box is vibrating at a different frequency. This pear is vibrating at a different frequency. The grapes are vibrating at a different frequency.

Everything you see is vibrating, and everything is vibrating at a different frequency, because everything is energy.

That is the first concept.

The second concept is that your brain transmits frequencies, energy, or vibration, whatever word you want to use, and also receives them. This is how you can learn how to TAP INTO THE ETHER and pick up ANYTHING from the "field."

The third concept is that you have the ability, by conscious, deliberate intent, to use your brain and create any frequency you want and transmit it on the WEALTH wave. When you do that, the frequency you broadcast is put into the zero-point field and thus is EVERYWHERE INSTANTANEOUSLY. There is no time lag. Distance does not matter.

And most importantly, THAT frequency you deliberately broadcast on the WEALTH WAVE acts like a magnet, ATTRACTING the same frequency back to you. You virtually are commanding the universe to CREATE and manifest what you desire.

You might be asking, "Well, how do I do that?" Hold that question. I am getting to that. I am just making sure you understand the concepts first. This is critical.

You have the ability to dial into your brain the frequency that you choose, and transmit it.

You also have the ability to transmit that frequency softly, with very little power and intensity, or blast it with huge amounts of power and intensity.

Because your brain is a transmitter, you effectively have a volume control or power control over it. You can crank up the power and transmit a beam that is so strong, so intense, and so powerful, it will affect everything in the universe massively and quickly.

Your brain transmits frequencies similar to a satellite transmitting frequencies, a cell tower transmitting frequencies, or a radio tower transmitting frequencies.

The difference is that the frequency levels that your brain is putting out are much higher than those put out by cell phones, a radio transmitter tower, or a satellite.

Remember, those frequencies primarily go in a relatively straight line, but they can still pass through solid matter in most cases.

They appear to travel instantaneously because they are so fast, but there is still a time delay. And distance DOES affect their power and intensity. The farther you are away from a cell tower, the weaker the signal is.

The frequency that your brain puts out is different. It is MORE powerful and has unique properties. It does not travel in a straight line. It permeates everything in all directions and passes through EVERYTHING, even lead. It actually travels through the Earth, to the other end of the Earth. It goes in all directions. And it goes throughout the universe. It is as if space and distance do not exist.

And when your brain transmits a frequency, it virtually is everywhere instantaneously. There is NO time lag. And unlike a radio transmitter, where the further you get away from the tower, the weaker the signal, the frequency that your brain broadcasts is everywhere with the same power and intensity. It does not matter if a person is five feet away from you or on the other side of the globe. They will pick up the frequency you broadcast with the same power and intensity level.

Now, let's go back. Who Do You Listen To? Someone who has what you want and has been where you are. Someone who KNOWS, not just knows about.

There is another distinction here on this critical basic. If you listen to someone who has what you want because THEY DID IT and have the results in their life to prove it, you still must listen with DISCERNMENT. Why? Because maybe they are just telling you what worked for THEM. That is good. You can learn a lot from that. But maybe what worked for THEM in the PAST, will not work for YOU or will not work NOW.

At the live event, the attendees got to meet real people who are using these methods and producing results RIGHT NOW. They could see with their own eyes the real results. They could testify that everything I was teaching was true. This isn't theory, this is real. It works. They saw the evidence.

What is your Teachability Index? What is your willingness to learn? What is your willingness to accept change? Right now you are probably focusing on "What is my willingness to accept change?" because I am giving you some data that some people have a hard time grasping.

But here's the goofy thing. Remember the *Star Trek* communicators? "Scotty, beam me up." They had this little hand communicator, which was like five times bigger than a cell phone. Back in the 1960s we looked at that as nothing but science fiction, pure fantasy.

How could there be such a thing as a "communicator?" Today's cell phones are even MORE advanced than those fantastical science fiction "communicators."

So, what I am talking about here is not mystical, magical, or something you have to believe in. What I am explaining is not fantastical; it is no more impressive than explaining how a cell phone works to someone sixty years ago.

Look at the old DVDs. Think about it. You take a DVD, a little disc, push it in a box, and like magic, images and sound appear on a screen. Try to tell someone fifty years ago that those would exist.

Look at a computer. Look at all the technology that we have today that we just take for granted because we see it and we use it.

I am telling you how your brain works, and some of you are thinking, "Huh? I don't know if I can believe that, Kevin."

Wait a minute. Turn on your cell phone. How does it work? It is not magic. It is not science fiction. It is real. It uses an invisible frequency. The cell phone tower is blasting a frequency, and your cell phone is picking it up.

I'm just suggesting that your brain is putting out the same thing. The evidence is very clear. Your brain is made up of atoms, which means your whole body is made up of atoms. Which means your whole body is nothing but a frequency. It's a vibration. Every organ in your body is vibrating at a different frequency.

Does this make sense?

So your brain puts out frequencies. You can decide the frequency you want to put out. If you put out a poverty frequency on the Beta wave, then you will ATTRACT poverty. If you put out a frequency of something you want on the Alpha/Theta wealth wave, then you will attract that which you want.

Your brain's frequency is different than radio or cell phone frequencies because it has more power and is broadcast in the quantum field, the zero-point field; therefore, it can go more places, faster.

Your brain's frequencies permeate everything. Nothing can block or stop it.

The brain transmits frequencies, and those frequencies are—not maybe—are picked up by other brains, and it does—not maybe—it *does* affect physical matter.

So when you put out a frequency, it affects physical matter and, in fact, ALL matter in the universe.

YOU are awesomely powerful, more than you know.

Is there scientific evidence to back this up? Yes. There are thousands of research studies that have been done around the world. The most well-known, in Western countries, were talked about in the movie *What the Bleep Do We Know?* and in the book *The Field*.

And if you have not seen that video, *What the Bleep Do We Know?* or read the book *The Field*, I suggest you do. They give you the hard evidence and proof.

The bottom line is there are thousands of scientific experiments that measure vibration of matter—whether it is a piece of granite, a piece of steel, a diamond, a flower, a bottle of water, a glass of wine, a book—anything at all.

All of these have been measured with scientific instruments. The scientific instruments show that each thing has a different vibration. Those vibrations are constant. They always stay the same, unless something alters or affects the "thing," and thus the vibration will change.

If you are looking at a piece of gold, the vibration is always the same. It is a constant, unless ***something affects it.***

Take a piece of gold and shoot it with X-rays, which by the way, are frequencies you can't see. Think about this: a magnet. Does a magnet have a frequency around it? Yeah, it is called a magnetic field. Science can't see it.

If you take the most powerful instruments available today and look at the magnetic field, nothing registers. NO instrument can SEE a magnetic field. BUT IT IS THERE.

The north and south magnetic poles are different. We know that because they affect things differently. But there is no difference in the atoms between a known north or south magnetic field.

Scientists say the atomic structure is the same. Magnetic fields DEFY explanation. Magnetic fields are frequencies that are different. Science cannot detect them yet.

For years, scientists said, "We can't determine any difference between the north and south magnetic fields with our instruments. The atoms are the same at the north and the south poles. EVERYTHING SEEMS to be the same."

But quantum physics shows the frequencies of those atoms ARE different, even though they look the same with the microscope. The "beyond the physical" invisible frequency, or vibration, is different. This has been discovered now.

Scientists have taken physical matter and measured the frequency of, let's say, gold, and it is a constant. But when they bang it with X-rays or Gamma rays, or even radio waves, the vibration DOES change.

So, here we have physical matter, a piece of gold or a piece of silver or a rock. It has a constant vibration. Every day it is looked at and measured by the scientists, and the vibration is the same.

Then one day they blast it with a radio wave, and the vibration changes slightly. They blast it with an X-ray, and the vibration changes slightly.

So, that vibration can be affected by an outside source that is BROADCASTING a frequency that is powerful and intense.

Multiple materials—from gold, silver, iron, plants, a book, and many other things—were tested to find their unique vibrational signature. Again, their vibrations did not change in day after day of testing.

Then a human subject would look at the gold and emit a vibration with deliberate intent, broadcasting a frequency from their brain on the Alpha/Theta wave.

Don't worry, I AM going to show you how to do this.

Remember, the brain is a transmitter of vibration.

Guess what happened to the gold? It physically would look exactly the same. The atoms looked exactly the same. But in the testing, just like when it was bombarded with X-rays or radio waves or Gamma rays, *the vibration of the gold bar changed.*

This means that YOU have the power TO AFFECT MATTER with deliberate intent, just by THINKING THE RIGHT WAY!

The same results were found with the flowers, with the glass of water, with the peach, and a book. Einstein and Edison were right.

The brain DOES transmit frequencies.

The brain is a transmitter and receiver of frequencies, and those frequencies are picked up by other brains, and those frequencies do affect physical matter.

Another great research study, one discussed in the video *What the Bleep Do We Know,* was testing water and seeing if a PERSON could change the STRUCTURE and VIBRATION of water with their THOUGHTS or even with a WORD!

This test is VERY visual. You can SEE the dramatic results.

I Love You

Truth

Thank You

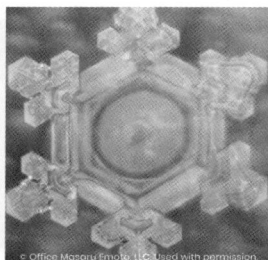

You Make Me Sick

Evil

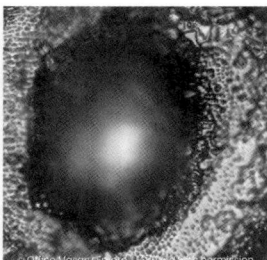

You Fool

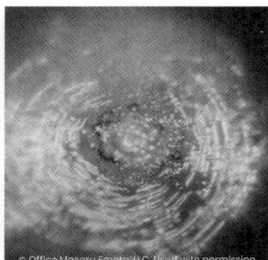

Photos © Office Masaru Emoto, LLC. Used with permission.

Various waters were tested, including tap water, spring water, and various forms of filtered water, including distilled water. The water was then frozen and then sliced. You could see the very distinct crystallization of the water. No matter how many times the water was frozen, sliced, and viewed under a microscope, each kind of water had the exact same crystallization pattern, thus the same frequency. Spring water was always the same, but it was different than the tap water or the distilled water or the filtered water.

Then a HUMAN PERSON would simply LOOK at the water and SEND a specific frequency from their brain to the water, with deliberate intent. Various frequencies were tested, like love, hate, and anger. Each one CHANGED the structure of the water!

The bottom line is that there is massive physical evidence, scientific evidence, that proves beyond a shadow of a doubt that the brain transmits frequencies and those frequencies affect physical matter.

BREATHE and SMILE.

Now, BACK to our NEW basic concepts:

Everything on the planet is made up of atoms. And all atoms are made of electrons, protons, and neutrons. All electrons, protons, and neutrons are really just vibration, frequency, or energy.

Therefore, everything on the planet, including you and me, is made up of the same thing.

We are all nothing but energy, just vibrating at a different frequency.

Everything is just energy that vibrates at a different frequency.

That's why everything looks or appears different. Yet everything is really all the same: energy.

But everything **is** vibrating at a different frequency.

That's the first concept.

The second concept is that our brain transmits and receives frequency or energy. It transmits and receives energy, and it can transmit that energy at different vibrational frequencies.

We can transmit any frequency we want with as much or as little power and intensity we want. That's the third concept.

The fourth concept is when our brain transmits frequencies, it's picked up by other brains, and it does affect physical matter in the universe.

When our brain transmits frequencies, it's picked up by other brains, and it does affect physical matter in the universe.

You may be thinking, Why isn't this taught in schools? Actually, it IS taught in the HOME schools of the elite class. I personally have been in palaces teaching this to the children of royalty.

But regular schools? Well, who runs the schools? Governments. Do you think that the government wants YOU to release YOUR personal power and become totally self-reliant? NO.

The government doesn't want you to read, never mind learn this. That is something I go into at higher levels of training.

As you read this book, you are in school right now. You are in the real school.

When you think about it, reading this book is like you being in the Harry Potter School of Magic. You are becoming like Merlin, being able to conjure into existence whatever you desire.

This is real, and it has been kept a secret from you.

At the live event, many of the attendees were amazed at the famous people I brought in to show and prove that this is real, that MAJOR people from around the world were in the Brotherhood.

I kept hearing attendees say to one another and me, "I didn't know he was in. I didn't know she was in." If somebody is super rich and powerful and happy and successful, they are probably "in."

But when you are in those societies, like the Brotherhood, like I was, we would have conversations with one another, and it would be completely different than a conversation we'd have with everybody else who was not in our organization.

It would be like we had two lives. It was really amazing. We were part of our group, and we weren't part of the general population. It was like we were aliens in a way. It was really quite amazing.

The very first time you use the techniques you are learning in this book and you manifest something in your physical universe that you want, you will be amazed at the untapped power that you had within you all this time.

Next basic concept: Law of Attraction.

So now that you understand how the universe and brain work, there is one other element you need to understand. That is the Law of Attraction.

The Law of Attraction is a senior law to the laws of the physical universe. It is actually a quantum law. We have physical laws, but some of those laws are superseded by more powerful or senior laws.

The Law of Gravity is a law, but it is superseded by the Law of Lift. The Law of Lift does not defy the Law of Gravity; it supersedes it. That is how an airplane flies. When the airplane flies, the Law of Gravity doesn't go away. The airplane is flying because it is using a more powerful law, a senior law to the Law of Gravity called the Law of Lift.

So, we have laws in the physical universe. Some of these laws are actually just agreements that you've made because you think that's how things work. In many cases, you've created your own set of 'laws.' More on this later.

So we have things in the physical universe that we believe to be true, like the Law of Gravity.

I am here to tell you that the Law of Attraction is senior to any of the physical laws, because it is a quantum law.

The Law of Attraction is the most senior law.

It is the most powerful law. It supersedes everything.

The Law of Attraction makes everything else go away. No other law has any effect when the Law of Attraction is fully activated.

The Law of Attraction says: vibrations or frequencies that are the same, attract.

Interestingly enough, Samuel Hahnemann, of Germany, invented a medical science or healing art called homeopathy, which is based on the same thing. Homeopathic remedies, when you get them, contain nothing. It is just some saline solution or another kind of carrier solution.

Scientists looked at five different homeopathic remedies for different ailments. They fully analyzed them. They all SEEMED TO BE exactly the same.

But the homeopath said, "No, they are NOT the same. The frequency, the vibration is different."

The way that a true homeopathic remedy is made is that a substance is taken, such as poison ivy. Now, if you rub poison ivy on your skin, what will happen? You'd get itchy, you'd get red marks. Right? You'd have an allergic reaction, effectively, to the poison ivy.

Homeopathy says, if poison ivy will give you itchiness and redness, then if you have those symptoms or similar symptoms, the homeopathic remedy that would cure you of those symptoms would be a HOMEOPATHIC version of what would GIVE you those symptoms. So the FREQUENCY of poison ivy would CURE you of those symptoms.

Hahnemann's theory was, like cures like. Which is the Law of Attraction: like attracts like.

To make a homeopathic remedy for itchy skin and red rashes, you have to get the FREQUENCY of the element that GIVES you those symptoms.

So the homeopath would take poison ivy and put it in some alcohol. You would let it sit to develop what is called a tincture. The alcohol pulls out the poison ivy essence. The alcohol would extract from the poison ivy all of its key elements.

Then the homeopath would take one drop of that tincture and put it in a five-gallon jug of water. Then what he would do is succuss it. This means to shake in a very specific way. The power of the remedy the homeopath wanted would determine how many times it was succussed. It could be once, or up to several hundred times. The more you succussed it, the more powerful it would become.

After the succussion process, he would then take ONE DROP from that jug, and put that one drop in ANOTHER five-gallon jug of water. He would then succuss that.

Then he would take ONE DROP from THAT jug and put that ONE DROP in another five-gallon jug of water and succuss that.

This was repeated many more times.

When he was done, the tincture of the poison ivy was so diluted that you effectively had just a jug of water.

With the most advanced scientific instruments today, if you analyzed the jug, you would just find water and nothing else.

But the frequency in the water was different.

Then, when a person was given this water, this homeopathic remedy, the person was cured of itchy skin and red rashes.

That is how homeopathy has been used for hundreds of years. Guess who are major users of homeopathy? Members of royal families and the elites.

This is because they understand energy. The reason they understand energy is because we have been taught about energy and frequency for thousands of years, so the concept of homeopathy makes complete sense.

When homeopathy was developed, guess who jumped on it and knew right away this would work because it is energetic healing? People who were members of the secret societies, who of course were members of royal families.

The Law of Attraction says a vibration will attract a similar vibration. Like attracts like. Vibrations or frequencies that are similar always attract. That's where the magnetic pull comes from.

The closer the vibrational match, the stronger the magnetic pull. That's what the Law of Attraction is.

Everything in the universe is a vibration. Every single thing that is vibrating is actually putting out into the universe a magnetic force, drawing in similar vibrations.

If you can imagine being in a room, everything you physically see is vibrating. Everything is emitting a unique vibration or frequency. Everything is then calling forth, or like a magnet, pulling into itself similar vibrations.

YOU, however, have a unique ability. Unlike a flower, for example. A flower is putting out one vibration, but that frequency is weak and not very intense.

But you and I have the ability to use our brain with deliberate intent and transmit whatever frequency we choose, with power and intensity.

Whatever frequency we transmit with our brain will be attracted into our lives and become our reality. That's the Law of Attraction.

Some of you are thinking, "I want to start using this."

Well, let me tell you the good and the bad news.

The good news is that you can now choose which frequencies you WANT to transmit from your brain, WITH deliberate intent.

The bad news is you *have* been using this from the moment you were born. But NOT with DELIBERATE INTENT.

You are just now learning HOW to use it.

The fact is, you are ALWAYS transmitting frequencies with your brain, twenty-four hours a day, seven days a week. Your brain is transmitting or broadcasting frequencies and vibrations ALL THE TIME.

Everything in your life is there because of what you've transmitted with your brain. Everything in your life has been attracted into your existence, into your experience, and into your life because of the frequencies and vibrations that you have been transmitting.

There are a couple of caveats here. There are three basic elements of transmitting frequencies or vibrations. Remember, whatever frequency you transmit, is being attracted to you. However, whether it comes in or not, or the speed in which it comes into your experience or not, is dependent on a few factors.

A key element is, what is the intensity or power of your transmissional frequency? Is it weak or strong? Is it focused? You *are* transmitting frequencies all the time, but the question is, at what intensity are you transmitting that frequency? And with how much power are you transmitting that frequency?

That's a key element. Power and intensity.

Another key element is, how *often* are you transmitting that frequency?

And another key element is, are you broadcasting your frequency on the Alpha/Theta wave, the WEALTH WAVE, the BILLIONAIRE BRAIN WAVE, or are you broadcasting on the Beta wave, the SLAVE and POVERTY wave?

The most important element to attracting things into your life, like a magnet, and creating things, is of course to transmit the frequency of what you want, NOT WHAT YOU DON'T WANT.

You are going to learn in this book exactly HOW to do this, so don't worry.

The frequency of what you want must be transmitted with intensity and power, on the Alpha/Theta wave, as often throughout the day as possible, WITH DELIBERATE INTENT.

The more power, and the higher the intensity of transmission of the frequency of what you want—and the longer and more consistently that it is being transmitted, will determine how fast you get what you want manifested in your life.

When you transmit a frequency, this is your command. Remember I said your wish is your command? When you wish for something, find the frequency for that which you want and then command it to come by broadcasting that frequency, with power and intensity, on the Alpha/Theta wave, as often as you can.

The command is transmitted into the ether by your brain. Increase the intensity and the power as high as you can and keep that transmission going for as long as possible, almost constantly.

That will determine how fast it manifests in your life.

Now, there is something that will block your transmission. There are COUNTER-INTENTIONS that will slow the manifesting of your desires or even stop them from becoming your reality.

I will talk about those later.

Remember Earl Nightingale, "You become what you think about most of the time"? Earl Nightingale's *The Strangest Secret* basically tells you everything I have said is true.

He effectively says you become, or you get, what you think about most of the time. When you are thinking about something, you are transmitting a frequency.

When you are thinking about what you want, you are transmitting the frequency of what you want. If you are worrying, which is thinking about what you DON'T want to happen, you are broadcasting THAT frequency.

And if you are thinking about what you want a lot, then it will be attracted into your life. This is an oversimplification, because there are several more key ingredients to this formula. I will give you everything in this book: the success or manifesting system that never fails.

You become, or you manifest, what you think about most of the time.

Whatever your dreams are, you can manifest them. I have seen thousands of people just like you apply these methods and create more success in their lives than they have ever imagined possible.

When you finish this book and apply this system, some of you are just going to be so blissfully happy because everything in your life is going to get better.

Your relationships are going to get better.

Your health is going to get better.

Your body is going to look and feel better.

And yes, you are going to manifest lots of money and material things.

But you are going to feel so much happier and fulfilled that money almost becomes irrelevant.

And quite frankly, money is irrelevant.

Some of you are thinking, "It is easy for him to say, look at all the money he has."

You will find out that money does not give you happiness. Attaining or acquiring MATERIAL THINGS does not give you peace of mind or true fulfillment. The act of creating gives joy. Success is a journey, NOT a destination. The JOURNEY is the reward.

At the live event, someone asked what the collective net worth was between myself and the people I brought there to share with the group. One of those people was the king of a country. It was estimated that the amount of money that those people had or controlled was over 1 trillion dollars.

But don't be in awe. Those were just people, just like you. Because you are learning the same information that they used to manifest that wealth, the only real differences between them and you are the size of their dream and time.

Shoot for the moon, because even if you miss, you will still wind up among the stars.

Don't let anyone steal your dreams.

LESSON 9

The First Steps
to Manifesting

You might be thinking, "What about people who are not members of secret societies, who have not been taught about the Law of Attraction—don't know anything about it—but have had incredible success in their life? How do they achieve that?"

The answer is, the Law of Attraction works whether you know about it or not.

Your brain transmits frequencies twenty-four hours a day, seven days a week. It does not matter whether you're consciously, with knowing, deliberate intent, broadcasting the frequencies of what you want. You ARE broadcasting frequencies all the time because that's what your brain does.

Everything on the planet vibrates whether you know about it or not. So whether you know about the Law of Attraction or not, and whether you're using these concepts consciously or not, they still exist.

The fact is, the Law of Attraction is working in your life, and everyone's life, whether they know it or not.

When you fully understand how it all works, by the time you finish reading this book, you'll understand *why* you have succeeded at times, and *why at times* you have gotten things in your life that you wanted, and also *why* you've gotten things in your life you didn't want or *why* you haven't succeeded.

You will soon see and have the cognition that you have been doing this unconsciously all along. You will see that the Law of Attraction has been working all along.

So for those people who don't know anything about the Law of Attraction or how this technique works, they're actually doing this anyway. They're just doing it instinctively. It's in their DNA. They're doing it automatically, or in some cases learning WHAT to do by trial and error.

Look at great athletes, for example: great golfers or various musicians that have "natural talent." When a coach or teacher looks at what they're doing, these individuals have figured it out on their own. They're doing it, not knowing that there's a law or a principle, or that this is how the physical universe is constructed. They're just doing it.

So that's the reason that some people who don't know about this are getting incredible success in their life, getting the things they want, are blissfully happy, have great relationships, etc.

But it's much easier when you actually know the mechanics and the recipe so that you can apply it.

Another comment that comes up often at this point is, some people can't believe how easy and logical this is.

Those who were in the room had a slight advantage over you reading this book, in some ways. They were from all over the world. They not only heard this information but could ask questions. They were also seeing the physical evidence that this works, and they had the luxury of meeting some famous wealthy people. These people were at the highest levels in both world governments and in business, including royalty. These were people who some of you have heard about, read about, and know about. They were able to get information and validation directly from them and see that this is not pie in the sky, not guru land or motivational speaker world or that type of thing, but the real deal.

I think this is the first time in history since Napoleon Hill was taught this information by Andrew Carnegie, a member of the Brotherhood, where true insiders are revealing the secrets from the secret societies about how to manifest what you desire.

Hill's information was strictly on the manifesting money side and the financial or economic side. But this is the first time in history that so many people have come out from the various societies and collectively bound together as we have to form my private club, the Global Information Network (GIN), and have been willing to reveal to the masses these methods for those people who are serious.

We made a commitment that we would not just share this with every single person and shove it down anybody's throat. We would make this information available to those who are serious about manifesting their goals and dreams.

You have to have a high willingness to learn, which means you're going to have to be willing to give up the things you love, including some time and money.

What is your willingness to learn? How do you determine this?

I think one of the easiest ways, as I mentioned, is you're willing to give up something you love for a short period of time, so that you can have total time and financial freedom.

If you love golf, if you love TV, are you willing to give that up for a period of time to learn this?

But there's something else. Are you willing to give up some money?

I'm going to talk about why it is very significant that you ARE willing to give up some money to learn this information and get educated, because that really determines how high your willingness to learn is and how teachable you are.

And then, of course, what is your willingness to accept change?

This information can be radically different than what you've thought about in the past. Being willing to really accept change, do things differently, and think differently is going to create different results.

We've talked about how the universe works. Everything is made up of energy that vibrates at different frequencies. That's all everything is, including us.

Our brains can transmit and do transmit frequencies twenty-four hours a day, seven days a week.

We have the ability to choose those frequencies, and we have the ability to determine the power and intensity of the frequency and the duration that frequency is being broadcast. We can also choose to broadcast that frequency on the Alpha/Theta brain wave.

Now, how long is that frequency being broadcast? When you put out a frequency, if you increase the power and intensity and increase the duration for which that frequency is broadcast, then a matching frequency will come to you like a magnet, as fast as you can imagine.

When we put out a frequency with our brain, with power and intensity, over a long duration, on the Alpha/Theta brain wave, then everything on the planet and everything in the universe begins working together to match that frequency and bring it to us.

It can happen incredibly fast, or it may take a little time. You are planting a seed in the universe. Sometimes it takes time for that seed to germinate, grow, and manifest.

With practice, when you get to unconscious competence, it'll happen faster and faster and faster. You'll be able to dial in the frequency exactly the way you want, increase the power and intensity, broadcast on the Alpha/Theta wave, and keep the duration long enough so that it activates everything in the universe. Then it is drawn to you like a magnet and comes rushing towards you.

Think about it this way.

What you want, wants you.

All you have to do is activate it and it comes rushing to you. There's a magnetic pull. You can attract money like a magnet. You can attract your lover, the best relationship you have ever had, like a magnet.

You can attract things into your existence. Friends, social status, accolades, success, achievement, happiness, bliss.

You can attract anything and everything you want.

You can be, do, or have anything you want.

As Napoleon Hill said, "Anything the mind of man can conceive," which means anything you can dream, anything you can imagine, anything you can desire.

"Anything the mind of man can conceive, and bring itself to believe, it can achieve." This means any and everything you can dream of, any and every desire you have, anything and everything you want to be, do, or have can be brought to you.

But you have to believe or have confidence that it will manifest. This is a key element that I will talk about later. If you "believe" you will achieve it, you will have it.

The method by which that is achieved, the method by which you command your Genie to give you what you want, is by putting out the frequency of what you want, increasing the power and intensity of that broadcast, broadcasting it on the Alpha/Theta wave, and keeping the duration of that broadcast long enough—WITHOUT COUNTER-INTENTIONS— it will come rushing towards you.

It has to by law.

It's the Law of Attraction, which is senior to the Law of Gravity or any law in the physical universe. It's how everything works. You cannot deny it.

You can't scientifically push it away. Quite the opposite. Because of quantum physics, every bit of scientific evidence and proof shows this is how it works.

Napoleon Hill put it this way. He said the key to success can be broken down to this:

Define your dream and get a burning desire for its achievement.

One, define your dream. That's number one: define your dream.

That means clearly know or define what you want. Be specific. Get a clear definition of what you desire.

In order for you to achieve things in your life, you need to know what you want. You can't hit a target you can't see. Nor can you hit a target you don't have.

You go to a restaurant and get the menu. You need to decide what you want so you can order it. You could just say, "Bring me some food." You may want food, that's fine, you'll get some food. But it may not be exactly to your liking. If you want something specific, you have to ask for something specific in the restaurant. Order it and it will come to you.

Life is the same way.

Define your dream, determine and define exactly what you want.

That's the first thing Hill said: He said one critical key that he learned from Carnegie was, "Define your dream."

And then second, "Get a burning desire for its achievement."

This was language used back in the early 1900s. Let me translate this into today's modern language.

Define your dream, determine exactly what you want, clearly identify what you want, and then get a burning desire for its achievement.

So the question is, what is the definition of burning desire?

What is the definition of "define your dream?" How do we define our dream? How do we get a burning desire?

This is really a key element.

Now we're getting into the specific techniques on how to apply the basic principle, which is, "Use your brain, transmit a frequency with power and intensity, keep that transmission over a long duration, broadcast it on the Alpha/Theta wave, and then it will come."

If you go to any success seminar or read any of the success books, I think you'll find now that many of them are misguided and missing key ingredients.

They may appear to give you some of the elements of what we're teaching here, but they may include other elements that basically make the method not work.

I am giving you a very specific, proven recipe. This recipe works all the time, when followed. If you start changing the recipe, if you start changing the ingredients, adding or subtracting ingredients, changing the proportion of the ingredients, or changing the order in which the ingredients are mixed together, you're not going to get the same result.

So I am giving you the pure, secret recipe that has never been released to the public with all of the ingredients in the exact proportion that produces results 100 percent of the time.

You can read thousands of books and you can get bits and pieces, but there isn't one out there that I, or any of the people I brought to the live event, have been exposed to that gives this exact recipe.

Therefore, the evidence also shows that there's nothing else out there that has delivered these superior results. Nothing has been proven to help someone manifest with the speed and effectiveness that this system has. Using THIS will get you what you want faster, with less effort, than anything else available. This is it. This is what you have been looking for.

First, define your dream. Exactly what do you want?

When I ask people this, they will say things like, "I want a car. I want a house. I want a better job. I want to be debt-free. I want to be happy. I want to travel all over the world. I want a better relationship. I want a relationship. I want to have a better relationship with my kids. I want to have a better social standing. I want to lose weight. I want better health."

All these different dreams come up.

But there's one thing that is senior to everything when we are talking about "define your dream." It is the one thing that we are going to be focusing on as our template.

It's the most important thing.

This is number one, number one, number one.

It is always the most important.

And that is this: You must always have as your NUMBER ONE goal … which is your goal subconsciously anyway … *to feel good right now*.

Your goal, your biggest dream, should always be, I want to feel good right now.

Not tomorrow, not when you get your raise, not when you get your new car, not when you take your vacation.

Your number one goal should be to feel good right now. Feel as good as you can, NOW.

Now, let me define what "feel good" means.

Feel good, first and foremost, means being outrageously happy.

Let's use some different words to describe some various emotions.

This is an emotion, not a physical body feeling.

Boy, my body feels good, you might say. When your body feels good, don't your emotions feel good too?

We're not talking about the physical body first.

We're talking about emotions.

Feeling good. Being happy. Being content. Being settled. Feeling secure. Feeling confident.

Feeling grateful. Feeling blessed. Feeling bliss. Feeling contentment. Feeling joy. Feeling exhilaration. Feeling exuberance. Feeling enthusiasm, motivated, inspired, at peace, fulfilled.

Think of those different words.

They all describe different feelings, don't they? There's a difference between feeling exhilaration and feeling contentment. They're both pretty good feelings, but they're different.

So the complete definition for you is, feel *good* now. That encompasses many emotions.

If you want to clearly define that even more, it's *feel as good as you can right now.*

And if you want to define that even more, your goal should be to *feel good now and keep feeling better,* because you have to be moving towards something.

Does this make sense?

Your number one goal should always, always, always be to *feel good now and keep feeling better.*

That's what your number one goal should be.

Based on your current situation and your history, your specific definition of feeling good will change sometimes from hour to hour, day to day, week to week, or month to month.

Sometimes feeling good means you really just want to feel secure. For you, at a specific time and place, that's going to be the best feeling to feel, because maybe you've been dealing with a lot of insecurity.

For some of you, the best feeling that defines feeling good is to feel content because you haven't been feeling very contented.

For some of you, the best feeling to feel *good* is to feel love because you've missed that.

You've missed hugs and feeling appreciated by people and feeling loved by people. So you're craving *that* specific feeling.

For some of you, the best feeling to feel *good* is to feel exhilaration because maybe you have felt bored and you're really craving something more like exhilaration.

There isn't a right or wrong *good* feeling.

Each one of you will select the feeling, knowing that it will sometimes change from hour to hour, day to day, week to week, or month to month.

The key is, you want to feel as good as you can.

Do you wake up in the morning with a smile on your face and feeling how excited you are about the day? Do you jump out of bed and start whistling for no reason or singing in the shower, feeling how lucky you are, how happy you are, how blessed you are, how wonderful life is, and how excited you are to experience all these incredible things today in your life?

For most people, that's not the case.

Feeling as good as you can should be your number one goal.

Do you go throughout the day with eyes open, observing things, taking things in, looking at the tree outside, and feeling excited and awed like you did when you were a child, filled with wonder?

You can feel excitement, joy, and happiness no matter what the external conditions are.

I've been fishing up in Canada in a tent and I feel joy, happiness, and wonder.

There's really not one experience better than another. Every experience in life is different.

Your feelings can be the same no matter what the experience is.

Your ultimate goal is always to feel good right now, as best as you can. This is your major indicator that you are on track.

Remember this. *Feel good now, feel as good as you can, and continue to feel better.*

This is your first objective: to feel good now, as best as you can.

So, when you're defining your dream, when you're defining what you want, you have virtually three options.

The first option in defining your dream is, be specific.

The second option is not to be specific at all, be general.

You can be very specific with your desire, or you can be general.

There is a third option: You can virtually not define anything, but just define feeling good as the goal and objective.

All three of these work, and they all will create a very good life for you.

I'll explain the differences.

First, let's talk about defining your dream with specificity. Let's use something tangible that we can all see. Let's say you are wanting a specific thing. You may want a better relationship. You may want a better career. You may want a Mercedes SL convertible.

Some of you may say, "I want clarity. I want a purpose. I have no purpose in my life. I want to find my purpose." That could be your goal, to find your purpose. That is specific.

Let's say that you want a new car.

You can be general and just say, "I want a new car."

Or you can be specific and say, "I want a Mercedes, a new Mercedes." You can be general and say, "I just want a new Mercedes. I don't care what kind of Mercedes. I don't care what color. I just want a new Mercedes."

Or you can be specific and say, "I want a black S-Class Mercedes."

You can be even more specific. "I want a NEW black S-class Mercedes with a black leather interior and a sunroof." You can be as specific as you want.

So the first thing is defining what you want. You must have a target, a goal, an objective.

"Define your dream and get a burning desire for its achievement."

"Whatever the mind of man can conceive and bring itself to believe, it can achieve."

"You become or get what you think about most of the time."

So if you want a black Mercedes, a Law of Attraction "expert" would say all you have to do is think about that Mercedes and do nothing. By magic it will manifest in your life. This is THEORY and is NOT how to apply this formula in real life.

THEY say, just think about the black Mercedes. Think about the black Mercedes. Think about the black Mercedes. Think about the black Mercedes. When you're thinking about the black Mercedes, what is your brain doing? Yes, your brain is transmitting a frequency of the black Mercedes. Thus it must be attracted into your life and must manifest.

But there are some KEY missing ingredients they don't know about.

With what intensity and power are you transmitting the frequency? They never mention power and intensity.

Are you broadcasting the "Mercedes" frequency on the Beta wave (the slave or poverty wave) or the Alpha/Theta wave? They never mention that.

How are you FEELING when you are broadcasting that frequency? Are you feeling bad or good? Do you feel AS IF you are already in possession of the Mercedes? Or are you feeling the LACK of NOT having it now?

These are KEY ingredients.

AND, does the broadcasting of that frequency motivate you to ACTION? It SHOULD if done right.

When you are doing this right, the HOW you are going to get the money to buy that Mercedes WILL present itself and thus you are MOTIVATED and INSPIRED to take ACTION to MAKE IT HAPPEN.

So with THEM, you are NOT getting the FULL, complete recipe. Thus you will probably not get great results. They are CLOSE, but they are MISSING KEY INGREDIENTS.

Years ago, a book was written, *As a Man Thinketh.* The book gave the factual statement, actually made by either Edison or Einstein, "Thoughts are things."

A thought is a physical thing. It sends out physical particles.

I've been calling them frequencies, vibration, and energy.

Thoughts have unique and peculiar characteristics. They are particles AND waves. They are physical particles that go out into the universe that have magnetic pull, according to Einstein and quantum physics.

This is not some mystical guru or hippie thing. Not that the spiritual guru, the enlightened master, is wrong, but most people have an easier time believing a scientist who has evidence than someone who says, "You just have to believe me on faith."

Thoughts are things.

So theoretically, based on what we've been talking about, if you just think about black Mercedes, black Mercedes, black Mercedes, black Mercedes, black Mercedes, you're transmitting the frequency of black Mercedes. And it thus SHOULD magically manifest. *But we all know it won't.* Anyone who has tried it knows it does not work. That is why so many people got disillusioned with the book *The Secret.* It is theory that SOUNDS GOOD, but does not seem to really work in real life.

Let's fill in the missing pieces of the manifesting puzzle.

According to Napoleon Hill, you must first "Define your dream." You did. You defined it as a black Mercedes. Hill goes on to say you must then have a burning desire for its achievement.

This can be defined as high-intensity broadcasting, high-power broadcasting of the frequency followed by ACTION. Burning desire is DRIVE. It is a NEED TO HAVE SOMETHING. It is a feeling that you will stop at nothing to get what you want. It is a feeling that says, "I am going to get it, THAT'S IT, PERIOD!"

If you have a burning desire, you're going to have high-intensity broadcasting of the frequency, high-power broadcasting of the frequency from your brain about black Mercedes, black Mercedes, black Mercedes. And if you have a burning desire, you're going to be thinking about it all the time. You are going to be OBSESSED with HAVING a black Mercedes. THIS will MOTIVATE and INSPIRE you to take massive and immediate ACTION to MAKE IT HAPPEN.

Earl Nightingale said, "You get what you think about most of the time." Which means you should be broadcasting the frequency of what you want as often throughout the day as you can.

I want a black Mercedes. I'm thinking about black Mercedes, black Mercedes, black Mercedes, black Mercedes, which means I'm putting out this vibration.

But I just don't *want* the black Mercedes.

That's not going to work, because if you just *want* a black Mercedes, you're going to put out a vibration that's very weak, with low intensity.

And if you just *want* a black Mercedes, you won't even be thinking about it that often.

If you just want something, you don't have a burning desire for it.

Some people WISH they had something. This is the weakest.

Others WANT something. This is also weak.

People who manifest things, NEED to have something! This is power and intensity. It is a burning desire.

When it becomes a NEED, you will get it.

So first, define your dream. Then second, get a burning desire for its achievement. That burning desire will mean you don't *want* the black Mercedes. You *need* to have the black Mercedes. You are OBSESSED with having that black Mercedes.

When you start having that true burning desire for that black Mercedes, the intensity of the transmission that's coming out of your brain, that you're broadcasting, will be very high and the power will be very high.

Because you have a burning desire to have the black Mercedes, you're going to be thinking obsessively about it all the time. So the broadcast is very frequent. It is consistent.

Do the right things, long enough, consistently.

When you do this, the HOW to have the Mercedes will be presented to you by the universe. You will see THEN, HOW you CAN have that Mercedes. Then you are MOTIVATED and INSPIRED to take massive and immediate ACTION. AND, you will LOVE doing the action steps to make it manifest.

Therefore, the black Mercedes should come into your experience and manifest.

Now someone says, "But wait a minute. What if I can't afford a black Mercedes?"

You are focusing on the HOW when you should be focusing on your THOUGHTS and vibrations. The HOW WILL present itself in time. You're on the wrong side of the Training Balance Scale if you are thinking about the HOW now.

When your attitude's right, the facts don't count.

Another way of saying it is: You don't need to know the how NOW because the Law of Attraction will present the how to you, and help you manifest your desire.

How does the Law of Attraction make it manifest?

It basically will create and put into your life, events, circumstances, people, situations, and conditions that you can't even imagine, that will help you and show you HOW YOU can create and manifest what you want.

Think, "If it is to be, it is up to ME."

The Law of Attraction will move mountains to put into your existence what you're asking for. The Law of Attraction has to work because it's a law. It works, period.

The Law of Attraction will affect virtually trillions of different variables and start shifting things around that you're not even aware of or thinking about, to create the ideal conditions so that a black Mercedes will be in your life.

You don't have to know how right NOW.

Think about a radar screen. Most people live their life looking at their radar screen. They are looking at what they can see on their radar screen.

This is one major reason people fail.

Most people base all of their decisions and beliefs on what they can see on their radar screen.

Someone says, "I have $50,000 in credit card debt. How can I pay that off? I'm looking at my income. I'm looking at my expenses. I'm looking at my prospects for getting a new job or getting a raise. I see nothing. I don't see a way out (on my radar screen). There's no way that I can pay off my credit card debt. It's impossible."

All you're doing is looking at what you see on your radar screen.

Now, if you imagine that the radar screen is this small screen, maybe about three inches in diameter, what you can see on your radar screen is VERY limited. You cannot see what is BEYOND your radar screen. There is MUCH MORE outside the scope of your radar screen than on it!

You can't even imagine what's off the radar screen that you can't see. What's outside the screen is a world of ALL POSSIBILITIES where NOTHING is impossible. If you COULD see what your radar screen cannot see, then you would KNOW that ALL THINGS ARE POSSIBLE FOR THOSE WHO BELIEVE.

This means, TRUST THE UNIVERSE. Have CONFIDENCE in the universe AND yourself.

Your radar screen can only see so far. It is only a three-inch diameter screen. It only picks up a few things that are close to your current reality.

Imagine that your radar screen is a hundred feet in diameter and picks up everything in a ten-thousand-mile radius. You agree that you would be able to see more, MUCH more.

Understand that the vast majority of what is available to you is *off your radar screen.* You can't see it. You can't even imagine it.

But once you start activating the Law of Attraction, everything outside the radar screen starts shifting and moving. There can be virtually hundreds of thousands, if not millions or billions or trillions of variables that start moving and shifting to help you manifest your desires.

This happens when you transmit from your brain a vibration of what you want, with power and intensity for a long duration on the Alpha/Theta wave.

Everything in the universe starts shifting. And everything starts happening and rushing towards you. What you want wants you. What you desire has to, by law, start coming towards you.

The universe will do this because the Law of Attraction is real; it can move mountains.

It will create events and circumstances and put people in your life to make what you want manifest and become your reality.

Surprisingly, what you want will manifest in ways that you can't even imagine because it is not on your radar screen. You can't even see the amazing ways the universe will help you to manifest your desires.

So stop looking at the radar screen. This is one of the biggest problems people have.

This is why Napoleon Hill said, "Whatever the mind of man can conceive or whatever you desire, you can have it, as long as you *believe you can have it.*"

There are several things that could slow down your manifesting or stop the technique from working.

Let's go back to the technique and I'll tell you what's going to cause it to NOT WORK.

The technique is, you define your dream. You define what you want. Black Mercedes.

You get a burning desire for its achievement. You really want it, want it, want it. And you move to NEED IT.

That allows you to transmit that frequency of black Mercedes with intensity and power.

When you have a high desire, which means you NEED TO HAVE IT, you will become obsessed with getting it so you will think about it all the time. You will have a long duration of transmission.

So where's the block?

The block is, if you don't *believe* that you will get it, then that lack of belief, or lack of confidence, stops it from coming into your life and manifesting.

When you don't have confidence that you will, in fact, HAVE the Mercedes, then you are broadcasting on the BETA slave wave and broadcasting the LACK of having a Mercedes, instead of the feeling of actually HAVING the Mercedes.

When you don't believe you will get it, you will not be obsessed with getting it, thus you won't be thinking about having the Mercedes very often. The duration of the transmission won't be very frequent.

When you don't believe you will have that black Mercedes, the intensity and power of the transmission won't be very strong.

When you don't believe you'll have that black Mercedes, you are in actuality putting out a counter-intention transmission. You are effectively broadcasting, "Black Mercedes, stay away."

Without belief, without confidence, you have intention (needing the Mercedes) and counter-intention (I don't believe I will ever get a Mercedes) being broadcast simultaneously.

They neutralize each other.

The black Mercedes *is* coming but being ***pushed away at the same time***. Thus it does not manifest and you get frustrated (stop feeling good now).

Does this make sense?

You might be thinking, "That's fine, that's good. But how do I get the high desire? How do I get the high belief and confidence?"

The answer is, as I said at the beginning of this Lesson, your first goal is to feel good now.

You must use your feelings as your guide. You must use your feelings as your gauge. You must use your feelings as your indicator. You must use your feelings to see if you are lining up. You must use your feelings to find out if you are in the sweet spot.

Don't worry, I am going to put this all together soon and give you the STEP by STEP recipe so you GET IT and can APPLY it without any questions. Be patient. We are getting there. I am still laying out the foundation and groundwork. Remember, you can only build as high as your foundation is deep.

Remember too that this book is not just teaching you the methods, it is written in a special way, using spaced repetition, hypnotic language patterns, and embedded commands to eliminate your negative failure programming and REPROGRAM you for SUCCESS.

How do you get what you want?

You must define your dream, have a burning desire for its achievement, and a high amount of belief or confidence that you WILL HAVE IT.

And here's the kicker. Some of you right now might actually want a black Mercedes. But you can't bring yourself to believe you'll actually HAVE a black Mercedes. Then you'll never get a black Mercedes. *So stop thinking about a black Mercedes.*

No one else in any books will tell you this secret.

And this is the secret.

You need to define what you want, but it has to be something *you can believe that you CAN attain.*

Let's say you were to write a list of all the things you want. If you look at that list, there may only be a few of those things that, right now, you actually KNOW that you can attain. There might be only a few that you have confidence that you CAN attain in time. You might only be able to BELIEVE you can actually HAVE just a few of them. The others are TOO BIG for you to believe you can attain them right now.

In a moment I will ask you to write a list of all the things you want if money wasn't an object, and you knew you couldn't fail. Imagine you hit a hundred-million-dollar lottery. Write down everything you would buy. Write down everything you WANT to be, do, or have.

Some of you might put down: new refrigerator, eat at a certain restaurant, go to Hawaii, get a private jet, get a black Mercedes, get a new wardrobe, quit my job, start my own business, I'll open up a restaurant, whatever. Maybe lose twenty pounds.

Make a list of everything and anything you want, material or non-material.

Maybe you will write down: learn a foreign language, learn to play the piano, be a great singer, whatever. Learn how to paint. Make a list of everything that you want.

Okay, do this now and limit your time to ten minutes. Do this now. Stop reading and do this now, and then come back in ten minutes to continue reading.

Welcome back.

Okay. Now you have your list. I want you to scan that list and ask yourself, on a scale of 1–10, with 10 being the highest, how much confidence do you have that you CAN ACTUALLY HAVE THAT in the next twelve months? Give each one a number as to your level of belief that within twelve months, you CAN attain that thing.

Do this now and come back when you are finished.

———

Welcome back.

When we did this exercise at the live event, very few people had a lot of 10's.

Here's the point. When you are starting this process, you can't focus on the things on your list that are at a "1" on level of belief, because you have no belief you'll achieve them.

This is one of the reasons why people who read the book *The Secret*, people who read *Think and Grow Rich*, and people who go to various Law of Attraction seminars, miss the whole point. You go to goal-setting seminars, success seminars where they talk about dreaming big. Get your dream bigger, they say.

It is true, you should dream big and be able to use your imagination and expand the size of your dreams.

BUT, there is a difference between a DREAM and a GOAL.

But people are teaching you to get this outrageous big dream and focus on *it*.

This is TOO STEEP a GRADIENT.

They give you all these techniques to focus on this big dream. But you don't really subconsciously believe you will ever get that. You are broke and in debt, and they tell you to focus on owning a private plane. That is TOO STEEP a GRADIENT. You go through ten years of your life, and it never manifests.

You get frustrated because you don't believe you're actually going to get what you desire and it's never going to come in because you're vibrating—you're transmitting—an intention of getting it and a counter-intention of you don't believe you will ever get it. Therefore it's never going to manifest.

The method that we were taught in the societies was very simple.

This is not a race. Everyone is different. Some people can believe that they can become a billionaire the day after they graduate from college, or halfway into college, or when they're twelve.

Another person may *never* really believe they can be a billionaire.

So what you need to do is, you need to start working on manifesting dreams, goals, desires, or objectives that you can believe that you CAN actually achieve.

Now let me tell you what the sweet spot is.

If you look at the list you wrote of the things you want, which ones should you focus on? You should focus on the things that have a belief level of 10. Start there.

However, there is a *sweet spot.* Let me explain what the sweet spot is.

The desire that you want, the goal that you want, the objective that you want, the dream that you want, the thing that you want that will come to you the fastest, is a dream or goal or an objective or a desire that's in the sweet spot.

What is the sweet spot?

The sweet spot is something you NEED that gives you a very high level of excitement and desire, and gets the juices flowing. It gets you excited when you think about having it. It gets you motivated, it lights your fire, and at the same time, you absolutely believe you can get it.

Now, the sweet spot ideally should be in both. It has to be big enough to excite you and small enough that you KNOW you CAN achieve it.

Let's walk on both sides here and let me show you the differences.

Let's say you had on your list, "I want to go to a certain fancy French restaurant." You've always wanted to go there, and you know it's going to cost several hundred dollars. The thought of going to this restaurant turns you on and excites you.

When you think about going to the restaurant, you say, "Oh, how good I would feel if I could afford to go to that restaurant."

Aha!

Remember when I said the most important thing is to feel good now? Aha! That's why I said that, because the sweet spot is also a place where you would feel good when you get it.

You also KNOW that it is POSSIBLE for you to earn enough extra money to be able to afford and go to that restaurant.

Right now, maybe you only have the ability to look at your tiny radar screen, but even on that, you can see that that you might have a Christmas bonus coming up. Or maybe you see that you could get some money for your birthday. So you can already see there is a way for you to attain your goal of going to that restaurant.

However, if you are thinking this way, you're still too focused on the *how.*

BUT, you ARE at a place where you can see that you CAN attain this goal. You're already figuring out ways to make it happen, and this makes your belief that you CAN attain it go up.

You see, when you get to unconscious competence, the *how* becomes irrelevant at the beginning of this process.

The more you do this, you will reach a point where you will think of a desire, and the HOW becomes not important. You KNOW that this works, so your belief that you CAN attain your desire is automatically high. You just know from experience that whatever you want, happens.

But you can't do that now because *success builds confidence*. In the beginning, you have to get some successes.

Some of you might have on your list of desires that you want to achieve, "I want to meet a mate." You may say, "Look, I *know* I'll meet a mate. I don't know how, but I know it'll happen. I don't know when, but I know it'll happen."

The thought of meeting a mate and being in a passionate, loving relationship, a fulfilling relationship, is really exciting to you. Maybe you have a high level of belief and a strong desire for it. And when you think about having a wonderful relationship with a wonderful person, you get excited. It makes you happy thinking about it.

That goal IS in your sweet spot. I am sure you get the idea of what kind of goal is in the sweet spot.

A sweet spot goal might be to start your own business. When you think about starting your own business, you think that you definitely COULD do that. You think of other people you know that have started their own businesses and become successful. You think, if they can do it, I can do it too.

You think about how much you would enjoy having your own business and being your own boss. You get so fired up and excited when you think about starting your own business that just thinking about it makes you happy.

This is another example of a goal being in the sweet spot.

Let me tell you what's *not* in the sweet spot.

Let's say you have the goal of starting your own business and the thought of it gets you excited and motivated. You love the idea of being your own boss.

BUT, do you BELIEVE you actually COULD start a business and succeed? All of a sudden, all this doubt pops into your head. You recall some people you know that TRIED to start a business and FAILED and had to file bankruptcy. You recall your friends and relatives telling you that YOU aren't smart enough to start a business and succeed. You start asking yourself, "Where am I going to get the money to start?"

You start thinking, "What if I lose all my money?"

You start to have massive doubts and your belief that you CAN do this crashes.

That goal right now is *not in your sweet spot.*

A sweet spot goal has to be a goal that you are really excited about, really fired up about, that you know will make you feel fantastic when you attain it, and you feel good now just thinking about it. And you KNOW that you CAN actually attain it. You need BOTH for a goal to be in the sweet spot.

If the goal is in the sweet spot, it is easier to attain, and you will manifest it faster.

Most goals and objectives make you feel good when you think about having them.

So to determine if a goal is in the sweet spot, think about having it and ask if that gets you excited, motivated, and makes you feel good. You're looking for a goal that makes you feel really good, really excited, really motivated. You need to have a strong desire to attain it. A BURNING desire.

Remember Napoleon Hill: "Define your dream and get a *burning desire for its achievement.*"

So the first question is, which of your dreams and goals do you have a burning desire for?

Not just, oh, I'd like to go to that restaurant.

So which of the dreams and goals on your list do you have a burning desire to have when you think about it?

Then which of the ones that you have a burning desire for do you have a high level of belief that you actually CAN attain them? Those goals and dreams are the ones in the sweet spot, right now.

Some of you are thinking, "Boy, I don't have very many." That's OK. Because there is a success cycle that is going to help you. It's a motivation cycle that INCREASES your confidence and belief.

When you do this manifesting process for the first time and see it work, see the success, actually manifest something you wanted, your belief and confidence that this DOES work goes up.

Once you start seeing the magic happen, once you start seeing something manifest that you didn't know *how* it could possibly manifest, THEN your belief and confidence increases.

When you looked at your radar screen and did NOT see HOW what you desired could become a reality, and then it DOES become a reality, all of a sudden, you start believing more is possible. You develop more confidence that this process works.

Then the dreams that you have burning desires for all of a sudden now start getting matched up with a high level of belief that you *can* actually achieve them.

A critical *key* ingredient in this formula is BELIEF— CONFIDENCE that what you want WILL manifest.

Now, this is a scriptural, spiritual principle as well. In many holy spiritual texts from different traditions around the world, it is said, "Ask and you shall receive." The texts also say, "You get not because you ask not."

Asking is you putting out into the universe what you want. Putting out into the universe what you want means using your brain to think about what you want, which puts out into the universe a transmission of a frequency.

You do that with high power and high intensity, with a long duration, on the Alpha/Theta brain wave, *with belief,* without any counter-intention, and it WILL manifest. You will GET what you ASK for.

Holy spiritual texts say, "Ask and *believe* that you WILL get what you are asking for, you shall receive and have whatsoever you ask."

That's scriptural. Not just from ONE holy book, but MANY spiritual texts from many religious and spiritual traditions.

Virtually all religious texts give these same principles because they are universal and they're physical, or quantum laws of physics.

So the key to getting whatever you want is this: First, define what you want.

There are three ways to define what you want. Very specific, general or just ... I just want to feel good. Those are the three ways to define what you want.

Next, think about what you want. Get a picture in your mind of yourself in possession of what you want. When you think about your desire, you have to have a burning desire. Does thinking about yourself in possession of your desire get you excited, motivated, and inspired? Do you NEED to have it?

If you don't have a burning desire ... then it will be hard to manifest something that you just "wish" you had.

You might be saying, "Kevin, there's really nothing I want that gives me a burning desire."

Do you want to feel good? Does that give you a burning desire?

If there is nothing that you NEED to have, don't worry. Later I will show you how to MANUFACTURE a burning desire and a NEED to GET SOMETHING.

Okay, you need to get a burning desire for something, but the first step is to *define what you want.*

Here is the process to do that.

Take a piece of WHITE paper and a pen with BLUE ink. Do not do this on a computer or your phone or some electronic device.

Then for ten minutes, write down anything and everything you want.

Ideally you would get yourself a notebook or some type of spiral-bound book where you can rip out pages and add pages. It could be a small one, it could be a big one. I like the 8½ x 11 size. In Europe, we use an A4.

Call this your dream book.

Anytime you think of something you want to be, do, or have, no matter how crazy, how outrageous, whatever it is, just write that down and add it to your lists of dreams and desires.

And then every once in a while, ideally every week or so, scan these goals, these dreams, these desires, and decide which one is really giving you a burning desire.

And then decide, what is your belief level on those dreams. Find dreams that are in the sweet spot.

I'm going to show you soon how to start slowly getting this belief level up. There are some specific processes you can do that will help you achieve that.

But the first thing is defining your dream: either something specific, something general, or just feeling good.

The dream that you define, you have to have a burning desire for, which means something that really gets your juices flowing, something that you really, really, really, really NEED to have.

Then match it up to make sure that dream or goal is in the sweet spot. This means you have a high level of belief that you CAN and WILL actually attain that goal.

Then the first part of the process is for you to focus on what you want, and believe you will receive it.

Let me run a process on you that will help you manifest your goals and dreams.

Go through your list of goals and dreams and pick one. Pick something that you have a high desire for, something that you REALLY want, and ideally you feel you REALLY NEED to attain. Something that you have a burning desire to have, and one that you have a high level of confidence or belief that you actually CAN attain it. Do that now and then come back.

Welcome back.

I'm going to show you what the physical manifestation is.

What I want you to do in a moment, with your eyes open or your eyes closed, is, when I say BEGIN, I want you to picture what you want in your mind. Get as clear and detailed a picture as you can. See yourself IN POSSESSION of that thing you desire. Make your picture vivid.

Picture what you want and picture it in color. And I want you to not only see it in color, but also look at it with your mind's eye and listen to the sounds. Then imagine how you would FEEL if you were in possession of that desire. Smell any smells that might be there.

Maybe some of you have a desire to go to an island on a luxury vacation. If there are smells, make sure you smell the smells.

So when I say begin, see yourself in possession of what you desire. See that mental image and picture as clearly and as defined as possible, with as much detail as possible. And feel now AS IF you WOULD feel if you were actually in possession of that desire. BEGIN. DO THIS NOW AND COME BACK AFTER A FEW MOMENTS.

Welcome back.

When I did that process at the live event, everyone in the room was smiling. You might be smiling right now. You probably feel good.

We are going to run that process again in a moment. Wait until I say BEGIN.

In a moment, I want you to do it again with more intensity. I want you to imagine that you already have your desire. If it's a car, I want you to physically imagine that you're driving the car and how you are feeling driving the car. Feel the emotions. Imagine how great it's going to feel and how good it *does* feel. Picture yourself in possession of your desire with clarity and feel NOW AS IF you WOULD feel if you were actually in possession of your desire. Do this with INTENSITY. After you are done, come back. BEGIN.

I bet you feel better than you were just a couple of minutes ago. Don't you feel great?

If you feel bad, and some of you might, that means your level of belief that you CAN attain that desire is not high. If you feel bad now, it means that goal is not in the sweet spot.

This is important to understand. Many people set a goal, and then when they think about it, they feel sad that they don't have it or that they never will have it. You are in that case, broadcasting LACK and the I DON'T HAVE IT AND PROBABLY NEVER WILL HAVE IT frequency. And the universe WILL make sure you NEVER have what you want.

The method, so far, to use so that you GET what you want is:

– Define what you want.
– Make sure that your desire is in the sweet spot.
– Have a high burning desire for its attainment.
– Have a high level of belief that you can achieve it.

You'll know if you are in the sweet spot when you think about what you want, and you will feel good. If you think about that goal or that dream or that desire, and you feel better, then you're in the sweet spot.

If you think of something you want and your feelings get lower, if you get depressed, frustrated, angry, or annoyed, that means that goal is not in the sweet spot. It means you don't have a high level of belief or confidence that you can actually get it right now.

It doesn't mean you'll never get it. You just have to change your level of belief. I will teach you exactly how to do that.

Henry Ford said, "If you think you can or if you think you can't, either way, you are right, it is your level of belief that makes it so."

The bottom line is this. You must define your dream. It can be specific, it can be very general, or it can be just, "I want to feel good; that's my objective."

BUT specific IS better. More on that later.

You must also have a burning desire for that dream. Otherwise, you won't be able to put out a transmission that is powerful enough or intense enough and for a long enough duration to affect matter in the physical universe and have a strong magnetic pull or creative force.

And you must believe or have confidence that it will actually manifest.

I am going to teach you how to get your level of belief up, because that's one of the biggest critical ingredients.

We're also going to talk specifically about how to get your desire up for the dreams. How you can get that burning desire.

You CAN be, do, and have whatever you want. You DO have the power, and it is ready to be unleashed!

LESSON 10

The Power of Belief: *Your Thoughts Shape Your Reality*

Many people at the live event pointed out that, even though they found meeting, shaking hands with, and talking to the incredibly powerful, famous, wealthy, successful, happy people that were in the room, and listening to them validate everything that I was teaching, was giving them great benefit, they actually found that they were getting more benefit and an increase in belief that this works from talking to other attendees who were learning this for the first time.

There's a reason for that. When you start actually listening to other like-minded people who are at the same level you are, and getting their first impressions as well, you can see that you're not the only person thinking certain things.

Many of you reading this are already amazed by this material, sometimes skeptical of this material, but probably excited to see if this material really works.

It will be very interesting to see what's going to happen to you over the next couple of weeks. When you start applying this material in real life, you will see how things in your life are going to change.

You are going to be making some changes in your thought patterns, actions, and activities.

Remember, if you want things in your life to change, whether it's your finances, your relationships, your health, your weight, or the way you feel, you have to change things in your life.

You can't continue to think the way you've always thought.

You can't continue to believe like you've always believed.

You can't continue to do all the same things the same way, such as waking up at the same time, eating the same foods, doing the same routines, saying the same words, thinking the same thoughts, or hanging out with the same people.

You ARE going to see some tremendous changes and improvements in your life over the next few weeks and months.

By the way, at the live event, somebody grabbed me at the break and asked, "Did you call that man King?" Yes, I did. But the official title is Your Royal Highness. But we know each other, and that's how I refer to him. I just call him King.

We were blessed to have royalty in the room. I was particularly pleased that many amazing individuals took time out of their schedules to come to that special event. They came because they know the importance of this material and the significance of me teaching this to people who were not "insiders" and members of secret societies. We all agreed that getting this knowledge out to more people who can start using it to better their own lives will better the world in general.

We are all very excited to be part of this movement with my private club, the Global Information Network (GIN). We think it's an incredible mission with a powerful purpose that will improve the quality of life and standard of living for potentially millions of people all around the world.

By sharing this information and getting you to grasp onto it and apply it, we think it is going to be very helpful to not only you as individuals, but also all of your respective countries where you come from and the world as a whole.

Some of you think I am going slowly and repeating things too often. Remember, you have been PROGRAMMED to FAIL. Your DNA has FAILURE programming. Your MIND has FAILURE programming. This book is written in a VERY specific way to reduce or eliminate those FAILURE programs and REPLACE them with SUCCESS programming.

One critical element is that you should *understand* how each ingredient works.

You should fully comprehend HOW and WHY the process works.

The process is the procedure, the technique, the steps on how to make whatever you want manifest in your life, how to get whatever you want.

An interesting thing about the Training Balance Scale. If you noticed, we haven't talked that much about the *HOW*. We haven't talked much about the SPECIFIC techniques or procedures because those are not that important at this point. I WILL get to the actual SPECIFIC action steps you DO to make this system manifest your desire.

Remember, 90 percent of success is getting your thinking right. It is getting your attitude right. It is your ATTITUDE, not your APTITUDE, that will determine your ALTITUDE in life.

When you understand the Law of Attraction and you understand that your thinking is 90 percent responsible for creating what you want in your life, the *how* becomes less relevant at the beginning of the process. You know that the universe, AT THE RIGHT TIME, will present the perfect HOW and motivate you to the correct actions.

If you desire to manifest and have a Cadillac, and if I were to ask you *how* you are going to get it, there may be no rational, logical, visible explanation that explains how you could possibly get this new Cadillac.

If your desire is to pay off all your credit cards and to get out of debt, and if I were to ask you "how you expect to do that?" you may look on your radar screen which shows you everything you know in your life, and you may say, "I can't see HOW I can pay off my credit cards. In fact it looks impossible. Based on what's on my radar screen, it appears that there is categorically no way on God's green earth for me to get out of debt."

If you say you want to lose forty pounds, you may say, "Listen, I've tried every diet and exercise program in the world and on my radar screen I don't see HOW I can ever lose weight and keep it off. I have no willpower, my metabolism is low, my thyroid doesn't work properly, and everybody in my family is overweight. I've tried to lose weight before and failed. I hate exercise. I love to eat."

If your desire is to get a better job, you might say, "Based on my skills, experience, and level of education, I don't see how I can ever get a better job and earn more money. The economy is bad, no one is hiring, I've been fired from my previous three jobs, and I have a terrible resume. I don't think anyone would hire me."

Based on all the facts, it would be easy for you to say, "Kevin, there's no rational way that I could explain to you why I will get a better job, a better, high-paying job, a more fulfilling job. I cannot tell you *how* that could possibly happen."

And that's the point. In these examples, you would be looking ONLY on your radar screen for the HOW. When you look on your radar screen, you cannot find any rational reason why or how you would be able to manifest your desire.

You need to understand that this system of manifesting works because when you correctly fire off and transmit from your brain a vibration and a frequency of what you want, the Law of Attraction will make the thousands of negative variables and "facts" that make it seem that you could not possibly get your desire, CHANGE in your favor.

Everything is in play, and everything will start moving and changing in your favor. And remember, 95 percent of what is out there is NOT on your radar screen. You can't see it, anyway. You can't even imagine all the things that are off your radar screen.

There are trillions of bits of data, information, variables, situations, coincidences, circumstances, and people that are off your radar screen that are being affected by your thoughts.

So when you put that thought out there, when you put out that vibrational frequency of what you want with power and intensity, with consistent duration of transmission, it will cause everything to start moving in a manner which you cannot comprehend, all in your favor and all designed to manifest your desire. The universe is CONSPIRING to make your desire your reality.

Even the highest mathematical genius or most powerful AI computer in the world cannot figure out all the patterns, the synergy, and the coordination of movements.

No one and no machine can figure it out, but the universe does. The Law of Attraction says: That which you put out, the vibration you put out, will attract that vibration back.

It's the Law of Attraction.

Everything will start shifting and moving in your favor to manifest in your physical reality that which you desire. And provided you have no doubt, which is belief, which means provided you have a high level of belief that it's going to happen, and you are sitting in a place of expectation as if it's already happened, then it comes flying into your life at record-breaking speed.

Your desire will manifest at the right point in time, the best point in time for you.

You should understand how this works, in general, broad-stroke terms now. Everything is a vibration. Our brain transmits and receives vibration or frequency.

If you broadcast a frequency on the Alpha/Theta wave, with intensity, power, and for a long enough duration, whatever frequency you broadcast DOES affect physical matter, and is picked up by other brains, thus influencing other people's thoughts and actions, and attracts back into your life a similar vibrational match.

When you understand how it works and why it works and that it works every day in your life, whether you are doing it by deliberate intent or by default, that's when you start increasing your level of belief that you CAN manifest your desires.

This is why understanding how it works and why it works is so important.

And that's why going back to the five basics—which are Who Do You Listen To; the Teachability Index; the Training Balance Scale; the Four Magic Steps, which means understanding that you are going to have to initially use conscious competence, which means applying this consciously with some effort initially until you get to unconscious competence, which means it's happening automatically and then it's happening absolutely effortlessly; and mastering the first Four Basics—is so important. It is the foundation from which we will build.

You also now know the basic procedure which you can do anytime, anyplace, anywhere, to get anything you want. The basic procedure can allow you to be, do, or have anything and everything you want.

Let's dive a little deeper into the basic procedure before we start adding some other key ingredients.

The basic procedure, to recap, is:

1) Define what you want. Define your dream. Define your goal. Define your desire.

You can do it three ways. You can define it specifically in great detail, generally, or just feeling good.

Someone asked me which is better. The answer is specificity is always best if you can't get to 100% alignment. Want a *particular* watch. Want a *particular* car.

But you shouldn't focus all your attention on a specific, clearly defined goal. I know you're all saying, "But that's not what all the goal-setting books say. They say you need to be very, very specific and set a deadline for its achievement."

Well there IS a place to be very specific with a SHORT-TERM GOAL and yes, setting a deadline is important. But those goals have to be things that you can control, not OUTCOMES. You can be specific with a goal such as exercising for twenty minutes a day. You control that. And you can set a deadline, such as, "I will exercise for twenty minutes a day for thirty days in a row." But you can't say, "I WILL lose twenty pounds in thirty days." You control your activity, NOT OUTCOMES. There is a huge difference between a short-term goal and a long-term DREAM. I will talk about this huge distinction later.

When you are wanting a specific thing, you are limiting the universe. You are not letting the universe give you what is going to give you the best feeling and what is ultimately the best for you.

I'll give you an example. Joe meets Mary, and Mary is a beautiful girl who's fantastic. Mary is single. Joe is single. Joe decides that Mary is the perfect girl for him. But Mary is only lukewarm on Joe. She's not that interested in Joe. But Joe says, I'm going to use this technique to get what I want. So he defines what he wants. I want

Mary to fall in love with me. I want Mary to be my wife. I want Mary. I want Mary. I want Mary.

Joe uses the technique, and he specifically defines what he wants. He puts out that vibration with power and intensity. He has a burning desire to have Mary fall in love with him and be his wife. Joe uses this technique over and over again, day after day. He's putting out that frequency with a long enough duration. And he has no doubt in his mind. He believes this will work.

But what Joe doesn't know is next month, Susie is going to get a job at his office. And Susie is ten times better for Joe than Mary. Susie is going to fall madly in love with Joe and make him the perfect wife. Susie and Joe are a much better vibrational match. Susie will make Joe ten times happier. And Joe will make Susie the happiest woman in the world. But Joe doesn't know that because Susie is off his radar screen.

So what is a better way for Joe to manifest his goal and what really should his goal be?

Here is the better way to set and achieve goals. Remember, you don't know what you don't know. You don't know what is off your radar screen. What you THINK you want may NOT be the BEST thing that could come in your life. What you THINK you want may not REALLY make you happy and fulfilled.

Imagine you are looking to buy a house. You look at lots of houses and you find the PERFECT house. Your dream home. You can FEEL that this is the PERFECT house. You know it is the house for you. You REALLY want THAT house.

Well, I'm telling you this, you ain't that smart to KNOW that THIS is the PERFECT house for you. Maybe you really like the house, maybe you LOVE the house. It makes your heart sing when you think about owning that house. And of all the houses you've seen, maybe it was the best house of the bunch.

But maybe there's a *better* house that you haven't seen yet that's off your radar screen.

And maybe NOW is NOT the best time to buy a house.

The UNIVERSE KNOWS MORE THAN YOU DO.

TRUST THE UNIVERSAL INFINITE INTELLIGENCE.

Imagine you go to a restaurant. You love the meal, and you think it's the best restaurant in town.

You start telling everyone it is the BEST food in town. Well, you haven't eaten at every restaurant in town, so you don't know if it's the best restaurant in town, do you?

The universe knows of all things outside your radar screen and ALL the POSSIBILITIES. It knows infinitely more than you do.

Over 95 percent of all the stuff is off your radar screen. You don't know what you don't know.

Your main objective is not to get *that* house. Your main objective is not to get *Mary* to fall in love with you. Your main objective is not to get that *particular* car. Your main objective is not to get that specific promotion at your office. Your main objective is not to pay off your debt *this month.* Your main objective is not to sell your house *this month.*

That's not what you really want. What you want is to *feel amazingly good.*

You THINK subconsciously that attaining those things will *MAKE YOU FEEL GOOD.*

So let me tell you the better way to use this procedure of defining your dream.

The best way to define your dream is to be as specific as you can but be OPEN to OTHER POSSIBILITIES and be FOCUSED on the REAL goal, which is to ultimately FEEL GOOD.

Example: You're a single man or woman, and your goal is to have a relationship. You want a relationship because you think it will MAKE

YOU FEEL GOOD. So you really want to feel GOOD, maybe feel loved, wanted, desired, secure, safe, or content. And you THINK you will FEEL those emotions IF you are in the relationship. So you have a desire for a relationship. But remember, the underlying desire is to FEEL GOOD. That is what you REALLY want.

So, make the objective specific. Write down exactly the kind of relationship you want. Write down everything you want in a mate and how that mate is going to make you feel. And write down how your mate is going to feel when they are in a relationship with you. BE SPECIFIC. Clearly define your perfect mate. Imagine you are placing an order with the universe. The universe says, "What kind of woman do you want? How tall? Age? Hair and eye color? Personality traits? Education?" The list could go on and on.

Then when you think of this IDEAL person and relationship, you are putting out a VERY specific frequency to the universe. BUT, there might be something better. So you add in a feeling of being OPEN to something BETTER that the universe has for you. That slight modification makes all the difference.

If you meet Mary and you think Mary is great, don't put out a request to the universe to give you Mary. Mary seems to be terrific. But you want a wife that makes you so incredibly happy, and you want a wife that is incredibly happy with you. Mary may or may not be that person.

You really want to be in a relationship where both of you are madly in love with each other. You laugh together, you have great sex, you enjoy many of the same things, you enjoy each other's company, and you live a lifelong, happy, fulfilling, satisfying, adventurous, loving, committed, secure, safe relationship. That's what you want.

It may be with Mary, or it may not be with Mary.

So you can clearly define what you want, BUT be OPEN to ALL possibilities that you can't even imagine.

If you're looking at a house and you see the house of your dreams, you may think this is a wonderful house, but you have to know that there may be a house that is even better, off your radar screen.

Maybe what you want is a home that makes you feel just so safe and secure, that gives you the freedom to enjoy your hobbies, that's big enough so that you can have children and have a backyard and a place where they can just play and enjoy.

And you have FAITH and confidence and belief that that house will come at the right moment, at the right time, into your life. So when you put out the desire for a particular house, BE OPEN to the universe saying NO to THAT house because it has a better house at a better time for you.

While being specific can indeed be very powerful—especially when you're feeling good and aligned—it's important to remember the broader context of this teaching. Specificity is often best for short-term goals or when your belief and vibration are already in harmony with the desire. However, for larger or emotionally charged desires, getting too specific can sometimes activate resistance. In those cases, stepping back into a more general focus—and especially focusing on the feeling of what you want—can be even more effective.

In fact, as originally taught, specific is good, general is better, and feeling is best. This progression still applies, even with the added nuance: specificity has its place, but alignment and emotional resonance are ultimately what determine your results.

Here's another example. Let's say I want to pay off my debt. Maybe paying off my debt this month is a goal that seems too impossible to achieve. Maybe setting a goal to pay off my debt in six months is more realistic, and setting a goal to pay it off in twelve months is something I feel I definitely can achieve.

No matter when I set a "deadline" for paying off my debt, I still don't know *how* it's going to happen because the how is off my radar screen. I actually don't really see HOW I could pay off my debt based on my current income and expenses, even in twelve months.

I really don't understand or comprehend how it could happen, but I have confidence that it will SOMEHOW, SOME WAY.

So I would define my dream as "I am DEBT-FREE!" I don't set a timeline for that to happen, because right now, if I did, DOUBT would spring up. My belief and confidence that I am going to be debt-free by a certain date is low. But my confidence is HIGH that I WILL be debt-free, SOMETIME in the future. I know the HOW will present itself at the right time. I don't have to worry about the how RIGHT NOW. This is how you define your dream and "set a goal."

You'll notice in my examples I don't put a time limit on things. Some of you are thinking that all the goal-setting books, all the success guru seminars you went to, they all said that you had to clearly define your dream with specifics and set a time limit on its achievement.

You can't do that RIGHT NOW. After you get fully trained and get many small successes under your belt, THEN you can do that. BUT there are still several nuances to clearly defining EXACTLY what you want and setting a SPECIFIC deadline for its achievement. That is a very advanced manifesting technique that will ONLY work if ALL the key elements are being used, and if they are being used by someone who is quite proficient in using these manifesting methods.

You have to crawl before you walk and walk before you run.

I'll give you a good example of why you should not set a time limit (at the beginning of your training).

When I was younger, learning this from my wealthy mentors, some of my friends and I had philosophies about manifesting. We were go-getters. Our philosophy was, "We put the round peg in the square hole. We make things work."

As I began to learn this technology, I found that that's the wrong way to do it. If you have a round peg and you have a square hole, yes, you can figure out a way to put the round peg in the square hole. But it will never be a perfect match.

But if you use the manifesting technique I am teaching you, that was taught to we correctly, then if you have a round peg and a square hole, you will use this manifesting technique to manifest either a SQUARE peg that fits perfectly in your square hole, or a ROUND hole that your round peg fits perfectly into. Then at the right time, at the right moment, when you need it, when it's perfect timing, the universe will deliver.

And that's the point.

The universe delivers exactly what is perfect for you, at the perfect time. Because the universe knows what you REALLY need and when *you're ready* to receive it.

When are you ready?

When you have no more doubt. Because if you still have doubt, if it comes in, you weren't ready to receive it. It's going to fall apart. It's not going to work anyway.

The universe does not do things TO you, it does things FOR you.

I remember I was trying to sell a house. I was convinced that this was the best time to sell the house, and I was going to use this technique to sell the house right now.

And I used the technique, and I used the technique, and I used the technique.

As I was trying to manifest selling the house RIGHT NOW, I'm thinking, it just doesn't feel right. Something is off. I don't feel like I'm in the sweet spot. I don't feel lined up. My desire to sell the house seems weak. My belief that it WILL sell NOW is a little bit weak.

I'm not lined up, but I'm trying to get lined up, but I'm not. The universe was telling me now is not the time. So I stopped.

Everyone around me, all my advisors, were telling me now is the time to sell, the house must be sold now. We have a time limit here. We have a window of opportunity. Everyone was telling me why now was the best time to sell.

I told them all that I can't line this up. My desire and my belief are just not lined up. When I say lined up in the sweet spot, it means you have a high, intense desire for what you want, and you're so excited about getting it. And your belief level is at a very high level that you're actually going to get it. You actually believe you've already got it. You can taste it and smell it. It's right there in your reality, and you're happy and excited when you're doing the technique.

But I wasn't any of those things. I wasn't feeling right.

So I stopped trying to manifest the house being sold RIGHT NOW. I took it off the market.

Six months later, my Realtor called me up and said, "There's a major Hollywood producer who's looking for property in town. I had told him about your ranch and the house, but that it wasn't on the market at this time. But I took him for a drive by it so he could see the ranch and the house from the outside. He fell madly in love with it. He said he's got to have it.

"Now, this producer is super-wealthy. Price is not an object."

I had it on the market earlier for several million dollars, which I thought was a good, fair price.

I told my Realtor to get an offer, but I really was not that interested in selling now. It would have to be an insanely high offer for me to accept.

He came back that afternoon with an offer two and a half million dollars more than I had the house on the market for just six months earlier.

That is how the universe works.

All my idiotic advisors were wrong. I listened to my gut intuition, my emotions. These things are your monitor, your guidance system, your regulator, your green light, red light, and yellow light.

Your emotions and feelings will tell you what to do. They'll tell you when you're lined up. But you have to train yourself to be able to READ those feelings. I will show you HOW to train yourself to READ your internal guidance system.

So the technique, the basic manifesting procedure, is, number one, define what you want.

You *can* be specific.

You want that gold Breitling watch with the black alligator band. Nothing wrong with being specific, but you can also be general. You just want a gorgeous watch that you're really going to enjoy wearing, and it'll present itself at the right time.

Or you can be completely general and say, "You know, there's nothing specific that I want in my life. I just want to feel exhilarated, or I just want to feel content, or I just want to feel secure, or I just want to feel bliss. Or I just want to feel Nirvana. Or I just want to feel love. Or I just want to feel laughter and happiness. I want to feel joy. I want to feel like singing. I want to feel like skipping down the sidewalk."

You can throw out a feeling you desire and guess what? The universe will then present to you situations and opportunities and people that will give you that feeling.

And when you think about it, this is probably one of the most exciting things because you have absolutely no disappointment and no stress. You have NO doubt or pressure.

Because you're not looking at a particular thing wondering if it's going to come in or not, where you start having doubt as time passes.

This way, when you wake up, you say, "I wonder what exciting opportunities are going to present themselves today."

Wow. Every day is like opening up a Christmas present. You say, "I know something wonderful is going to be presented in my life today."

And then you drive down the road and get a flat tire. And you're thinking, "How is that wonderful? When was the last time I got a flat tire? My God, twenty-five years ago. This is an exciting experience. Maybe I'll meet somebody. Maybe I'll meet somebody new that'll put us in a big business deal. Or maybe I'll meet some wonderful person and share some great experiences and develop a new friendship. Or maybe where I was going, something screwball was going to happen. And maybe I'm being prevented from going further on this road at this time for a reason. Maybe getting a flat tire is saving me from some disaster."

You see, when you start thinking in these ways, life becomes magical.

So define your dream. Define exactly what you want. Either be specific, general, or just a feeling.

Whatever you're defining, whatever you want, you must have a burning desire for it, which means a really strong need to have it.

You have to have high intensity and high amounts of power. Because if you have a strong desire for something, the frequency that you're going to be transmitting from your brain is going to have high intensity and high power.

That will create strong magnetic attraction. Then it will come to you much faster.

2) You need to transmit that frequency on the Alpha/Theta wave. I *will* show you HOW to do this later in this book.

3) You need to transmit that frequency for a long enough duration of time. You can't just do it once for five seconds.

Now the question is, how long? Should you sit down for an hour a day and just focus on this like a mantra? "I want a new car. I want a new car. I want to pay off my bills, or I want a great relationship. I want a great relationship."

The answer is, you could do that. But none of the people I know that manifest easily and fast do that. But you could do it. It is not wrong. Focusing on what you want, seeing it in your mind's eye, picturing yourself in possession of what you want, and feeling NOW AS IF you WOULD feel if you actually were in possession of your desire for a long, sustained period of time, and repeating that process throughout the day, is fine.

You become or you get what you think about most of the time.

You want to be thinking about what you want in this manner, with intensity and power, and with a high level of belief or confidence that it actually WILL manifest.

When you think about what you want in this manner, when you're beaming out this energy, when you're beaming out this frequency, you have to be feeling good.

That's the indicator that you're in the sweet spot.

How long do you think about what you want in this manner? As often as possible, and for as long as possible each time.

If you're driving in a car, you could be thinking about what you want in this manner and thus beaming out that energy, broadcasting that frequency. As you do that, it should make you smile, and it should make you sing. It should make you feel GOOD.

You could be thinking about what you want in that manner when you're cooking, when you are exercising, when you are watching TV, when you are in the bathroom, or taking a shower.

IDEALLY you want to be thinking about what you want in that manner right before you go to bed and as soon as you wake up.

The more often, the better, and the longer you MAINTAIN the FEELING each time, the better.

Remember, don't worry about WHEN it will manifest or HOW it is going to manifest. Don't think about that. Don't say I want this new car by Friday. You don't know if Friday is the best day for that car. There are a trillion reasons why it may not be the best for you.

Don't put time limits on your desires, YET. Later I will show you HOW and WHEN to put DEADLINES on attaining the things you want to manifest.

Right now, don't put pressure and stress on yourself to attain or manifest something with a strong deadline.

4) You must believe and have no doubt that what you desire WILL manifest. You need a high level of confidence that you WILL attain that which you desire.

The opposite of belief is doubt. If you have doubt, this usually means you're focusing on the how, or the desire is TOO BIG at this time.

You start thinking something like this: I want that new car, I want that new car, but I don't know how I'm going to get it. I mean, I don't have any money. I may get laid off from my job.

That's doubt, that's lack of belief, that is a low level of confidence.

Faith is the substance of things hoped for, the evidence of things NOT seen. You have to have FAITH that your desire WILL manifest even when you don't see HOW it could be possible.

ALL things are possible for those who BELIEVE.

You have to have belief in your dream. You have to believe in yourself. And you have to believe in the process.

How do you know if you're really *in alignment?* How do you know if your desire is really what's best for you? How do you know if you have a high level of belief? How do you know if you have strong burning desire?

The answer is, when you do this procedure, which starts when you think about what you want, how do you FEEL?

If what you want and your strong desire for its attainment are lined up with what's best for you, you will FEEL good.

If you have a burning desire for that desire or that want, and if, when you think about what you want, you have a strong level of belief that it will actually manifest, you will feel better. You will start getting excited. You KNOW it is coming. You feel like Christmas is coming. Presents are going to be under the tree with your name on them. You keep feeling like it is getting closer and closer, and you get more excited and more excited.

Do you understand?

Imagine it's the 24th of December. Tomorrow's Christmas. You know you are getting presents.

Do you have any doubt? No, it's the 24th. Tomorrow, it's Christmas. You're getting presents. You know that. NO doubts.

If it's the day before your birthday, you know that tomorrow is your birthday, and you are getting presents.

If tomorrow's paycheck day, you know you are getting your paycheck tomorrow. You have no doubt about it.

Do you understand?

If you place an order on Amazon, and you get an email confirmation that your order was received and that order has been shipped, you KNOW it is ON THE WAY, and you ARE getting what you ordered.

When you do this procedure, you are placing an order with the universe. If you do it right, the order WILL be received and shipped. It may take some TIME before you get it, but IT IS ON THE WAY.

So when you're doing this manifesting process for a new car, better relationship, losing weight, new house, whatever, if you're in the sweet spot, you will feel like that. You will feel like IT IS COMING. You will start feeling exhilarated. You'll start getting excited with anticipation because you know it's ON THE WAY. AND you SHOULD feel NOW AS IF you WILL feel when you actually get it.

The trick is, don't put the timeline on WHEN it will arrive. The car is coming if you ordered it. You may not know *when,* and you may not know *how* it will manifest, but you do know it WILL.

People who manifest what they want easily and quickly don't know when it will arrive and don't know how it is going to happen, but they just know it WILL manifest into their life and they WILL HAVE IT.

When you do this process correctly, you feel GOOD.

Think about what you want and FEEL as if you've already got it.

That's the key. FEELING NOW *as if* you already are in possession of what you want.

So the monitor to determine if you are in alignment is, when you do this process, do you feel good? Now, if you start feeling bad when you are doing this process, that means one of two things. Either, a) your want is really not in line with what's in your best interest, or b) it's because you're starting to doubt. Your level of belief is going down because you're focusing on the *how*. You start thinking, "I don't understand **how** I am going to get what I am desiring."

You're focusing on your radar screen. You're focusing on the facts. You're focusing on only those things which you can see. And based on what you can see, you can't imagine HOW it will manifest.

And it's true. Based on what you can see, based on what's on your radar screen, it won't happen, because based on what you SEE, it CAN'T possibly manifest.

But we're not interested in what's on the radar screen. Since 99 percent of the stuff that's going to make it manifest is off the radar screen and you CAN'T see it, it's completely irrelevant what you SEE on the radar screen.

Let me say that again. Ninety-nine point nine percent of the things that will take place to cause what you want to come into your life, are off the radar screen.

You can't see them and you can't even imagine them. You can't even dream of what they are.

So what you see on the radar screen is completely irrelevant.

When I am talking with my colleagues and we're doing something, it means we're *creating* something. Creating something means we have a **want or desire**. We are creating in our life whatever it is we want. When we do this, we speak in a certain way, a CREATIVE way. Our thinking and words CREATE what we want in our lives. We have certain speech patterns.

However, when we deal with underlings, which means people who are not part of the society and don't know this manifesting process, the conversations are VERY different.

Here's how the conversations go when society members are together. Four of us are sitting around in one of the members' mansions in Barbados. We're talking about doing a business deal where we need $450 million. We have some of the accountants and lawyers there, who are NOT society members. They work for us.

It's a long meeting, and the accountants are looking at each other very concerned, and they say, "Where are we coming up with the $450 million?"

The senior guys in the meeting, who are members of the societies, who know the technique, all smile at one another because we really can't talk to the accountants like we talk amongst ourselves. We say to them, "Oh, don't worry about the money."

The accountants shoot back, "But how are we going to raise the money? Where is it coming from?"

"Don't worry about it," we reply.

"Well what do you mean, don't worry about it? Where is it coming from? Because we can't see, based on our global financial picture, where we can come up with that cash," say the accountants.

"Don't worry about it," we say again.

"But where is it coming from?" they press.

Finally we break down and tell them, "Okay. Do you want to know the real answer? The answer is we have no freaking clue where the money's coming from. We have no earthly idea. We can't tell you where the money is coming from. As a matter of fact, it looks like there's no possible way that we can raise this money. But don't worry about it, because it will come in when we need it. We're doing the deal. That's it, period."

The accountants look at us like we're insane. We are looking at them like they're insane. In fact, they're just uneducated. We know that the money will come in when we need it, because we are all in alignment. We are anticipating and excited about this deal. We know it's going to work. It doesn't matter HOW we are going to raise the money right now. We will figure that out later. The money will come in when we need it, and if it doesn't, NO BIG DEAL. Who cares?

The money will manifest. It'll all work out. It always does. We don't have to worry about the money.

At that point in the meeting, we didn't want to talk about where the money was coming from or HOW we could raise the money. "But couldn't we have discussed the possibilities?" NO. Not at THAT point. Because if we're discussing the possibilities of where the money could possibly come from, we're going to be focusing on HOW too soon, and doubt or disbelief could start to creep in.

We couldn't even imagine where the money was coming from at that point. So it would have been a futile discussion to try to look at our radar screen and come up with HOW we could raise the money.

We know that the money is coming from off our radar screen in ways and in methods and in circumstances that we couldn't even comprehend or imagine today.

So there's no reason to have a stupid discussion about it, wasting time and energy. We let the UNIVERSE figure out the HOW. WE LET GO.

Let go and let GOD.

This is being in a state of ALLOWING. A receptive state of surrendering to the universe.

Remember, I am still painting broad strokes as I explain the manifesting method. There are MANY distinctions and nuances to this formula that make it work. By the time you finish the book, you will know all the steps and understand each step clearly. You are learning how to crawl first, then walk, and then run. Be patient. Stick with this. At the end, I will go over ALL the steps in order, but you must read the entire book first.

Every story is told for a reason. Each example is there for a reason. The repetition of the concepts is there for a reason. Trust the processes of reprogramming you for total success in life.

Think about this as you start to define your dream and use the formula for manifesting.

You only see things that are on your radar screen. But by using your feelings, you can tell if you are in alignment. And by using your feelings, you will, in time, be able to FEEL the things that are off your radar screen.

When I do this process, I can *feel* it. How do I know it's there? How can I feel it? Because I'm so excited. I feel GOOD. I am smiling. We are all so excited about the Barbados deal. We know it's going to happen. It's a knowingness. That means the money is there, that means it's coming in. We don't have to worry about how.

Do you understand that? That's how it works.

That's the basic procedure. Over the next few Lessons, I am going to give you many more distinctions and nuances and several more key steps. The recipe is NOT complete yet. The formula is NOT ready for application YET. There is MORE to it.

Let me give you one critical key point here.

Success in life is nothing more than a decision away.

In order to get the universe REALLY MOVING, all matter in your favor and working FOR you to manifest your desire, you have to be serious. You have to be determined to attain it. You have to be committed to doing whatever it takes.

In that Barbados scenario, by the way, it virtually happened just as I described it to you. Some of my colleagues at the live event were laughing when I used that example because they were there.

Success is a decision away. It is a decision that says, "I am going to do it, THAT'S IT, PERIOD." When you make the decision to do it and you're in the sweet spot, you know what you want, and you have a high level of belief, and you focus on your desire, and you feel out-of-control excitement, that means it's going to happen.

A critical element is making a decision. You don't care about the how in the beginning. You don't know HOW it will manifest. In fact, it may seem impossible to manifest based on the information that's on your radar screen. But it doesn't matter because you have made the decision that you are going to MAKE IT HAPPEN. And you BELIEVE it WILL happen.

When you make that kind of decision, you feel strong and AT CAUSE over your environment. You no longer feel AT EFFECT of circumstances.

My feelings tell me it's going to happen because I *know* it is going to happen. My feelings tell me my belief level is high, and my desire is lined up with what's ultimately best for me. And I KNOW it is going to happen *at the right time, in the right way.* It'll all work out perfectly. And it'll probably work out in a way that I can't even think of right now.

And if there's a twist or turn along the way that I don't anticipate, it doesn't mean that I'm not getting what I want. It means I am getting exactly what I need and what's best for me. Because the universe is working everything together for my best need. The universe does not do things TO me, but FOR me. I know that because I feel good.

So it comes down to this.

Everything is energy, everything vibrates, and everything in your life is in your life because of the Law of Attraction. You, with your own thoughts twenty-four hours a day, seven days a week, have put out and transmitted frequencies, consciously or unconsciously. Up until now, unconsciously probably, not with deliberate intent.

You've put out frequencies of what you want, and you've also put out frequencies of what you don't want. All the frequencies that you've transmitted from your brain, if you've transmitted them with power and intensity over a long enough duration, those frequencies have manifested something in your own life.

Which means you, you, you, you, and only you have created everything in your life.

If you have disaster in your life, you created it. If you have good things in your life, you created it. If you have a divorce, you created it. If you have a car wreck tomorrow, you created it.

This might be hard for you to accept. It may go against the way you have thought before. Think about the Teachability Index. What's your willingness to accept change?

You may be thinking, "What do you mean, I created the car crash? I stopped at the red light. The guy behind me crashed into me. How did I create that?"

Here is the answer.

You didn't think of a car crash. You didn't throw out the frequency of car crash, car crash, car crash, car crash, car crash, car crash, car crash, into the universe with your brain.

You did not do that. You may have, but it's unlikely. Why did that car crash occur? How did YOU manifest it?

The answer is simple.

When the guy crashed into you, you were parked minding your own business at the red light. You were doing the right thing. YOU did nothing wrong. You stopped at the red light and the OTHER guy crashed into you.

Here's the question: How did that make you *feel*? You say, "I felt so frustrated. I felt like my whole day is ruined. I felt like I'm not going to be able to get everything I need done. I thought, I can't believe this is happening to me. I felt angry and annoyed. Those were my feelings."

Okay, good. This is how you created that car crash.

You were feeling those *feelings* earlier. Maybe hours, days, weeks, or months earlier. Your FEELINGS are a frequency that you were transmitting without DELIBERATE INTENT.

You have a negative circumstance or experience and say, "How did I create this?"

Maybe you tripped down a flight of stairs, or got fired from your job, anything that appears to be negative. Ask yourself, "What feelings did I have when this negative situation happened?"

You will come up with a series of feelings. What was the most prominent one? Now, think about over the last few days or weeks, what have you been thinking about that gave you a similar feeling?

Oh, my gosh. Yes, I was thinking about my brother-in-law's problem. Or I have been thinking about such and such situation that gave me a very similar feeling.

So the answer is all the thoughts and FEELINGS you have are vibrations and frequencies that you are broadcasting. The universe will manifest in your life situations, events, circumstances, situations, and people that will give you MORE of that FEELING.

If you're thinking of a situation, a negative situation that happened twenty years ago when some guy screwed you in a business deal, guess what?

You're going to continue to attract into your life circumstances and events that give you similar feelings.

This is why people continue to have bad relationships. They keep attracting the same type of person in their life. They can't attract anybody new because they keep focusing on the feelings that they got with the person that they were with in the past.

That's what they're throwing out into the universe. Instead of defining what they want, they're focusing on what they didn't want to happen. And by focusing on what you didn't want to happen, that means you're still thinking about it.

Remember, you get what you think about most of the time.

If you're thinking about what you don't want, something that you don't want to happen, that's what you are transmitting out of your brain. And you continue to attract what you DON'T WANT.

You will attract experiences and situations that give you the same feelings.

Do you understand that?

It's the feelings that actually have the vibration and frequency that you transmit.

That's why, when you think about a specific thing you want, you are really broadcasting the feeling that you want. Remember, when you want something, you really want a certain feeling.

Then what manifests in your life maybe isn't exactly the thing that you were thinking about, but a circumstance, or thing, or event, or person manifested in your life that gave you the feeling that you were transmitting. Which is what our ultimate objective is anyway, to feel a certain way.

If you are feeling bad NOW, you're going to attract circumstances and events which give you similar bad feelings. Thus FEELING GOOD NOW is critical.

Think about it this way. Whatever you really, really, really, really, really want and NEED to have, and you feel good when thinking about it, and believe you WILL get it, then YOU WILL GET IT.

When you have strong desire for something, feel good when thinking about it, and believe you WILL get it, your brain is going to be pulsating and transmitting powerful, intense vibrations of what you want, thus causing the universe to manifest it for you. What you want, then wants you. You are attracting your desire into your life.

All the ingredients are important. You should have a feeling of excitement and anticipation when you think about what you desire, and you have to believe you'll get it.

But here is the other side of the coin. Whatever you really, really, really, really, *don't want*, you'll also get that. Because that means you're focusing on it. That means you're thinking about it. And that means your brain is pulsating and transmitting vibrational frequencies of what you don't want combined with the feelings associated with it.

Then what you DON'T want will start coming into your experience as well.

Understand that your brain, twenty-four hours a day, seven days a week, is pulsating or broadcasting frequency or vibration. Throughout a twenty-four-hour period of time, you will be thinking about what you don't want some of the time. And you will be thinking about what you DO want some of the time.

The idea is to be thinking about what you DO want MORE OFTEN with HIGHER INTENSITY AND POWER than the thoughts of what you don't want. Thinking about what you *don't want* is putting out a neutralizing counter-intention to the thoughts about what you DO want.

If you have lots of counter-intentions being broadcast, then what you want is not going to come rushing into your life and manifest because you have too many neutralizing counter-intentions, and probably more powerful ones compared to the frequencies you are broadcasting for what you DO want.

Remember, you get what you think about most of the time. But this is not really 100 percent accurate. If you are thinking about what you want with power and intensity only 20 percent of the time, but the other 80 percent of thoughts do not have much power and intensity, then you will get what you want.

You are thinking random, weak thoughts all day. You think without deliberate intent. You probably have billions of thoughts a day. So those little thoughts that you don't think about very often, don't worry about them.

Understand that your brain transmits vibrational frequency at various levels of intensity and power. You will attract and manifest the HIGH intensity and powerful thoughts you broadcast.

Let's discuss The Ten-Second Miracle.

The ten-second miracle is the moment that you understand that you now take 100 percent responsibility for everything in your life:

If you take 100 percent responsibility for everything in your life and know without judgment, without getting mad, without getting frustrated or angry, that everything in your life is there because YOU created it with your THOUGHTS.

And if you've created it, you can change it just as fast or faster.

When you *know* that and take 100 percent responsibility for EVERYTHING in your life, your whole life, changes. You will never claim you are a victim ever again.

And you stop using "mysticism." This is blaming outside influences for your circumstances.

The way the masses have been controlled is to get the masses to believe that it's not their fault and to blame some outside force or person.

It's the government's fault. It's the economy, it's the banks, it's the interest rates, it's the political powers that are in control. It's their mother and father. It's the trauma they had when they were a child, when they fell off a runaway horse, that traumatized them and that still affects them today. They did not get enough love as a child. The teacher treated them badly. They did not have a good enough education. It's always some excuse.

And they start saying, "It's this, it's that, it's this, it's not me. I am a victim. It's not my fault."

That's how the masses are controlled, by getting the people to believe that it's not their fault. Because if you get people to believe it's not their fault, that their situation is not caused by themselves, you're telling them they have no power and no control to change it. And you keep them wallowing at a level where they will never rise up.

I am empowering you in the same manner I was empowered.

When I was told and understood that I have 100 percent creative ability, that I'm a creator, and that I'm responsible for everything in my life, positive or negative, and that whatever has happened in my life, I created it, THEN I realized that I could CHANGE IT to ANYTHING I WANTED.

I became FREE. I realized the "bad" or negative in my life was no big deal because if I create a disaster, I can just as easily use my brain, emit frequencies, and turn that disaster into the greatest triumph of all time. Faster and with more gusto. And I can enjoy the process of attracting, manifesting, and creating. And I can absolutely have the most fun playing this game we call living on Earth.

It frees you when you know that you have that power and that you are, in fact, the creator of your own destiny and the creator of your own experience. You need to take 100 percent responsibility. I will teach you more about this later.

So there are a couple of key points here for you to think about.

The first question is, how do you increase desire? How do you increase that "I want, I really, really, really, really want it," to the point where you NEED to have what you want?

On the list of things you want that you wrote earlier, there are a lot of things.

If I were to ask, "At what intensity do you really want these things? Do you have a burning desire for any of them?" a lot of people may say, "I don't have a burning desire for anything."

So, how do you get a burning desire? How do you increase the burning desire? When you have a burning desire for things, life becomes a lot more fun.

First is to reduce the doubt that you'll get it. One reason you don't have a strong burning desire for something you say you want is because you doubt that you'll get it.

So if you increase belief, which is in effect reducing doubt that you'll get it, burning desire goes up. That's a very important key.

What exactly is doubt or lack of belief? In effect, it's you looking at the other side of the Training Balance Scale, focusing on the how.

Doubt or disbelief is you looking at your radar screen and only looking at what you can see. You're looking at the current facts. When you only look at the facts, you would easily doubt because you could easily say that this can't happen based on this information, and it's true.

So the key is, you have to understand that 90 percent of what is possible is off the radar screen and you can't see it. But you can *feel* what's there. You can learn how to feel what's there.

So you just have to *know*, just know, just know, that when you want something, if you look at your radar screen and try to figure out a way it's going to happen, just know that there won't be a way. So don't be upset or shocked by this.

Whatever you want, start by saying, "I know there's probably no way for me to look at the facts in my life right now or, looking at all the information I see on my radar screen, that I will be able to see HOW what I want is possible to achieve. There will be nothing that can justify me believing I can get this. There's no rational reason, there's no way, there are no facts that can show me that there's any method, any way that I can get this. I know that because I can only see what is on my radar screen. But I know that 90 percent of possibilities are off the radar screen. I can't see it, but I know it's there, and I know the Law of Attraction works. So I know if I do this process, all the things that are off my radar screen will start moving in manners which I couldn't even comprehend or calculate. And what I want will come into my existence in ways I couldn't even imagine."

When I deal with people who are very successful and trained in this powerful manifesting technology, and we're looking at situations, we think and speak very differently than you do.

I had a friend of mine who had a major legal "problem." He was owed huge amounts of money.

We were discussing it and he said to me, "I need this money. I can't pay my bills. And based on what my lawyers told me, and the way the courts have been ruling on my case, there's no way this is going to settle for at least twelve months. And I need the money within a couple of months. There's just no way it's going to settle."

And then he said, "But I'm going on a vacation because I know it'll all work out. I have no idea how. But it's going to be really interesting and amusing to me when it does work out. I'm curious to see how the universe is going to make it work out for me. So I don't need to worry about it. I'm going on a vacation. I have tried everything I know to sort this out with no results, now I am letting the universe figure it out."

And he took off.

Within a few weeks I received a phone call while he was on holiday, having a great time, enjoying himself, feeling good. Remember, when you're feeling good, you're not thinking about what you don't want.

If you're thinking about what you don't want, you're putting out vibrations of what you don't want and you are going to attract that into your life.

That's why I said earlier, the number one goal is always feel good now. Because if you're feeling good, you're never putting out vibrations of things you don't want.

So while he was feeling really, really good, he was only putting out positive vibrations into the universe, which were making his dreams come to him faster. He had no blockages, no counter-intentions.

And thus he called me and said, "I got a miracle. I have no idea how it happened. My attorneys can't figure it out, but the deal is done. We settled. I got my money."

It was no surprise to us because that's how it works.

If he had been feeling horrible, it wouldn't have worked out.

He could have said all day long it's going to work out fine, but as long as he felt horrible, that meant he was putting out vibrations of what he didn't want.

Doubt is when you're looking only at what you can see on your radar screen.

So if we break this down to one final concept, it's this.

You must always, always, always focus on one thing.

If you want to make this super simple, you focus on one thing every day, as much as you can throughout the day. You focus on feeling good.

If you're not feeling good—if you're feeling frustrated, angry, depressed, unstable, unsure, confused, fatigued, drained, exhausted, or grieving—you are slowing down the manifestation of your desires.

If you're in emotional pain, if you're not feeling good, you are putting out counter-intentions that are preventing what you desire from manifesting in your life.

There are really only two thoughts. Feeling good and feeling bad. And all degrees of that.

If you're not feeling good, which means if you're feeling bad to any degree, you are stopping what you want from coming into your life.

Here's what's happening.

If you're feeling bad to any degree, you are thinking about what you don't want, or you are thinking of NOT having what you want, feeling the LACK of what you want. This means your brain is transmitting the frequency of what you don't want.

Or you may be thinking about what you DO want, but you doubt you'll get it or you believe you won't get it. Which, in effect, means you're thinking about what you don't want.

So anytime you're feeling bad, it always comes down to one thing.

You're thinking about what you don't want to happen.

And it breaks down two ways. You're thinking about specifically what you don't want or you're thinking about what you DO want, but the emphasis is you're doubting you'll get it. Which means, in effect, you're thinking about what you don't want.

So always, always, always, anytime you're feeling bad, just know that you're thinking about what you don't want or doubting you will get what you DO want.

And so the question then is, how do I feel better?

How do I, most of the time, feel good to varying degrees?

And if I do feel bad, what is the specific thing I can do so that I feel good?

Let me tell you where you are. You're just starting this.

The Law of Attraction says whatever frequency you transmit from your brain will attract a matching frequency.

Here is what happens first when you transmit a frequency.

Let's say you are thinking of a black Cadillac, black Cadillac, or a black Mercedes, black Mercedes, black Mercedes. Or a new car, new car, new car.

Whatever it is you're transmitting, the first things that get attracted are *matching thoughts.*

When the matching thoughts keep coming in, that means the power and intensity of your transmission get stronger and stronger and stronger and stronger and more intense and more intense and more intense.

And the duration of that transmission can get longer and longer and longer.

When it reaches the tipping point, where your INTENTION is bigger than your COUNTER-INTENTION, that's when the physical manifestation happens, and you actually see it and touch your desire with your own hands.

But before what you want manifests, before you see it and touch it with your own hands, the first thing that happens is when you consciously transmit that thought and consciously add power and intensity to it, which is strong desire, strong belief, anticipation, excitement, then other matching thoughts begin to come in.

Example: You start thinking new car, new car, new car, new car, new car.

The first thing that could happen might be, you start seeing the car you're desiring everywhere.

You start transmitting that new car, new car, new car, new car, new car frequency, and all of a sudden, you're seeing ads, "Lowest interest rates on car loans in the last twenty-five years."

And you're thinking, "You know, boy, these interest rates look good." Then you start seeing ads like, "New lease programs available."

As you continue to transmit the thought, new car, new car, new car, new car, new car, all of a sudden, you're driving down the road, and you see a sign, "Home-based business, new car program available. We make the payments for you."

And you're like, "Wait a minute. I could probably do a home-based business and make enough money for the car of my dreams." You start expanding what you think or believe is possible.

Now, because you are transmitting new car, all of a sudden, things start coming into your radar screen that you did not think of before. Your belief that you actually CAN get a new car starts going up.

That little ball of energy for new car gets bigger and bigger and bigger. And as the energy, which is thoughts, starts to pile on one another, the ball of energy for a new car gets bigger and bigger and bigger.

And the bigger the ball of energy—which is just a whole bunch of thoughts—gets, the stronger its magnetic pull for more like-minded, matching thoughts.

Matching thoughts come in faster and bigger. And that ball of energy gets bigger and bigger and bigger. And the bigger it gets, the stronger the magnetic pull, which means more similar thoughts come in faster and bigger. It's exponential.

Your belief keeps going higher and higher. Your anticipation keeps going higher and higher. This big ball of energy gets bigger and bigger and more powerful and stronger. Your transmission of what you want gets more powerful and more intense.

And the duration of that transmission, instead of being twenty minutes a day, it's now all you're thinking about. You are consumed with NEW CAR.

You have an obsession with this new car. The anticipation of you actually HAVING the new car is VERY HIGH, even though you still have no idea how it's going to happen.

You start smiling all day and whistling as you think of NEW CAR.

And all of a sudden, in three weeks, you drive away in that brand-new car.

Someone will say, "But how could you afford that?"

And you would say, "It's the funniest thing. You wouldn't believe it. I was walking down the road and I saw a briefcase lying against the building. And it was just sitting there. I picked it up and there was a guy's name and phone number on it. He had a business card attached to the briefcase. I called him up from my cell phone. And I said, 'Sir, I'm here on the street. I found this briefcase.' And the guy says, 'Oh, my God, I didn't know where I left it. I don't know how I lost it. Oh, thank you. My whole life is in that briefcase. Where can I meet you? What can I do to repay you?' 'Oh, nothing, sir.' 'Great, let me pick it up. I'll be there in twenty minutes.' And the guy comes, picks up the briefcase, and says, 'You know, I can't believe you're such a Good Samaritan. You didn't even open the briefcase. I didn't have it locked. But you have no idea what I had in here was valuable. And I want to give you a reward.' 'Oh, no, sir. I don't need a reward.' 'No, please, please let me give you a reward.'

And the guy gave me a check for fifty thousand dollars.

"I hopped in my car and I went down to the Mercedes dealership. I traded in my car, put down a down payment. I got lower payments now than I had before with my old car. I got a brand-new car, and I got cash in the bank."

That story, by the way, actually happened. True story.

The reason I bring this up is, right now, you have probably been using the Law of Attraction the opposite way.

You have been thinking mostly negative thoughts. Oh, I could never make that happen. Oh, that could never work for me. Oh, this won't happen.

The more negative thinking that you do, the more counter-intentions you put out, the more negative transmissions you broadcast, means you will attract other negative thoughts, which attract more negative thoughts.

You have a black ball of negative counter-intention energy growing.

That ball ALSO has magnetic pull and power, so it attracts more negative counter-intention thoughts and forces that prevent what you want from manifesting into your life.

You do this out of HABIT. And you do this SUBCONSCIOUSLY.

Right now you actually have neural pathways that developed in your brain that are negative patterns.

Over your lifetime, you have developed failure habits and patterns. Right now you probably have this huge mammoth block of energy that you're carrying around consisting of negative thoughts and counter-intentions.

And you have these huge, well-grooved neural pathways in your brain, which make thinking negatively so easy. It is probably automatic. You do it subconsciously without deliberate intent.

In fact, you are unconsciously competent.

You are unconsciously competent when it comes to thinking negatively. Thinking, speaking, and acting negatively happens automatically for you. You're a genius at thinking negatively and putting out counter-intentions which neutralize your desires, wants, and dreams.

You're brilliant at self-sabotage. You are very proficient at instantly thinking a negative thought and thinking why it won't work, or why what you want can't manifest.

You are great at coming up with all the reasons why things won't happen and making all the excuses as to why you are not manifesting your goal.

Failures are always good at one thing … making excuses.

You are an expert at focusing on what you don't want. You've been doing it your whole life. And you do it without deliberate intent. You don't even know you are doing it. You do it automatically and subconsciously out of habit.

When you start using the techniques in this book, you're starting off with a very small positive energy ball, which means you have to be consciously competent. You have to do this with deliberate intent, and do it consciously. You have to concentrate and focus. You have to start changing your HABITS of THINKING and SPEAKING.

The more you focus on the positive, on what you want, and feel GOOD when you are thinking about your desire, the negative energy ball that IS there will only continue to attract things if you engage and activate it by thinking *that* way.

When you start thinking of the positive, of what you want, in the PROPER MANNER, you're now developing new neural pathways in your brain. The old neural pathways will still be trying to pull you to think like you've always thought.

That negative ball of energy, those old failure thinking habits, like a magnet, are pulling you to think the way you've always thought, because that's your pattern, that's your habit.

So conscious competence is required for about a month of doing this.

As you do this CONSCIOUSLY with DELIBERATE INTENT, you start developing new neural pathways in your brain and new habits of thinking.

You start getting that positive energy ball bigger and bigger and bigger. And as it gets bigger, it starts attracting matching thoughts and the negative ball of energy starts diminishing.

Your counter-intentions' attractive power starts diminishing.

Over time, your habits and patterns of thinking negatively, and the neural pathways that have been grooved so much about thinking negatively, start losing all their power.

You start developing positive thinking habits. You start thinking positively, unconsciously competently, automatically.

And THEN the magic will happen in your life. The day and the moment that that positive energy ball gets bigger than that negative ball, your life will change.

For the first time in your life, probably, you're experiencing positive energy—positive thoughts such as: 'Oh, I *can* make that happen. I don't know how, but I know this works. This can happen. Good things always happen to me. I'm lucky.'

When you start thinking like this AUTOMATICALLY because it is who you are, and you actually KNOW those statements are TRUE, your wish can be virtually your command.

When you instantly and automatically say, "Listen, I don't know how it's going to work out. Oh, this may look bad. But I KNOW that it will all turn out just fine"—that is when you have POWER. That is when you are at CAUSE over your environment, and not at effect.

When you say something like that and completely believe it in your core, that is when that positive energy ball within you is bigger than the negative counter-intention energy ball.

That's the tipping point. There's a shift. Like a titanic earthquake in your being. You're now thinking more positively than negatively, and it is your NEW HABIT.

You have crested. A shift has occurred. Everything in your life then changes. It's the moment that you *wake up* and come out of your trance.

That is why we say *success is a decision away*.

That's the day when you can make the decision, "I'm going to do it. That's it, period. I don't care what the circumstances say. I don't care what the facts say. I'm going to do it. That's it, period. Watch my stuff, baby. Oh, it doesn't matter what people say, what people think. It doesn't matter what the facts say. I have no idea about the how. I don't know how. My radar screen tells me it's impossible. Oh, man, it's going to be interesting to see how this thing actually works out, because it's going to work out just fine."

You start feeling so unbelievably powerful and confident. You start feeling so joyful and blissful. You start skipping and smiling throughout the day. You start waking up in the morning and jumping out of bed and singing a tune thinking, "I don't know why I'm so happy. I have no idea why, but I am. Everything in my life is going terribly wrong. Why am I so happy? The reason is because I know it will all just work out fine. Everything will turn around, and I have no idea how, but I just know it will."

That's when your life becomes magical.

That's why it's so vitally important to focus on feeling good now. Feeling good now.

There are many techniques and specific things you can do to feel good now, which I'm going to share with you. All of them are things that we've done within the societies.

This is just the beginning. You are on a journey that will take you to the promised land. You have greatness within you. You are more powerful than you know. Smile. Your future is bright!

LESSON 11

How to Eliminate Negative Counter-Intention Thoughts

When you are using the manifesting formula, out of habit it is normal for you to start having thoughts such as, "This can't work. How is this going to work? I don't think I will ever attain my desire." You will start to doubt the manifesting formula and yourself.

The solution is to work on getting the ball of positive energy bigger than the negative ball of counter-intention energy that you've been establishing your whole life, which is probably very large and powerful at this point in your life.

How do you get the positive ball of energy bigger than the negative ball?

By the time you finish reading this book, you will be at the conscious competence level. You're going to be consciously aware of the techniques and consciously aware of how you have to think and how you have to apply these procedures.

You want to get this material, the methods and techniques, to the unconscious competence level so that you are DOING the methods AUTOMATICALLY and SUBCONSCIOUSLY, because it is WHO YOU ARE.

It is not when you got into this book, it is when this book got into you.

Thus, it is important to read this book over and over again. Get the audios of the original seminar that I taught and listen to those audios over and over again.

As you read this book, you will learn the daily things to do so that you develop NEW ways of thinking that will replace your old failure habits of thinking.

These simple, fast, daily "to-dos" will cause you to focus on these techniques and will cause you to be thinking the right thoughts. By the Law of Attraction, when you're thinking the right thoughts, you will start attracting MORE "right thoughts." You will start developing new neural pathways in your brain. You are REPLACING old failure thinking habits with NEW success thinking habits. Your ball of negative counter-intention energy will get smaller, and your ball of positive energy will get bigger.

This is a process. It is like bodybuilding. If you are skinny with no muscles and you want to have a bodybuilder body, you will have to go to the gym every day and work out hard. After the first week, you might not notice any difference. But if you are consistent and persistent with your efforts, in two years, your body will look totally different. You WILL build big muscles.

Do the right things long enough, consistently.

Remember, when you think, whatever you think about, your brain is then transmitting a frequency. Every thought that you have is your brain transmitting a frequency. Every time you think a thought, your brain transmits a frequency.

The more intensity you put into that thought and the more power you put into that thought, the stronger the attraction power of the frequency is.

Let's define: What is intensity and what is power?

When a thought is focused and large, and when there's a lot of emotion attached to that thought, you are broadcasting it with intensity and power. Now, if that emotion is hate, anger, excitement, thrilled, it doesn't matter whether it's a good emotion or a bad emotion, the more emotion that's attached to the thought, and the more focused you are when you think that thought, that is what increases the power and intensity of that thought.

Additionally, the longer you think that thought, that is the duration. Thinking a thought for ten seconds is less powerful than thinking that thought for two minutes. Thus, thinking a thought for two straight minutes a day is better than thinking that thought for ten seconds, twenty times a day.

Every time you think a thought it puts out a vibration. Your brain is transmitting a vibration. Every time your brain transmits a vibration, it is attracting, first, other like-minded thoughts.

So the more you read this book or listen to the audios, the more often you will be thinking the "right thoughts" to reduce the size of your negative ball of counter-intention energy and increase the size of your positive ball of energy.

As you read this book over and over, and listen to the audios over and over, you are going to start attracting more of the right thoughts, and then your positive ball of energy is going to get bigger and bigger and bigger, and the negative counter-intention ball of energy is going to get smaller and smaller.

Remember, you don't know what you don't know.

Right now you're consciously competent, or close to it, when it comes to using the manifesting steps that you have learned so far. At some point you will start to notice yourself thinking the wrong thoughts or saying negative things.

When you do, simply say "CANCEL CANCEL" and REPLACE that "wrong thought or words" with the "right thoughts and words."

How do you know when you're thinking the wrong thought? Answer: based on how you feel.

That's why I said, earlier the first, most important thing, the only thing you do to make this super stupidly simple, is every day, monitor how you feel.

If you feel good, the objective is to feel better.
If you feel bad, the objective is to feel BETTER.

This is important. You can't go from feeling depressed to feeling super happy. That is too big a jump. It is too steep a gradient.

Your objective is simply to feel BETTER.

When you feel bad—and that could be on the low end of the scale such as depression or sadness, or just bored, unsure, afraid, feeling grief, anger, hate, or any negative emotion—be aware that every time you feel an emotion, the universe is telling you something!

If you feel bad, the universe is telling you you are thinking WRONG thoughts.

If you feel good, the universe is saying you are thinking the RIGHT thoughts.

Just catch yourself whenever you feel bad. Be AWARE that you feel bad. Say "CANCEL CANCEL". And then the procedure is to ask yourself: "Okay, I feel bad, how do I feel better?"

I'm going to teach you how to feel better. Just remember, when you are using the manifesting steps and thinking about what you want to manifest, your ultimate goal is to feel GOOD, but your FIRST goal is to feel BETTER.

The basic procedure for getting what you want is to first define what you want. You can be specific, general, or have a desire to just feel good.

There is actually a powerful SECRET step to do BEFORE you define what you want. This step is NOT talked about in ANY book on manifesting or success. Quite frankly, NO success "expert" or Law of Attraction "expert" knows about it. WE, in the societies,

KNOW it and USE it. It really is a key MISSING ingredient that makes this all work. I will share that with you later in this book.

You must have a burning desire for what you want, which means you have high intensity and high power when you broadcast your desire from your brain.

This means you have high emotion, high expectation, real excitement. When you think about what you want, you feel you NEED to have it NOW. Your juices are flowing. You are on FIRE. You have an obsession with attaining your desire.

You think about being in possession of your desire. When you do this, you feel GOOD, motivated, and inspired.

This means you're going to be thinking your desire all throughout the day with excitement and ANTICIPATING it manifesting into your life.

If you're feeling bad when you do this, that means you're doubting. If you're feeling good, that means you're believing. You must BELIEVE you WILL attain your desire. You have to have CONFIDENCE that your desire WILL manifest.

Belief is a key component to getting what you want. There is MAGIC in BELIEVING.

The key element here is, once you define what you want, when you think about what you want, how do you feel? You want to increase the feeling to complete excitement, exhilaration, and you ideally want to get to the point of complete expectation. You KNOW what you want WILL manifest.

The ideal feeling you should have when you think about what you want to manifest is as if there's completely no doubt that it will manifest.

Actually the IDEAL feeling you should have when you think about what you want is as if it was ALREADY in your possession. You ideally should feel that it ALREADY MANIFESTED.

A good example is, how do you feel on Christmas Eve knowing tomorrow it's Christmas and the presents are ALREADY under the tree with your name on them?

There's no doubt at all that you will receive presents. They are already there. You have a feeling of complete excitement KNOWING that you can open your presents tomorrow.

The only difference here is when you have that feeling of anticipation, you don't have to worry whether it's tomorrow, next week, or next month because the time when it's coming in is completely irrelevant. You have placed your order. You received an email saying your order has been shipped. YOU ARE GETTING IT. IT IS COMING. NO DOUBT.

The timing as to WHEN you will receive it is irrelevant. You ALLOW your desire to manifest when it's supposed to manifest. Don't put a deadline on WHEN your DREAM will manifest.

Does this make sense?

Let's talk about specifically how to feel good now, because this is the number one challenge you will face. How to feel good now, or how do you feel BETTER now working toward feeling good?

First and foremost, always monitor your emotions; they are your guidance system. Every day, I always monitor my emotions.

If you're not feeling good, that means you're not thinking properly, and that means you need to change your thinking and start feeling better. When you start feeling better, you start attracting more like-minded positive thoughts.

The more you CONSCIOUSLY do this, the faster you will get to the unconscious competence level where this method of thinking is happening automatically.

You will start thinking this way automatically when you've done this process enough times and you develop enough new neural pathways in the brain so that the positive ball of energy is bigger than the negative ball of energy.

Let me give you a specific list of things you can do to feel better now and work towards feeling good now.

Some of these might surprise you. But these are the things that we in the societies have learned that work incredibly effectively. Some of these are simplistic and easy, but you'll be surprised at how well they all work.

First, if your body feels bad, it's going to be hard for you to feel good mentally and emotionally. So first and foremost, having your body feel good is an important element for success in life.

To have your body feel good, consider doing these things:

Eat good-quality food.

The number one cause of death throughout history has been famine, lack of food. The second cause of death has been disease, which overcomes the body due mainly to nutritional deficiencies and a weak immune system. This is caused by a lack of good-quality food.

This is not a book about nutrition or health. If you want all the information about how to have the body feel great, read my #1 *New York Times* best-selling book, *Natural Cures They Don't Want You to Know About.*

A good general rule for eating is to eat food in a form that is as close to what nature intended as possible. So avoid processed food. Eat fresh vegetables and fruits. Fresh is better than canned or frozen. Organic is always better. Non-genetically modified organism food (non-GMO) is MUCH better.

Organic grass-fed beef is better. Organic rice from Thailand or Japan is best. Organic buckwheat and barley are good. Free-range organic chicken, organic lamb, duck, and fish are all good.

Here are some things to avoid.

ALL corn products, high-fructose corn syrup, MSG, hydrogenated oils (trans fats), and artificial sweeteners should all be avoided. Fish that do not have scales and fins should be avoided as they absorb toxins. Pork is very hard to digest and should be avoided. Oils from seeds should be avoided (canola, for example).

Eat at least three times a day.

"Bad" food with chemicals and toxins block your ability to think and actually make you feel bad and depressed because they're blocking neural pathways in the brain.

Eating good food is really significant and important. Read *Natural Cures*! www.KevinTrudeau.com

Next, you should consider taking nutritional supplements to address the nutritional deficiencies that you DO have.

Everyone has nutritional deficiencies because we're not eating as well as we should. Even if you are eating 100 percent organic food, you are still not getting all the nutrients your body needs. This is because today's food, even the best 100 percent organic food, has less than half of the nutrients than that same food did fifty years ago. Our food is simply LOW in nutrients compared to years ago.

When your body has all the proper nutrients, and you are not dealing with nutritional deficiencies, you feel better. You have more energy. You are sharper. You can concentrate more. You are more enthusiastic. You think clearer, can focus better, and you can transmit vibration better. Thus you can manifest faster and easier.

You will always feel better when you have all the nutrients you need. World's Best Nutritionals and Organics manufactures and sells products that I developed, and I believe are the best WHOLE FOOD supplements and organic products in the world. For more information, go to www.KevinTrudeau.com.

When you are taking an organic whole food supplement, you are simply taking concentrated food with all the nutrients FROM real food. This means you are getting the nutrients in the form nature intended in the exact proportions to each other that nature intended.

Next, drink pure water. There is tap water, filtered water, distilled and spring water. ALL tap water is loaded with toxins. Avoid tap water. Don't use it to make coffee or tea, as you are STILL ingesting toxins. Boiling does not eliminate the toxins in the water.

There are many ways to filter water such as reverse osmosis and carbon block. Not all filtered waters are good, but they are all better than tap water.

Distilled water should not be consumed except in the case where you are doing a specific cleanse and under the direction of a health-care provider.

Spring water is my choice. But not all spring waters are the same. Some are better than others.

Also consider NOT drinking any water that comes in a plastic container. Glass is better.

It is ideal to drink about two liters of WATER a day. Water is water. It is not tea or coffee or juice. Water stops being water as soon as you add anything to it including squeezing some lemon in it.

Drinking a LARGE glass of water when you first get up in the morning FEEDS THE BRAIN and makes your brain work BETTER.

Next, one of the reasons you feel bad and one of the things that will block your ability to focus is the toxins you have in your body. EVERYONE has toxins in their body. These come from prescription and nonprescription drugs, recreational drugs, smoking, poor air quality, and virtually all the food you have eaten your whole life.

Toxins also include heavy metals such as from mercury fillings. Candida is a toxin in the body. All the food you've eaten your whole life was filled with pesticides and herbicides that are NOW in your body, in the FAT cells of your body. Your brain is mostly FAT and water. Thus your BRAIN is FILLED with toxins that are reducing your ability to broadcast. The toxins also reduce your ability to FEEL GOOD.

In the water there are toxins such as chlorine and fluoride. When you shower or bathe in water, you are absorbing all the toxins in the water. Your skin is the largest organ in the body. Anything you put on the skin is absorbed into the body. Think about all the soaps and lotions you have put on your skin. Perhaps hair dyes. ALL are toxic and they DO NOT LEAVE THE BODY. They are stored in the fatty tissue of the body and continue to accumulate over the years.

The number one toxin that you're dealing with today is drugs. This includes prescription, nonprescription, and recreational drugs. I'm not going to get into this whole discussion, but getting people to use pharmaceutical drugs, nonprescription and prescription drugs, is something that the "elites" want because taking drugs, even an aspirin, will weaken your ability to focus and transmit vibration.

So the more drugs "they" can get you to take makes you powerless. It reduces your power to create. So if you're taking nasal decongestant, cold and flu medicine, statins for high cholesterol, a drug for high blood pressure, pain medication, cannabis, psychedelics, all these things reduce your ability to transmit vibration.

The bottom line is we're loaded up with toxins and these toxins keep you broadcasting in the Beta brain wave, which is the slave wave, the poverty wave.

Therefore, you should be doing some type of cleansing to get these toxins out.

There are many different cleanses including a colon cleanse, a liver/gallbladder cleanse, a kidney cleanse, a parasite cleanse, a candida cleanse, a fat cell cleanse, and a heavy metal cleanse. Those are the basic ones. Read my book *Natural Cures* for more information about all of this, including what to eat, what not to eat, and cleanses.

We in the societies do fasting and various cleanses on a regular basis to make sure that we always have power to broadcast on the Alpha/Theta wave, and have the ability to concentrate, focus, and maintain our power.

It's similar to taking your car in, getting a tune-up, and getting the oil and filter changed.

If you're going to race a car and you want to win the race, you want to make sure that the engine is operating really powerfully and is at peak performance.

Here your engine is your brain and your ability to focus and transmit vibration on the Alpha/Theta wave.

The next thing, which is very interesting, is today you're bombarded by electromagnetic frequencies such as 5G.

Remember, I told you about the experiments where various things, from a bar of gold to a glass of water to a piece of metal, were hit with an electromagnetic frequency from a radio wave, a microwave, a wireless device, or a cell phone.

These waves affect vibration, and they change the vibrational frequency of what they touch.

You are being bombarded twenty-four hours a day, seven days a week, from all the satellites that are beaming electromagnetic waves, all the cell phone towers, all the radio transmissions, and when you are in your homes, you are also affected by all the electrical wiring in the house because it also emits radio waves.

All wireless devices emit frequencies that affect YOUR BRAIN and YOUR FREQUENCY in a NEGATIVE WAY.

We can't avoid them anywhere on the planet.

These frequencies are affecting our own vibration and our ability to transmit vibration.

So what do you do? You can't eliminate it, but you can neutralize it. They're called electromagnetic chaos eliminators. There are many devices that you can purchase. Some are better than others. This is something to consider.

Next is exercise, moving your body. You always feel better when you exercise, for many reasons. When you exercise, you are flooding the body with oxygen and releasing the "feel good" hormones. Stretching also opens up energy channels so that "chi" energy can flow more easily, thus making you feel better.

There is one thing that ALL successful people have done for centuries to make them feel better.

That is, go for a walk outside and as you walk, look at things far away. First, you're getting the sun. The sun is vital to making you feel better. I don't care what month it is; if it's cold, put on clothes, because the photons from the sun will pass through your clothes into your body. Get outside and go for a walk.

Throughout history, the wealthy always went outside. They always walked, with rare exception, and those who didn't, such as Howard Hughes, became crazy.

Going outside for a walk or riding a horse is powerful, but no one today has a horse sitting around, so walking is great.

The aristocracy always rode horses. If you have a horse, go for a horseback ride and look at things far away.

When you walk, it doesn't have to be a fast walk. It'll make you feel much, much better.

Modern research shows that the number one, easiest, fastest way to cure any type of depression or low feeling is going for a walk outside for about an hour and looking at things far away. The natural body movement of walking, the air, oxygen, the sun, and the fact that you're looking at things far away, all combined, actually can help with sadness and depression better than any type of drug or any type of known treatment.

Another effective way to feel better is rebounding. This is jumping up and down on a little mini trampoline, called a rebounder. This is a cellular exercise. It flushes toxins out of the lymphatic system. Within just five minutes of jumping on a rebounder, you feel dramatically better.

There is also something called a vibration plate. The popular brand is PowerPlate. Hypervibe is also good. You get on this device and just stand on it as it vibrates. It vibrates every cell in the body and releases endorphins, making you feel tremendously good.

Also, there's something called an inversion table. Teeter Hangups is one of the best, invented by Roger Teeter. An inversion table is something that you can get for your home. You can stand on it and you slowly start shifting as you begin to hang upside-down. You don't even have to go all the way and hang completely upside-down.

But you're getting inverted to some degree so that your head is below your feet and you're inverting yourself. This process makes you feel tremendously better. It releases lower back pressure, makes you taller and decompresses the spine.

For more information on all the things you can do to make your physical body feel better, read my book *Natural Cures They Don't Want You to Know About* or join my private success club, the Global Information Network (GIN).

Now let me give you some other things that you can easily do on a regular basis that will make you feel better.

I strongly recommend that every day you should be reading books. Even if it is only for five minutes a day. Leaders are always readers. At the end of this book, I will give you a recommended reading list.

Even reading one page a day gets you to focus on positive thoughts and focus and believe in yourself. As you read the books I suggest and reread this book, you'll start thinking thoughts such as:

I can change my situation.

I can create anything I want in my life.

I can do it.

I can manifest my desire.

If others have done this, so can I.

Reading books on a regular basis is absolutely vital.

Listening to audios also gets you to focus and think the right thoughts and start building up that positive energy so you get to unconscious competence.

If you join the Global Information Network (GIN), you will have access to the best audios available anywhere in the world that will motivate and inspire you to succeed. You will learn vital skills and techniques that you can use that will create results in your life and help you manifest your goals and dreams faster and easier than before.

This includes my Success Mastery Course audio series.

I would highly suggest and recommend that you join the Global Information Network (GIN) so that you can be plugged into a "system" and get the success information from me and my colleagues directly.

As a member, you get a weekly "Member Development Series" audio, weekly update audios, and other information and updates on world events and what's *really* happening, directly from the "insiders." But primarily we will be teaching you more in-depth manifesting knowledge and training you how to create the life you want.

As a member of the Global Information Network (GIN), you'll also have access to all of our global live and virtual events, such as our annual cruise where we take over an entire cruise ship for a week for members only. There are also three other major weekend events at luxurious resorts. Additionally we have four virtual seminars and rallies and hundreds of live and virtual local chapter meetings all around the world.

At these events you can come and listen to people, either myself or others, who will share more about this information and answer your questions. You get to meet, in person, the major players from around the world. You will also meet and develop powerful relationships with other like-minded people who are members of the Global Information Network (GIN).

When you come to one of our events, one of the advantages you get is that your mind starts attracting other, like minds. It's the Law of Attraction. But a unique thing happens when you're physically in a room with other people who are like-minded.

When minds are connected in a room physically, you actually create a NEW mind that is a combination of everyone in the room.

Napoleon Hill called this the Mastermind. He learned this from Andrew Carnegie himself.

Creating a "Mastermind" is a technique that the wealthy have used throughout history because they know that even though they themselves have incredible power, there is a thousand times MORE power in a Mastermind.

The Mastermind creates a synergistic effect.

When they start attaching themselves on a regular basis by physically being in the presence of other like-minded people and start sitting down with them, they create another mind, a Mastermind, which is much more powerful than each one independently.

You're all going to be energized more than you can imagine when you leave an event. You get permanently changed by going to events. Events are where decisions are made. Remember, success is a decision away.

Coming to an event is much more powerful than, let's say, sitting at home watching an event on the internet. That's very good, but it's much, much better to physically be in the room.

So I would suggest you join the Global Information Network (GIN) because if you do, you're going to be part of a very unique, powerful group, almost like a secret society that's now going to be available to all people and not just the elite class.

The relationships you will develop will be a major component to your success. Your income is always the average of your five best friends'. Think about that. Aristotle Onassis said the single most important ingredient to success is associating with successful people. Success rubs off. When you are a member of the Global Information Network (GIN), you will associate with, and become friends with, powerful, successful people from all over the world. These "connections" will prove vital for your success in life.

Another way to feel good if you're feeling down, is by listening to music. Listen to your favorite music, the music that gives you a lift and makes you feel better.

If you're ever feeling blue or feeling bad, playing your favorite song can change the way you feel dramatically. Singing can dramatically change the way you feel. People don't sing because they are happy, they are happy because they sing! Think about that.

Baroque classical music is powerful because it synchronizes the left and right brain hemispheres and puts you in an Alpha state. It does not instantly make you feel better, but it IS very effective in the long term.

Use the power of music to help you feel better.

There are many other things that wealthy people do to make themselves feel better. I will not list them all here. As a member of the Global Information Network (GIN), you will get access to ALL the methods we use in the secret societies to "feel good now" and thus increase your ability to manifest goals and desires.

The reason I am giving you these tools to feel better is that when I, or another member of the societies, have something occur in our lives that we did not expect or do not like, and it "triggers" us and makes us feel bad, we have a tool box of things we can do to "feel better." Feeling better is a key.

Because we've been trained so well and do this at the unconscious competence level, when something makes us feel bad, we do the following steps:

We ACKNOWLEDGE IT, and we don't DENY IT.

We WELCOME THE BAD FEELING, and we don't RESIST IT.

We use that negative energy to allow us to contract and concentrate energy so that we can THEN clearly define what we want.

We THEN transmute the negative feelings by using one of the tools in our toolbox that will help us FEEL BETTER.

Imagine I get an email that says, "Bad news in court." Such and such just happened. I look at that, and think, well, that certainly appears to be bad news. I get angry or frustrated or scared. I acknowledge that feeling. I don't deny it.

I welcome that feeling and allow myself to fully feel it. I then use that negative energy to clearly define what I DO want and see myself in possession of that and FEEL NOW AS IF I were in possession of what I want. I put an instant smile on my face, and I think, "I have no idea how, but I know this is going to work out to my ultimate advantage. Something outstandingly good is going to come from this, and I don't know how."

I might go for a walk, or jump on my rebounder, or listen to some music, or shoot pool, or go fishing, or golfing, or cook a nice meal.

But years ago, when something like that would happen, I would feel instantly bad, because I had developed the habit of feeling bad. And positive thinking says, DON'T FEEL BAD, try to "reframe it." So I would DENY I was feeling bad. If someone asked me how I was, I would say "GREAT," even though I did not feel great.

Then you start focusing on the "bad situation" and, oh, my God, fear comes in.

You start thinking, "This is not good." You get STUCK feeling bad instead of USING that negative feeling to clearly define what you want. And you DENY your bad feeling. Once you deny you are feeling bad, IT WILL STAY AND INCREASE.

You may feel bad because you're focusing on your own radar screen. You are falling into old habits. So go through the process with confidence IN THE PROCESS.

Then to feel better, you go for a walk, or you listen to your favorite song, you start singing, and you start changing the way you feel right away.

Because the most important thing is every day, as often as possible, that you feel as good as you can right now, no matter what the situation. Remember, it is GOOD to feel BAD, but you don't LIVE in the bad feeling.

In the same way, you must DREAM, but don't live in a dream world.

You VISIT the bad feelings, and you VISIT the dream, and you LIVE IN THE MOMENT. Live in the NOW, the PRESENT TIME, and TAKE ACTION while FEELING AS BEST YOU CAN NOW.

Hugs. Do you want to feel better? Hug somebody. Most people today don't get enough tactile contact with other human beings. Shaking hands is good, but hugging someone is really valuable, and that can make you feel tremendous. Even hugging a pet is powerful!

Laughing. One of the most powerful things you can do to help you feel better is LAUGH. When people in our circles, get disastrous news, they don't focus on the disastrous news. They go through the process and sometimes very quickly, in a matter of a minute or two.

They know if they can change their vibration, they can change that situation. The way you change your vibration is you feel BETTER.

When you're feeling as good as you can in the moment, you're vibrating "good," and something "good" will happen. You will attract it.

Sometimes you can read funny books or watch funny movies or TV shows or just start laughing.

The more you laugh, the better you will feel. If you laugh through-out the day, as a new habit, for no reason, you will feel better. Laugh-ing is one of the healthiest processes you can do. Laughter is the best medicine.

There was a great book written by Norman Cousins called *The Anatomy of an Illness*. The author was diagnosed with cancer. The doctors all told him it was incurable and that he was going to die. He went home and he started laughing because he said, Before I die, I'm just going to laugh my way into the grave.

Well, six weeks later, when he was supposed to be dead, he went back to the doctors, and they said his cancer was in complete remission.

Laughter itself is healing to the body. It creates an alkaline state where disease can't exist in the body. Laughter is very powerful.

Smiling. If you can't laugh, at least smile. Try to smile as often as you can, even for no reason.

Most people walk around with a scowl on their face, which is evidence of what they're vibrating, what they're transmitting SUBCONSCIOUSLY. Scowling means you DON'T FEEL GOOD. You may subconsciously feel fear, pessimism, sadness, and uncertainty.

When you smile, you change that vibration. Just the act of smil-ing can change your vibration.

Getting a massage will also make you feel tremendously good. Take a sauna—hot sauna or wet steam. Get a pet if you don't have a pet or play with your pet. All these things will make you feel better.

Paint if you like to paint. Do some type of arts and crafts. Do gardening. Chop wood. Do something physically with your hands. Create something with your hands like painting or pottery or arts and crafts.

Dance. You don't have to go to a ball. You can be home and just start dancing. Believe me, if you turn on some music and start danc-ing by yourself right in the midst of a catastrophe in your life, you will start feeling better. You will start laughing and, believe me, as if by magic, your situation will begin to change.

Cook. When you cook you're creating something with your hands. For some people, cooking can be very healing.

Music. I mentioned listening to music. You can also play music. If you play a musical instrument, playing it in the middle of a trauma can be very healing.

Play in a garden or plant a garden. When you start planting living things yourself, with your hands in the soil, something magical happens to you. Very powerful.

And the last couple of items in your "feel better toolbox", I want to talk about are some things that you absolutely should consider.

There is a technique developed by Dr. Roger Callahan called Thought Field Therapy (TFT).

Roger was a very close friend of mine. One of Roger's apprentices is a man by the name of Gary Craig, who developed an offshoot (or a simplified version) of Roger's method.

I suggest Roger's original method as it is by far the more effective.

TFT is one of the most powerful and fastest techniques of changing the way you feel.

As a member of the Global Information Network, you have free access to a three-hour seminar I did teaching you the fast, simple method you do to yourself anytime you feel "bad." In virtually five minutes you can eliminate fear, anxiety, sadness, grief, phobias, stress, and any other "negative" feeling or emotion.

And I'll explain generally how it works here. This is a very important technique to learn and use because, especially in the beginning, you are going to feel bad at some point, and you need to have a tool that can turn that around very quickly.

When you're feeling bad, the reason you're feeling bad is because you're focusing on something you don't want or something in your "energy field or memories" is triggered.

When you are thinking about what you DON'T want or something is triggered, you are transmitting energy, a vibration. The vibration that you're transmitting is a vibration which is different than what you DO want, and that frequency opposes the things you DO want.

Everything you want is in your "energy field." So you're vibrating everything you want right now.

But if you're transmitting an opposing vibration, they don't mix. That counter-intention then blocks the free flow of energy in the body, and you feel horrible.

These are the general mechanics of how it works.

So theoretically, all you have to do is think about something you want that you believe you'll get, and you will feel better. But the counter-intention vibration is an uncontrollable feeling and many times irrational. You can't shut it off. And it is usually MORE powerful than your INTENTION towards what you do want.

If you think about the worst possible scenario that could happen to you, you feel terrible. And you usually can't stop it. If you start thinking about something you want, what will instantly happen because you're feeling so bad and the counter-intention is so strong, is that you might start thinking, "I'm not going to get that," which will make you feel bad again.

Because of the Law of Attraction, your negative thoughts keep attracting more negative thoughts.

So, yes, theoretically you can change the way you feel by consciously shifting and focusing on something that you DO want, something good, something that will make you feel happy, something you believe you can get, and keep focusing on that. Then the negative will just, over time, begin to diminish and go away. So you are REPLACING by WILLPOWER your thinking about what you DON'T want with something you DO want.

But because the negative can be so powerful in terms of its attractive pull, it is, for a lot of people, very difficult to use WILLPOWER to create good results. That is just THEORY.

Imagine you just got served with divorce papers, and you're devastated, you're heartbroken.

It will be very difficult to focus on something positive like "Well, my life will be better, and everything will be fine," because you have had thoughts about this person for such a long time and those thoughts are very powerful, so they will keep drawing you back there.

So it's going to sometimes be difficult for you to change the focus, or change your point of focus, so you can focus on something good that you believe in to make you feel better.

So you can use the TFT technique, and you can eliminate or dramatically reduce those negative feelings. Those feelings will be transmuted or "blown" out of your field. You WILL feel BETTER.

Of course you can use some of the other tools in your "feel better tool box." You can go for a walk, you can listen to some music, you can sing, you can laugh, you can dance.

Absolutely those are very powerful techniques, and you should employ them on a regular basis regardless of how you're feeling to maintain a "good vibration and feeling." If you do the things I mentioned above, they are going to keep you in that good feeling state.

But when you do have that horrible feeling, you don't want to wallow in it for hours or days or weeks. You want to eliminate it, or at least dramatically reduce it, because that will allow you to focus on the things you DO want powerfully with anticipation, and thus be able to create good things very quickly, changing your situation for the better.

The Callahan technique (TFT) is a technique to use anytime and ideally every time you're feeling bad. This way you get rid of those things that "trigger" you PERMANENTLY.

When those frequencies that are lying dormant are gone, you can begin vibrating and sending out broadcasts for those things you DO want without counter-intentions. If the counter-intentions are still in your energy field, even if they are not activated or triggered, you are STILL sending out counter-intention vibrations SUBCON-SCIOUSLY that will neutralize the vibrations you consciously send out for the things you DO want to manifest.

So with these counter-intentions, you have "opposition" and you feel horrible because the free flow of energy is blocked through the body.

To use the Callahan technique (TFT), you simply tap on a series of acupressure meridian points in the body, in a very specific sequence. It takes less than five minutes to do this process.

You can do it anywhere. Doing this will break up the blockages in the physical body and make that negative vibration virtually dissipate or dissolve and leave you. Then you INSTANTLY feel better.

In a matter of minutes, we've had people who were completely depressed start laughing and feeling better than ever. And they can't get that depressed feeling back because it's physically gone. TFT takes that negative blob of energy and virtually dissipates it and breaks it up.

You need to have this tool in your pocket to use on an ongoing basis.

Join the Global Information Network (GIN) to get all the training on HOW to do this for free.

Next is a process called dream building. This is where you're building up your dreams, goals, and desires, making them more real and very solid. This technique is done multiple ways.

First, dream building is done by looking at things that you could potentially want, which means expanding your mind to possibility. It gets you thinking BIG. It is easy to look at physical things.

So you can get a book or a magazine, such as *The Robb Report* or *duPont REGISTRY*, which have fine homes and cars. You can look at magazines which have luxury items from clothes and jewelry to watches and different things. You can look on the internet at private jets, luxury resorts, and various pictures of very expensive things.

By looking at expensive, opulent things over and over again, you start expanding your ability to DREAM. What is POSSIBLE becomes bigger. This is because you start seeing that people are actually getting this stuff. This is real. What others have done, you can do also.

So looking at magazines, brochures, or pictures on the internet of opulent things, even if they are things that you do not want, is critical to making "you" and your imaginative power bigger.

The pictures do not have to be of things. They can be "lifestyle" pictures. Maybe it's pictures of happy families. Maybe it's pictures of colleges. Maybe it's pictures of people who are physically fit, if that's a goal you may want.

Or look at pictures of people that look young, happy, healthy, and vibrant. Pictures of people that are laughing, people that are enjoying social settings and being with other happy people. Pictures of people that are doing things you may want to do.

Look at pictures of luxury cars, homes, jewelry, clothes, exotic locations around the world, and the places you may want to visit someday.

It is critical that you do this "dream building" process of looking and looking and looking at PICTURES of things and lifestyles that are beyond your current realm of what you think is possible for you right now.

Interestingly enough, when you do this, you're going to notice your feelings. Because sometimes when you do this, you actually get depressed because you start believing, "I can't have that. I can't have that. I can't have that."

When and if that occurs, then stop the process. But you've already put into your subconscious mind these images and pictures, and your negative feelings will slowly start to turn around over time. This needs to happen. You are deprogramming yourself and expanding what your subconscious believes is possible.

So on a regular basis, every day ideally, you should be doing some type of dream building, such as looking at pictures in magazines, brochures, or on the internet.

You could also be watching videos like *Lifestyles of the Rich and Famous,* or various shows on the Travel Channel that show you what others have attained and what is available to those who "believe." You start to see different things that you COULD be experiencing. You see people who have luxury yachts and luxury homes around the world, the top ten beaches in the world to travel to, private planes, and amazing, world-class, opulent lifestyles.

Watching videos and looking at pictures is part of the process of dream building, where you start expanding the possibilities and your ability to DREAM BIG DREAMS.

The BEST process of dream building occurs when you physically go window-shopping. Go to a car dealer and see and touch an expensive car. Go to an open house at a $10 million luxury home. Go to a jewelry store and look at expensive watches and jewelry. Doing this makes it REAL.

Go into luxury shops where there are expensive items. Walk by expensive restaurants and look at the menus, or go online instead and look at the menus of restaurants you may want to visit someday.

I'll give you one other powerful technique. The closer you can get to the item physically, the more powerful this technique is.

So going to a car dealership to look at a car is one thing, but to sit in the car is another. You begin to smell the smells and feel the textures with your own hands as tactile contact. That's very powerful at expanding your mind and your belief. Your subconscious WILL change.

It happens over time. It doesn't happen the first day, but it happens over time. This is especially true if you specifically want something, and you go physically look at it and touch it. This makes it more real and will bring it into your existence faster.

This is because when you physically see it and touch it, it becomes more real, and your belief level starts going up. The anticipation that it can be yours starts going up.

The most powerful part of this technique is to believe or imagine how you're going to feel when you're driving that car, or how you're going to feel when you're living in that house, or how you're going to feel when you're wearing that watch.

Go to a jewelry store and try on a ring. Try on the watch. Go to the clothing store and try on that jacket. Try on that fur and imagine how you're going to feel when you're wearing this in real life.

The closer you can get to it, the more you can get the anticipation, the better you will feel.

You will also start getting mad you DON'T have it now. THIS IS PERFECT. You turn your wish into a want and then into a NEED. That is powerful.

When you NEED to have something, the more these things start coming into your life.

How often should you do this dream-building process, where you go and touch things in real life instead of just looking at pictures? The more often and consistently, the better. Do it every week if you can. Some of you will do a little of this every day.

Dream building should be a constant, ongoing process.

Do you know the richest people in the world do dream building DAILY?

I was chatting earlier with one of my friends, a billionaire, one of several billionaires I was with from Malaysia, and we're constantly dream building. Every time we're together, we do some dream building.

He has enough money that you assume he can buy anything he wants, but we're still out there dream building.

We're still looking at things, expanding our capacity to dream BIGGER; we're still experiencing NEW things, we're still touching and seeing NEW things because we're still always working on building up our dreams and increasing our power of imagination.

Dream building is a very effective and critical technique.

The last technique I will share here to "feel better" is to use the power of gratitude and appreciation.

This is something you should do automatically every morning and every night. You should do this as a habit every morning and every night, no matter how good or bad you feel.

You need to understand that every single person on the planet has something that they should be thankful for, that they should be grateful for, that should make them feel blessed, that they should appreciate.

Here is the drill. Every morning, as soon as you wake up, ask yourself the question, What am I thankful for? This gets you focused on something.

No matter how bad things are in your life, there's absolutely something you can focus on that you can be thankful for. And it doesn't matter what it is.

I'm thankful for my great health.

I'm thankful for having such a wonderful, lovely wife.

I'm thankful for all of the experiences I've had up until now.

I'm thankful for living in a beautiful world.

I'm thankful for this gorgeous, sunny, magnificent day.

I'm thankful for that tree that I can look at and enjoy.

I'm thankful for this beautiful river that goes by outside of our windows that we can look at.

I'm thankful for that beautiful meal we had.

I'm thankful for these shoes I'm wearing.

I'm thankful for my wonderful mother and how much love she's given me.

I'm thankful for the success I've had in my life.

You can pick anything to be thankful for.

I'm thankful that I'm still alive.

I'm thankful that I'm breathing.

I'm thankful that I have the ability to think.

I'm thankful that I have the ability to think of things that I'm thankful for.

Go through this little exercise every morning for just a few minutes. One or two minutes in the morning and one or two minutes right before you go to bed. Just think, what am I thankful for?

When you think of that, everything starts to change because you're now putting out and transmitting vibrations of love and appreciation and thankfulness. And the universe will start moving heaven and earth and even start moving mountains to give you MORE things to be thankful and grateful for.

Remember this power that you have. When you put out a vibration, that vibration relates to a feeling, and the universe will give you circumstances, situations, conditions, events, and people in your life that will give you matching feelings. Feelings that will match the vibration that you're putting out.

So if you are putting out a vibration of how lucky I feel, how blessed I feel, how lucky I am, how blessed I am, how thankful I am, how much I appreciate this … Thank You, Thank You, Thank You, Thank You, Thank You … If you put out the vibration of Thank You, Thank You, Thank You, Thank You, Thank You … guess what's going to happen in your life?

You have no idea what they will be, but those things that will come in will be situations, circumstances, events, people, and conditions that give you the same feeling of: thank you, thank you, thank you.

If you're vibrating thank you, thank you, thank you, thank you, guess what comes in your life?

Circumstances and events that make you feel MORE thankful, MORE grateful, MORE appreciative.

If you're vibrating "That makes me mad, I'm so frustrated," guess what's going to come into your life?

More events, circumstances, and people that make you feel, "That makes me so mad, I'm frustrated."

Do you understand? That's why the simplest way to create a magical life without going crazy is to just simply transmit feelings without any specific attachment to a thing or a time. It makes life so much more of a wonder.

Yes, you can focus on one thing and say, "I really want that."

But balance it out throughout the day by focusing on feelings of gratitude, appreciation, and thankfulness.

Thank You, Thank You, Thank You, Thank You, Thank You, Thank You.

Thank you for the miracles in my life.

Thank you for the wonder in my life.

Thank you for this wonderful feeling of just feeling great.

Thank you for the amazing things that are happening in my life.

Thank you for the feelings. Thank you for the feelings.

Thank you for making me feel so good.

Thank you for making me feel so good.

Thank you for making me feel so good.

Thank you.

I feel so great.

Thank you.

I am so lucky.

I feel so lucky.

I feel so lucky.

I feel so lucky.

When you start doing this, you are now transmitting that feeling with power and intensity. And guess what's going to be coming into your life? Throughout the day you're going to have more thoughts of things that will make you feel lucky. Thankful. Blessed. Wow. Wonder. Excitement. Gratitude. Appreciation. Happiness. Joy.

And then you're going to start getting events, circumstances, and people which make you feel that exact same way.

That's how it works.

So you must feel as good as you can, now. It is the most important thing every day.

Number one is to feel good now. And when you don't feel good, use the tools I gave you to feel BETTER. You should be using as many of these tools as you need on a regular basis.

If you use the tools I gave you, you will start to establish a high base level of feeling good. Your default feeling will be higher than it is now. You will feel good as a baseline. This way it will be rare that you feel bad.

So if you're eating right; if you're taking nutritional whole food supplements; if you've done some cleansing to get toxins out; if you have some electromagnetic chaos eliminators; if you're walking on a regular basis, ideally every day, but a couple of times a week; if you're using a rebounder on a regular basis or vibration plate or inversion table; if you're reading books every day; if you're listening to audios every day, even for fifteen minutes; if you're going to seminars on a regular basis, maybe once a month or once a quarter; if you're listening to your favorite music; if you're playing musical instruments; if you're outside getting some sun; if you're hugging people on a regular basis every day; if you're laughing every day; if you're smiling every day; if you get massages once in a while; if you're getting a sauna once in a while; if you have a pet and you play with your pet on a regular basis; if you're doing something creative with your hands, like painting or pottery, something creative on a regular basis; if you're dancing on a regular basis, by yourself, for those of you who think, "I'm afraid of dancing in public," once a day, dance for a little bit; if you're singing on a regular basis, just sing in the shower; if you're cooking on occasion to create something with your hands, if you enjoy that; if you're planting things on a regular basis; playing in a garden … guess what? If you're doing all those things on a regular basis, you're going to be feeling better and better and better.

If you're doing dream building on a regular basis, and ideally physically touching things, going to places, doing that as an exercise, you WILL be working on deprogramming your subconscious mind.

If you use the Callahan tapping technique when you feel bad, you WILL start to eliminate those stored energetic imprints that get keyed in or activated and make you have uncontrollable and irrational emotions.

And if you're doing what we call the appreciation drill every morning and every night, first thing you do when you wake up, and right before you go to bed, where you say "What am I thankful for?" And just start saying, "I feel lucky. What do I feel lucky about? I feel blessed. What do I feel blessed about?" And you start doing this every morning and every night, guess what? You're going to feel so much better every day and every day and every day and every day, and that ball of positive energy is going to get bigger and bigger and bigger and bigger and bigger.

Your ability to focus, your ability to transmit those things that you want, dramatically go up.

Then, when you do feel horrible, which will happen from time to time, when you get slapped with those divorce papers or you find out you have some horrible physical illness, or somebody that you loved died in a car crash, and you feel terrible, use the Callahan technique. Make sure you have access to that.

Join Global Information Network (GIN) and get access to the free seminar at www.GlobalInformationNetwork.com.

Learn how to do this on your own and use that technique; it takes less than five minutes and it permanently eliminates that trauma. You need this powerful tool. When you use it, you will immediately feel better.

When you are feeling "good" and you don't have counter-intentions distracting you, you can focus on manifesting your desires. You can focus on what you WANT.

"You know, I want to get out of debt." Okay. Now you focus on what you want: "I want to get out of debt." You don't put a timeline on it YET, you just start transmitting that with energy. And the energy is: "I'm *getting* out of debt."

Then think, "How am I going to feel when I get out of debt?" And you'll start getting that emotion of anticipation and feeling good. You will begin to notice that it's going to be much easier for you to believe that you can achieve your goals and objectives.

When you're doing all these techniques you will start feeling good every day, every day, every day, because your ball of positive energy is going to get bigger.

When you build up your dreams, you just begin to KNOW that it CAN happen even though you don't know HOW just yet. You stop focusing on the how in the beginning of this process. You know the HOW will show up in time, if you just have FAITH NOW. You know there are things OFF your radar screen that you can't even imagine now. So you TRUST the process and feel good now.

It's perfectly okay to say, "I'm getting out of debt, and I don't know how," because that's true. You don't know HOW.

You can say, "I have no idea HOW I am getting out of debt. As a matter of fact, based on the information that I have, it doesn't appear that I will be able to get out of debt. I can't imagine how I'm going to get out of debt, but I know I *will,* and I know it will happen exactly at the right time. And I know everything is going to be perfect, I feel good now, and I know getting out of debt is going to happen, and it's going to happen because the Law of Attraction works. I'm putting out that energy, that vibration, that frequency, and I'm feeling NOW AS IF I WILL feel when I AM out of debt. I have no idea how long it's going to take, and it doesn't really make a difference how long it's going to take."

How long should you actually do that exercise? You want to do it at least for a minute and a half, at least for ninety seconds. CAN you consciously do that? Yes. WILL you consciously do that? That is YOUR choice alone. You have within you the power of life and death. You have the power to create or destroy. It is YOUR choice. Your wish is YOUR command.

If you DO engage the process, you will start activating the Law of Attraction. The more you do the process throughout the day, the better it is. Why?

Because you become or you get what you think about most of the time.

So a key element is: Feel Good Now. Actually feel as good as you can right now. Work on feeling a little better. Then, just a little better. THEN, just a little better. One step at a time.

Feeling good allows you to increase desire. It will motivate and inspire you to action. When you feel good, you become happier. You become energized. You become more enthusiastic. You start to get a bounce in your step. You become a little more confident.

Let me give you two other things that you can do to help increase *desire* so that you start focusing more on those things that you want instead of those things that you don't want.

We talked about dream building, but I would suggest two additional elements to dream building.

One is called a Dream book. I would get a three-ring spiral binder with pages you can put in and take out. I would make this your Dream book.

Anytime you think of something you want or desire, WRITE IT IN YOUR DREAM BOOK. Anytime you have an idea of something you want in your life, no matter how crazy it is, WRITE IT DOWN IN YOUR DREAM BOOK.

You may think, "I want to learn to speak German." Just grab your book and on the page just write: I want to learn how to speak German. This does not mean that dream will ever become a GOAL that you set out to achieve. This book contains just your DREAMS.

You may think, "I want to learn how to cook a soufflé. I want to get out of debt. I want a Ferrari. I want a yacht. I want to travel to Vienna and have coffee there. I want to have a luxury jet." No matter how crazy it is, write it down in your Dream book.

It could be something as simple as I want to lose thirty pounds, or I want to drink Cristal Champagne for the first time in my life. I want to have a private chef. I want to have a better relationship with my kids.

Whatever it is, all throughout the day, when you think of anything that you might possibly desire, WRITE IT DOWN IN YOUR DREAM BOOK.

You should have this book with you always, because it forces you to think of things that you want. It forces you to dream. It forces you to think of things you want instead of things you don't want. It makes you feel better.

WRITE DOWN YOUR DREAMS AND DESIRES. Write them down, write them down.

Then, every once in a while, grab that whole list and rewrite it. Clean it up, if you will, because some of those dreams that you had maybe you don't want anymore. Write it down on white paper with blue ink. Don't use a computer.

Magic happens when you do this. Something magical happens when you take a thought which is in the ether and transfer that thought into the physical universe by writing it down on white paper with a pen with blue ink.

There's a reason why writing IN CURSIVE is much more powerful than typing into a computer.

When you type, your fingers actually create only eight neural pathways in the brain. So you think a thought, you type it, but you're taking that thought and only establishing and using eight neural pathways in the brain because you have only eight effective movements when typing.

But when you physically write IN CURSIVE, there are THOUSANDS of neural pathways established in the brain. THIS MAKES ALL THE DIFFERENCE. It does not matter what language you are writing. Whether it's English, German, French, Russian, Chinese whatever it is, Arabic, it doesn't make a difference.

When you physically write something down on paper, you're actually feeling the thought because the hand is actually moving. You are transferring THOUGHT into the PHYSICAL PLANE of existence. When you write in cursive, there are over ten thousand various intricate movements that can happen.

So you start creating over ten thousand neural pathways in the brain, *new* neural pathways that correspond to your THOUGHTS, to your DESIRES and dreams. When you WRITE DOWN what you want, you are virtually planting INTO YOUR BRAIN what you desire! And your brain will begin to broadcast that frequency twenty-four hours a day, seven days a week. Your subconscious then starts working on manifesting your dreams, even when you are sleeping!

Writing down your dreams and desires is much more effective and will produce faster results.

Almost all the richest people always write, write, write, write, write. We don't type things into the computer that often. Yes, we use technology, when we write things on our phone's "notes" or into various digital documents. I am typing this book on a computer. BUT we ALL use massive amounts of pens and white paper. We WRITE things on PAPER constantly.

It's interesting to note, our EMPLOYEES, the people who work *for us*, all type things into the computer. They rarely write things down on paper.

People who have the top positions write ON PAPER. Usually with a pen with blue ink and usually with white paper.

So, writing dreams down by hand is really an important key ingredient to manifesting your goals and dreams.

Now you have a dream book. It is really a book where you write down a list of what you want or maybe want. You should be writing in this book VERY often, daily if possible. Constantly THINKING about potential things you WANT.

Then from time to time, go through your dream book and clean up. REWRITE your dreams. Eliminate things you don't want anymore. This will re-energize you.

One pro tip. DON'T SHARE YOUR DREAM BOOK WITH ANYONE. Don't share your dreams with others. KEEP THEM TO YOURSELF.

Next ...

The next powerful tool you NEED is what's called a dream board, sometimes called a vision board.

Your dream board is for YOU to look at, NO ONE ELSE. So put it where NO ONE WILL SEE IT, but where YOU can see it OFTEN. You COULD put your dream board in your dream book.

Your dream board is where you put *pictures* of things that you potentially want.

Pictures of an island because you want to travel to the Caribbean. Pictures of a yacht because maybe you want a boat. Pictures of your dream house. Pictures of a fur, jewelry, cars, maybe pictures of happy families. Pictures of someone with the body you dream about with YOUR face.

You create this with your hands. You do it yourself. You cut out pictures and put them on your dream board.

Ideally you have yourself in the pictures. When you go to the car dealer, have someone take a picture of you sitting in your dream car. Put that picture on your dreamboard. When you visit your dream house, have someone take a picture of you in front of your dream house. Put that picture on your dreamboard.

This whole process of creating your dream board with your hands is POWERFUL. It will help you manifest those dreams faster and easier than you can imagine. Doing the process of MAKING a dream board forces you to think about these things that you want, with emotion, for a longer period of time.

Remember, you get what you think about most of the time.

Does that make sense?

You get what you think about most of the time.

So what we're trying to do here is get you to think about what you want most of the time and feel good about it when you think of it.

This technique is really: Think about what you want, with power and intensity, and feel NOW AS IF you WOULD feel if you were actually in possession of your desire.

When you look at this dream board creating technique, what are its components when you break it down?

Think about what you want and feel good about it when you think of it. Because if you're feeling good when you think about what you want, that means you **believe** it will manifest. If you feel bad, that means you don't believe it will manifest.

If you feel bad when you think about what you want, this means your dream is too big. It's not in the sweet spot. Or it means you still have to work on your belief by doing the various things that we talked about. That means your ball of negative energy is way too big.

Does this make sense?

So basically, think of various ways that you can do things that will force you to think about what you want most of the time.

Some people think, "Well, I'm going to put a picture of my key, most important dream on my car visor. This way, when I'm driving to work for an hour, I'm staring at it." Perfect.

"I put it on my mirror in the bathroom, so when I'm shaving and getting ready in the morning, I'm looking at it." Perfect.

"I put it on the ceiling in my bedroom. So when I'm in bed, right before I go to bed, and the first thing when I wake up, I look up and I see it, and I'm reminded to think about my desire and feel good." Perfect.

"I make a habit of going through my dream book a couple of times a day." Perfect.

"I put a card in my jacket pocket, or I carry it with me in my purse or pants pocket. I have it laminated because I want to feel it and remember that it's always there. This will remind me to look at it." Perfect.

"I put it on my keychain so that I'm always reminded about what I want. So that I'm thinking about it." Perfect.

"I put pictures of my dreams on my refrigerator, because I live alone, and I am the only person to see it." Perfect.

When you look at that picture of your desire, think about what you want, and feel good about it, you are putting out a vibration into the universe. And the Law of Attraction will make it manifest in your life and become your reality.

As long as you don't worry about the time frame, about WHEN it will manifest, and you just feel good about it NOW, it *will* manifest.

Here's the other thing. I want to emphasize this.

If you're thinking about one particular thing, such as "I want *this* new watch," you have a feeling attached to getting this new watch. It's a specific feeling. So when you're putting out that vibration, that vibration is for the new watch.

But the ***good feeling*** you have for that new watch is also being put out into the universe as simply a GOOD FEELING. So the universe will not only manifest for you the new watch, but the universe is going to bring into you circumstances, events, and people that will give you the same or similar *feeling* that you're vibrating.

So when you're broadcasting vibrations and frequencies of feeling GOOD, you're getting good vibrations and good situations back in your life.

Very, very powerful.

So, there are two basic concepts here. First is, you must ***look at*** PICTURES of what you want as often as possible. You get what you think about most of the time.

What you want should be in the sweet spot, as I have previously described and defined the sweet spot. You will always know you are in the sweet spot because you will feel good when you think of what you want.

Does that make sense?

And if you want to focus on one thing all day, it's feel good now, or feel as best as you can. Work on feeling BETTER.

Anytime you don't feel good, that just means that you're not thinking about the right thing, or some energetic imprint is activated, keyed in, stimulated, or one of your "buttons is pushed."

If this happens, USE THE CALLAHAN TECHNIQUE. It is the SINGLE MOST POWERFUL and FASTEST way to eliminate negative feelings. Within five minutes you can go from crying and feeling horrible to laughing and feeling pure happiness.

You may say to yourself, "I feel horrible. I just got this bad news, and I have no idea why it's going to be good. And I can't even make myself feel better about it. So I don't want to think about that. Let me think about something else. What can I feel good about? Well, what do I feel lucky about in my life? I CAN'T think of anything positive. I CAN'T change my thoughts or emotions." If this happens, SOMETHING IS KEYED IN. You are HELPLESS and POWER-LESS. You have an uncontrollable emotion. It may even be irrational.

This is when you NEED the Callahan technique. It will work when nothing else will, and it will work in under five minutes. Your negative feelings will VANISH. Use this powerful tool. Join www.GlobalInformationNetwork.com to get the three-hour seminar where I personally teach you how to use this method FREE.

Only when your uncontrollable emotions have been neutralized will you be able to find something positive to think about so you can change your thoughts. Your new thoughts will cause you to start transmitting a new frequency, a new vibration, which will attract more like-minded, good-feeling thoughts.

This is how you can turn yourself around and take CONTROL over your emotions and life instead of having your emotions and thoughts control you.

Initially, you're going to be at the conscious competence level at doing this. But after a short period of time, you're going to get to the unconscious competence level of doing this. And then it just happens like you are on autopilot.

This is why, when I deal with people at the highest levels of awareness, consciousness, and success, we're sitting around laughing and joking most of the time, regardless of how THINGS in life might be going. We are in CONTROL of our thoughts and emotions. They do NOT control us. NO ONE can make us angry or feel a certain way. WE decide how we are going to feel and what we are going to think.

One time I was with a successful friend. We're telling stories and we're laughing. We're having dinner. This guy is a billionaire from the Middle East. A high-ranking member of a royal family.

And we're just laughing and laughing and laughing.

And then I asked, "So, what's going on in your businesses in China?"

He said, "All disaster, disaster, terrible, terrible. It looks like it's all crumbling. I will lose most of my money. I had almost everything invested in this venture. I made a terrible mistake."

And he's laughing as he is telling me this.

I said, "It doesn't seem like you're worried about it."

He replied, "Oh, it's terrible. It's the worst I've ever seen. I have no idea how things are going to turn around. But I know it'll all work out. It always does. So maybe I have to live in tents for a while. I don't know."

That's the difference between winners and losers. Winners and losers both get knocked down. Losers stay down. Winners get up. They never quit. Winners never quit and quitters never win.

Successful people are not people without problems. They are simply people who OVERCOME their problems.

We do this method automatically. It is part of us now. It is in our DNA. It is in our subconscious. We are unconsciously competent in the application of this method. It is like we are on autopilot. You can get there too.

The situation, no matter how bad it is, ***doesn't make us feel bad for very long***. We know that there's some reason for it happening and that we created it. In every situation you either WIN or LEARN. We never look at a situation as BAD. It is always either a WIN or a learning experience, so in effect ALL situations work to OUR ADVANTAGE. This is the BILLIONAIRE MINDSET.

We understand that all situations in our lives are things WE created.

Someone will ask, "Well, how could you create that disaster when you're feeling so good all the time?"

Here is the reason. Sometimes you need to tear something down before you can build a new structure. If you want something NEW, you first have to create space for it, a VOID. You can't build a new building until you tear down the existing one.

Sometimes you have to destroy things FIRST. Sometimes things have to be destroyed before you can build a new structure.

The universe knows the best way to get us to where we want to go. TRUST the process. Have FAITH in the universal intelligence and the Law of Attraction.

You don't know how, in the grand scheme of things, everything is being worked out for your benefit. In the Bible it says, "All things work together for GOOD for those who love and serve the lord."

Imagine you're putting out into the universe a vibration: "I want a new house. I want a new house. I want a new house. I want a new house." Then all of a sudden, your house catches on fire and burns to the ground. It seems like a disaster. But it IS NOT. Believe me, the universe is working it all out FOR YOU and setting it up so that you're getting that new house. The first step was to create this fire and get rid of your existing house. Maybe it was because you needed more intensity in your broadcasting of your desire and a greater sense of urgency of NEEDING a new house.

The universe does not do things TO us, it does things FOR us.

You have no idea the intricacies and the variables that are being put in play. There are trillions and trillions of puzzle pieces that the universe has to manipulate to manifest your dreams and desires. TRUST THE PROCESS.

You don't really have to worry about anything.

Does that make sense?

TRUST THE PROCESS.

And remember, THE UNIVERSE DOES NOT DO THINGS TO US, IT DOES THINGS FOR US!

LESSON 12

Power Words and the Essence of Manifestation

We have covered a lot of material so far. Yet it is just the tip of the iceberg. My training in the Brotherhood lasted from 1969 to 2009, including spending seven months in a cave in the Himalaya mountains. I trained a minimum of twenty hours a week. Many weeks, I would spend eighty to a hundred hours engaged in the most rigorous "training" you could imagine. When I left the Brotherhood, I continued my training with the spiritual masters: enlightened, self-realized beings that had taken me beyond the veil. I am, and will always be, a student.

In the Your Wish is Your Command live event, this part of the book was the start of the second day. I remember everyone was smiling. Everyone was so happy. They FELT different. So many attendees came up to me sharing stories of how the manifesting method was ALREADY working and creating results.

I recall this one particular gentleman who was single, had just never been able to attract or manifest a fulfilling romantic relationship. He was working on that as a primary objective.

It's great to be in a relationship. He was really focusing on that. That was the one thing he was working on manifesting. Then the previous night, he went off by himself to a restaurant, and a woman just came right up to him and started chatting. They got into a conversation and ended up having dinner.

I asked him if he was amazed, and he was, but he also was NOT amazed, because he was EXPECTING good things to happen after the first day of the live seminar.

People always ask when you do this, are you surprised at the results? And the answer is, if you're doing this effectively, you are not surprised at the results because you expect it.

So it's no surprise that you start manifesting what you want. That is what is SUPPOSED to happen.

You are not surprised when you manifest what you want, because you've actually experienced HAVING IT in your mind first, as if it's already happened. So when it DOES happen, when it DOES manifest, it's actually no surprise.

In the movie *The Empire Strikes Back*, the Jedi Master Yoda was training the young Jedi apprentice, Luke Skywalker. In one particular scene, Luke Skywalker's X-wing fighter had landed in a swamp. Yoda was teaching Luke how to use the Force to lift the fighter out of the swamp with his mind and move it onto dry land so he could take off.

Luke said, "I'll give it a try." Yoda responded, "NO. Do or do not. There is no try." Luke tried to do this, and the X-wing began to lift and then went back down into the swamp and sank.

Yoda then, frustrated with Luke and his inability to grasp this, used the Force, lifted the fighter out of the swamp with his mind and moved it onto dry land.

When Luke saw Yoda do this, Luke said: "Oh, my, I don't believe it!"

Yoda said, "That is why you fail."

Luke failed because he did not BELIEVE. And that's why he couldn't do it in the beginning, because he didn't believe it.

From a scriptural standpoint, there's an interesting story in the Bible about Jesus, who was walking on water. Peter the Apostle was looking at Jesus walking on water and was so excited, he went out of the boat to greet Jesus.

The Bible says that Peter walked on water. It says *as* Peter was walking on the water, Peter looked down and saw that he was walking on the water by himself. He saw the waves and the water, became frightened, and began to sink.

Now, this is exactly what we're talking about. When you start thinking about what you don't want to happen, when fear and doubt come in, when you take your eye off what you WANT, all of a sudden you get the opposite result.

There are many Bible stories about belief. A woman with an incurable issue of blood said to herself, "If I can just touch the hem of Jesus's garment, I will be healed." She did and she was healed. Jesus looked at her and said, "Your FAITH has healed you."

The Bible said Jesus traveled throughout Israel and healed ALL who were ill. But when he went back to his hometown of Nazareth, where everyone knew him from the time he was a boy, the Bible says Jesus could perform NO miracles because of their DISBELIEF.

There is power in belief. Miracles happen because of your BELIEF, or confidence that what you want WILL happen. This is faith. This is trusting the universe and the universal laws.

Remember what you really, really, really want, you'll get, but also what you really, really, really don't want, you'll get that too. Whatever you're thinking about, with intensity, emotion, and belief, you'll get.

And if you're thinking about what you don't want to happen, you will know that because you feel crummy. When you feel crummy, what you DON'T want is coming into your life and will manifest.

So, to get what you REALLY want in life, anything and everything you REALLY feel like you NEED, just do the procedure. Engage the formula with deliberate intent.

You define what you don't want anymore in your life, that thing that you will not tolerate anymore. Then you define what you DO want. You picture it in your mind. You see yourself in possession of your desire. Focus on that with intensity and power, which means emotion, positive anticipation, as if you already have it. You BELIEVE it WILL happen. You feel good NOW.

Do that process for a certain duration every day. The more the better, at least for a minute and a half each time. Most importantly, you have to believe that what you desire WILL manifest in your life without any doubt.

Which means you just need to focus on what you want and not what you don't want. And you know you are doing the process correctly because as you do that procedure, you'll feel good. You will feel like you just placed your order, your credit card was charged, and you got the email saying YOUR ORDER IS ON THE WAY. You KNOW it IS coming.

Do the procedure, which is defining what you do NOT want anymore in your life and contract the energy into a NEGATIVE energy, then think about what you want, see a picture in your mind of you in possession of your desire, feel now AS IF you were in possession of your desire, and anticipating that you've already received it. You then feel good now.

You know you're doing the procedure correctly if you're excited and you feel really good. See yourself in the picture of you already in possession of your desire and feel now AS IF you actually were in possession of your desire, and if you're feeling as if you've already achieved it, that's the ultimate.

Then throughout the day, always work on your emotions and work on feeling good as much of the time as you can, because that will get your positive energy up and make the procedure easier to apply, making everything happen faster.

At this point in the live event there were several questions about actions, the how versus the thoughts. Now we all know that thoughts are 90 percent of this process.

But people wonder if they can sit home and just think and create anything they want without physically doing anything. Don't you have to *do* something?

And the answer is, no, you don't *have* to do anything. However, when you're using this technique, you will *want* to do things. Actions become a joy and a pleasure. The JOURNEY is the reward. You get the ultimate pleasure NOT from attaining your desire, but rather when you are in the act of CREATING and manifesting your desire.

But here's the trick. If you're doing any actions to make something happen because you think you have to make it happen, you are missing the point.

Sometimes people go out there with a feeling of, "We have to do things." They feel like they have to work, work, work, work, work, work to make it happen.

If you're doing any actions to make something happen that you want and you feel frustrated or bad or annoyed doing the actions, your actions will be fruitless. They're not going to create any results.

Your actions should be a joy and a pleasure, even if you're working eighteen hours a day. When you look at all the successful people, we all say the same thing. We love—not just like, but rather, we love—what we're doing.

Doing the WORK, taking the action steps, gives us incredible joy and exhilaration. It is our bliss, because we are in alignment with who we really are. We are living our purpose. We are in the sweet spot.

But the thought process is first and critical. And when the actions become frustrating, that's when people decide, "I'm not going to focus on the actions, because that's making me think about what I don't want to happen and making me feel bad."

So they say, "I'm going to go golfing. I'm going to go to the movies. I'm going to take a vacation. I'm going to go to the beach."

People will look at you and say, "We're in the midst of a crisis. How can you be taking a vacation?"

Because for me to go into the office and start working in the midst of this crisis, I'm going to feel absolutely horrible at this moment in time. So I need to do something so I can feel BETTER because feeling good makes it all work.

So the actions are not that significant, but they ARE important and critical.

And this is why focusing on the how is not ideal to manifesting your dream. When you're looking at your radar screen, and you're thinking, "How can this event work out to my advantage? How am I going to turn the situation around?" you are NOT in the sweet spot. You are NOT broadcasting your desire on the Alpha/Theta wealth wave.

If you are focusing on the HOW, you are only seeing what is on your small radar screen. But remember that 90 percent of all the stuff that's available to the universe to manifest your "impossible desire" is off the radar screen. If you were to see everything OFF your radar screen, you would KNOW with 100 percent certainty that everything you desire is not only possible but can 100 percent manifest into your life.

The universe will provide you with the circumstances, conditions, people, situations, and events needed to manifest your desires because of what you have been vibrating. Everything will work to your advantage IF you BELIEVE.

And when you have that "knowingness" that everything WILL work out, IN TIME, you'll feel good. You will have a sense of peace and inner certainty that is beyond your current comprehension. You'll start saying, "I have no idea how that's going to happen. I don't know why this negative thing is actually a good thing. But I KNOW that everything will work out."

When a bad thing does happen, we understand it's not necessarily a bad thing. As a matter of fact, it never is a bad thing. Remember the scripture, "ALL things work together for GOOD ..."

There's a story about the man many years ago in China who had a son. He said to his friends, "I want my son to be safe and live a long life. There is so much chaos going on in China and so much famine and war. I'm afraid for my son. I'm afraid he could be killed. I'm afraid he could be killed in war. I'm afraid we could die of famine, or he could get sick. I just want my son to live a long, healthy, happy life."

He clearly defined what he did NOT want. He contracted that negative energy. He got MAD. He then clearly defined what he DID want and saw himself in possession of that. He felt NOW AS IF what he wanted was a reality.

The man had one horse. It was everything to the family. Without the horse, the family could not plow the fields and would starve.

One day the horse broke out of his corral and ran away. All the man's friends said, "I am so sorry you lost your horse. That is a terrible tragedy."

The man replied "Maybe bad, maybe good. Things will work out."

A week later the horse came back, bringing with it ten wild horses. The man corralled them all. Suddenly he was rich. All of the man's friends said, "You have such good fortune. It is so good you have all these horses and you are now rich."

The man replied, "Maybe it is good, maybe not."

One day his son was trying to break one of the wild horses and fell off the horse and broke his leg. All of his friends said, "Oh, what a terrible thing. Your son fell off the horse and broke his leg."

The father smiled and said, "I don't think it's a terrible thing. I don't know why, but I think, actually, it's a good thing. I feel good. I am grateful my son did not die."

The next day, the Chinese Army came riding into town, and they took all the young men to fight in the war, which meant almost certain death. But they didn't take this man's son because he had a broken leg.

The story goes on and on and on to talk about how each situation that happened to the man which appeared to be bad at the time turned out to be a blessing. But you could not SEE HOW the bad thing would turn out to be a blessing at the time it happened.

The key is, you don't need to know how a bad thing will turn out to be a blessing when it happens. You have to have FAITH.

In every adversity is the seed of a greater benefit.

The key is your thought process, how you think. The evidence of how you're thinking is twofold.

Number one, how are you feeling? If you're feeling good, that means your thought process is right. If you're feeling bad, that means it's not.

The other evidence is what you're saying. What are the words you're saying? Are you looking at things as they are? Are you focusing on what you don't want or what seems to be terrible? Or are you looking forward and creating tomorrow with anticipation?

The words that you say really are a strong indicator of your thoughts.

Using spoken words correctly is another powerful technique that will help you manifest your desires. Use your words wisely and say things in a way which will help focus your thoughts.

The words you speak out loud and the words in your head that you say silently are very important because they help focus your thoughts.

They do two things. They show you what you're thinking SUB-CONSCIOUSLY, but they also help create and focus your thoughts.

By using certain words, with conscious, deliberate intent, in a certain way, you will increase your ability to focus your thoughts in the correct manner.

In the Brotherhood, we did very extensive work on activating and illuminating words. This is a time-consuming process where you take a word and look it up in a large, detailed dictionary. You read all the definitions of the word. You see the history of the word and its origins. You learn about the original meaning of the word. You then use the word in several sentences so you "feel good about it." This will ACTIVATE and ILLUMINATE that word, releasing the energetic vibration of the word and allowing you to use words like a magician. Your spoken words then have creative power.

When people join the Global Information Network (GIN), Members get free access to my written course, the Science of Personal Mastery. This is the actual Brotherhood training I received over many decades. Included is the Activating and Illuminating words processes. This is extremely powerful.

When you speak out loud, you have creative power. The tongue is a creative force. What you SAY is what you GET.

I've been using certain words in this book and giving you a lot of phrases. When I use a word, it is full of active energy, frequency, and vibration. That is why when you read this book or hear me speak, you feel changed from the inside.

Listening to the audio version of this book is very powerful because you HEAR me speak using activated and illuminated words that have creative power.

This is another reason why reading this book over and over or listening to the audios over and over is so effective at deprogramming you from your failure habits and reprogramming you for SUCCESS!

Being able to speak with creative power takes some time. You have to start developing NEW speech patterns, NEW neural pathways, and a NEW vocabulary that you use with deliberate intent. This is another reason why you need to associate with successful people. You speak in a similar manner as your friends and the voices that you listen to. If you listen to the right audios from successful people and start hanging around successful people, you will HEAR successful words and speech patterns. You will then start duplicating those patterns.

THIS IS CRITICAL. Remember, your income is the average of your five best friends'. This is why joining a club like the Global Information Network (GIN) is so vital for you if you want to succeed in life. You have to have success-oriented friends and you have to be LISTENING to audios from successful people who are using SUCCESS words and speech patterns.

THEN you will get to the unconscious competence level and start speaking the correct activated and illuminated words automatically. You will start using the correct "magical" speech patterns that manifest goals automatically.

The words and speech patterns are automatic for me and the other people in the societies.

You need to start using activated and illuminated POWER WORDS and start developing new POWER MANIFESTING speech patterns. This will start developing NEW neural pathways in your brain and get you broadcasting on the Alpha/Theta billionaire brain wave. You do this by reading material from someone who is USING power words that have been activated, and illuminated and using these specific manifesting and success programming speech patterns. Also you need to LISTEN to speakers who are using these words and speech patterns, so that you start mimicking and modeling their words and speech patterns.

When you read and listen as I described, and with deliberate intent, start using those words and speech patterns when you speak out loud and THINK thoughts, you will start developing NEW predominant thought patterns, which will start developing NEW predominant constant vibrations that you're transmitting out of your brain. This will then create more like-minded positive vibrations, making this manifesting process work better and faster.

There are various things that you have to say OUT LOUD, verbally with your mouth, daily.

I suggest you start right now and read these OUT LOUD. I also suggest that later you take the keywords in each phrase and do the activating and illuminating processes I described. Then come back and read the phrases again. I also suggest you write these down and read them OUT LOUD daily.

Everything always works out for me.

I'm lucky.

I'm blessed.

This appears to be really negative, but I know everything will work out fine.

Everything will work out fine.

Everything IS fine.

I don't know how, but everything always works out fine in the end.

All is well.

Everything is just fine.

I expect miracles, and I get miracles.

Everything always turns out to my advantage in the end.

This will ultimately work out to my benefit.

Every day, in every way, I am getting better, better, and better.

I am a winner.

I am a champion.

If I think I can or think I can't, either way, I am right; it is the
thinking that makes it so.

I was born to win.

I am winning.

I can do it.

I am doing it.

Winners never quit and quitters never win. I am a winner.

When the going gets tough, the tough get going. I am TOUGH.

Those are the type of speech patterns I am talking about. You can
call these phrases "Nuggets of Gold." I have a list of hundreds of these
available to you for FREE. Visit www.NuggetsOfGold.com or buy my
book, *Nuggets of Gold for Total Success*, at www.KevinTrudeau.com.

When you understand the incredible concept that using activated
and illuminated words with proper speech patterns actually gives
your WORDS creative power, life becomes so much more of a pleasure, and life becomes so much easier as you go forward. You begin
to realize that your wish is virtually your COMMAND.

Does that make sense?

At the live event, a question came up at this point. Someone asked,
"What if I'm doing everything? I'm doing the technique. I seem to
be doing everything. I'm doing everything on the list. I'm going for
walks. I'm eating right, I'm doing the Callahan tapping technique,
I am doing all these things. I'm really doing this technique, and I'm
feeling really good all day long, but nothing seems to be happening.
I'm not getting what I want. I'm thinking about it all the time, but
it's just not manifesting. Nothing in my life seems to be changing.
Am I doing something wrong?"

Another similar question came up where someone asked, "What
if I do all these things and something bad happens? Like I'm really
feeling good today, tomorrow, and the next day. Then out of nowhere

something horrible appears or what I want just doesn't seem to be coming in."

Number one, don't put a time frame on things. These questions show that the person does NOT have belief. DOUBT has crept in. Doubt can sink a ship.

Also, these people were giving me an example of something that hasn't really occurred. It was a "What IF" question. They were just thinking, what if this occurs?

If you think of WHAT IF, you have DOUBT. You do not have faith or belief. You are NOT broadcasting on the Alpha/Theta billionaire manifesting brain wave. You are broadcasting on the Beta, or slave or poverty brain wave.

Over the decades of using this material and seeing thousands of others use this material, I can say I have seen it all. Some people start using this technique today and tomorrow and they say, "Hey, it's the third day. Where is it? How come what I want has not manifested yet?"

Remember, at this point in the training, don't put a time limit on WHEN your desire MUST manifest. Don't put a time deadline yet because the universe is doing everything at the perfect speed for you, to give you the feeling you want that's ultimately for your benefit. The universe is working on manifesting your desire, but YOU might not be READY yet.

RELAX. Let go. Surrender to the universe. Be in a state of ALLOWING. Be RECEPTIVE.

So don't put a time frame on things, YET. We will get to how and when to set deadlines.

My friend Herb Cohen wrote a book called *You Can Negotiate Anything*. A wonderful Jewish guy from Chicago who taught his seminars while smoking a cigar, in NON-smoking hotels (he NEGOTI-ATED being allowed to smoke his cigars in the seminars).

With his heavy Chicago Jewish accent, he would say, "In life and in negotiation, you have to care, but not that much."

You have to care, but not that much.

That's really the type of attitude you have to have as you go through life.

Don't sweat the small stuff—and it is ALL small stuff.

Most people major in the minors. Major in the majors. And NOTHING is really major.

You have to care, but not that much, when it comes to the time. Because once you start putting emphasis on time deadlines and trying to make it happen, as you get closer to the deadline, doubt starts to come in. You start focusing on what you *don't* want, and THAT really stops the whole process from working anyway.

So you're not getting the benefit when you put a deadline on WHEN what you want is going to manifest. So don't worry about the time deadlines just yet. We will get to that when you are ready. Now, that is too advanced for you. You can't handle it. You are too weak. You have too much negative programming. Your ball of negative energy is too big.

Don't worry about how fast what you want is manifesting, because it *will*. If you do everything right, your order will be placed and on its way to you. RELAX and FEEL GOOD NOW.

If you do this properly, you will not even care that what you are trying to manifest is not physically in your life, because you're experiencing it in your mind and feeling NOW AS IF it actually were in your life. If you DO THIS CORRECTLY, you don't care that you don't have what you are trying to manifest because you FEEL LIKE YOU DO HAVE IT.

And when you're at that point, it'll come in so fast, it'll be ridiculous.

As you start using this technique, manifesting will happen faster and faster and faster because you'll have less and less negative thoughts, counter-intention, doubt or lack of belief, which is going to hinder the process and slow the manifesting of your desires.

What you desire WILL manifest. THIS WORKS. It is PROVEN and has passed the test of time (thousands of years).

Keep in mind, when you're focusing on a particular thing that you want, you're adding the emotion that that thing is going to give you when you get it.

Remember when you do this, the first thing that's going to start coming in is other thoughts that mimic that emotion because of the Law of Attraction.

The next thing that comes in or manifests is the physical experience of circumstances and events, situations, and people that allow you to feel that emotion.

This is why you don't want to be transmitting hate towards somebody, because if you transmit hate or anger towards somebody else, that's going to come into your life and you're going to experience situations or an event where you feel hate and anger.

But if you transmit love towards people, happiness, or if you transmit thoughts about the things that you want that give you great feelings of exhilaration and pleasure, then experiences and situations are going to come into your life that give you that exact same emotion.

So let's say you're happy today, tomorrow, and every day as much as you can be, if you are feeling glee, you're singing, you're dancing, you're feeling great, and you're saying, "I don't know how things are going to turn out, but I know they're going to turn out great. I just know, I can feel it. I'm so happy things are going to turn out fantastic. I don't know how, but I'm looking for this big win. I know I'm going to get this. I don't know WHEN or HOW it will happen, but I KNOW it WILL happen. I just feel great about getting this promotion even though I don't have it yet. And things are going to work out great for me. And, man, I'm getting out of debt. I don't know how, but I'm using the technique."

And a week later, you not only don't get the promotion, but you lose your job. And you think, "How could that have occurred?"

Believe me, when you are vibrating, "I want that promotion. I want that promotion. I want to get out of debt," what you're vibrating is "I want the feeling of having more money and greater status and a better job and working experience."

You are broadcasting, "I want more money, maybe more freedom, more responsibility. And I want to get out of debt."

And all of a sudden, you lose your job. Believe me, the universe got you out of that job. It created a void. It manifested a situation where you get mad and contract energy and more clearly define exactly what you DO want. The universe created a situation where you're going to get a better job or decide you REALLY want to start your own business or a create some other off-the-radar better opportunity you have not even thought of yet.

That's how it works.

That's like the story of the Chinese man and his son. Every situation is neither good nor bad but working TOGETHER for GOOD and helping you ultimately attain your desires.

No situation is bad, although it may appear that way and feel that way. What you think is bad isn't, as long as you're feeling good. There really is no good or bad news. All there is, is news. YOU choose if it is good or bad. That is YOUR decision. Choose wisely.

When something that appears or seems negative happens, don't look at it as bad. Look at it with anticipation and excitement and say, "Wow, it's already happening. Things ARE in motion helping me attain my desires. Things are MOVING. The universe is not doing things TO me but FOR me. And I don't know how this is going to turn out to my advantage, but I KNOW that it is. Something

GOOD is happening for me. Because I feel good, this event can't be bad. All things work together for GOOD."

There is an old saying, "Everything will be fine in the end. If it seems not fine right now, then it is not the end."

We always say during trials and tribulations, "Someday we will look back on this and laugh." That is TRUE. So, knowing it is true, why wait until "someday"? Laugh NOW, in the midst of the challenge you are facing.

That's a very important concept.

And there's one other concept here. When you think things are bad or you lose your job or you come down with an illness, you *think* that's bad. No. Because when you have in your life something that you don't think is good, it forces you to really clearly define and focus on what you want. BAD THINGS ARE A GIFT FROM THE UNIVERSE.

Negative situations create the best opportunity for you to manifest the things in your life you really want. In every adversity are the seeds of a greater benefit.

ALL successful people created the majority of their success OUT OF a NEGATIVE, BAD experience.

When things are not going well, you also have the best opportunity to contract energy and create something that you will NOT tolerate. You clarify exactly what you do NOT want and will not accept any longer.

This is the WHY behind the WHY. Winners love to win. But they HATE losing MORE. We move AWAY from pain with more intensity than we move TOWARD pleasure.

A negative situation also allows us to clarify what we DO want, focus on those things, and create more of them. It will always give us an opportunity to broadcast our desires with more intensity.

So anytime something negative happens in your life, take it as an absolute blessing because it is. Negative or bad situations force you to focus on what you want.

The key here is, when something bad happens in your life, something negative, something that you didn't anticipate, something you don't think is good, here are the steps to take.

Acknowledge it, don't deny it. If it makes you mad and you think it is bad, acknowledge what IS. Don't bury your head in the sand or see everything with rose-colored glasses. CONTRACT energy. FEEL the pain. But you don't LIVE HERE in the state of constantly feeling pain.

Next, WELCOME these negative feelings and emotions. WELCOME the pain and fear. Don't resist it. What you resist, persists. FEEL the pain, the disappointment, the embarrassment, the fear, fully. USE this negative energy to get mad, to MAKE A DECISION that you will NOT TOLERATE THIS ANYMORE.

Then use this negative energy to clearly define what you DO want. SEE yourself in your mind's eye in possession of your desire and FEEL NOW AS IF you were actually in possession of your desire.

This allows the negative energy to TRANSMUTE.

If you are STUCK feeling bad, USE THE CALLAHAN TECHNIQUE.

So the first thing you do is you acknowledge it as what it is. DON'T DENY WHAT IS or your feelings.

"Okay, this happened, and I feel horrible."

Welcome those negative feelings. Allow yourself to feel them fully. DON'T RESIST the negative feelings.

Then, start using your inner POWER to change your thoughts and perspective. Say OUT LOUD something like, "I don't know why this is happening, but this will turn out to my advantage. And I'm going to take this opportunity now to focus on what I want because I know I don't want this. I don't want more of this. I will not take this anymore. Let me think about what I really want."

This really allows you to clarify exactly what you DO want.

In relationships, for example, this happens often. Everyone has experienced the pain of a breakup. No one is immune.

You're in a relationship with somebody and you're arguing, you're fighting, you're not feeling fulfilled, you're not being heard. You are irritated that things just aren't going well. Then your lover leaves you and you are in desperate pain. You feel horrible and alone. You feel unloved and lied to. Feeling this pain is hard. You might be stuck in this negative state. This is the ideal time to use the Callahan technique. In less than five minutes you will feel MUCH better.

When you experience the pain of the breakup, try to take that as the best opportunity in the world to manifest what you DO want. Acknowledge the situation. Don't deny it. Welcome the emotional pain and upset. Try to say out loud something like, "OK, this person left me. I DON'T want to be alone. I will NOT be in a bad, unfulfilling relationship ever again! Now I can clearly define exactly the type of relationship I want because I know exactly what I DO NOT WANT and will NOT tolerate. I was in a relationship, and I wasn't getting my needs met. NEVER AGAIN."

Then, rather than continuing to focus on what you were not getting from this relationship and how terrible it was and how terrible this person was, now clearly figure out, based on your experience with this person, what do you really want NOW?

STOP TALKING ABOUT THE PAST. STOP TELLING YOUR STORY! The more you talk about the past, the more something similar will manifest in your future.

Start talking to yourself about the FUTURE, NOT the past, and talk to yourself about what you WANT NOW.

At this point you can really clearly define what kind of person you want to be in a relationship with. You can clearly define exactly what kind of personality you want in a lover and what kind of life you want. You can define how you want to be treated and how you want to feel.

Any time you go through something "negative," any time you taste bitterness, you can more clearly define what you want, and then manifesting becomes easier and faster.

You go to a buffet and you start tasting some food. You might notice that "I don't like this, I don't want that." You LEARN what you do NOT want and more clearly define what you do want.

When you are at a buffet and you taste different things, if you taste something you hate, it's good. Because now you know what you don't like. Now you can clearly define what you do want.

Life is the same way. Every day life is going to give you experiences and then you can determine your preference.

Do I want this, or do I not want this? Do I like this? Do I not like this? Does this make me feel good? Or does this make me feel bad?

If it makes you feel bad, good. Now you've established that's what you don't want. And when you look for a moment at what you don't want, you can now more clearly define and focus on what you do want.

This allows you to more clearly dial in the proper frequency of what you desire and transmit it, and thus manifest your desire faster and easier.

That's what life is. But most people live in the past, and thus it continues to repeat itself. You LEARN from the past, but don't LIVE in the past.

Yesterday is history, tomorrow is a mystery, but today is a gift— that is why it is called the present.

Life is going to give us a series of things that we don't want, that make us feel bad, and a series of events and circumstances that we do want. This allows us to clarify what we want.

And as time goes on, we become more focused on what we want and on transmitting the frequency and vibrations of what we want. Then we continue to get more and more and more and more and more of what we want.

When something comes into our life, or we observe something that's maybe not in our life but in a friend's life, something that we can imagine we wouldn't want, something that doesn't give us a good feeling, these situations continue to help us clarify what we *do* want and allow us to focus on those things.

When something bad happens in your life, you should pop the champagne.

I can tell you this. When something bad happens, the bigger, the better. The worst things allow you to really focus on what you want and help you manifest what you DO want faster and easier.

The really BAD experiences in your life help you to transmit a beam, with massive power and with massive intensity, of what you do want.

When you can take negative situations and USE them to your advantage, your life will become magical. You are then *capable.* It is ONLY at that point that you become *capable.*

It is only then that you are capable of really generating massive power with your manifesting vibration. Only then can you broadcast with massive intensity a vibration and frequency of what you want.

Only then can you really focus.

In the Brotherhood training, we were "set up" with many massively negative situations in our lives. We were given tremendous amounts of adversity to deal with. THIS is where the rubber meets the road. In these scenarios, manufactured by our "handlers," we were tested. In these situations, the training revealed itself. Most of us passed. Some passed with flying colors.

I was taught that everything you know at the top, you learn at the bottom. It is in the depths of despair where you find yourself and your inner strength. What does not kill you makes you stronger.

A diamond becomes a diamond because it withstood massive amounts of pressure over time. YOU can be a DIAMOND.

When you go through adversity, you think, "I don't want this. I'm sick of this. I'm sick and tired of being sick and tired. I am NOT going to take this anymore."

This is the point where everything can change for you. It is the point where you make a DECISION. This DECISION changes everything. This is when you say, "I am going to do it, THAT'S IT, PERIOD!" Nothing will stop you. Every person will either get out of your way or help you achieve your goal. This is when the entire universe wakes up and takes you seriously. This is when all heaven and earth will conspire on your behalf and make your desire a reality.

Success is a decision away.

Get to the point where you are sick and tired of being sick and tired. That's the point where you stop looking at what you don't want and stop talking about your past. You stop "telling your sad story where you have been the victim."

And the bad circumstances and situations in your life? That's the moment that you stop looking at them. You turn your back to them.

Then you say, "I'm sick of *that.* THIS is what I really want."

And that's when massive desire is developed. That's when you get on fire and get the "burn." When you are on FIRE, people will come from all around just to watch you burn. When you are on FIRE, you GET WHAT YOU WANT IN LIFE.

Massive clarity and desire of what you want is developed. That's when the vibration is thrown out from your brain with massive power and massive intensity, on the Alpha/Theta wealth manifesting wave. This is when you can *focus* on your desire, and you become obsessed with it.

Which means you're thinking about what you want all the time. And you get what you think about most of the time. Because what you're vibrating most of the time is what is being attracted into your life.

Make sense?

But you might be thinking, what if I'm feeling depressed all the time? And I'm having a really hard time feeling good? What if people easily push my buttons, or if the smallest of setbacks make me feel bad?

Well, first off, what that means is you've really developed a lot of NEGATIVE neural pathways, and a lot of failure thinking habits of focusing on the things you don't want. People do this all the time out of *habit.* One thought attracts another like thought, with a like feeling. And then another like thought with another like feeling.

You have failure habits. You can't eliminate failure habits. You must REPLACE them with SUCCESS habits. This book IS deprogramming you from your failure habits AND helping you by PROGRAMMING you with success habits. But you must DO the mentioned processes with deliberate intent, ideally daily, so that over the next few weeks or months you'll REPLACE your failure habits and programming with success habits and programming. This is on YOU.

Repeat out loud: If it is to be, it is up to me!

Say that three times out loud.

I see people all the time who are negative. They are thinking about the negative all the time. When they speak, it is always negative. They don't realize it. They are not aware of it. They are ASLEEP. It's their habit and their pattern.

This means they have this huge ball of negative energy that they're walking around with.

Example: A person walks into a meeting. He has a cup of coffee. He puts the coffee cup down on the table. And the first thing he says, virtually to himself, but loud enough for others to hear it is, "Now watch me spill this."

See, he's instantly thinking about: I'm going to spill the coffee. Which he does. People are always putting a negative spin on everything. They see the cup as half EMPTY instead of half FULL. When you get to the advanced training, if you looked at the cup, you would NOT think it is half empty OR half full. You would think, "I can always REFILL THE CUP!"

Because of habits and the neural pathways in the brain they have established, most people are thinking about what they don't want. They're thinking about what they hope won't happen.

Worry, thus, is simply negative goal-setting. Worry is simply thinking about what you don't want to happen. Worry is a HABIT. Worry will SLOW down the process of manifesting your desires.

At this point in your life, you have developed a huge negative habit pattern. For you to go from where you are to complete bliss is an impossible jump. It is too steep a gradient.

Whatever negative emotion you are feeling, all you want to do is feel a little better, a little relief.

If you're depressed, wouldn't it be better if you felt anger? Because that's a little bit better than feeling depressed. If you're depressed, you actually are feeling better if you're feeling angry. You are moving up on the emotional scale.

Your objective is always just to feel a little better. To feel some relief from the negative feelings you have now. If you're feeling completely depressed and you're having a hard time feeling good, what do you do?

Well, first, I would start doing all the things on the list that we talked about. Go for a walk, get some sun, do the Callahan technique. The Callahan technique is a miracle cure.

It is extremely powerful and effective. And it works FAST. Most times, the positive effects last a very long time. In many cases the positive results are permanent, such as in the curing of phobias.

If you are feeling sad, low, depressed, or have a case of the "blues," first look at the drugs you're taking. Depression is a side effect of many drugs. Do some cleanses. It may take a few weeks or a few months before you actually start getting to a better place.

Do the appreciation process. What can you be appreciative for? Do that every day, three, four, five, six times a day. What can I be appreciative for? That will start forcing you to focus on something good and positive, which will mean, by the Law of Attraction, more like-minded thoughts will come in and your positive ball will start getting bigger and bigger and bigger.

You're at the conscious competence level now so you have to do it with conscious, deliberate intent. If you want things in your life to change, you have to change things in your life.

You won't get to the unconscious competence level until you get to the point where your positive energy ball is bigger than your negative ball.

Associate with positive people. Surround yourself with those who uplift, support, and encourage your growth.

One great way to do this is by joining the Global Information Network (GIN). www.GlobalInformationNetwork.com

Does this make sense?

This is why it's important to understand, if you're doing the technique, you're defining what you want, and as you're thinking about what you want, you are feeling bad, that means you can't focus on that desire because that goal then is too big. It is out of the sweet spot.

As you think about what you want, and you feel bad, at that moment, your subconscious mind is spending too much time thinking about the how and the *lack* of having what you want. You are actually subconsciously thinking that you DON'T have what you want to manifest.

Do you understand?

When you're thinking about something you want and you feel bad, that means your subconscious mind is convinced you're not going to get it. You're focusing on the *lack* of it.

Your subconscious mind is focusing on the fact that you *don't* have what you want, and now you're vibrating: I don't have it. I don't have it. I don't have it. I don't have it.

And when you're focusing on that, that's what you get more of. The universe will make sure you DON'T have what you want. It will stop it from manifesting.

It's perfectly okay if you say, "Well, I'm massively in debt. I don't have much money." That is acknowledging what IS. But you have to use the rest of the formula as I described.

Let's say that's your situation and you want more money, and you want to get out of debt. It's okay to say right now, "I am massively in debt, and I don't have much money."

That's the situation.

But what most people do is, they continue: "… and I have no idea how I'm going to get out of debt. I don't know how I'm going to get more money. I just keep getting worse in debt. I just keep getting worse and worse. Nothing goes my way. I'm so unlucky. Everything is working against me. I don't understand why everything is so bad. It just keeps getting worse and worse. I'm worse off today than I was a year ago. I just keep getting further and further in debt. I don't understand why or how this is happening to me. Maybe I'm a compulsive spender. I am such a loser. Maybe it's the banks, maybe it's the interest rates. Maybe it's the fees. It's my job. I can't get a raise. I can't get more money. I'm always getting sick. Every time I'm getting close to doing something, it just works out against me."

This is how most people think and talk. They paint themselves as a victim and take little or no responsibility. They act as if they are helpless and powerless.

But guess what? By talking and thinking like that, you're vibrating that into your life and that's what you're going to get more of.

Instead say, "I'm massively in debt and I don't have much money, and I have no idea RIGHT NOW how I'm going to get out of debt or get more money. But I know something will present itself. I don't know how or when. So right now, I know that in time—and I don't know when—everything will work out fine. Everything always works out fine. I don't know how, but I'm sure things will work out OK."

If the glass is half empty or half full, it does not matter. YOU always have the power to *refill* the glass!

In the midst of something bad in your life, you're just trying to get some feeling, some thought, that makes you feel better. You are looking for some RELIEF.

Maybe for you, you have to say, "Okay, I'm in debt. I don't have much money and maybe I'll never get out of debt. Maybe I'll go through the rest of my life and never get out of debt and never have much money. But you know something? That's okay. That's not so bad. At least I'm not living in some country where I'm sleeping on dirt every day. So maybe I'm in debt. It isn't so bad."

Maybe that is the only thing you can grasp onto to get some relief and feel better. Maybe you say, "I'm sure things will turn around. Maybe I'll slowly get out of debt. Maybe little by little, maybe something will happen."

See? You start thinking just a little better thought. The key is to feel BETTER now, get some RELIEF. Then work on feeling better still. Until you can get to the point of feeling GOOD.

But the real key is, don't focus on feeling spectacular. The real key is when I say feel good now, it's feel *better* now. Feel some RELIEF. You should always be working on feeling a little bit better than where you are because you're all at different levels.

Does this make sense?

Another question that was asked at the live event was, "How important and powerful are words?"

We talked a little bit about words. In my courses, the Success Mastery Course and The Science of Personal Mastery Course, both offered exclusively to GIN Members, I talk A LOT about the power of words. We do many DRILLS that activate and illuminate words and get you to be able to use words and speech patterns that have creative power with deliberate intent. You learn how to virtually create with your words.

The words you use are important. Having them activated and illuminated is powerful. Using those words with specific language patterns moves energy and creates. Your tongue is a creative force. You are hung by the tongue. What you SAY is what you GET.

Because what's really relevant is the INTENTION you have when you are speaking words. Words do have vibration, but when you're speaking words, it's the attachment of the vibration to the word that's more important. You can broadcast energy when you speak from your mind/brain, and/or from your heart, and/or from your creative center two inches below your belly button. I teach this to GIN Members in the Success Mastery and Science of Personal Mastery Courses.

If I use a word and you use the same word, we may use the same word but have a completely different vibration attached to it. And the vibration might be broadcast from different centers. Most people broadcast word frequency from their throat. This does nothing. It must be broadcast from one of the three centers I mentioned. I broadcast from all three simultaneously when I speak. This is the most powerful.

For you at this point, the real key is use words that, when you're saying them, make you feel good, make you feel better. Start there.

Everyone has different speech patterns and words that they use. Using the same phrases and speech patterns that successful people use is one step that will help you achieve more success. There is magic in the words they use and the patterns of speech that they use.

Unsuccessful people all talk in a similar way and all use similar words. Successful people use words and speech patterns that unsuccessful people do not. Think about this.

Some of my phrases that make me feel much better are:

"Everything always works out."

"Everything always works out for me in the end."

"I don't know how, but it will always work out."

"All is well."

"Things always work out."

"I don't know how, and I can't explain how, but I just know everything always works out because I'm feeling good and I'm putting out a good vibration."

"Things will always just work out fine because they always do."

So words are important, and speaking is important because when you say words, you're reflecting what your thoughts are. Your subconscious mind is revealing itself.

You CAN also use words to help change your thoughts, thus changing your feelings and emotions.

So choose words wisely.

"Oh, it'll be fine." That's a great phrase. It'll be fine. It'll work out. I don't know how it'll work out, but it will. I love my life. I love being me. Things are exciting!

Those are all great phrases.

When someone asks you, "How are you?" Do you just say, "Fine, how are you?"

Instead, consciously, with deliberate intent, say a word or phrase that makes you feel better.

You could say something like, "I'm good and getting better." "If I felt any better, it'd be illegal." "I'm getting better every day." "I'm feeling great." "Every day, in every way, I am getting better, better, and better."

You can say something that makes you feel good, but don't lie. Don't say something that makes you feel bad.

Let's say you had a rough night last night, and I ask, "How are you?" And let's say you feel horrible. Don't say, "I feel great." Because you don't. You feel horrible.

You could say something like, "Well, you know, I was feeling really terrible, but I'm getting better. I'm working on getting better. I think today is going to be better than yesterday."

That's a more accurate statement.

"I was really feeling terrible. I got some bad news this morning, and I felt like I got hit in the stomach, but I'm working through that and I'm getting better."

See, that's an accurate statement. You can feel good about that statement because you're telling the truth. If you say, "I feel terrific, I feel fantastic," you're lying. And actually you'll feel worse if you say that because your mind is going to be focused on the lack of feeling terrific and you'll be thinking about the negative situation you are in. You will feel bad because you are LYING to the person AND yourself.

Make sense?

Another question that came up in the live event was about when you're using this technique in relation to another person. Let's say you want this person to give you a raise or you want this person to do something. Aren't their thoughts, goals, and desires affecting the process?

The answer is yes. Remember, when you transmit a vibration on the Alpha/Theta wealth manifesting wave, that vibration is picked up by other brains and affects physical matter.

When you're dealing with another human being and you're putting out a vibration, and this human being, for example, is going to give a raise to somebody, or this person is going to decide whether he's going to buy your house at a certain price, and you're trying to put that vibration out, they may be putting out a counter-intention vibration, or somebody else may be putting out a vibration to them as well that's affecting them.

This is why it's important that the ultimate DESIRE is not a particular outcome, but rather your desire is for YOU to experience something that gives you the FEELING you are seeking.

The feeling that you think you will have when you get what you desire is ultimately what you're vibrating. This is why when you are trying to manifest something, you have to care, but not that much. I will talk more about this "releasing" secret powerful ingredient to the manifesting formula later.

When you understand that other people can be putting out counter-intentions that are in opposition to your desires, you will see why wanting one specific thing in a specific time frame is not the ideal way to send out a vibration, but rather, a more general vibration of how you want to feel is better in most cases.

Having the knowledge that there are things outside the radar screen that you don't know about that are probably much better for you than what you can even consider allows you to "release attachment to a particular outcome at a particular time." This will get you to the point where you care, but not that much.

Let's say I'm dealing with a person, and I *want* this person to invest in my company.

Well, do I want *this person* to invest in my company? Or do I want investment into my company? And do I really want investment into my company? Or do I want my company to grow and prosper and I just THINK I NEED an investment? Or do I really want to make more money and I think if my company grows, THAT is the WAY I will make more money?

Do you understand?

You may think that you need *this guy* to invest in your company in order for it to grow and prosper and for you to ultimately make more money and get rich. You may THINK that unless you get an investment NOW, your business is going to crumble.

That's the wrong thought process. Maybe you THINK you need investment into your company for it to grow and prosper, and for you to be ultimately successful, but maybe that's not true.

So what you ultimately want is, you want your company to grow and prosper so you can be ultimately successful. But that's not true either.

What you really want is for you to feel powerful and successful and feel that you've achieved something, and become ultimately wealthy.

That's what you really want.

You don't want this guy to give you an investment. You think that's the HOW to get you to the ultimate objective, which is, you want to feel powerful, feel that you've achieved something, and become wealthy. *That's what you want.*

You think you want this guy to give you an investment. That's not what you want. So when you're vibrating, "I want this guy to give me an investment," that's really not correct.

When you actually look at what you want, it's much better to say, "What do I really want here? Do I want this guy to give me an investment? No. I *think*, based on what I can see on my radar screen, that this is what's needed to get me to my ultimate goal."

Guess what, gang?

You ain't that smart.

This is why you can't assume things that happen or don't happen are good or bad: because you have to really think to yourself, what do you ultimately want here? And then let the universe use the best method to get you to where you want to go.

So in this example, you don't want this guy to give you an investment, and you don't want an investment, and you don't want your company to prosper. What you're really looking for is you want to feel that you've achieved something, that you've created something, and you ultimately want to become wealthy.

So focus on *that* without the specifics, because the method and the way that you think that's going to happen probably is not the method that is best and the way it will work out anyway.

So don't even focus on getting THIS guy to invest. Keep thinking and focusing on "I want to be wealthy! Universe, YOU figure out how." Does this make sense?

If you think, "I want this guy to buy my house"— no. You may think, "Well, I want *somebody* to buy my house." No. You may say, "Oh, yeah, I want to *sell* my house." No.

THINK. Why do you THINK you want to sell your house?

You may say, "So I can have enough money so I can buy a new house." Ah! Eureka!

So what you really want is *to buy a new house*.

You think the method of selling your house is the one that will get you to the place where you can buy a new house. You THINK you have to SELL your existing house first. Maybe that is true. But you DON'T KNOW THAT!

Maybe selling your house or buying a new house is not the right thing. Maybe this is not the right time. Maybe the universe has a BETTER plan. Maybe the market is going to change in six months in a way that you don't know about, but the universe does!

The universe may be thinking that it will be much better for YOU if you don't sell the house now and buy a new house because if you just WAIT there's going to be a great new house that's going to be given to you at a spectacular deal and you can rent your existing house out and have a fantastic income investment property.

You understand? Remember, YOU DON'T KNOW WHAT YOU DON'T KNOW.

You don't know the BEST method to achieve your ultimate goal. The universe does. Think of the universe as GOD, the Force, Infinite Intelligence, All-That-Is, the Atman, Allah, The Field, or whatever name you choose to use.

So it's USUALLY, in the beginning, much better to be general with your wishes without a particular deadline and release attachment to a particular outcome at a particular time. RELAX. Enjoy the ride. The journey is the reward.

Success is the progressive realization of a dream. Success is a journey, NOT a destination.

It is always critical to ask yourself, "Why do I really want this? Why do I think I want this?" And keep going up the line and ask, "OK, why do I want *this*?"

Why do I want this watch? Because that's the watch I want. And why do you want that watch? Because I think it looks gorgeous. But WHY do you want THIS watch? Because of the way you will FEEL when you are wearing it and showing it off to your friends will make them feel that you are a somebody and a great success.

You justify that you want the watch because it goes with your clothes and it looks gorgeous and it's totally unique. And you just like the way it looks. And of course, you like the way people will react when they see you wearing it.

So now you know it's not a watch you even want. What you want is something that makes people look at you as very unique and special, and maybe have money, and you want to feel good. You want to feel special.

Do you understand? It isn't that particular watch that you really want. It isn't even a watch at all that you want. It isn't even a piece of jewelry. You seek a FEELING you think the watch will give you.

Doing this process of asking, WHY do I want THIS, will be eye-opening to you and very revealing of your inner insecurities and low self-esteem. This is VERY helpful self-awareness.

So when you start moving up the line asking, WHY do I want THIS, and start focusing on the REAL desire, life becomes much easier. You will start releasing attachments to particular outcomes and deadlines. You will care, but not that much. You will be in a state of allowing.

You will start letting the universe provide for you the best things at the best times, instead of what you think is what is best for you.

Now, there is nothing wrong with saying I want that particular watch because that's the watch I want. But if you lighten up a little bit and let the universe provide for you, life is much, much, much easier.

Does this make sense?

And I can tell you, not only easier, but better, because you get better stuff. The universe is smarter than you.

The universe will give you better things than what you think is the best, because the universe sees EVERYTHING, not just what you see on your tiny radar screen. The universe knows the best METHOD of attaining your desire, because what you think is the best method ultimately almost always isn't.

Which is why I'll tell you a little secret. When you start wanting things and you get them, most people think, "This is not what I thought it would be." Remember this axiom of truth: *It will not be what you attain that gives you your greatest joy; it will be who you become.*

When you ALLOW the universe to give you things that are for your highest good, because you're at a high level of consciousness and awareness of who you really are, you will feel so much better about the things you do attain.

Another question that came up at the live event was about the importance of writing down, on white paper with blue ink, the things you desire to manifest.

I can just tell you this. You should always have lots of paper, white paper, and pens with blue ink. Write things down. Write your goals down. Write your wishes down. Write your dreams down. Write your "to do" list down. Write down your plans.

Plan your work and work your plan. Do this by first writing things down on paper.

Magical things happen when you take a thought and you put it on paper in words, ideally writing in cursive. I can't spend a lot of time on the subject in this book. But the bottom line is, if you're writing things JUST into a computer or on your phone, you are completely missing out on one of the best opportunities for creation.

Your brain will put out a vibration much stronger, with much more intensity, with much more clarity, when you take your desires from the ether and you write them down on paper. This is because you're actually transmitting through your whole DNA structure, not just your brain, the feelings you want to attain, through the kinetics of cursive writing. You don't get this when you type.

There are over ten thousand different movements when you write in cursive, so more new neural pathways begin to be established and become activated. You feel better. You remember the information you write down better. You focus on the information better. You're bringing greater clarity to the information by writing than by typing into a computer.

So write things down.

Another question that was asked at the live event was, "Can you predict the future with this?"

Well, you're predicting the future because you're creating the future. That's how you predict the future. Predicting the future is nothing more than creating the future.

People have always said to me, "Kevin, you have an uncanny ability of predicting the future. You must be the world's greatest psychic."

I would always smile, because the fact is I'm creating the future. I know what's going to happen because I'm creating it. You will be able to predict the future because you're going to create your tomorrow.

What's going to happen next month? You're going to create it because when you are using this technique, you're creating your future. And as you use this technique and feel good, what occurs is that as things get closer to your radar screen, you can *feel* them.

You begin to *know* what's going to happen because you've created it. And now you're *feeling* it coming in because the anticipation goes up and up and up. And actually when the anticipation goes up and up and up, you KNOW it's getting closer and will manifest SOON.

And when you feel bad about something, you *know* that what you want is going further away, or that something that you don't want to happen is going to happen because you're feeling bad.

Your feelings are your tracking system, they're your guidance system, they're your predictor, they're your thermometer, they're your Geiger counter. In time, the more you do this and the more training you get, the better you will get at FEELING and SENSING what is going to happen.

You can learn how to walk through life and *feel* your way through life because you know when you're feeling good, only good things will happen and you're going to be just fine. And even if something happens but it doesn't *appear* good, know that it *is* good because you're going to be just fine in the end.

You begin to have a sense of *knowingness* that the "bad" thing that happens that seems to be horrible, is actually the BEST thing for you and IS getting you closer to manifesting your desire in the best way possible and for your highest good.

You realize and KNOW that something big is changing in your life for your highest good. You KNOW that something big is in the process of manifesting for your benefit and it's right around the corner. When something happens that you don't *think* is good, just know that now I have a great opportunity to clarify exactly what I want and create a transmission from my brain with more power and more intensity than ever before.

What you want will then start to come into your life faster than ever before because your broadcast will have more magnetic pull than ever before.

So that's predicting the future.

Another question that came up in the live event was about how much time it takes to manifest a desire and setting deadlines.

How much time it takes to manifest a desire is completely irrelevant. If you are focused on the WHEN it will manifest, you are not in a state of allowing. You are in a state of DOUBT. You do not have enough belief. And you are not feeling NOW AS IF you WOULD feel if you actually were in possession of your desire. If you were feeling that way, you would not CARE how long it took, because you feel no lack NOW.

If you want a new car, if you want to get out of debt, when will it occur? The answer is it doesn't matter when it occurs. In fact, if you are doing this correctly, you will not even care IF it manifests, because you are FEELING GOOD NOW.

When will I get my lifelong soul mate into my life? I have been single for so long. I've had relationships, but I've never found my soul mate. When am I going to find my soul mate?

If you are asking these questions, you are vibrating the LACK of that person; therefore, you will NOT manifest a relationship. You will continue to manifest situations and circumstances that will make you feel MORE of NOT having a relationship and having the feeling of LACK of a relationship.

When you start *believing* that you WILL find your perfect romantic partner and feel no LACK of not having that partner now, it will manifest at the right time.

You have to wonder—why isn't it the right time NOW?

Remember, when the teacher is ready, the student will appear.

You may have to go through multiple relationships and experience more things that you don't want before you can completely clarify what you do want. And when you completely clarify what you do want, and then put out that vibration with anticipation, and feel good when you think about having it, even when that person is not there, THEN it will manifest.

When you feel so happy being alone, knowing that your soul mate will come in at the exact right time in your life, THEN it will manifest. You will find yourself skipping through life feeling happy with complete glee even though you are alone, because you *know* that the soul mate is coming. That is when it will manifest.

You KNOW that Christmas is tomorrow. You don't know when that tomorrow is for the soul mate, but you know it's there. When you get to that point, your soul mate will come. In the meantime, enjoy the process and FEEL GOOD NOW. Just know that everything will work out fine.

If you think you will feel better WHEN you manifest your desire, then it WILL NOT MANIFEST. You have to feel NOW AS IF you WILL FEEL when you are in possession of your desire.

You can't get caught up in the timing. Don't be thinking that you KNOW what's the best time for the manifestation of your desire.

"But I really want it now!"

Okay, what you're doing is you're feeling bad because you're focusing on the lack of what you want; therefore, you'll never get it.

Do you understand? Care, but not that much.

You can't put that much attention on what you don't want or what you don't have. That is putting out a frequency of lack, thus you will attract and manifest more LACK.

Why does this technique fail to manifest desires?

The method does not fail. It is the success system that never fails. If you follow the formula correctly, it always works. It always has. It is science. It is quantum physics. It is proven, tested, documented, and substantiated. It has passed the test of time. The only time it APPEARS not to work is when someone is NOT following the formula correctly or they have so many counter-intentions in their DNA and memory bank (their energetic field).

Let's recap the steps of the recipe we have gone over so far. This is the formula for manifesting.

Define what you DON'T want. Contract energy and get MAD. Find the pain that you MUST eliminate from your life. Find the thing that you will not tolerate anymore. This is the WHY behind the WHY.

Define exactly what you want. You can be specific, general, or just a feeling. Clearly define what you want. When you define what you want, make sure you know WHY you want that thing. Ask yourself, do I really want *this* guy to invest money, or do I want an investment? Or do I want my business to succeed? Or is what I really want to have a feeling of achievement, that I've created something, that it worked, and I want to be wealthy and respected?

So define what you want, but define it in such a way that you have as much freedom, flexibility, and openness to the options that the universe may present to you.

Write down on white paper with blue ink what you want to manifest.

Make a DECISION that you ARE going to manifest your desire, THAT'S IT, PERIOD. Make the decision that NOTHING is going to stop you. Become OBSESSED with the attainment of your desire.

Think about what you want and see yourself in possession of your desire. Feel NOW AS IF you would feel if you were actually in possession of what you want. You have to feel good when you are thinking about being in possession of your desire. Make sure your desire is in the sweet spot. If you don't feel good when thinking about what you desire, you're thinking about the lack of it and you're thinking about all the reasons why it probably won't come in. You're doubting and your level of belief is down.

So you must focus on what you want, but be feeling good about it. No timeline. Have a lot of emotion when thinking about having your desire. The best emotion is anticipation. You should feel like you ordered something, and it is ON THE WAY TO YOU. Feel like Christmas is coming, where you get the things you asked for. It's already in a box. You've seen the box. It's under the tree. And when Christmas Day comes, it's already there, waiting for you.

Start feeling and anticipating you have already attained and are in possession of the thing you desire. Feel NOW AS IF you ALREADY HAVE IT.

KNOW that if you have something you want and you're doing this, you're putting out a beam, you're transmitting a vibration of what you want with complete anticipation, as if it's already here and it is going to come rushing towards you. What you want wants you.

But if you're thinking about what you want, and if you're completely unclear of what you really want, that means the beam you are broadcasting is very weak.

If you're clear about what you want, but you're not feeling that good and you're having doubt, that means you're focusing on the lack of it, the fear of not getting it. You're focusing on the fact that you don't have it and you don't know *how* you're going to get it. That's the doubt that stops the process from working.

Then RELEASE ATTACHMENT TO THE OUTCOME. Put yourself in a state of allowing and surrender to the universe. I will write more about this later.

Make a dream book with your desires and dreams, of the things you want, written down.

Make a dream board with pictures of the things you want to manifest.

Go dream building.

Listen to positive motivational audios daily.

Read positive books daily.

Go to events with other positive, motivated people on a regular basis.

Associate with successful people, winners, people who are going for their dreams.

Use words and speech patterns correctly and SAY OUT LOUD positive statements and affirmations. Speak into existence what you desire.

Does this make sense?

Do you KNOW this material yet? If you think so, then close the book and write the above formula by memory. I bet you can't. You are not at the unconscious competence level yet. I am writing this book without notes. I am writing it from memory, from my KNOWINGNESS. This material is a part of me.

It is not when you got into this book that matters. It is when this book gets inside of YOU that makes all the difference.

You can have, be, or do anything and everything you want.

It's available to you. It's right in front of you. This is a method that must be activated by you, by USING IT. Everyone reading this has a big, huge ball of negative energy. You have installed in your brain failure habits. You all have negative patterns of thinking. You've established multiple neural pathways in the brain that aren't working for you to your advantage. They're not creating what you want. They are not helping you manifest your desires. Those negative habits of thinking and speaking are giving you in life what you don't want.

Everything in your life is there because you've created it with your own thoughts, not with your actions. You've created your life with your thoughts first. You've created everything in your life with your thinking. Then with your words. Then with some actions. But it STARTS with your THOUGHTS.

You have in life what you THINK ABOUT most of the time. That's the fact.

So you can create anything and everything with your thinking.

Let me say that again.

You've created everything in your life right now with your thinking. Do you like and want everything in your current life?

Well, you've created it, so TAKE RESPONSIBILITY FOR ALL OF IT.

Taking responsibility for everything in your life is the ten-second miracle. If you can do that, EVERYTHING IN YOUR LIFE WILL CHANGE FOR THE BETTER. You will attain ULTIMATE POWER and CONTROL over your ENTIRE LIFE.

If this is true, which it is, it means *you can create everything you want for the future.*

You create everything anyway. Nothing happens by chance. You are a creative force. YOU are the ultimate creator.

Everything that will happen to you for the rest of your life, you will create with your own thoughts, whether you like them or not. Most people create without deliberate intent. Start creating your life with DELIBERATE INTENT. YOU are the master of your destiny. Acknowledge your awesome creative power.

You create what you're focusing on. Whatever you really, really, really want, you'll get. And whatever you really, really, really don't want, you'll get that too.

In the Bible, the book of Job, everything in his life was destroyed. He lost his wealth, his family, and his health. He said, "That which I feared most has come upon me." What you FEAR is what you will

GET. Because when you FEAR something, you are THINKING about it and thus attracting it into your life.

If you think you really want something, the problem that most people have is when they really want something, their focus really is on the *lack* of it, that they don't have it. Therefore, they create more lack.

How do you know if you're thinking about the lack or about the anticipation of getting it?

The answer is, how do you feel when you think about it? If you feel good, you're thinking about getting it. You are actually imagining you HAVE it. There is no lack.

If you feel bad, you're thinking about the lack of it, you are thinking about the fact that you DON'T have what you desire, and you're stopping yourself from getting it.

That's how it works.

So you must always monitor your feelings. Feelings are the key and the most important. You will get better at trusting and reading your feelings the more training you have. You will get there. Then life will be magical.

This technique will work for anything and everything in your life. If you want a romantic, loving, passionate relationship; if you want a better relationship; if you want a better relationship with your kids, your friends, family; if you want a better job, more money; if you want better health—anything you want, you can manifest.

This works in the physical body just as well. Physical health. Weight, energy.

If you want lucky things that happen in your life, you can manifest that. I have seen it. I have seen people become uncannily lucky.

You can manifest all the physical things that you could possibly want. Cars, boats, planes, jewelry, money. Getting out of debt. More fulfillment. Learning a skill.

Anything that you want to be, do, or have, you can manifest.

We talk a lot about attaining THINGS. But you know what it comes down to at the end of the day? None of the *stuff* matters. Because when you really start doing this technique and you realize that you can create anything and everything in your life, when you realize WHO you REALLY are, what everything really comes down to is: How do you feel?

Who cares if you have three Rolls-Royces and a private jet and a 200-foot mega-yacht and your own island in the Caribbean?

If you're depressed, if you've got cancer, and you don't even talk to your kids anymore, those THINGS mean NOTHING. Who cares about all the stuff? The stuff doesn't really matter.

What really matters is, how do you feel?

Do you wake up in the morning with a smile on your face saying, "What a glorious, beautiful day," even if it's pouring rain?

I'm living on this planet. I'm enjoying my life. Life can be like going to an amusement park every day and getting on a different ride. Today may be a roller coaster, but how thrilling!

You see, life is like the roller coaster, because when you're going straight down, you scream, aaahhhh! But you know you're not going to die. When something bad happens in your life, just imagine that it's a roller coaster going down and you can scream aahh! But with a big smile on your face saying, Wow! What an experience I'm having!

In life, as you go through the excitement and thrill of living, feel like: I don't know how it's going to turn out, but it'll turn out just fine.

Do this and you can feel exhilarated by the challenge and the adventure that life is.

You can have, be, or do anything and everything you want.

Remember, you become what you think about. You get what you think about most of the time.

If you're thinking about what you want correctly, you'll feel good. If you're thinking about what you don't want, you'll feel bad.

But either way, you get what you think about. If you're thinking about what you don't want to happen or lack of something, you'll get more of it, you'll feel crummy, and you'll keep getting more of what you're focusing on. You get what you think about most of the time.

When you're thinking about what you want, you feel good.

When you're thinking about the lack of what you want or when you're thinking about what you don't want to happen, you feel bad.

So if you're feeling bad all the time, that means you are vibrating and transmitting what you don't want. So if you feel bad all the time, guess what? You're thinking about what you don't want, and you get what you think about most of the time.

That's why I've said, and I'll say it again. Your number one. Number one. Number one. Number one. Number one. Number one objective is to feel good now. Feel as good as you can. Work on feeling BETTER. Work on feeling RELIEF. Aim toward feeling good most of the time.

Because if you're feeling good most of the time, you will be thinking better thoughts. These attract more like-minded good feeling thoughts. That means the vibration that's going out is on things you want.

If you're feeling good most of the time, that means you're vibrating what you want. That means you're thinking about what you want CORRECTLY most of the time.

Do you understand how simple it is?

Just feel as good as you can, good all day. Work on THAT. Laugh, sing, try to feel great all day. Use the tools I gave you. They will help you feel BETTER. Feeling good is a HABIT. You can develop that habit, and it will change your life.

If you feel good, that means you are thinking about your desires and believing you'll receive them. You will be in a state of gratitude, appreciation, and thankfulness. This is the state where your desires manifest.

If you're feeling good most of the day, that means you're focusing on and thinking about what you want, and you're believing that you'll receive it.

And if that occurs, guess what? You get it. You get what you think about most of the time.

So the procedure is so simple: It is, feel good as much of the day as you can. If you're laughing and singing and feeling good all day long, you are thinking about what you want most of the time correctly.

If you're feeling bad most of the time, that means you're thinking about what you don't want and you're thinking about NOT having what you want, and you're going to continue to NOT have your desires.

What you're thinking about most of the time is what you're going to get. Does this make sense?

LESSON 13

Keys to Making Money

We will be talking about money now and focusing on manifesting money. We talked about the Four Basics and the Fifth Basic, which is master the Four Basics.

Who Do You Listen To?

Teachability Index.

Training Balance Scale.

The Four Magic Steps.

You can see how that is the foundation of everything we're learning here. If you understand those basic concepts, then you will learn how to apply these concepts better. You will be happier and manifest your goals and dreams faster and easier.

The Training Balance Scale says on one side, it's the why; the thinking, the thoughts, the motivation—the attitude—that you must focus on.

And the other side is the how; the techniques, the skills, the methods, the strategies, the actions—the doing.

We pointed out that 90 percent of making money, or getting anything that you want, or being, doing, or having anything in your life and creating anything and everything in your life, comes from focusing on the thoughts.

It's using your brain to put out a vibration or frequency on the Alpha/Theta wealth manifesting wave, without much counter-intention. And then, by Law of Attraction, the universe will give you circumstances, situations, events, and people to help you manifest your desire and bring into your life that which you're vibrating.

Remember, the universe will give you events, situations, and people which match the feeling you are vibrating, in order to give you circumstances that match that feeling.

This is why people always say, "I wasn't vibrating or thinking about a car crash. I wasn't thinking about falling down the stairs. But that is what happened to me."

But the question is, what feeling did you have when that event occurred? You were vibrating that FEELING. Whatever feeling that event gave you, that's what you were vibrating. You were vibrating that emotion and feeling.

You can create a specific thing by the vibration or frequency you broadcast. When you're putting that out, the universe will give you circumstances, events, situations, and people which match the feeling that you're vibrating or broadcasting.

That's what we have to be aware of.

Now, when we're talking about manifesting money, how do we specifically apply this?

I am going to give you a couple of specific "hows," or techniques, that you can apply specifically to manifesting more money in your life.

However, the action steps I will share are really not that relevant. If your thinking is not right, the actions will not produce great results. Because there are virtually millions of different strategies to make money, it's really stupid and impossible for somebody to say, "I'm going to teach you THE specific way to make money." That specific method that I would teach may apply to you but may not apply to someone else.

It may be something you really enjoy and want to do, but someone else wouldn't. So what is more important is for you to find the various methods and techniques of making money that you enjoy, that give you the feeling that you want.

When you set as a desire making more money, the universe will bring into your life exactly the right method for YOU.

But I am going to share with you some things to help you think about some certain things, and focus on some certain things, so you can bring into your life more money.

The first, most important thing about making money is to want *money.*

That's the first, most important thing. You must want and desire *money.* You must be obsessed with making more money. You must NEED more money. You have to have a burning desire for more money.

Again, the first rule, or the first step, in the manifesting process is find your pain. You need to be fed up with your current financial situation. You need to get to a place where your current amount of income and assets makes you mad as hell, and you are not going to take it anymore.

Then, clearly define exactly how much INCOME and money in the bank you NEED to have. You must define exactly what you want.

So if you want money, how much money do you want? How much income and how much money in the bank (in cash, stocks, bonds, crypto, etc.)? Get specific.

That amount has to be a number that, when you think about it, you feel good. If you feel bad when you think of that number, that means it's out of the sweet spot. It may be too big and out of your realm of possibility. You have to have a reasonable number.

If you come up with a number, for example, "I want a million dollars in the bank and a million-dollar-a-year income," then when you think about that you feel bad instead of happy and excited, that means you're not ready to focus on that amount because you're going to be pulled into thinking about the lack of it. Doubt will creep in.

You will think, "How am I going to get that? That'll never happen to me." And then you're focusing on and vibrating LACK.

You will know you are not in the sweet spot because you will feel bad when you try to see yourself in possession of that money. You will not attract that money; you will attract and draw into your life more of lack.

Everyone's amount of money that will be in the sweet spot is different. Some of you may say, "I just want enough money to help start paying down my debt." This is not good enough. You need to come up with a specific dollar amount of money that you want that you can focus on and that you feel good about.

You can take a different approach. You may say, "I want to FEEL financially secure and FEEL like I am financially free." You can start here, but when it comes to MONEY, you really need to come up with a specific dollar amount.

Remember, the three ways you can define your dream or define your goal or define your *want* are with specificity—a specific dollar amount—or a general desire or feeling. With money, being specific is much more powerful.

When you decide how much you want, you CAN set a deadline. BUT, that deadline MUST be REALISTIC and something you KNOW you can achieve.

Before I go on, I want to explain a key new point: the difference between a dream and a goal. Dreams are BIG, with no time limit. It is something that you have no idea HOW you could ever attain it. In fact, you might look at your dream and say, "There is NO way for me to EVER attain that." That is OK for a dream. You NEED to dream BIG and have BIG, unrealistic dreams. Shoot for the moon, because even if you miss, you still end up among the stars.

BUT, you THEN need to set a GOAL, a target, a chief aim, a primary objective. This is something small enough that you KNOW you CAN attain. It is totally realistic. If you have been earning $100,000 a year, it is totally realistic to set as a goal earning $110,000 a year, and set a deadline of "within five years." THAT is TOTALLY realistic.

So think about what your DREAM income is, and what is your DREAM amount of money you have in the bank, THEN set a REALISTIC GOAL that you can focus on. When you hit the goal, you are closer to your dream.

Desiring money in a general way is not ideal. If you say, "I want MORE money," that is not good enough. With money, being specific is better.

The second best is to desire the feeling that more money will give you. I want to feel secure in my finances. I want to feel financially free. I want to feel safe. I want to feel stable. I want to feel stress-free. I want to feel in control and powerful. These are FEELINGS you might think more money will give you, and that is what you are ultimately seeking.

By the way, when you're focusing on your wants, make sure you focus on what you WANT and NOT what you DON'T want. Don't say, "I want to feel *no* burdens financially. I don't want to feel any more financial pressure." Those things can't be a goal, because whatever you think about, you'll get.

If you're thinking about a goal such as, "I don't want to feel financial pressure," you will be thinking about financial pressure. Do you understand that?

If you say, "I don't want to have any more financial burdens," you're thinking about your financial burdens, so by the Law of Attraction, you will get more of that.

This applies to everything you desire. When you think of anything you want, you must think of what you WANT, NOT what you DON'T WANT.

If you're desiring a relationship, for example, you can't say, "Okay, I want a person who doesn't drink and doesn't smoke." No, because you're thinking about a person who's smoking and drinking. That's the vibration and frequency you are broadcasting. The universe will deliver to you a person who drinks and smokes because you're focusing on that.

You would rather say, "I want a person who lives a very healthy lifestyle, like me." You must always put wants, desires, dreams, and goals in the positive. Don't say, "I want somebody who doesn't do this," or "I want no more of this," or "I don't want this."

When I ask most people, "Tell me what you want in life," they actually tell me what they DON'T want. "Well, I don't want to be overweight anymore." No, you *want* to be thin. See the difference? "I want to stop having food cravings." No, you *want* to have a normal appetite. "I don't want any more stress." No. You *want* to feel secure and content and relaxed.

Do you understand?

You always must put your wants, goals, dreams, and desires in the affirmative, in the positive sense. That way you're focusing on what you want. Always remember that.

It is the same with your words and what you say. Say things in the positive, NOT the negative.

So ideally you will have a money DREAM, and then a specific amount of money you desire as a GOAL. The amounts will change from time to time as you go through the process. Your dreams will change, and your goals will change.

Over the next days, weeks, and months, you'll start changing the amounts and always be changing the amounts as you increase your belief and confidence in the method and in yourself.

You'll always be fine-tuning your dream and what you want because you will be experiencing things that you don't want; thus you clarify with more specificity what you actually DO want.

As you do this, your vibration gets more focused and more specific. The more specific and focused your vibration and broadcast are, the more powerful and intense they will be. Then your belief goes up. Thus you manifest what you want faster.

It is important to DREAM and have financial or money DREAMS. But then it is critical for you to set a specific dollar amount of income and assets as a target, a goal, a primary objective, or a chief aim.

Chief aim in this sense means a primary, focused goal. That should be a specific amount of income (either weekly, monthly, or annually) with a VERY reasonable deadline for its achievement.

One of the keys to manifesting your desires is, you become what you think about most of the time. Which means if you really want things in your life, you have to be OBSESSED with having that which you seek. It must be a NEED. It cannot be a wish or even a want. It has to be a NEED.

One of my mentors, a man worth billions, invited me to one of his homes for a week. I asked him many questions and observed how he lived and operated his businesses. I learned a lot. On the last day we were in his pool. I asked him if there was ONE thing that was a KEY to success, one thing that is REQUIRED for success. He smiled, then violently grabbed my head and pushed it under the water. He was a big, powerful, and very strong man. I fought to get free but could not. I was panicking. I thought I was going to drown. I actually inhaled some water. Then he pulled me up. I gasped for air and was in shock. He just laughed. Then he said, "When you want something as bad you wanted to breathe and live, THEN you will manifest it." Think about that.

Having a magnificent obsession with attaining and manifesting your desire is critical.

People always talk about living a balanced life or about having a balanced life. You want a great relationship. You want great health. You want a great family. You want a great social life. You want great intellectual stimulation. You want great emotions. You want great finances. You want a great career. You want to be fulfilled. You want friends. You want to travel and enjoy vacations. You want your golf or tennis game to get better. You want to spend time enjoying music, movies, or fine dining. You want it all.

Well, if you're thinking of *all* these things throughout the day, the question is, what are you thinking about most of the time? The answer is, you're not focusing on anything. You're putting out so many different vibrations of all the things you want that none of them are getting any focused attention. You are not obsessed with any ONE thing. You are spreading yourself out too thin.

All these vibrations are good; when you think of them you feel good, but none of them, therefore, can be very intense or very powerful. None of them can be broadcast out of your brain for a long, continuous duration.

One of the secret keys to manifesting that nobody will talk about, is to have a magnificent obsession with the attainment of your desire.

Everyone wants to talk about the importance of living a balanced life. A balanced life is a LIE. NO ultra-successful athlete, musician, or business tycoon has ever lived a balanced life. They were OBSESSED with attaining their goals and spent most of their time working on achieving their CHIEF AIM. That is all they thought about. That is all they talked about. All their activities were focused on attaining their desire.

One of the secret keys we learned in the "societies" is that you become what you think about most of the time. The key, therefore, is, you can't live a balanced life. You must be focusing on a chief aim most of the time.

If that's your health, that's your health.

If that's your family, that's your family.

If that's your finances, that's your finances.

If it's your relationship, it's your relationship.

If it's your intellectual pursuits, it's your intellectual pursuits.

You become what you think about most of the time.

Therefore, you must always have a chief aim.

Look at the various areas of your life. You really have to ask yourself, what is your CHIEF aim? Is it finances? Is it relationships? Is it health? Is it your spouse? Is it your career? Is it your intellectual pursuits? Is it golf? Is it family?

What is your chief aim?

The fact is you *can* want all those things. But you *must* have a chief aim.

This was taught to Napoleon Hill by Andrew Carnegie. It's something that has been overlooked throughout history. You must be obsessed with attaining what you want. That's the only way you can focus your broadcasting vibration with enough intensity, power, and consistency, and broadcast that frequency for a long enough duration, for it to manifest.

You must be obsessed with what you want. You must be thinking about your chief aim ALL THE TIME. That's the only way you can continually clarify it, broadcast the vibration with power and intensity, and have the duration long enough to create it in your life.

You must be obsessed with your chief aim.

You get what you think about most of the time.

So if you're putting equal amounts of effort or equal amounts of thought across twenty different things that you want, all those things could ultimately come into your life, but very slowly.

But if you want something to really come into your life fast, you must broadcast it most of the time with intensity and power, and on the Alpha/Theta manifesting wealth wave. Which means you must be thinking about it most of the time.

You become what you think about most of the time.

You must have a burning desire.

Remember Napoleon Hill? Define your goal and get a burning desire for its attainment. Later he called it defining your CHIEF aim. And he later said, "define what you're going to be thinking about and what you want most of the time."

Define your objective AND have a burning desire for its achievement.

What's burning desire? Burning desire is massive obsession. It is NEEDING something so badly you will do anything to get it. You will do whatever it takes. There is no stopping you. You are determined. You are committed. You have made the decision that you are going to do it, that's it; period! You will be consistent and persistent in your efforts. You will never quit.

You can't have a burning desire for something if you're not thinking about it most of the time. You need to be obsessed with attaining your chief aim. You need to be talking about it, thinking about it, living it, breathing it, tasting it, touching it, and anticipating it as if it's already yours.

You become what you think about most of the time.

You need to define your CHIEF aim and become obsessed with it. Have a burning desire for its achievement and focus on it most of the time. That's how you create it. That's how you manifest it.

Tiger Woods, arguably the greatest golfer that ever lived, was obsessed with golf since he was a little kid. He didn't have a balanced life. If you look at all the great athletes, all the great musicians, all the great people in any area that have achieved greatness, they didn't have balanced lives.

Now somebody said, "Well, I don't want that. I want a balanced life." That's fine and that's very good. So you could make good money, and have a good relationship, and be happy, and have a nice family life, and have a nice social life, and have a nice church life—all these different things—and have a wonderful, balanced life.

That's a good CHIEF aim. Your CHIEF aim could be, "I want to have a balanced life. I want to be really balanced and enjoy so many different things in my life." That's perfect.

Maybe you want to make massive amounts of money, or have a spectacular physique, or have the most brilliant relationship in the world. You need to pick ONE to be your CHIEF aim. That means you're going to be a little bit unbalanced in your life. You're going to be focused on and obsessed with that one thing, which is your CHIEF aim.

CHIEF aim is overlooked. Obsession is never talked about. But the fact is, you must have a magnificent obsession for ONE CHIEF aim. Doing so will get you results faster. And you will be happier, because you are living your purpose. You are living your life with PASSION.

In order to manifest something, you have to think about it most of the time and feel NOW AS IF you were already in possession of what you desire.

You must define what you want and have a burning desire for its achievement, which means you're obsessed with it, which means you're thinking about it most of the time and feeling good when you're thinking about it.

Now, if you're thinking about your CHIEF aim most of the time, and you're feeling good most of the time, guess what's going to happen? You're going to get exactly what you want with record speed. That's how it works.

It isn't the actions or the activities that will manifest your desire per se; it's the vibration that you are broadcasting that will create the events, situations, people, and circumstances in your life that make it happen.

Doing this properly WILL motivate you to ACT and DO THINGS. You will WORK long hours on the attainment of your chief aim, but it will NOT feel like work. It will be a pleasure. All the actions you do working on your chief aim will give you joy. You'll be thrilled and excited to do the "work" and "put in the time and effort." The journey will be the reward. You will be engaging in the act of creating, which always gives you the most inner joy and fulfillment.

If you're not enjoying doing the 'work' and 'putting in the time' to make your CHIEF aim come true, it means you're not feeling good—and you're not in alignment. Your CHIEF aim isn't in the sweet spot. You're focused on the lack—on not having your CHIEF aim right now—and you're doubting whether you'll ever get it. You probably feel like you are wasting your time because you feel sub-consciously that you are NOT going to manifest your desire.

Make sense?

So first and foremost, you must be obsessed with your chief aim.

Do this process. Grab a piece of paper, ideally white paper, and get a pen with blue ink. On top of the page, write DREAMS. I want you to write down anything and everything you would buy or do if money was not an object. Imagine $5 billion was deposited in your bank account. I want you to do this for ten minutes. Set a timer. When you are done, come back and continue reading. Ready? BEGIN.

Welcome back.

How did you FEEL when you were doing that? Before you con-tinue reading, tell me OUT LOUD how you felt doing that process, then continue reading.

Thank you.

Now, take another piece of paper and write on the top, CHIEF AIM. When I say BEGIN, write down in detail what your No. 1 chief aim is. This is something you want to manifest within the next six months. When I say BEGIN, you will have five minutes maximum to do this. Set a timer. Ready? BEGIN.

———

Welcome back.

Tell me out loud how you felt doing that.

Thank you.

You now have a target. Get obsessed with obtaining that goal. Think about what you want with power and intensity. You must feel good when you think about your goal. The techniques that will help you think about your chief aim most of the time include getting pictures of what you want, ideally with yourself in the picture.

This is why a dream board is good. A dream book is also good. These are VERY effective tools. USE THEM. They are KEY ingredients. If you leave ingredients out, you will not get the results you seek.

If you want lots of money to do a lot of things, looking at all the pictures you put on the dream board or in your dream book will create good results. If you make a dream board, you can put many pictures of the many goals you have, but put the biggest pictures of your chief aim in the middle so you FOCUS on your chief aim and the MAIN target.

Reviewing the list of things you wrote down that you would buy or do if money was not an object will help remind you to think about money, money, money, money, money. As you read your list or look at your dream book or dream board, you will think, "I'm bringing in money." FEEL the anticipation and exhilaration as if you already have it.

You become what you think about most of the time.

Just looking at a picture of something you want, ideally with yourself in the picture, over and over and over again, and feeling good as you imagine yourself in possession of your desire, WILL change you from the inside and help you manifest your goal. It is LAW.

If money is your chief aim, having pictures on the ceiling so you see them right before you go to bed and seeing them as soon as you wake up is extremely powerful. Looking at your dream book or dream board before you go to sleep programs your subconscious to work on attaining your goals WHILE YOU SLEEP.

Looking at your dream board or dream book as soon as you wake up is extremely powerful because your brain will be in the Alpha/ Theta brain wave state; thus you will be broadcasting your desires on the WEALTH WAVE, the MANIFESTING brain wave, which will activate the Law of Attraction to manifest what you desire.

CREATING a dream board and a dream book is important. Do this yourself, with your hands. Take time to do this. Put in some effort. You are creating a blueprint for your future. You are placing an order with the universe for the things you want. Whatever you ORDER, you will get. So order wisely. Do this process with deliberate intent.

The actual process of creating a dream book and dream board with pictures and images of what you want keeps you focused on your desires and gets you excited, motivated, and inspired. It will make you FEEL GOOD. And it allows you to broadcast from your brain the frequencies of what you want to manifest.

You can put pictures of your chief aim everywhere. The visor in your car. In your office. On your computer or phone as a screen saver, anyplace so that you're looking at these things much of the time. BUT, ideally you don't want others to see YOUR dreams or chief aim. That is between you and the universe.

Having your dream book with your dreams and goals written out, and reading those dreams of what you want throughout the day, causes you to focus on what you want while feeling good doing it, thus broadcasting the frequency of your desires into the universe on the Alpha/Theta wealth-manifesting wave.

In the beginning, you will be doing this with deliberate intent at the conscious competence level. But you are starting to establish NEW success habits in your thinking and actions. If you want things in your life to change, you have to change things in your life. If you continue to think, speak, and do as you always have, you will continue to get what you have always gotten. Is it enough?

Going dream-building, as described earlier, allows you to focus on new things and expand your ability to dream. If you go dream-building on a regular basis—looking at things, touching them, sitting in the car, feeling how you're going to feel when that car is yours, looking at homes—you will EXPAND as a BEING. Your MIND will get bigger. Your imagination will get stimulated. Dormant energy inside of you will be awakened.

Use the internet to expand your power to dream. Watch things like *Lifestyles of the Rich and Famous,* or shows on the Travel Channel about luxury yachts, exotic destinations, mega mansions, and opulent lifestyles. Start expanding your imagination and ability to dream.

Now you may say, "Well, I'm watching shows about luxury yachts, but I don't want one." Perfectly fine. But what you're seeing is that money is available; other people are getting money. Other people have the money to buy these things. Money IS being manifested by others. What one person has done, YOU can do also. If THEY can do it, YOU can do it.

When you do these processes, your belief level goes up. Your belief level in the PROCESS, this method, and the Law of Attraction goes up. Your belief level in yourself goes up. You start to believe that YOU can manifest too. The confidence in yourself goes up. Your self-image improves. You see yourself differently.

Does this make sense?

Ninety percent of success is in your thoughts. It is your *attitude*, NOT your *aptitude*, that will determine your *altitude* in life.

The success secret that they don't want you to know about is that it's all in the mind.

This is what they, the elite class, don't want you to know.

The major secret to making money is that you must have a burning desire, an obsession with making money. You must be thinking about making money most of the time and feel good when you think about HAVING money.

That's the secret of making money and becoming wealthy.

Andrew Carnegie, a member of the Brotherhood and the richest man in the world, taught this information to Napoleon Hill, who wrote the book, *Think and Grow Rich*.

The book was entitled *Think and Grow Rich*. Not *Work Hard and Grow Rich*. Not *Get More Education and Grow Rich*. Not *You Must Know the Right People and Grow Rich*.

It was *Think and Grow Rich*.

This is because Andrew Carnegie, the richest man in the world, taught Napoleon Hill that the number one key to success was all about thinking. Success was all about HOW a person THINKS. A person succeeds and makes money based on HOW THEY THINK.

When people who are rich work hard, they're not working. They may put in long hours, but they LOVE what they do. It gives them pleasure. They are doing what they love. They're enjoying every step. They LOVE the journey.

Carnegie was in the steel business. Most people don't know that he went to the office at ten in the morning, and he would leave to go home at four in the afternoon.

Back then, they didn't have telephones, Blackberries, mobile phones, or laptops. So he did his business from ten to four. Monday through Friday. He did not go into the office on the weekends.

He took an hour or longer for lunch, and he went home every night. He did not work nights or weekends.

In the summer, he took three months off and he went to Scotland. He did not work while in Scotland. No phones, no telexes, no fax machines, no emails, no instant messaging, no cell phones. He was somebody who "did not put in a lot of physical effort or activity."

But he became the richest man in the world because, as a member of the Brotherhood, he understood what I am teaching you here. He understood the power of the mind. He knew he could use his THOUGHTS to create as much money as he wanted. He knew that success is created in the mind. He was taught, as I was, by high-ranking members of the Brotherhood, this secret training. When you put out that vibration from your brain, it attracts into your life and creates people, circumstances, events, and situations to give you exactly what you want.

Now, if you believe that you have to work seven days a week, twenty hours a day to become successful, guess what? Then it's true. And you might ENJOY working like that. Most successful people do put in that amount of time working on attaining their dreams. The point is, as you can see with Carnegie, it is not required.

Henry Ford, who was also a member of the Brotherhood, said it this way: "If you think you can or if you think you can't, either way, you're correct. It's the thinking that makes it so."

It's the thinking that makes it so.

If you believe and you're putting out, "Well, you can't be successful unless you work really hard," then that is what will be true for you. The universe is going to give back to you and put in your life circumstances, events, situations, and people which will prove that you must work hard and long hours in order to be successful.

If you put out, "I know that the Law of Attraction works, and 90 percent of making money is just how I think and what I broadcast from my brain, therefore, I can make large amounts of money, and I don't have to work that hard; and if I do put in a lot of hours simply because I'm absolutely enjoying it and loving every minute of it, I do so by choice, but it's not required"—then for you, the universe will put into your life circumstances, events, situations, and people which will prove that THIS IS TRUE.

Does that make sense? It is always the *thinking* that makes it so. What you BELIEVE to be true, IS true.

You could stop reading this book right now, use what you learned, even though it is just the tip of the iceberg, and go on to manifest your desires and get rich. But I know you want more. I know you really do want to become a magnificent manifester. So keep reading.

You may notice that I am using spaced repetition, repeating certain things in specific intervals, throughout this book. I told you that. It is to both deprogram you from your failure programming and REPROGRAM you with success programming. Spaced repetition combined with certain words, hypnotic language patterns, and embedded commands will help you manifest your dreams faster and easier. Combine this with the ENERGY and FREQUENCY I have embedded in this book, and you have in your hands a powerful transformative tool that will change you from the inside out in a major positive way. Welcome home.

To recap, so that you GET IT, first find your pain. Find what is in your life that you will not accept anymore and that you MUST change. Remember, we are more motivated by wanting to avoid or eliminate pain than by attaining pleasure.

Then you basically define what you want, how much money you want, or a feeling you want to have if you had more money.

Focus on that chief aim as often as you can and feel good when you think about being in possession of your desire.

Become obsessed with it. Get a burning desire for its achievement. Feel like you NEED it, just like you need to breathe. Make a decision that you WILL get it, that's it, period! Nothing is going to stop you. You are DETERMINED and COMMITTED to get it. One person with a commitment is more powerful than a hundred people with an interest.

When you think about your chief aim, feel great. Feel exhilaration and anticipation like it's already in the present, like you actually have it now. Use the power of your imagination.

Imagine that your chief aim is a Christmas present already in a box. It's got your name on it. It's under the tree. And when Christmas comes, it's yours. You know it. You have no doubt. No one's taking it away from you. It's there. It's yours.

You just do that, and you'll manifest all your dreams.

Now I'm going to give you a list of some additional things to think about. These are some techniques, some methods, some strategies. Here are some of the "hows." None of these are required for you to make tons of money.

But here are some things that you may want to think about and consider. Certainly they HELP you get your thinking right and help you manifest your dreams.

They will hopefully raise your level of belief because you are probably still stuck in needing to know HOW you are going to manifest money and what you should DO to make money. When you learn some of these things, some pressure might come off and some fear or doubt might be reduced.

But doing these things is not required to make money. The only thing that's required is what I just told you. Get your thinking right.

Broadcast the frequency of what you want on the Alpha/Theta wealth wave. Get a chief aim regarding money. Focus on it. Use the method to activate the Law of Attraction.

What you have learned so far is the secret that Napoleon Hill shared in *The Law of Success* and *Think and Grow Rich*. The richest, most successful people in the world used it, including Andrew Carnegie, Henry Ford, Thomas Edison, Albert Einstein, Elon Musk, Bill Gates, Jeff Bezos, Warren Buffett, and many more. Every super-successful person in the world uses that one manifesting technique that I have described.

Let's look at some other key elements of manifesting and making money.

There's a *U.S. News and World Report* collector's edition called *Secrets of the Super Rich: The 15 All-Time Richest Americans. Modern Moguls. An Inside Look.*

And there is a little-known book called *Seven Secrets of the Super Rich*.

Keep in mind that the material in the magazine article and book is not 100 percent accurate because they were written by journalists who talked to and observed these people for a very short time. But they do give you a little bit of insight. I will fill in the blanks.

Here are KEY things to think about when it comes to manifesting, achieving your goals and dreams, and making money.

1. Perseverance beats education. J.D. Rockefeller said perseverance is OMNIPOTENT and overcomes everything, even nature! Look up the word perseverance and read the definitions and history of the word. It will enlighten you. It will activate the power of the word, so you have that power in your life to use to your advantage.

It doesn't take superhuman intelligence to become super-rich. The bottom line is some people think you have to be smart to be rich. No. Throughout history, superhuman intelligence didn't matter when it came to making money.

What is MOST important is perseverance. And what is perseverance? Perseverance is basically being obsessed with what you want, believing you're going to get it, and NEVER giving up.

Which means get a chief aim and focus on what you want most of the time.

You become or you get what you think about most of the time.

2. Make your own luck. Create your own luck. How do you create your own luck? The universe makes you appear lucky when you're focusing on what you want. Money-wise, believe you're going to get it. Have complete anticipation and expectation that what you want wants you and IS coming into your life. The universe will then create and give you lucky circumstances and situations in your life.

3. Gamble, but wisely. Successful people follow their feelings. They listen to their gut. They make decisions and choices based mostly on feelings, NOT data. If it feels good—if they feel good about doing it without fear or anticipation—which means they're not thinking about what they don't want to happen, then they do it. They're thinking about what they *do* want to happen.

When they do things, they do things based mostly on how it makes them feel. Am I going to go in this direction? Am I going to invest here? Am I going to try this business? If they're feeling great about it, it always works out fine because they are then predicting the future.

You are predicting your future because you're creating the future. To somebody else it may look like you are taking a risky gamble, but nobody else can know how you feel.

So if you're about to do something and you're feeling bad about it, don't do it. It may be the most brilliant idea in the world, and it may actually work. But the fact that you're feeling bad about it means your doubt level is high, your belief is low, and you're thinking about it not working.

This means even if it's a brilliant idea, it won't work for YOU at this time. You must follow your feelings.

4. Know your market intimately. Successful people associate with people and situations that revolve around what their particular market is. They are curious. They ask questions. They always want to know more. They study their area of business. They know what their competition is doing. They study the trends. They attend conferences, symposiums, and workshops. They read trade journals. They join Mastermind groups that are focused on the market and business they are engaged in.

They know their business intimately. They have a sense, a feeling, about the market they are involved with.

All this means is, when these very wealthy ultra-successful people think about doing things in their particular business, they're following their feelings, which is how this all works. Trust your feelings. Learn how to FEEL energy and have a KNOWINGNESS of what is off your radar screen.

It's not about being smart or intelligent or educated. You don't have to know every detail about your business or industry because most of it is irrelevant.

You must learn how to get out of the "think stage" and get into the "emote" or "feeling" stage. Then trust your feelings. Be a Jedi Knight. Use the "force," the energetic field, universal intelligence, the ether, GOD.

Knowing details is important. Data is important. But always remember, when your attitude is right, the facts don't count. Your attitude, your thinking, the vibration you are broadcasting, supersedes facts and data.

If you're going to *do* something, take some action step; even if all the facts may say that what you want to do—the actions you want to do—will not work, but your feelings tell you that it WILL work, trust your feelings. Your feelings will tell you that the Law of Attraction IS working, and what you want to do will produce results. This is how ultra-wealthy people operate.

5. Focus obsessively. This was the first time I saw someone say "be obsessive" when it comes to manifesting.

Wealthy people focus obsessively on what they are trying to manifest. They concentrate. They do hard thinking. This focus usually results in wealthy people spending eighty to a hundred hours a week "working" on the attainment of their desires. But they LOVE the activity. It is NOT work.

They focus obsessively on their chief aim. They keep their eye on the target. They are not distracted. They put blinders on.

When you think about what you want to happen—attaining your chief aim—most of the time, and feel good when you do that, you will be motivated and inspired to "work" more than the average person. A living is made 9 to 5. A fortune is made at night and on weekends.

The massive amounts of time and effort you put in "working" on manifesting your chief aim should give you so much more pleasure than almost anything else. You'll *want* to *do* actions almost all the time. You will be the person who can't wait to get up in the morning so you can WORK on manifesting your chief aim. You will stay up past midnight, loving doing the "work" to make your dreams come true.

6. Timing is everything. Bill Gates, co-founder of Microsoft and at one time the richest man in the world, was being interviewed on *Larry King Live* on CNN. Bill was asked what was the secret to success?

Mr. Gates said, "Well, basically a couple of things, Larry. First TIMING, you have to be at the right place at the right time. Then you have to have vision; you have to see the potential in something. Then you have to take massive and immediate action."

In that interview, Bill explained that depth of vision is being able to see the future. Bill went on to say that if you want to be successful, you have to know exactly what you want with total clarity and SINGLENESS OF PURPOSE.

Mr. Gates explained, "When I was looking at the computer business, there were a lot of people that were at the same place I was. We were all looking at the computer business, but they didn't see the potential in the computer business—I did."

So you have to see the potential in things. This is why expanding your ability to dream is so important. Increasing your power of imagination is critical.

Depth of vision is really going beyond looking at what you see in the current state. It is seeing what it could become. It is seeing the POTENTIAL.

Years and years ago, I was in Denver, Colorado, and I was talking to the past president of one of the largest corporations in America. I asked him, "What is one of your secrets to success?" He said, "Depth of Vision. Seeing the potential in things. Being able to use your imagination and DREAM big dreams."

I asked for clarity on exactly what he meant. He responded by telling me to not just look at things as they *are*, but to look at them as how they could become; to see their potential; to have *depth* of vision.

Then he gave me an example. "Kevin, make believe you're looking at an acorn. If you look at an acorn with depth of vision, trying to see the POTENTIAL in the acorn, what do you really see?"

So I said, "I don't see an acorn. I see a tree." With a smile he said, "Very good. But Kevin, do you know what *I* see when I look at that acorn? I see a forest."

That, my friends, is depth of vision. Rich people have it; poor or average people do not.

I then responded, "Well, you could see in that acorn houses being built all over the world using wood that will come from that ONE acorn." He shook my hand and said, "You will be very rich someday."

That's called depth of vision, seeing things further down the track as they COULD be. Seeing the TRUE potential in things.

When Bill Gates told Larry King that the first key to success is timing, being at the right place at the right time, he also added, "And luck has a lot to do with that."

Remember, luck is created. YOU create your own luck.

So when you want something and focus on it obsessively, the universe will give you circumstances, situations, events, and people to help make your desire manifest.

In other words, *the universe will put you at the right place at the right time*. The universe will take care of the timing.

Yes, the universe will present to you the perfect set of circumstances, events, people, conditions, and situations, making sure you are at the right place at the right time, but it will be up to you to trust your feelings and take massive and immediate action. DO something.

There's a story about a minister who was in Louisiana at his church. The levees broke and a massive flood came. Officials evacuated the town. But the minister believed in the Bible and God and said, "No, I don't have to be evacuated because God is going to take care of me."

So he stood there at the church waiting for GOD to save him. But the water continued to rise and rise and rise. A boat came by and the officer yelled, "Preacher, we evacuated the whole town. Hop in this boat and let's get out of here. This is dangerous."

But the preacher said, "NO, GOD will save me. I'm not worried."

As time passed, the waters continued to rise and rise and rise. The preacher was on top of the church's roof, praying to GOD to save him. Another boat came by and said, "Preacher, this is getting worse. It isn't getting better. We're here to rescue you. Get in the boat."

Again the preacher said, "No, I am committed to staying because God's going to take care of me. I trust God and his word."

So the boat left. The waters continued to rise.

As the preacher sat on the roof of the chapel praying for God to save him, a helicopter came by and said, "Preacher, it's getting worse. It ain't getting better. You could die here if the water rises any more. Get on the ladder and get in this helicopter so we can get you to safety."

Again the preacher said, "No, God's going to take care of me. I'm sure everything's going to be fine."

Well, the water continued to rise, and the preacher drowned.

When the preacher woke up in heaven, St. Peter was there waiting for him. The preacher was mad. He yelled at St. Peter, "I don't understand this. I believed in the Bible. I believed in God. I prayed. I thought God was going to take care of me, but I died. What happened?"

St. Peter said, "You idiot, God sent you two boats and a helicopter!"

Do you understand that?

So, in your life, when you use this method properly, circumstances and situations will present themselves. The universe will present you with opportunities. Your prayers are being answered. But most people are just not paying attention.

You're wanting something and wanting something and wanting something and wanting something. You are broadcasting the frequencies and vibrations of what you want.

And all of a sudden—BOOM—an opportunity or circumstance, or a person comes into your life, but you don't "see" it for what it is, and you don't take action. So you must take action when the opportunity presents itself.

7. **It's not just or even mostly about the money.** People who are super-wealthy know it's not really about the money. It's about wanting the feeling you think having money will give you. So they're really working on how they want to feel. They want to feel like they are a

powerful creator. The act of creating is what gives us the most pleasure. Sex is an act of creation, even when it does not result in pregnancy.

People who are super-wealthy want to feel like they are someone who's adding value to society. They want to feel like they accomplished something. They want to start and finish a cycle of action. They want the feeling of fulfillment and being on purpose.

Attaining the money really is secondary. It really just is used to keep score.

What I am referencing is a great little book that talks about the richest people of all time in America. I know most of you reading this are not American, but from all over the world. In the country where you live, there are very wealthy people as well. This applies to ALL wealthy people around the world.

The richest Americans of all time include:

John D. Rockefeller, estimated net worth in today's dollars: $700 billion.

Andrew Carnegie: $450 billion.

Cornelius Vanderbilt: $268 billion.

Bill Gates, John Jacob Astor, Elon Musk, Jeff Bezos, Sam Walton, Warren Buffett, Richard Mellon, Frederick Weyerhaeuser, Marshall Field, Jay Gould, Henry Ford, Andrew Mellon, and the list goes on.

All these people have used the method that you are learning in this book. If you pick any of the people that are on the Forbes 400 list of richest people in the world, *all of them* are using the techniques that I'm sharing with you in this book. They all use their THOUGHTS to create wealth.

This is not guru land. It is not theory. It is not "sound good" advice. This is not some fictional fantasy.

These techniques are what the wealthiest people on planet Earth use to create their wealth. Period, end of story. You can argue or disagree, but then, who is the fool?

If you think you're going to achieve massive amounts of money by *not* using this system, you are living in fantasy land. Yes, you can make money to varying degrees if you don't use this system exactly as outlined. But if you do make some money, you will be using it to some degree.

Anyone who makes lots of money *is* basically putting out a money vibration. The vibration you broadcast from your brain is what's making you the money. It really isn't anything else you're doing. It is actually not the action steps you are taking. It's the vibration you are broadcasting.

You may think it's your effort that is giving you the results. You may think it's the genius that you are, how smart you are, how persuasive you are, and how many good skills you have. None of that really matters.

The fact is, what's really making the money in your life is the frequency you are broadcasting.

You may think it's everything else, but it's the fact that you are putting out a vibration that matches the thing you want without counter-intention.

You may not realize it, but you ARE thinking about what you want, you're broadcasting the frequency of what you want, and the universe is putting what you want into your life. You may not think it's this, but it is. It's the thought process, whether you're consciously doing it or just doing it automatically and subconsciously, that is giving you the results you want.

When you ask most people, "Do you know about the Law of Attraction, or the book *Think and Grow Rich*?" they say no. But they make half a million dollars a year. So you ask them, "Why do you think you're so successful?" If you listen to their answers, you find that they ARE using this system to some degree but don't even know that they are. They really do not KNOW why they achieved great success. They THINK they know, but they don't.

I've talked to hundreds of people like this. They're all using this method to some degree. They have some pain that they will not tolerate. They're thinking about exactly what they want most of the time, and they feel good when they think about it. That is the technique that they're all using, whether they know it or not.

Let me give you a couple of key distinctions that will help you "get this."

Remember, if you want to make money, the key is you must be thinking about HAVING money most of the time.

Some of you are thinking, "Well, Kevin, I really don't want to make millions. I just want to make a little bit more. I just want to make enough money to get out of debt." Fine. Focus on that.

You're not less of a person if you're not rich. As a matter of fact, the only thing that's important in your life is that you're happy and feeling joy and fulfillment. It doesn't make a difference if you're $100 million in debt. It doesn't make a difference if you file bankruptcy. It doesn't make a difference if you have to live in a tent for a while.

Heck, I pay big money to go fishing in Canada, and when I am there, it's like I'm living in poverty.

Like a third-world country. And I have the best time in the world.

I remember the first time I went fishing. It was supposed to be for three days. I stayed there for three weeks, sleeping on the ground, using a hole in the ground as a toilet. I was having so much fun, and I was living virtually like a pauper. But I was having the most joyous, wonderful time in the world.

So it's not about the things or the money, or the homes or the cars. It's about a feeling inside you're looking for. That's what life is really all about, how you FEEL.

You will have desires to *do* things. You will desire to manifest things. You will have desires to HAVE things or achieve goals. You'll have desires to create. You'll have desires to add value to society, to work with children and help other people. That's what life is really all about. The secret to living is GIVING. You will find that this is true in time.

Money is only one small part of true "success."

But some of you also, right now, DO have desires of making money. That's OK. Go for it! You can do it!

Some of you want to make a million dollars a year. Some of you want to have $10 million in the bank. And some of you can't even think that big.

When I was twenty years old, a billionaire told me, "Kevin, the difference between you and me is the size of our dream, and time." Think about that. I will say the same to you.

If you can't dream big right now, when you think about it, all it means is right now your level of belief is low. Don't worry, it WILL grow. The fact is, there are lots of people making a million dollars a year. There are lots of people no smarter than you that have $10 million in the bank. If they can do it, YOU can do it.

You know, relatively recently, there were only 15 billionaires in America. As I write this book, there are over a thousand. And around the world, there are thousands more.

And believe me, that is a LOW number. The people with the real money, no one even knows their names. They are not on any list. What one person has done, you can also do. All you really have to do is BELIEVE. Believe in your dream. Believe in yourself and believe in the method.

You can be, do, and have anything you want.

So here are a few more things to consider when it comes to making money. First and foremost: again, when you think about having money, and you broadcast that frequency, the universe will give you circumstances, events, people, and situations that will help you manifest your desire. The universe will put in your life everything you need to manifest what you want.

But there are a couple of things to consider about making money and to be aware of. If you are employed by somebody, you're pretty much limited on the amount of money you can make.

The reason I bring some of these things up is because, when circumstances and events come your way, they may be so far off your radar—and outside your level of understanding—that you don't realize the universe is presenting you with exactly what you need. You may not know that what is presented to you is actually that boat or helicopter here to rescue you. **You just have to take action and seize the moment.**

If you really want to make some good money, you need to consider that your job is not really the place for making serious money. Yes, you can cut your expenses, work overtime, try to get bonuses, and use the extra money you have to invest. Over time you CAN become very well off financially. My dad was a union welder working for GE. He did not make a lot of money. But he kept his expenses very low and saved a large percentage of his income. He invested it. When he retired, he had over $1 million AND a good pension. He lived a great life.

Yes, you can use this technique of manifesting to get raises, to get promotions, and get better job opportunities with higher income. You can use this manifesting method to increase your earning power as an employee, no question about that. And maybe that is perfect for you, like it was for my dad.

But real money is going to come from owning your own business or by very aggressive investing or trading. If you look at the wealthiest people in the world, most own their own business or have large amounts of stock in companies. They invest in real estate, stocks, bonds, and crypto.

Let's start with a business. There's a difference between a business of your own and your own company. A business of your own is a business that you own, such as a florist, a restaurant, a dry cleaner, anything that's a business. So having a business of your own allows you to make a lot more money than having a job, generally speaking. There are exceptions to this. You could have a job as a major CEO, executive, or director of a large company where you're getting stock options, huge salaries, bonuses, and so forth. But that is rare.

Remember, if you're employed and you are using the technique to attain more money from your job, the universe might do things to increase your job income, BUT the universe may also put into your experience business opportunities or other methods of making money. When these present themselves, don't say no. It might be that boat or helicopter being sent by the universe as an answer to your prayer.

So, a *business* of your own is some type of business that **you** are out there generating money.

A *company* is your own company, but the *company* is out there generating money.

Yes, a business is technically a company and a company is generally a business. But please note the distinction that I am pointing out here. If you own a business, generally the business owns you. YOU are the one doing all the income-generating work. Your income is based on your activity, especially in small businesses.

A company, as I am describing, makes money FOR you. Generally this type of company that I am describing makes income from such things as investments. These could be in the stock market, commodities markets, other trading markets, crypto, real estate, or *investing in other people's companies.*

So a business of your own could be an internet-based business, it could be a multilevel marketing or other type of home-based business. These can be part-time businesses that you work to build up on nights and weekends while you keep working your job to pay your bills.

A business could also be a real brick-and-mortar business, like a restaurant, florist, coffee shop, dry cleaning, service station, hardware store, or owning a franchise.

These are examples of a ***business of your own***. There are home-based businesses and real, what we call brick-and-mortar, businesses. There are full-time businesses and there are part-time businesses. There are businesses that require lots of capital and money to get started and there are businesses that don't require lots of money to start. There are businesses that require a lot of experienced knowledge and time, and there are part-time businesses that don't require lots of knowledge or time.

So depending on your situation and what you are broadcasting, a business-of-your-own opportunity might be presented to you as an answer to your desire. Keep your eyes and ears open. Start being more AWARE and CONSCIOUS. Start PAYING ATTENTION more.

Be aware that having a business of your own or having your own company earning money for you is something that is a way to generate huge amounts of revenue and wealth. Either a business of your own or owning your own company, or both, are the ways most wealth is created.

I will give you one other little tidbit here. Keep in mind, I am just scratching the surface in this book. You may feel like this is a lot of information about manifesting desires and making money, but it is only the tip of the iceberg. Members of the Global Information Network (GIN) get in-depth knowledge on all of these subjects through my courses, the Success Mastery Course and the Science of Personal Mastery Course. These are available for free, exclusively to members. But you eat an elephant one bite at a time.

There are really only two ways to make money.

One is ***you*** earn money. Which means, you go out and make money. Your time and effort makes you money. If you work an hourly wage, the more hours you work, the more money you make. If you have a salary, you make money as long as you go to the job and put in the time. If you stop going to work, then they stop paying you. Your income is based on your time.

There is nothing wrong with that. Working at a job can be incredibly pleasurable, fulfilling, and lots of fun. However, there is a limit to the amount of time and effort you can do each day. When you are earning money based on your own efforts, even in a business of your own or your own company, there is a limit. And if you stop working, your income stops. Your income is based on YOU. YOU make money.

Let's say you have your own business that does trading, or you have your own business which is a restaurant, or you have your own business providing a service, such as an accounting firm. All of these businesses require *your* time and effort to earn money.

When you're earning money based on your own efforts, your money is limited to a degree. And you have no freedom. You are a slave to your business. The business really owns you.

To avoid this trap, to increase income potential and time freedom, what you do is *duplicate your efforts*.

If you have an accounting business and you are a one-man accounting firm, all of your income is based on your ability to work. It is based on how much time you work. If you stop working or take a vacation, you earn no money.

So you decide to hire some additional accountants who work for you. Therefore when people hire your firm, THEY can do the work. You pay them less than you get from your clients. Your clients pay you $200 an hour for accounting work, and you pay them $100 an hour. You keep the extra $100 per hour for your overhead and the rest is yours.

You have effectively duplicated your efforts. Now other people are making YOU money.

This is the second way to earn money. Either other people make you money or your MONEY makes money for YOU. Instead of YOU working for money, MONEY is working for YOU. *THIS IS THE SECRET TO FINANCIAL FREEDOM.*

Basically, this is investing. It is NOT trading. It is having money in some kind of investment where that investment PAYS YOU MONEY each month or quarter or year.

An example is when you have money and you put money into someone else's business as an investment. Without any time or effort on your part, that money begins to grow and earns you money. That money is working for you while you sleep, you are on vacation, and while you are playing golf.

This is how super wealth has always been created. This is how people attain total FREEDOM.

Imagine that you had $10 million in bonds or dividend-paying stocks, which send you 8 percent a year on your money. You would get $800,000 a year income and you NEVER have to work for it. Your money is earning you money. Every year, your $10 million makes $800,000 for YOU. This goes on for the rest of your life. AND, if you had that money in stocks, every year that $10 million might grow by 5 percent or 10 percent. So in twenty years, that $10 million could be worth $15 million, $20 million, or even $30 million or more.

Now, a lot of you aren't at the super wealth mindset yet. You can't DREAM this big yet. You just want to make a little more money than you are earning now. But this millionaire mindset seed must be planted. And it has been planted into your subconscious mind. Resistance is futile.

I'm just giving you this little tidbit as a tease, to tantalize and inspire you. The seed I have planted will grow. Riches can be yours. Financial FREEDOM can be yours. Your wish HAS been granted.

Even though riches, wealth, and financial freedom may not be a desire that you think about all the time or most of the time, it could be a desire that you begin to think about little by little.

Maybe you could be imagining, "I do want to be at a place financially where I don't have to work. I want to be at a place where my money or company is giving me an income of twenty, thirty, forty, or fifty thousand dollars a month WITHOUT me WORKING FOR IT. I DO want my money to be working for me and earning money for me. I DO want financial freedom. I do want to start doing all types of different things, like travel. I do want to look at new businesses for fun and fulfillment. I do want to learn how to paint and I do want the time and money to do that."

I'm planting that seed right now. In time, you may start desiring different things. Your dreams might get bigger. And you might start transmitting those new, bigger dreams into the ether, and then actually manifest them into your life.

There are a couple of other basic concepts you want to consider. I will be planting more magical seeds into your subconscious. None of these are required, but here are some things to consider. Again, the reason I'm giving them to you is, I'm planting seeds. I have actually been planting seeds into your subconscious from the moment you started reading this book.

At the live event, on the second day, many attendees came up to me and asked, "What the heck did you do to us? We feel VERY different. We are feeling so empowered, so confident, excited, and so fantastic."

As I said earlier, I'm using certain activated words and specific language patterns, which are putting embedded commands into your subconscious for you to consider and evaluate. I am programming you for success. I am planting seeds so that you start thinking in a new, positive way. I'm giving you a lot of positive things to think about. I'm planting a lot of seeds and doing it on purpose with deliberate intent for your benefit.

There are a lot more techniques that I'm employing in this book to help you succeed. These new thoughts are beginning to germinate inside your mind, and for many of you, you are already beginning to think in a new way. Some of you will have a hard time sleeping tonight.

As you think about and ponder and evaluate these things, even just a little bit, your brain is putting out that vibration, which is causing an attraction of more like thoughts. And these thoughts feel really good, because the thoughts I'm giving you feel good.

Therefore, like-feeling thoughts come in and they begin to start to build up and grow. This is why the more you read this book, or listen to audios of this book over and over and over and over and over again, and read the other books I suggest, and listen to the other audios I recommend—such as my Success Mastery and Science of Personal Mastery Courses—your positive ball of energy will grow and get bigger and you will more easily manifest your desire.

If you become a member of the Global Information Network (GIN) and plug into the "system," you WILL attain the success you seek faster and easier than you could ever imagine, because your THINKING will change. As part of the club, we're planting so many seeds and getting your brain working almost on autopilot, that you will begin to attract more like-minded thoughts. Your constitutional vibration will change. You will become a "success magnet."

So I'm going to give you a couple of things to consider here. A couple of concepts that will help you in terms of wealth creation. Making money.

As one of your goals, and maybe your chief aim, consider putting some focus on getting out of debt. Now, there's a difference between *debt* and *credit*.

Debt is bad. Credit is good.

Debt is basically owing lots of money that has been borrowed and spent on depreciating assets or no assets at all.

Basically what this means is, you buy a car and you're paying on that car, and every year the car's value becomes less and less. The car continues to go down in value, but you keep paying on it. So you basically borrowed money (and have to pay interest) and then used that money to buy an asset (car) that goes down in value (depreciates). So you owe money on a depreciating asset. The money you owe is DEBT. Wealthy people do not do this. Broke people do.

The money you owe on your credit card, that you are paying interest on, is debt.

A home mortgage is not debt. That's credit. When you borrow money, with interest (mortgage) and use that money to buy an asset (house) that should go UP in value, you are buying an APPRECIATING asset with the borrowed money. This is the proper use of credit. But mortgages are terrible credit vehicles and not the best way to buy a house. The wealthy do NOT buy homes with mortgages. They use other methods where they pay a FRACTION of the interest. I explain this to GIN Members as part of the "Subject Specific Area" in the Members Only section of the GIN website.

So credit is good. Debt is bad.

Ideally, in order to free up the flow of energy, you should have very little debt. Debt creates fear, stress, anxiety, and pressure. Being under any kind of conscious or subconscious financial pressure will STOP money from flowing into your life.

Your thought process will flow more easily when you have reduced your debt. When you're on the way out of debt and you're only using credit properly, to your advantage, all your thoughts flow easier and energy around money flows easier.

So an objective or a goal should be to reduce or get out of debt.

GIN Members have free access to all the debt-reducing methods including, how to fix your credit rating and clean up your credit report. We also teach GIN Members how to use credit as the ultra-wealthy do and how to get access to millions in credit at favorable rates and terms. Membership in GIN has its advantages.

So consider working toward getting out of debt. The good news is, no matter how much debt you have, you *can* get out of debt and reduce any financial pressure you might be experiencing.

You can start reducing your debt by simply using this technique, saying as a chief aim, "I want to be debt-free." Don't say, "I want to get out of debt," because you're focusing on debt.

Say, "I want to have all my bills paid in full. I want to be debt-free. I want a zero balance on all my credit cards. I want my loans paid off in full." Get it? Then do the entire manifesting process regarding THAT goal.

Next, learn and understand this key concept. You have heard the phrase, "Live within your means." This means don't spend more than you make. This is a lie that will keep you broke. The truth is you must LIVE BELOW YOUR MEANS. This means you spend a lot LESS each month than you earn. You always have EXTRA each month that you DO NOT SPEND. YOU INVEST IT.

You should consider, starting right now, saving 10 percent of what you earn and investing it. Just take 10 percent off the top of whatever you get, EVERY time you get paid, and put it away in a savings account. GIN Members learn how to invest their money so they make extremely good returns. Imagine if you were given the opportunity to invest in Apple, or Microsoft, or Walmart, or Google when they first started? GIN Members get access to these kinds of potentially great investment opportunities. It is not just WHAT you know, but WHO you know. Imagine turning a $1,000 investment into $100,000 in just a few short years. This could happen to you.

For now, you can just put it in a savings account or invest it in blue chip stocks or bonds. You can use that money and buy gold or silver, and just put that in a safe. Investing your savings varies greatly based on your age, income, risk tolerance level, your family, your financial goals and dreams, and many other factors.

But just start shoveling away 10 percent and *never touch it*. When you do this, you begin to free up energy because this process starts to increase your level of belief in the fact that you could start accumulating a net worth, some wealth, and someday actually become financially free, where your money is working for you, giving you an amazing annual income so you can live the life of your dreams.

This little technique dramatically changes the way you think. It is very powerful. Start saving 10 percent NOW. If you can't afford to, that means you must cut your expenses. Reduce your overhead. You MUST live BELOW your means. Start TODAY on the road to financial freedom.

Next, you want to reduce the amount of taxes you pay. How do you do that? There are many strategies to reduce taxes. This is not a book about all the legal ways to reduce the amount you pay in taxes. Tax laws are different in every country. And by the time you are reading this book, many of today's laws will have been changed.

GIN Members are kept up-to-date on the best tax strategies. The reason this is an important issue to consider is, I can assure you, you are paying TOO much in taxes. Real tax experts can look at almost anyone's tax situation and save you thousands of dollars a year in taxes.

If you save $2,000 a year in taxes, that means you just EARNED an extra $2,000 a year. Most people who earn $100,000 a year can probably save $5,000 or more in taxes. These savings are real cash in your hand. Saving on taxes is the quickest way to increase your income and put more money in your pocket. Money you can use to MAKE YOU MORE MONEY.

Next is, you want to reduce your insurance premiums. If you were to just sit down and look at all the insurance premiums you pay, review your policies, and just start doing some shopping comparing rates, every one of you can dramatically save money on your insurance premiums.

You can potentially save thousands of dollars a year on insurance payments. So if you reduce the amount of money you're spending on insurance premiums, that's extra cash you are putting in your pocket. It's like you just got a raise.

If you reduce taxes, which you can all do very easily, and if you reduce insurance premiums, you've all just got an instant raise.

Next, use corporations for credit lines and OPM, which stands for other people's money. Setting up a corporation, LLC, or trust is what EVERY wealthy person does to help them attain total financial freedom. You have to start thinking like a millionaire BEFORE you are a millionaire. Start TALKING like a millionaire BEFORE you are a millionaire. Start ACTING like a millionaire BEFORE you are a millionaire.

There are major tax advantages to forming corporations, LLCs, or trusts. These kinds of entities also allow you access to lines of credit that you wouldn't have as an individual person. Most normal people do not know the power of these entities. When you set them up correctly, all of a sudden, almost instantaneously, you could have access to instant credit.

Not debt, but powerful credit. You could potentially get lines of credit up to a million dollars, which is really something to consider. GIN Members learn how to do this.

Next, there are some, what we call character traits, of the wealthy. These are things you should consider working on in yourself.

If you work on adding these character traits to your personality, to the image you see of yourself, you'll feel better about yourself and more confident and you'll attract more money in your life.

One is to develop a pleasing personality. There's a great book called *How to Win Friends and Influence People* by Dale Carnegie. Read the book. I would also highly encourage all of you to take the Dale Carnegie course.

When you develop a pleasing personality, you attract more and better people in your life. Whatever personality you have, you will attract like-minded people. Birds of a feather flock together.

If you have a pleasing personality, you will attract like-minded people. Things will be easier in business. You'll get more accomplished when you have a pleasing personality. People will HELP you and support you and your efforts.

Next, work on improving your communication skills, your persuasion skills, your sales skills, and your negotiation skills. In business, you will be using some of these skills. GIN Members have free access to all these types of training.

These skills are definitely on the right side of the Training Balance Scale. These are skills and specific techniques.

One communication technique, which is very powerful, is to learn how to ask questions and listen. God gave you two ears and one mouth; use them proportionally. Listen more than you talk. When you're meeting people, talk less, listen more.

When you're asking questions, use the six honest serving men and use them till you die. They are: what, when, where, who, how, and why. If you want to appear interesting to others, be interested IN others. Remember, people don't care how much you know until they first know how much you care. Being interested in others by asking questions and listening will serve you well.

I have many hours of training on all these skills and many more that are free to GIN Members.

Now, there was once a very successful man. He was successful not by accident. He was using the thought technique, the method I taught you, virtually unconsciously.

One day he wrote down what he was *doing* every day that he thought caused him to be successful. All he focused on was all his actions because he thought his actions were what caused his success.

He then taught a lengthy seminar, five days in a row, teaching people all of his *actions.* He taught communication skills, how to joint venture, how to partner up with other people to create joint ventures, how to market, how to run a business. He taught all the skills and actions that he did, that he THOUGHT created his wealth.

Later, he was frustrated because with all the people who went through his course, not one of them became successful and not one of them made any substantial increases in income.

He was upset and came to me saying, "Kevin, I gave them the gold. I taught them exactly what I DID. Why aren't they doing it? And if they are, why isn't it working for them like it worked for me?"

I said, "Because that stuff doesn't work *unless* your thinking is right. Unless you're focusing on what you want and obsessed with it and feeling good about it when you think about it. You see, unless the Law of Attraction is activated, all the skills and techniques you taught them won't work."

You see, these people were trying to apply and DO all his wonderful action strategies, but their thinking was all wrong. It is your ATTITUDE, not your APTITUDE, that will determine your ALTITUDE in life. They were not broadcasting the correct frequency on the Alpha/Theta wealth manifesting wave.

So when they actually did all the things exactly as he described, because their thinking wasn't right, none of it worked. None of it created new results.

So you can do every technique wrong, and if your thinking is right, it still works!

This is why in business, you find people who are incredibly successful yet have no pleasing personality, no communication skills, no negotiation skills, and no sales skills, but they are still successful because their thinking is right.

So I'm touching on these various skills, characteristics, personality traits, and strategies here, but letting you know that they actually are not *that* important. HELPFUL, YES. But mandatory, no.

I'm just planting some seeds.

Next, if you want happiness and wealth, manage your priorities. Some people call this time management. Time management is incorrect. It's really priority management. It's being able to get more done in less time, with less stress. It's not being stressed out about getting things done. It is having no feeling of overwhelm. If your thinking is right, if you are using all the techniques I have taught you so far, you won't even feel any stress at all.

But there is a good technique to reduce stress or the feeling of overwhelm. You have been so drilled and ingrained and have so many failure habits when it comes to getting things done. The key is to use some proper *priority management system*.

I would recommend a company called Priority Management. It is the system that I use. It is a paper-based system, but they also have a digital system. Writing things down is STILL the best way to manage priorities. You can combine writing things down on paper with digital technology, but know that ALL rich people, including most "tech" billionaires, STILL write things down on paper.

Being 100 percent digital is not as effective as using a paper-based system. So if you do use the Priority Management system, use the paper-based system and augment it with digital technology.

I actually gave a free presentation about HOW to do priority management, with daily "to do" lists, scheduling appointments, and having communication planners for each person you interact with. This is available on my YouTube channel, The Kevin Trudeau Show, at www.KevinTrudeau.com.

I also have many hours of free training on this subject available to GIN Members, including a full-day seminar by the founder of Priority Management, Dan Stamp.

Lastly, here are some of the things that you want to do that successful people do. Mimic and model success. Success breeds success. Follow a pattern for success. Success does leave clues. DO the things that successful people DO and you will soon be THINKING like successful people think.

These are four critical success habits of the ultra-wealthy.

1. Read positive, inspirational, motivational books every day. Even if it's just a page a day. Leaders are always readers. When you're reading books, it's causing you to focus positively on the things you want. It's raising your level of belief. And while you're reading, you are virtually blasting out positive vibrations because you will be feeling good. Therefore, you will be creating positive experiences to happen in your life via the Law of Attraction.

What books should you read? I'm going to give you a list of suggested books at the end of this book. I would also encourage you all to join the Global Information Network (GIN) and get free access to my written course, The Science of Personal Mastery. This is the best reading material you could have that will release your hidden abilities and "superpowers."

2. Listen to positive audios every day. If you drive a car, you can listen to audios while you are driving. You don't have to listen for hours and hours and hours every day. You can do that. The more the better. But listening even a little, consistently, daily, is really the important thing. Like reading books daily, listening to audios will feed your mind with positive thoughts daily.

Join GIN and listen to my Success Mastery Course audios.

3. Attend various live events such as positive motivational seminars. Something magical happens when you are in an inspirational live event with other like-minded people. A Mastermind is created, and your power is amplified dramatically. That's why the people who were at the live event where I delivered this material originally had a huge advantage over you just reading this book or listening to the audios of this book. Join GIN and you get a FREE ticket to a major weekend event where you will meet hundreds or thousands of other motivated GIN Members from all over the world. You will hear speakers that will inspire you and teach you more in-depth information about the keys and secrets of success. These events are life-changing.

4. Associate with successful people that have what you want. Associate with winners, with successful people, with positive, motivated, inspired people who are manifesting their dreams and following this success system that never fails. Build relationships and friendships with winners. Success rubs off. Your income will be the average of your five best friends'. Join GIN and associate with true winners. Meet and become friends with extremely successful people who will support you and ***pull for you***. Listen to them, observe them. Aristotle Onassis, one of the wealthiest people in the world, said the one thing he would do if he were broke was to go to places where wealthy people were and just be in their presence. Success does breed success.

Years ago I was taught this very important concept of association by the Brotherhood. One of my mentors said, "Five years from now your income is going to be based on the books you read and the friends you have."

Think about that.

Why? Because when you're associating with people, Masterminds are created, your brains are synchronizing, and if their thought process is low and their income level is low, that energy will affect YOUR energy. Your energy and vibration will begin to match theirs. Your income will match theirs. This is because thoughts and frequencies are what develop your income.

Many of you reading this may be thinking, "Oh God, I need to get some new friends." Guess what? Yes, you're right.

Associate with people that have what you want and always try to associate with people that have income levels that you want, and beyond—the higher the better. You'll begin to observe them and *do* observe them. Watch them, model yourself after them, listen to them, learn from them, and mimic how they speak and how they act. Mimic how they THINK. Just being in their presence will help your vibration and positively affect your brain. THEIR vibration and frequency WILL positively change you for the better.

Do this and you'll start developing new, positive, success-creating neural pathways like they have, and you will start achieving the results that they get. It's always the thinking that does make it so.

I'm planting a lot of seeds. A lot of seeds into your subconscious that will start to germinate. You'll see the results soon in your life, and it will be magical. Expect your miracle soon!

LESSON 14

Activating Your Power:
The Decision to Be Great

At the live event, after our break, when we started this section, all the attendees had smiles on their faces and were very happy. Hopefully you are smiling now too. Feels good, doesn't it? Feels good to know that you actually do have power. It feels good to realize that, yes, you do create everything in your own life. And it's good to know that everything that you've created can be changed. There's nothing that can't be different if you choose.

Success is really just a decision away.

When you have the attitude, "I'm going to do it, that's it, period," and you know you have the power, and you know all you have to do is focus on what you want and feel good about it with anticipation as if you've already received it, and start jumping up and down with happiness NOW—then you are broadcasting, you are transmitting a frequency with power and intensity for the thing you want to manifest, and you know it IS coming into your life.

And if you broadcast that frequency consistently, it will attract like-minded thoughts that give you like-minded feelings. And it will attract into your life exactly what you're transmitting. And what will be attracted into your life are circumstances, events, situations, experiences, and people that match that vibrational frequency.

Which means you will have in your life things that give you the emotions or the feelings that you are broadcasting.

413

And you will have in your life the actual *things* which you desire, and which you are focusing on, and which you are broadcasting because that thing, that thought of a thing, is a vibrational frequency. And when you attach an expectant emotion to it, you start getting other circumstances and events that give you the same emotional feeling as well as the thing that you're focusing on.

Isn't that exciting?

Isn't it exciting to know that no matter what happens in your life, there's no such thing as something bad? It's just a different experience. You've created it. And that "bad" thing is really probably very good because the universe put it there to HELP you to attain what you desire. The universe does things FOR you, not TO you.

Look at the emotion you are feeling at any time of the day, and if you like it, fine. And if you don't, you look at it, acknowledge it, accept and welcome it, and use it to clearly define what you DO want. At this point, you turn your back on the negative emotion you don't like feeling, and the thing you DON'T want, and focus on what you clearly defined as what you DO want. Then with deliberate intent, imagine yourself in possession of what you do want and feel NOW AS IF you WOULD feel if you actually did have what you want right now.

When you look at what you don't want, and your negative feelings, and fully CONFRONT them, it helps clarify what you do want. ***Whatever you can fully CONFRONT, you can HANDLE.***

What most people do is, they keep thinking about, and focusing on, what they don't want. They think about the lack of what they want. Which means they're thinking about not having it. So they think they're thinking about what they DO want, but they are actually thinking about the fact that they *don't* have what they want. They are seeing themselves NOT having their desire. They are seeing themselves WITHOUT what they want to have.

And they're talking about that. They are speaking that into existence.

They keep thinking and saying, "I don't have it. Why don't I have more money? Why don't I have more money? Why don't I have more money? I should have more money, but I don't have any money. I want money, but it's not here. I don't have money. I am so far in debt. I am struggling financially. I never seem to get ahead. Nothing works for me. Why can't I have more money?"

You're focusing on the fact that you don't have money, and that it's not coming in. It's hard to come in, and nothing works out your way. ***Thus, that's what you're creating.***

You know what your thoughts are by how you feel. If you're feeling good most of the day, no matter what the situation is, guess what? That's the vibration that you are broadcasting, a GOOD feeling. This is the same feeling you will have when you are actually in possession of your desire.

The more you feel good, more and more similar thoughts will start coming in that will make you feel better and better and "gooder and gooder." Then the physical manifestation of your desires starts coming into your life and you start seeing events, circumstances, and situations which reflect that, which give you MORE good feelings, because you SEE tangible evidence that it is working.

That's how it works.

Most people say, "I'll believe it when I see it." NO. This is a lie. The truth is YOU WILL SEE IT WHEN YOU BELIEVE IT. The believing has to come FIRST.

Fifty years ago I knew a very wealthy man. He had a great attitude. He would walk into a room with confidence. He smiled and seemed to not have a worry in the world. I told him that when I had his kind of money, I would have that attitude as well. He snapped at me, "NO. The money will NOT give you this attitude; it is the attitude that will give you the money. You have to have this attitude when you are broke, THEN the money will come."

Now, let me give you a little trick to help you feel good. When you feel really, really good, your body changes. Your posture changes when you're feeling really, really good. You stand tall, your head's up, you smile, your shoulders go back, you have a spring in your step, you skip, you whistle, you hum, you sing, and your body is moving and flowing with power and confidence.

Well, guess what?

When you're feeling bad, your body begins to change as well. Your shoulders get slouched, you begin to hunch over, you walk a little slower, you frown, your voice changes: It gets lower and sounds tired, depressed, annoyed, and fearful. "Oh my, oh my, oh my."

So, here's a little trick. When you're feeling bad, in addition to doing all the things I previously mentioned, like the Callahan technique, you can do this one little-known "hack" that will change how you feel almost instantly.

This "hack" is when you are feeling bad, *change your physiology*.

If you're ever feeling bad, if you pay attention, you will notice your physiology is bad too. You'll notice you're slouching, you're bent over, you're not walking with a spring in your step.

So, when you are feeling down, low, sad, depressed, angry, etc., just change your physiology to the same physiology you WOULD have if you were happy and motivated and enthusiastic.

Just say, wait a minute, I'm feeling bad. Okay, let me throw my shoulders back. Let me put a smile on my face. Just by putting a smile on your face will make you feel better. It actually happens instantaneously. Like wow, instantaneous.

So stand up tall, throw your shoulders back. Smile. Put a little bounce in your step. Whistle, hum, sing. Start moving your physiology into the space that it WOULD be IF you were actually feeling happy. ACT enthusiastic and soon you will FEEL enthusiastic.

And, when you ACT as if you were happy and change your physiology to match a happy person, all of a sudden, your emotions change.

You begin to FEEL happy. When your emotions change, that means internally your focus, your thoughts have changed, and you're now thinking about things that you want.

You are thinking positive, good thoughts, and now you're vibrating good feelings. That means you're going to be attracting more good feeling thoughts and more good feeling thoughts and more good feeling thoughts.

Your positive ball of energy is growing, your negative ball of energy is going down.

Remember, you don't sing because you are happy, you are happy BECAUSE YOU SING.

That's how it works. YOU CAN control how you feel. Most people let emotions control them.

The key element is, always feel good most of the time. Try to feel better. When you feel good, your thoughts are about the things you WANT, and you have an expectation that you WILL manifest them. You get what you think about most of the time.

Which is why, when you really, really, really want something, and you're obsessed with attaining it, you will be thinking about it much of the time. Thus, as long as you believe you WILL have it, and have the expectation that you WILL have it, and feel good when thinking about your desire, it WILL manifest.

But most people think they are thinking about what they want when, in fact, they are thinking about the fact that they don't have what they desire. They're thinking of the fact that their desire is absent from their life, so they feel bad. And they think they will feel good WHEN they actually GET their desire. That will not work. You can't believe it when you see it. You have to believe you have it when you DON'T have it. When you believe it, THEN you will see it. This is faith. Faith is the substance of things HOPED FOR, it is the EVIDENCE of things NOT SEEN.

You know which way you are thinking based on how you feel.

If you feel anticipation, happiness, joy; if you feel as if you've already received your desire—you can taste it and feel it, it's already yours—then that's when your desire is flowing into you, because that's when you're broadcasting your desire's frequency at full power and at full intensity. There's no resistance or counter-intentions on the lines to slow the manifestation of your desire.

That's when the Law of Attraction is activated and is bringing into your life your desires. That's when the universe is doing everything to make your desire manifest, things like you wouldn't believe because you can't see what is off your radar screen. The universe is working "behind the scenes," virtually conspiring with All-That-Is to manifest your desire. It HAS to, because you have activated the LAW of Attraction. It is LAW.

This is where faith comes in. Faith is the SUBSTANCE of things HOPED for. It is the EVIDENCE of things NOT SEEN. You can't see all that is off your tiny radar screen. You can't SEE the universal forces working on your behalf. You can't even imagine them. Your mind can never understand or comprehend what is BEYOND the mind.

But there are trillions of bits of data and information and particles flowing, moving, and being adjusted into trillions of different scenarios with trillions of different variables. This is happening in a dimension that is beyond time and space as you know or understand it. It is the quantum world, which is VERY real and TANGIBLE. Science today has proven this.

Everything is being done at this quantum level to get what you want. What you want, wants you.

It's a law. It has to happen. It is the Law of Attraction.

The Law of Attraction is pulling your desire into your reality. And your desire WILL come. It WILL manifest. It WILL be your reality.

When you do this properly, more like-minded thoughts will come to you first and you'll feel better and better. And *then*, at the perfect time that is in your highest good, the physical manifestation of your desire will occur. You will HAVE it.

Make sense?

I remember doing this many years ago. I wanted a Ferrari and a Rolls-Royce. I did this when I could not afford those cars. But I did the process properly. Later, I walked into my garage and was deciding which car to take: the Rolls, the Ferrari, the Mercedes AMG, the Porsche, the Range Rover, my classic 1976 Cadillac El Dorado convertible, or my classic 1970 Chevelle SS convertible with the LS 6 engine, one of only six in the world. As I looked at all the cars, all purchased in cash, I laughed at the time, a few years earlier, when I could not even afford one of them. THIS WORKS if you WORK IT.

At this point in the live event, a question came up about how to handle disappointment or failure or when somebody says "no" and rejects you or tries to stop you.

Know this reality. In life or in business, you WILL have what appear to be setbacks, obstacles, challenges, problems, delays, stops, disasters, adversity, and many situations that COULD make you FEEL disappointed, angry, afraid, stressed, or upset, or feeling like giving up.

Pain in life is inevitable, but SUFFERING is OPTIONAL. Suffering is your choice. Remember, if you have an emotion that you cannot control and it actually controls you, then you have an engram, an energetic imprint with encapsulated emotion keying in, or activating, or coming to surface. This is stronger than you are. You must eliminate it or at least reduce its power using a technique such as the Callahan technique or some of the methods taught in the Success Mastery and Science of Personal Mastery Courses available exclusively to GIN Members.

In life, you will have experiences which you want to go one way but don't. You will try things that fail. Unexpected negative situations will come up. Business will turn bad. You will lose money sometimes. Investments will go down. People will betray you. The list goes on.

And you CAN get a feeling of disappointment or some other "negative" emotion.

You're trying to do something, and you fail and you feel bad. Somebody says no to you about something, and you feel bad.

The first reason you feel bad when an external situation happens that you don't want or like, is based on the habit you have of REACTING to negative situations instead of RESPONDING with deliberate intent.

And the second reason is because some engram or samskara gets activated and comes to the surface. Samskara is a Sanskrit word meaning energetic imprint in your mind, or memory or energetic field—that has encapsulated emotion and can activate without your control—thus giving you an uncontrollable and mostly irrational emotion. Sometimes we say "They pushed my buttons" when we have an uncontrollable emotion activate.

When a situation doesn't turn out the way you want, you say you are disappointed. Now, there is a whole training program on this one point that I will give you a taste of here. Most people say things like, "I am sad. I am disappointed. I am angry." NO. YOU are not sad or disappointed or angry. You are FEELING sad, disappointed, or angry.

NEVER put anything after "I am" that is not positive, wonderful, and reflects WHO YOU REALLY ARE, especially NOT what you are FEELING. Don't even say, "I am happy." Say, "I am FEELING happy." You CAN say "I am love, consciousness, light." Those are accurate statements of who you REALLY are. I teach at length about this in my Success Mastery and Science of Personal Mastery Courses.

This is very deep and very powerful transformative material, in case it is something that resonates with you.

So when you do something and it doesn't work, you say it's a failure and feel like a loser. You feel bad. When somebody says no, you feel bad because you think they are stopping you from getting what you want.

The reason you feel bad is because your focus goes to the fact that you don't have what you want in your life. It is ABSENT. It is NOT there. There is a lack of it in your life. You do this out of habit.

You think of the fact that you don't have what you want, that it is NOT in your life. Therefore, you feel bad. And that happens many times because it's a habit of thinking. Neural pathways have been drilled into your brain, and thinking that way automatically, without deliberate intent, is a habit.

The fact is, if you look at the people who are operating and using this manifesting technology at the highest levels of effectiveness, like many of the powerful and wealthy people that were at the live event or at GIN events, we don't have uncontrollable negative emotions. We CHOOSE to feel negative emotions to our advantage and use them to contract energy, to clearly define what we DON'T want, and then focus on and clearly define what we DO want.

If you ask us, "How do you deal with disappointment?"

We say, "Well, I don't feel disappointment without wanting to or without using it to my advantage. I feel negative emotions and USE them, then STOP feeling them." You see, we visit the pain, and we visit the dream, but we LIVE in the present, and we choose how we feel. We control our MINDS, our thoughts, and our emotions. Most people have no control over their minds, thoughts, or emotions. For most of you, your mind, thoughts, and emotions control YOU. CHANGE that and change your life. You can!

And if you ask us, "Well, how do you deal with failure?" we say, "We don't have failure." Does this mean we succeed in everything? It is perspective. We know that you either succeed or learn. You either win or learn. There is no failure. There is no loss. When you don't WIN, you LEARN, thus you STILL WIN.

Think about Thomas Edison. He "failed" ten thousand times trying to create the incandescent light bulb. But when he was asked by a reporter how it felt to fail ten thousand times, he responded by saying that he did not fail ten thousand times, but rather, successfully found ten thousand ways that did not work.

You see, he understood that every time he found a way it wouldn't work, he was getting closer to his ultimate success. He LEARNED something valuable when it "failed." Thus he looked at every "failure" as a success. Those failures were not obstacles; they were stepping stones he was walking on, getting him closer to his dream.

So what you would call a failure, and you would feel bad, he looked at as a success. "Wow, this doesn't work. DAMN. But I'm getting closer."

Do you understand that? That kind of thinking is the habit that people who use this technology at the highest levels utilize.

When something doesn't turn out exactly the way you think it should, most people, out of habit, CHOOSE to FEEL disappointed.

But if you understand that the way you think it should turn out probably isn't the best way for it to turn out anyway, you will have a different perspective on it. You know that in every adversity, there are the seeds of a GREATER benefit. You look at challenges and adversity as a gift.

When something happens that isn't to our liking, what *we* do out of habit is USE that situation to contract energy, define what we don't want and will not tolerate any more, and use that powerful contracted energy to clearly define what we DO want and start the process. We DO feel negative emotion, but by choice and deliberate intent, and we don't feel that for more than a few moments or minutes. We THEN feel empowered and fired up. This type of situation gets us MOTIVATED, energized, and inspired. We feel like we are in a fight, and we are going to fight back and WIN. We don't feel disappointed.

We just say and think things like: "I caused this, what vibration did I put out? So do I need to change my vibration?"

Or "Wow, something incredible, even better than I could have imagined, is about to happen because I thought this was the best way, but it ain't working out, so something better is happening."

Or, "This sucks. I am so disappointed. Okay, I am NOT going to take this anymore. Enough is enough. I know EXACTLY what I want, and I am making the decision right now that I will NEVER quit. I am DOING it, that's it, PERIOD! Now let's go to work and win this thing!"

Or, "Oof, let's reevaluate. Maybe we are going down the wrong path. What can we learn from this? Let's take a step back and regroup and look at everything in a new unit of time. Let's see if we can look at this from a different angle. Maybe we are going down the wrong road."

So we don't feel disappointment. We don't look at these things as disappointing. We look at them as something with a seed of a greater benefit. We do this out of habit and because we have used the "processes" in the Success Mastery and the Science of Personal Mastery Courses to clear our "field" from the "samskaras" that can activate, giving us uncontrollable and irrational counter-intention emotions that STOP us from manifesting our dreams.

When somebody says "no" to us when we're expecting or hoping for or wanting "yes", we don't feel bad out of habit, and we don't have samskaras keying in or activating. That situation does not push our buttons, because we don't have buttons to push. We cleared them out of our energetic field. We are rational and in control of our emotions and thoughts. We just think, "I'm vibrating something incorrectly, thus manifesting what I don't want, because my broadcast—my transmission of vibration—may be incorrect, so let me look at that."

Or, if we are broadcasting correctly, we think, "This 'no,' which I didn't think should happen and I did NOT want to happen, obviously *should* have happened. It must be a gift from the universe because it is actually going to help me get what I want. This 'no' must be a prerequisite for me to really be getting what I want, because I don't know what's off the radar screen. Let me learn from this, use it to really clarify what I DON'T want, and use that to drive me to focus more on exactly what I DO want."

Do you understand that?

So, the answer is, anytime you are in a situation where you feel disappointment, know that you are feeling that way out of habit or because a samskara is keying in and activating.

Know that you don't HAVE to feel disappointment. Acknowledge it, don't deny it. Welcome it, don't resist it. Then USE that negative emotion as I have taught you.

Do this if you feel bad because of a failure. Or you feel bad because somebody said "no." But the key is, ask yourself, "Okay, why did this happen?" Are you vibrating or transmitting an incorrect vibration such as lack? Is a subconscious counter-intention that you have not cleared out, activating, and thus attracting into your life things you DON'T want?

Okay, so work on that first.

But then secondly, "Why am I feeling bad?" The reason you're feeling bad is because you're focused on the idea that you are NOT going to get what you want, and you DON'T have it now.

How do you change that thinking? How do you change the focus on your desire not manifesting? First have the awareness that you are focusing on NOT manifesting your desire. You have to have AWARENESS. You have to be CONSCIOUS. Pay attention!

Then by deliberate intent, think about what you want. Focus on what you want and work on feeling better. When you focus on what you want, you should feel better. If you focus on what you want and you don't feel better, that means you're really being pulled back into believing you won't get it. Or you have a samskara active and giving you an uncontrollable negative emotion.

Generally, what you want is probably not in the sweet spot. So what you are desiring has to be corrected or changed to something that you CAN believe you can actually achieve.

How do you change your belief level? Let's say you want something and feel bad. Then start saying to yourself out loud something like this, "Okay, obviously, I'm not believing that I'm going to get this because I am feeling bad, so let me change this. I'm focusing on lack, I am focusing on the fact that I DON'T have it, which is why I feel bad. So I want to feel better, and I really do want this thing. So how do I start feeling better? Okay, well, a way for me to actually manifest my desire is not on my radar screen. I don't see any way I can get this. And based on all the circumstances that just happened, it looks even bleaker. But that's okay. I don't have a time limit on attaining it, and I'm not putting any pressure on myself to get it right now. Other people get to have what I desire. Well, if other people who are less intelligent than I am, less worthy than I am, are getting this, then certainly I can. So I'm sure at some point I COULD possibly get this too."

And you start feeling better, you start moving again in the direction of feeling better. You are taking charge of your emotions. You are in control and command of your mind and thoughts.

The ultimate point you want to get to is, "Oh, I'm absolutely getting this." But you may not be able to get to that point right away. You may be able to only go up on the belief level scale one step at a time. But you need to *move* your emotions UP the emotional scale.

Go as far as you can see, and when you get there, you will see further.

Remember, the ideal scene is that you feel great most of the time, but the real focus is that you *feel better*. No matter how you feel right now, you're just trying to feel a little better. Just move yourself up the emotional scale with deliberate intent and willpower, and feel a little better.

If you can't do it on your own with your own thoughts and you really feel bad, then use the Callahan technique. It *will* help you. Do the other things I mentioned earlier to help you feel better. And if you're doing all the things on the list that I gave you, this may be a great time for you to listen to your favorite song, or go for a walk, or listen to one of our motivational audios so you can start changing the way you feel, and that will get you out of that funk.

It's the same thing with criticism. How do you handle criticism? When somebody criticizes you, when somebody says something to you that makes you feel bad, you may have so many neural pathways and habits that have been ingrained, that when somebody criticizes you, you cringe and you feel horrible, automatically. It is many times uncontrollable and often an irrational emotional reaction.

What I suggest is anytime somebody criticizes you, if you instantly and uncontrollably feel horrible, that means you have a samskara activating. Immediately use the Callahan technique, and blow out that charge that is activated. This will change the neural pathway in your brain because that's what the technique does, and it will blow out the *root cause* of that habit of feeling bad when criticized.

So the next time somebody criticizes you, you won't feel that bad at all, because there is no longer any button for them to push.

You then have control over your emotions instead of your emotions controlling you.

Rationally, if somebody is criticizing you, you shouldn't feel bad at all. It should be completely a non-issue. A guy can look at me and criticize me night and day, he can call me names, and say all kinds of terrible things to me, and I'm just looking at him in a state of neutrality. He can't push my buttons and get me to *react* because I have no buttons to push. He is wasting his breath. I have the power to *respond* in a calm, rational way of my choosing. I control HIM; he is not controlling me.

The way you think doesn't affect the way I think. And the way you think doesn't affect what happens in my life. I don't care what you think or say. It has no effect on me or my emotions. I create my reality, no one else.

If somebody is criticizing me, I *will listen* because maybe he's pointing out some things that I don't see, and maybe there are some things that I can do better. So I'm not offended in any way. But see, that's the habit that I have. Those are the neural pathways that have been established in my brain. That is how I am programmed now.

But if you get even the slightest amount of criticism, you may cry, you may get upset, you may get beet red. You may feel horrible. The reason that's happening is because it's basically activating a samskara, and all of the neural pathways in your brain light up, and all of the negative energy that is trapped in your "field" relating to criticism gets activated and keyed in.

The good news is you can now focus on starting to change, little by little, the neural pathways in your brain so you can establish new habits and new programming by using the technique of focusing on what you want in the manner that I have laid out for you. Use the Callahan technique to blow out the "charge" and encapsulate negative emotion so you don't have any buttons to push on this issue. This gives you the power to **respond** with deliberate intent to criticism instead of **reacting** uncontrollably. This also gives you the power to rationalize how this is just a criticism, "it is only someone's opinion, and what he thinks or says, doesn't affect me." And you have the power to actually listen and maybe gain some helpful insight that you can use to be better.

Anytime you feel bad about anything, anytime you feel like your "buttons" are being pushed and you are feeling an uncontrollable emotion, use the Callahan technique.

If your lover leaves you and you feel horrible, use the Callahan technique. You got "bad" news and you feel horrible, use the Callahan technique.

Anytime something "bad" happens and your state changes from a good state to a horrible state, all that means is you have many neural pathways that have been established in the brain and many patterns that have been ingrained in you, and so much negative energy that is now activated when that situation happens, you automatically and uncontrollably feel bad.

You need to get rid of all those things. You need to blow them out of your "field." You need to be "clear."

You can get rid of them instantly by using the Callahan technique. Or you can focus and spend one, two, three minutes, five minutes, and start using your own mind and willpower to say something like, "My focus, by the Law of Attraction, is being pulled to these thoughts so I feel horrible, because now I'm feeling lack and I'm vibrating that which is not who I am. All my hopes, dreams, and desires are vibrations; that's a part of me. But I'm vibrating now something different that doesn't line up with who I really am. Or I'm vibrating that I won't get it, or that I don't have it now, and that misalignment is making me feel horrible."

This is confronting. Anything you can confront, you can handle. When you confront anything fully, it vanishes.

So criticism or any of the things people say and do to you that are keying in and activating negative emotions are just telling you that you have a large ball of black negative energy in your "field" which you are going to have to reduce in size and power.

And every time you have someone push your buttons, or you feel something "key in," use the Callahan technique. For some of you over the next thirty, sixty, or ninety days, you could be using a Callahan technique almost every day because you have so many samskaras that need to be "cleared." You have so many different things that will come into your life which activate different parts of this big black blob of trapped, condensed and encapsulated energy, and you need to disempower it—to blow it out, to clear it. You need to make it dissipate. You need to make it go away. You need to "transmute" that negative energy into positive energy. This will then create a void.

Then you need to fill up all those old nonactive neural pathways and patterns and start replacing them with new ones. You need to establish new patterns, programs, and neural pathways which will give you new success habits to replace your current failure habits.

Make sense? Good.

Let me talk about a couple of other key issues when it comes specifically to making money.

A key issue which we addressed, but I want to hit again, is focus. We talked about obsession. We talked about a chief aim. We talked about "you get what you think about most of the time." Therefore, it's to your major advantage to have focus on one major thing as your chief aim.

This is called "singleness of purpose." It is a secret to achievement and manifesting something.

When you have a singular focus, most of the day, most of the time, you're focusing on that one thing in an obsessive way. You're thinking about it most of the time as if it absolutely, positively, 100 percent is already yours, and you *need* to have it.

And when you do that, you will feel amazing. If you're thinking about it and you're feeling bad, that means your shift is on the lack of having it—the fact that it is currently absent from your life. Or doubt and disbelief have crept in. Either way it means what you want is not going to manifest.

So you have to shift back to feeling really, really good, or at least better.

But *focus* is a key. It is the ability to concentrate. You never hear about this from "success experts" or Law of Attraction experts. The reason I bring this up is most people who are trying to make money, many times don't put any focus on any one thing. They are scattered. They are juggling ten balls at the same time. They are running around with no focus, working on fifty different projects simultaneously.

And every time a new exciting idea comes by, they jump on that one. And they're not putting any focus or attention on any one thing long enough for it to germinate and grow and produce results.

If you plant a seed, you have to water it and cultivate it and fertilize it. And water it and cultivate it and fertilize it. And water it and cultivate it and fertilize it. You have to focus on it and do all these things *before* it grows.

Same thing here.

When you're broadcasting a vibration that you want something to succeed or to have more money, and you're putting attention on a particular project—and all of a sudden a new project comes along— your tendency is to stop what you are doing and put attention on the new thing. You can't finish a cycle of action.

You're taking your attention and focus off the first one. You become distracted.

Basically, you're not thinking about anything long enough for it to really attract into your physical existence. You get what you think about most of the time.

So focusing on a chief aim is vital. Focus. Concentrate. Pay attention. Do the right things long enough, consistently. Persistence. Commitment. Perseverance. You should know the meanings of these words. Look them up. Activate and illuminate them.

I see people losing focus all the time. I can see it because people who aren't focused are not getting the results they want. Therefore they start getting frustrated, start feeling bad. They're vibrating bad. They are not manifesting their desires. They lose faith. They get angry and depressed, and it's a continual spiral downward.

They're never going to turn it around, ever, because they're not focusing on anything.

And then, slowly, over time, they shift into thinking about what they don't want to happen, or they keep thinking about the fact that they *don't* have what they want—the lack of it—and therefore they get more of NOT having their desires in their life.

Does that make sense? Do you understand that?

A question that came up at the live event was, "How long do I do something? At what point should I quit and move on to something else? I have heard that if you continue to do something that is not working, expecting a different result, you are insane."

That is an excellent question. If you're focusing on making money and focusing on a project, but it is not producing the results you want, and then a new opportunity comes around that looks really good, what do you do? Should you quit the first thing and start putting time and effort into this new great-sounding opportunity?

Perhaps that first opportunity was just a stepping stone for you to move on to this next one. At what point do you stop or quit? There's a saying, "Stop throwing good money after bad."

The answer is really simple. If you're doing something and it is in line perfectly with your thoughts and who you really are, you will be having so much fun doing the activity, the results don't matter. You will feel great as you engage in the *process of creating*.

Sometimes you focus on making money and you decide, "I'm going to do a particular business or activity that I think will make me the money that I seek." You've been doing this business for weeks, months, maybe a couple of years. You're enjoying every minute of it, but at some point, the enjoyment goes away. It has now become drudgery. It's no longer fun.

That's when you quit. That is when it is time to move on.

If it's no longer fun, you should consider moving on to something else. Life is too short. Do things that are fun. Enjoy your life. You don't *have* to do anything. Stop saying "I *have* to do this, or I *have* to do that." What you do is your CHOICE.

If you are in a situation where you are no longer having fun, first consider if you got your thinking off track. Did you change your thought patterns and are now focusing on the fact that it's not working fast enough? Are you focusing on your business *not* working or the feeling of lack that you have because you're not getting the results you want? Or is fear, lack of belief, or doubt creeping in?

First see if you can change your thinking so that the activity can go back to being fun again. Many times reevaluating your goals will sort this out for you and bring you clarity and certainty.

Maybe this reevaluation of your priorities and chief aim will make you *want* to stop the activity, quit, and look for something else that can give you pleasure. The main reason we do anything is for fun and fulfillment. We're all playing the game of life. That game is to have fun and to get as much fulfillment and joy as we can.

Another question that always comes up is, "How do I stay motivated?" First understand that as you go through your life, there are cycles or seasons that you will experience. This is based on your karma or destiny and influenced by astrological positions based on your exact time and place of birth. In advanced training, I taught at length about all the different cycles a person goes through. GIN Members get exclusive access to this information, as do people who do one-on-one live video sessions with me.

It is normal for a person to feel like they are in a "funk," or uninspired, or not motivated, and not feeling enthusiastic. This happens to all of us. Many times you just need a break. You need to rest and distract yourself for a while and let your subconscious sort everything out.

Many times you will be focusing on what you want, have a burning desire for its achievement, and you will absolutely feel motivated and inspired every day.

The first thing to know about how to *stay* motivated is if somebody says "I don't feel motivated," I ask, "What's your chief aim? Maybe you don't have one. You have to know your chief aim as well as you know your own name. In order to stay motivated you need a chief aim that is in the sweet spot. So get one."

The first reason people don't feel motivated is, other than being in one of the "down" cycles, is they don't have a chief aim, and/or that they don't have a burning desire for its achievement because that chief aim is not in the sweet spot.

The way to *get* motivated is to do all the things I suggest in this book, such as reading daily, listening to audios daily, going to live events on a regular basis, being part of GIN, and having motivated friends who support you and do all the other action steps suggested. Plugging into the system is critical so that you continually feed your mind with positive messages and programming. This will help you overcome your past failure habits of thinking and change your failure programming.

Additionally, the way to *get* motivated is to get a chief aim that is in the sweet spot and get a burning desire for its achievement. You need to be living your life with passion. You need to be living your life *on purpose*. You should have a purpose-driven life.

When you can find a goal, a chief aim, that can give you a burning desire, that's when you're the happiest. That's when you're motivated. That is when you are inspired. You are in alignment. You have clarity and certainty.

You are *truly* happiest when you're in the *process* of achieving your goal, *not* when you *attain* it. The journey is the reward. True happiness and success is your progressive realization of a worthwhile dream. It's the process. It is when you are in the process of *creating*.

The real process is when you have something that you NEED, that you MUST have, and you have a burning desire and obsession for its achievement. That's when you are the happiest and that's when you're motivated. You become a meaningful specific instead of a wandering generality.

That's the real key: to get and stay motivated.

Now, the way to fuel the fire and keep the fire of motivation burning is to read positive books and listen to inspirational audios every day, go to live motivational events on a regular basis, and associate with other positive, motivated, successful people.

Do the dream-building processes you learned. Dream-building will keep you motivated. It will keep you focused on your chief aim and keep that obsession and desire to achieve it high. Dream-building will keep fueling your fire of desire.

That's how you stay motivated.

And always, always follow *your own desires*. Follow that which gives *you* the greatest sense of bliss. If you always follow what gives *you* bliss, you will live an extraordinary life. You will experience a magnificent existence on this wonderful planet. Always, always, always follow *your* bliss.

When you evaluate your goals and dreams, consider that most people actually have goals that are NOT theirs, but someone else's. You want to get a PhD because your parents always dreamed and wanted you to get a PhD. You want a Rolls-Royce because you want other people to look at you in a certain way. It is not really YOUR desire. Your goals must be *yours* and yours alone.

A question that comes up often is about making money in various areas such as crypto trading, stocks, options, forex, franchises, online marketing, online affiliate marketing, MLMs, and real estate. People ask me if there are good courses available—produced by people that have actually succeeded in that particular area—that will teach specific methods and techniques and the "how" to make money in that particular area of business.

Yes. GIN Members get access to courses in all those areas.

You can learn how to buy real estate with no money down (even if you have bad credit), make amazing money, and generate wealth. Making money and becoming financially free as a real estate investor is something that many people have achieved. You can as well. IF that is your passion.

You can learn how to make money investing or trading in the stock market, or trading options, commodities, forex, and crypto. There are courses on how to make money on the internet. I have a course called Three Keys to Internet Millions. Having generated billions in sales worldwide, I know the keys and secrets to making money on the internet.

There are hundreds of *ways or methods* to make money. This is proven by all the people who actually *have* made money doing those things. What one person has done, you can do also.

Today, with the internet, you have access to more information on *how* to make money than ever before in history. In fact, it is *easier* today to make money than at any time in history. More people are making more money than ever. Yet, most people are still asleep and in a trance. They will never be successful because they have been programmed for failure and reject things like this book. They will always struggle financially and make excuses. Remember, failures are always good at one thing: *making excuses.*

There are many courses available that have good information, good techniques, and good methods, taught by people that have what you want and have been where you are.

You can follow their systems and profit immensely if you follow the formula and steps they outline, as long as you have the *right thinking and vibration.*

I know many of the people that have put those programs together, and some of them are good and some of them are great. Use discernment, however. Many of them are simply designed to SELL you the first course, usually at a very low price to get you in their "funnel," which then is really designed to sell you the NEXT course, and then the NEXT course, etc. So BEWARE and be cautious. This is why GIN Members have an advantage. We do all the due diligence and offer to our members the best of the best. It saves our members time and money.

A question that comes up is, "What business or moneymaking method is best, which one should I get involved with? Crypto? Real estate? Buy a franchise? Internet marketing? Multilevel marketing? Online affiliate marketing?"

The answer is, follow your own bliss. If you don't LOVE real estate, don't get involved. You won't succeed. You must do what you love. Actually there is a point that is the combination of what you love to do and what you are GOOD at doing. Find that point and then do, as your moneymaking activity, *that*, and you will not only make money but feel happy and fulfilled.

Use this technique. Believe me, the universe will point you in the right direction and present you with the right moneymaking course and area of business that's right for you.

You may have to go through several courses, and try several things, to find which one really zeroes into your own sweet spot in terms of really getting your juices flowing. The one that is a perfect combination of what you love to do and are good at doing. That "thing" that is in alignment with who you really are.

A lot of moneymaking courses teach real steps where everybody *can* make huge amounts of money. But people say, "Well, you know, a million people have bought that 'how to get rich in real estate course' and almost all of them did not make any money in real estate, therefore the course must not work, it must be a scam."

No, don't be silly. Let's look at the facts. A million people buy the "How to get rich in real estate course." The facts are, 90 percent of them don't even listen to even ONE audio. They buy it and never even start listening to the course. The other 10 percent will *start the* course, but won't *finish* the course. So, of course, they will not make any money. So you can't count them.

If you are looking for real numbers of what percentage of people actually make money with the real estate method taught in the course, you can only look at the people who not only FINISHED THE COURSE, but who actually followed the steps correctly for at least a year. If we look at those people, statistics show approximately 80 percent succeed!

Those who did not succeed, in analysis, we find that it was their thinking that was so negative that caused their actions to not produce results.

Because their thinking was "off," when they did put forth some action, they actually hated doing the activity because they were not using this technique and the Law of Attraction properly.

There's only a very small amount of people that actually do anything on a consistent basis. The failures did not do the right things long enough consistently. This is fact.

Let me just tell you exactly how it is. If you're using the technology and the mind techniques that we're teaching here in this book, you could get a hundred courses and close your eyes, pick one, do what it teaches, and you'll make millions. It doesn't matter which one you choose. One is not better than the other. When you use the techniques and manifesting formula in this book, they all work.

So if you want to make money buying and selling on eBay, Etsy, Amazon, Poshmark; or use the system in my Three Keys to Internet Millions; invest and trade stocks, options, crypto, futures, forex; or buy and sell companies; or real estate; or tax liens; or whatever you choose—all those courses taught by a person who actually did it and is still doing it will teach you incredibly effective methods that work when you use them.

If you learn the material in those courses and do what they say exactly as they say it, and don't change the recipe, combined with the manifesting technique in this book, you will get results. You will make money.

They all work and they're all wonderful, fun ways to make money. Some of these moneymaking methods do not need a lot of time and money to get started. You can keep your job and start part-time, with under five hundred dollars. You don't need a lot of knowledge or experience because they teach you what you need to know and *how* to do everything.

Another question I get often is, "I have no idea *how* to make any money. I am not good with math or numbers. I don't think I have business sense. I don't like doing paperwork or accounting. What do I do?"

The answer is you don't have to know *how.* You don't need any of those skills. Those can be outsourced. When you look at the Training Balance Scale, you see the first side is the thinking, the vibration you are broadcasting—your attitude. Ninety percent of success is what is on this side of the scale.

The how—the techniques, the skills—are only 10 percent of success. You don't have to know *how* right now. The universe will present the *how* to you AFTER you focus long enough on the first side of the Training Balance Scale. The universe will manifest the conditions, circumstances, events, situations, and *people* you need to manifest the money you desire. Other people will come into your life who know *how.*

So what you do is you say, "I want to make money." Now be more specific. "I want to make $500,000 a year income." Do that long enough and something more specific will come into your mind. Do you want to be in a business of your own? Do you want to make money from your home? Do you want to start your own company? Do you have any inkling of *how* you want to make the money?

No. Okay. Perfect. You don't have to know *how* yet. All you may know *now* is that you *want* to make lots of money and have freedom to do anything you want.

Basically, you might say you want to make money out of your home. You want to make money without investing a lot of time or money, right? Perfect. Guess what? You know exactly what you want and you're smiling. You are feeling good. You have a magnificent obsession for that which you desire.

Let's say your goal, your chief aim, is, "I want to be rich, financially independent in some business, in something that gives me massive amounts of monthly income without me putting up a lot of money, with low risk, and not putting in a lot of time, and without investing a lot of money. I just really want a lot of cash flow coming in without doing a lot of work and without a lot of effort. I want this so I have time freedom and can travel anywhere in the world whenever I want."

This kind of financial goal is right on the money. Perfect. It could be anything, but this is just an example.

If that's your chief aim, all you have to do is think about that all the time, get a burning desire for its attainment, a magnificent obsession with actually having it, and keep saying and believing that the universe will put this opportunity right in your lap at exactly the right time.

As you do this, something inside you may tell you to join GIN and go to a GIN weekend event that you get for free when you join. Think about this. Before you read this book, you put out to the universe a desire. The universe gave you this book to read. Your desire brought you here. You are not reading this by accident. This book and GIN are your rescue boat. It is an answer to what you have been asking for. Your wish has been granted. It is now up to you to say yes and take massive and immediate action.

Does this make sense?

The manifesting technique is easy. You find your pain. You then clearly define what you want, either with specificity, general, or a feeling. You get obsessed with it, a burning desire for its attainment. You *need* to have it more than anything, which causes you to think about it all the time. And when you think about it, you feel NOW AS IF you would feel if you were actually in possession of your goal, you feel good. You have anticipation and expectation that it WILL manifest. You have faith, belief, and trust. You *know*. You are confident that it *is* manifesting at the right time. And you release attachment to the outcome and feel good now, even though you don't have it presently.

And you say, "I don't know how it's going to happen. I have no clue. How it will manifest is not on my radar screen. Based on the information on my radar screen, I couldn't even imagine how this is going to manifest. But I know it will, I am confident that it will, at the right time for me."

That's the technique. That's the power.

Use that method and then things start coming into your life. What you desire will manifest. Your wish will be your command.

The block that prevents things from manifesting is the counter-intentions that are in your DNA, subconscious, and conscious mind. The blocks are that all of the patterns, the programming, the old neural pathways in your brain, the failure habits that you've established, all the negative thoughts, have attracted more negative thoughts, thus creating a vibration that you broadcast that repels what you want instead of attracting what you want.

Your desires are stopped from manifesting because you're walking around with this big ball of negative energy, which has huge magnetic power, attracting what you ***don't*** want.

And anytime you start thinking positive, anytime you start thinking outside of that negative pattern that you have in the past, that negative pattern keeps pulling you back because it is powerful.

What it comes down to is you then start doubting and you start putting limitations on yourself. You think consciously or subconsciously, "I can't."

Remember what Henry Ford said: "Whether you think you can or if you think you can't, either way, you're right."

Imagine an elephant. Do you know how to train an elephant? Did you ever go to a circus and see these big, powerful, magnificent beasts? They are chained up with what looks like a relatively small chain around an ankle. One ankle. And this chain around the ankle goes into a stake in the ground, and it's not in cement.

They just pound these stakes in the ground. The elephant is just standing; he's not trying to get away. Anytime the elephant feels the slightest pressure on his ankle from this small chain connected to the stake in the ground, he just instantly stops. He gives up. He accepts that he is chained and cannot move.

As I was watching this one time, I thought, "This is goofy. I'm sure this magnificent, powerful animal could just pull his leg and it would yank that stake right out of the ground." So I talked to one of the guys at the circus, and I asked, "Can't that elephant just yank that stake out of the ground?"

The keeper said, "Yes and no. He has the power to do it, but he *can't* do it."

I was confused. "What do you mean?" He went on, "You see, the way elephants are trained is when they're very small, we put an identical chain around their ankle, but what we do is we don't put it to a stake in the ground. We bolt the chain into cement. So no matter how much effort the elephant puts into trying to escape, he can't escape. You watch these little baby elephants struggle; they will pull and pull and pull, day after day after day, week after week after week, they will pull, trying to escape. Then one day, they give up. They realize that there's no way, no matter how much effort they put in, that they can escape. The elephant is trained at that point. You have conditioned him to fail. He has been programmed. All you have to do then is just tap a stake in the ground and tie a chain to one of his ankles. The moment the elephant moves his leg and feels even the slightest resistance, he stops trying. He has been conditioned that it will be fruitless. He quits at the slightest resistance."

That's why the big mammoth adult elephant, which has a hundred times more power than the baby, doesn't even try to break free from the chains that bind him. He could break free in an instant, but he doesn't know that. You see, the elephant is bound and chained in his *mind*. The chain is not holding him; his beliefs are keeping him a slave.

There is a great true story about the escape artist Harry Houdini. He used to go around the world and do magic shows. In order to drum up business for a show, he would do some publicity stunts, one of which was he would walk into the police station in the town where he was doing this show, and he would challenge the officers to put him in handcuffs and lock him in their best cell. And if Houdini could walk in just with his street clothes on, he guaranteed that he could escape.

He escaped from every cell. He did this challenge all over the world. One time in Cologne, Germany, they had built the most technologically advanced and secure maximum security cell anywhere in the world. They said that this cell was inescapable, the lock could not be picked, and no one could get out of this cell. It was the best, most secure cell anywhere in the world.

Houdini went and challenged the police department to put him in that cell and insisted that he would escape. This got lots of publicity. Lots of cameramen were there, and all the newspapers. This was before TV. To much fanfare, Houdini went into the cell. They shut the door to the cell, and they left.

What most people didn't know was that Houdini was a master locksmith. The reason he would go in with his street clothes is because in his belt, he had hidden a very thin piece of metal, like a wire, which he would use as a pick to help him open the lock.

Houdini took out this wire and other various locksmithing tools that were hidden in his belt, and he began to work on picking the lock and opening it.

Houdini, being a master locksmith, usually could pick locks within a few minutes. In fact he practiced so much that he could pick any lock in less than five minutes.

But after about ten minutes, Houdini still hadn't picked *this* lock. It was a lock he'd never seen before. He continued to work and work and work on opening the lock. Another fifteen minutes passed, and he still hadn't picked the lock.

The confident Houdini was now becoming less confident in his abilities. He began to panic. Not escaping would ruin and end his career. He could be a laughingstock. He continued to work on opening this lock for another half an hour and still couldn't open the lock.

One hour later he was still furiously working on this lock. He was dripping with perspiration from head to toe. He was physically, mentally, and emotionally exhausted.

For over an hour he had been working on opening the lock, without success. Totally exhausted and on the verge of giving up, Houdini virtually collapsed against the cell door ... which sprang open!

You see, with all the fanfare, with all the press taking pictures that were there, with all the commotion and people, the police department shut the door of the cell, but they forgot to *lock* the lock.

True story.

Houdini, when you think about it, was locked in that cell for over an hour as securely as ever because he *believed* it was locked. He was locked in the cell by his *mind.*

You and I are the same way. We get conditioned to failure in the same way as the elephant and Houdini, with our beliefs, programming, and conditioning. What we *think* is a limitation, IS. If you think you can or if you think you can't, either way, you are right. We simply put limitations on ourselves.

These self-imposed limitations that we put on ourselves stop us from succeeding, even though they are not true. They create fear and doubt. FEAR is False Evidence Appearing Real.

Whether you think you can or if you think you can't, either way, you're right.

A critical key to manifesting is you don't have to know *how* what you desire is going to manifest when you start the process. You will never know how in the beginning. You have to have faith, belief, and confidence in the method and in yourself.

That is the key.

There is a block that everybody has, every single person, preventing them from success.

When I sit down with someone, and I ask what do you want, 10 percent of the people say they don't know what they want. This is a major issue. You can't hit a target you can't see (not clearly defined). And you can't hit a target you don't have (not knowing what you want).

If a person thinks they do know what they want, when they are telling me their desire, they're really describing what they **don't** want.

Example: "What do you want?"

"Well, I want a relationship."

"Okay, what are you looking for in a relationship?"

"What I want is somebody who doesn't give me a hard time, who doesn't bitch and complain …"

"Stop. You're focusing on bitching and complaining and giving yourself a hard time. That is what you **don't** want. What is it that you **do** want?"

"Well, I want somebody who umm, umm, you know, who umm …"

They don't even know what they **do** want. You can't hit a target you can't see and you can't hit a target you don't have.

So, the first problem is, do you really know what you want? And is it clear enough? Have you defined your desire with clarity and specificity? Can you really describe it and see it in your mind's eye?

If you can't describe what you want, then it's not clear. You have not defined your desire. You can't put out a vibration for something that doesn't exist.

Does that make sense?

A major reason why people think they are using this method but still aren't getting what they want is, they don't actually know what they DO want. It's probably not clearly defined with specificity. If it isn't clearly defined, something you can see in your mind's eye, you can't put out a vibration of something when you don't know exactly what it is.

You need to know what you *do* want. Remember, not what you *don't* want. Do you understand that distinction? It is very important and a very common mistake.

You don't get in the car and start driving without knowing where you're going unless you're just going for a pleasurable drive to nowhere. But even then, you probably do know where you are going. And you know what you are doing. You *want* the pleasurable experience and enjoyment of driving your car.

You must know what you *do* want. It must be clear. *Define* your dream, goal, or desire.

"What do you want?"

"I want money."

"Good. How much?"

"I don't know."

That's fine. "What do you want the money for?"

"Well, I just know I need money."

"Oh good. For what?"

"Well …"

Stop! *If you have to think about it, you haven't clearly defined your dream.*

"I want money."

"How much?"

"I don't have a specific amount."

"Okay. What's it for?"

"I really don't have any specific requirements right now."

"Okay, so now we're talking about your feelings. How do you want to feel when you acquire more money?"

"I want enough money to give me a sense of complete security for the rest of my life. No matter what happens, I will always be able to take care of myself, feed myself, clothe myself, and have a roof over my head."

"Okay, good. When you think about that, how does it make you feel?"

"Fantastic. Safe. Secure. At peace. I know exactly what I want because I know exactly how I'm going to feel when I get it. That's what I want."

"Perfect. That's clear."

Do you understand the distinctions here?

Another example:

"You want money?"

"Yeah."

"How much?"

"I want $20,000 a month."

"Perfect. How do you feel when you think about it?"

"Well, I have no idea how I'm going to get it …"

"Stop. You're focusing on, I don't know how …"

Are you with me? Do you see how this goes? If I were to sit down with you personally, I could point out many things you are doing incorrectly with your words and thinking that are preventing what you desire to manifest. Without me sitting next to you or doing a live Zoom call, you have to increase your own personal awareness and consciousness.

So the first problem people have is they don't know what they *do* want, and it is not clearly defined.

If I were to ask you, "What do you want?" you better be able to describe it to me. You have to know what you do want as clearly as you know your address and your own name.

And as you describe what you do want to me, you should be seeing that in your mind's eye, smiling and feeling amazing.

That's the first test to determine if you are on track and doing this right. Most people fail right here and need correction.

Do you know what you do want right now? The way to determine that is to ask if you can describe it in detail and clarity, and do so instantly without thinking about it.

"I want a new car."

"Okay. What kind?"

"I really don't know."

"That's fine. It would be better if you knew exactly the car you want, including the color and all the options. But let's deal with this. How does it feel when you think of *having* a new car?"

You probably aren't going to feel spectacular because you don't have it clearly defined. You can't get a picture of a "new car" without knowing what make and model of car you want.

Again, the test is simple.

You define what you do want; you should be able to see it in your mind's eye, and when you think about it, you should feel amazing.

For most people, when it comes to a specific thing like a car, the more specific it is, the better it's going to make you feel thinking about it.

"Well, I'm not choosy, it could be a Lexus, it could be a Mercedes, it could be a Cadillac. I'm not sure. I don't care if I get a two-door or a four-door."

"That's fine. How does it make you feel?"

"Good."

"You want to feel better? Go look at Lexus. Go look at Cadillac. Go look at Mercedes. Sit in them, drive them, find a make and model that you do want and can get a burning desire for."

Why? Because if you're being completely general when it comes to your desire instead of specific, that's good to one extent and not so good on the other.

Remember when I said you have to FEEL NOW AS IF you would feel if you were already in possession of your desire? With that in mind, let's do a process.

Imagine that today, you just won a prize. You won a new car. But you have to pick a particular make and model. You have to choose the colors and options. Your new car can cost a maximum of $200,000. Now you get five minutes to choose which car you want, or you lose the prize.

Do you understand?

As you imagine this process, your feeling of excitement goes up dramatically. The feeling of anticipation as if you already have the car went up. You can probably see that defining your dream or goal with clarity, details, and specificity helps you increase burning desire.

Another reason you don't have what you want, what you desire is not manifesting, is because when you think you are thinking about what you *do* want, you're actually thinking about the lack of it. You're actually thinking of what you *don't* want. You're actually focusing on your desire not being there. You are focused on the *absence* of your desire.

The process of thinking about your desire not being there, is what is preventing you from manifesting what you do want.

You know whether you're thinking about what you *do* want or what you *don't* want, based on how you feel.

There's one key thing I need for you to understand when it comes to making money, when it comes to manifesting a relationship, when it comes to manifesting your desires and making all of your dreams come true. The cavalry is not coming. No one is coming to save you. There's no savior that's coming.

Stop looking at anything outside of yourself as the cause of your troubles.

The reason you don't have your desires is not because of the economy, not because of the politicians, not because of who your parents are, or the school you didn't go to, or bad luck.

The reason you are exactly where you are is because you've created it.

The key, the ten-second miracle that will change everything in your life and give you more power than you ever imagined, is you taking 100 percent responsibility for everything in your life.

It is coming to the knowingness that you can in fact create anything you want in your life. And that you HAVE created everything in your life. It is never about the other person. It is always about you. As within, so without. God dwells within you AS you. *You* are the creator.

You can be, do, or have anything and everything you want in your life.

If you can want it and categorically believe that you already have it, you can have it. Whatever the mind of man can conceive and bring itself to believe, it can achieve.

The problem for most people is even if they really want something, they can't actually bring themselves to truly believe they can have it. We talked about how to get a goal that is in the sweet spot so that you *do* believe you *will* have it. Set your goal big enough to excite and motivate you and small enough so you have total confidence and knowingness that you WILL manifest it.

Many times you have to set for yourself lower goals that are in the sweet spot.

You also have to work on knowing and believing that these techniques work. Joining GIN will expose you to people all around the world who have applied these methods and have experienced awesome results.

And you have to believe in yourself. You have to know that YOU can do it too.

You can be, do, and have everything you want.

Just use your own power that we are releasing as you read this book. Your future is bright. You have the creative power within you to make all of your dreams come true. You were born to win. You were designed for accomplishment. You were engineered for success. And you were endowed with the seeds of greatness.

Dare to be GREAT!

LESSON 15

Awakening the Genie Within

Do you think that you have your own Aladdin's Lamp? *Yes.* Do you think you have your own personal Genie that will grant you your desires? *Yes.* Do you think your wishes are now virtually at your own command? *Yes.* Do you think you can make your inner "Genie" grant you any wish you want? *Yes.*

Maybe you are beginning to. Maybe you are considering that this is true, and it could work for you like it has for millions of others.

You now have the power and the knowledge.

This is the beginning of the beginning for you.

This is the first step.

Over the course of this book, I have been sharing the details of manifesting your desires. It may seem like a lot of information. Each bit of data shared has many distinctions. You can go very deep on each concept and learn more and more nuances that make you understand the concept better, thus apply it better, and then get better, faster results.

But I have been just scratching the scratch of the surface. I have just been giving you a thumbnail sketch, kind of a bird's-eye view, or just the tip of the tip of the iceberg, here in this book.

There is so much more in-depth knowledge that is available to you when you join my private success club, the Global Information Network (GIN), or take advantage of the other books and audio and video material I have produced.

But with what you have right now, this is all you need. You can go anywhere in life you want to go, with what you have. You can manifest your desires by applying what you have learned.

You can achieve virtually anything and everything you want with the knowledge that has been presented to you and that you now possess. You can be, do, and have anything and everything you desire.

You can manifest making millions of dollars a year. You can be financially free. You can call forth your soul mate. You can have the most loving, spectacular romantic relationship that gives you bliss, happiness, and fulfillment beyond your wildest imagination.

You can have a magnificent relationship with your children, coworkers, friends, and family members. You can wake up ecstatic. You can have dynamic, vibrant health.

You can make businesses grow. You can create new businesses. You can come up with inventions and ideas. You can learn skills.

You can be, do, or have anything and everything you want.

You can have the car or cars of your dreams. You can have the boats or yachts of your dreams. You can fly first class or have your own private jet. You can travel anywhere in the world at any level of luxury you choose.

You can eat in the finest restaurants, drink the finest wines and cognacs, and eat the most expensive, luxurious foods. You can have butlers, maids, landscapers, private chefs, and chauffeurs if you choose.

You can have the wardrobes that you have always dreamed about. Custom-made clothes.

You can be traveling all over the world, shopping in the finest, most expensive shops if that is what you choose. You can have the physical physique you have always wanted. You can have flexibility and strength in your body. You can look younger.

You can be, do, and have anything and everything you want.

You can learn foreign languages. You can learn to play musical instruments. You can learn to sing. You can learn to paint. You can learn to cook.

You can, be, do or have anything and everything you want.

You can have the most wonderful, obedient, loving pets using these techniques. You can live in the home or homes of your choice using these techniques. You can be happier and feel more secure and more fulfilled than ever before. You can have peace, joy, and an inner sense of purpose and fulfillment.

You can experience any and every emotion you want. You can feel exhilaration, adventure, excitement, enthusiasm, and passion. You can feel power and feel achievement.

You can add value to society. You can help your community. You can begin to change the world for the better using these techniques.

You can be, do, and have anything and everything you want using this information.

All these things are absolutely available to you. They are yours for the asking. They are yours for the taking.

The manifesting technique is simple. It really does take only five minutes to learn, but it does take a lifetime to master.

Right now you are at conscious competence. You DO have to consciously apply the steps of this manifesting method. You DO have old failure patterns and habits that have to be replaced with new success patterns and habits.

You have old, well-established neural pathways in your brain.

You have many negative thought patterns, energies, and counter-intentions in your DNA and "field" that get activated when things occur in your life that you don't want, making you feel bad and stopping your dreams from manifesting. The "Processes" I offer blow these out permanently. Consider having us deliver to you in person the "Money, Relationship, Leadership, Communication, Health, Spiritual Awakening, and Dream Processes." Get more information on those if they resonate with you.

But right now you have the techniques and power that can begin to move you into a power vortex where you have total control over your emotions and life. Do all the things I suggested in this book. Remember, this is the beginning. A journey of a thousand miles starts with a single step. You eat an elephant one bite at a time. Go as far as you can see, and when you get there, you will see further.

Over time, if you are consistent and persistent with your efforts, if you do the right things long enough consistently, that big ball of negative counter-intention energy will begin to get smaller, its magnetic pull and creative power will get weaker, the old failure neural pathways in your brain that you have established, and all the negative patterns and programs that you have established in your subconscious, will dissipate and will get weaker, and weaker, and weaker.

They will no longer control you.

And over time, the positive ball of success energy will get bigger and bigger. New success-creating neural pathways and new positive patterns and programs will begin to be established in the brain. They will grow stronger and stronger and become bigger and bigger.

And at a certain time, which will be different for all of you, your positive ball of energy will get bigger than the negative ball of energy. That will be the tipping point.

When that happens, it is all downhill from there. When that happens, the momentum is on your side. All of a sudden, everything starts going your way. You instantly become lucky. You no longer feel like everything and everyone is against you. You no longer feel like you are swimming upstream or have a black cloud over your head.

You reach the unconscious competence level.

You start thinking and broadcasting the right frequencies and vibrations automatically. You start talking and acting the "right" way automatically. Instead of instantly popping back to the negative default patterns of your past—all of a sudden, now, instantaneously and effortlessly—you are popping into the positive habits and patterns. You have been programmed for success. Those programs work to MAKE you successful *automatically.*

And when something occurs in your life that you don't like or want, instantly you smile and think, "This is going to be good. I don't know how, but it is." You automatically feel GOOD. *You do this automatically. It is your new default.*

Before, without thinking, you would have automatically thought, "Oh my God. This is bad." And you would automatically *feel* bad.

This change, this powerful shift, *will* occur for you. Your life will get easier, more fulfilling, more exciting, and more fun. You will feel more secure, more content, more fulfilled, more in control, more loved, more acknowledged, more heard, more validated, more accepted and wanted.

You will experience increased levels and intensities of positive emotions, more so than ever before.

You have everything you need in your hands right now. What you need and have asked for and have prayed for is in the palms of your hands this very moment. Your prayers have been answered. *Your wish has been granted.*

The fact that you have this book means you are at the right place at the right time. Your *asking* has brought you here. The fact that you are reading this right now tells me that you have depth of vision. I am sure many people will buy this book and never read it. Or they will start to read it and never get to this point. You, however, are here reading this. YOU have vision.

But now it is up to you to take massive and immediate action and USE this material. The plan works if you work the plan. Follow this *pattern for success* and you *will* see the results in your own life.

You can see the power of this method. You can see the results from those who have used it. You can see the simplicity, and you can see that this method is using quantum physics "law." It uses science. It is *the success system that never fails.*

And whether you *consciously* apply this method *with deliberate intent* or not, it is STILL going to operate in your life every day anyway. Every time you think a thought, you are broadcasting a vibration and attracting a like vibration into your experience.

Every time you feel a feeling, you are broadcasting a vibration and you are calling forth and attracting more situations, events, people, conditions, and circumstances into your life that give you the same, or similar, feeling.

You can be a ship without a rudder and no engine, and be tossed around by the waves and the wind, and live life as a victim, blaming everything and everyone but yourself—being a master of excuses.

Or you can be the captain of your own ship, a nuclear-powered vessel with unlimited power. And you can steer that ship, by your own will, by your own choices, and with your own decision-making power.

You can point your ship in any direction and go anywhere, anytime, anyplace you choose, because you have the power, you are in control and command. You are the master of your destiny, the creator of your fate.

You now know what to do and how to do it.

So, where do you go from here? How do you take the next steps? I will give you a few things to do.

— Read this book again. Then again, then again.
— Get the audios of this book and listen to them as well.

Every time you read this book or listen to the audios, your under-standing of this information will go up. Your belief in the method will go up and your belief in the fact that you can do it will go up.

— Get some of the books on the recommended reading list and read a little each day. You can be reading parts of multiple books a day. Feed your mind every day. Leaders are always readers.

— Listen to positive motivational audios every day. Join GIN and have free, exclusive access to the best audio success training on the planet.

— Join my private success club, the Global Information Network (GIN) at www.GlobalInformationNetwork.com

The Club provides free exclusive information, courses, audios, videos, and seminars on subjects such as:

— How to handle depression.

— How to bring people into your life to do joint ventures with.

— How to invest.

— How to make money in real estate.

— How to make money on the internet.

— How to have dynamic health naturally, including longevity and anti-aging.

— How to cure disease naturally: The Natural Cures, "They" Don't Want You to Know About.

— The Weight Loss Cure, "They" Don't Want You to Know About: How to lose 45 pounds in 45 days.

— How to have better relationships with your spouse.

— How to have better relationships with your family and friends.

— How to get credit, loans, and financing, and improve your credit score.

GIN Members also get exclusive access to my two courses:
– The Success Mastery Course (audio course), Levels 1–12.
– The Science of Personal Mastery Course (written course), Lessons 1–100.

Also, we give GIN Members updated "insider" behind-the-scenes information on global events. Members get access to ground-floor "first in" opportunities, which in many cases are for "Members Only."

One of the advantages of being a member of a society was, we had access to people around the world. We had connections. "Your 'network' is your NET WORTH."

When opportunities presented themselves, we were always given first option, and first knowledge, of these incredible opportunities. We knew about the 2008 financial crash before it happened. We knew about Bitcoin and crypto before it was well-known. We knew companies like Apple, Amazon, Tesla, Walmart, and many more were going to be potentially huge.

When it comes to making money, the fact is this: Getting in at the beginning, at the ground floor, is a major, major, major advantage. That is the fact.

Those who make the most money are those who are plugged into high-level networks of people who are "in the know." We were then given opportunities to get into situations and deals, on the ground floor.

You have never had that opportunity.

These opportunities are exclusively made available to members of the societies. That is one reason why the rich get richer. It is through these associations, these "connections," that we were given, and had access to, these opportunities that you never get exposed to.

Through the Global Information Network (GIN), my colleagues and I are going to be presenting similar opportunities to members.

If you join GIN and become a member, you will also have access to our annual Leadership Cruise, where we take over an entire luxury cruise ship, for "Members Only." We also put on three other weekend events each year in magnificent locations and hotels around the world. We have four seminars and rallies each year in addition to hundreds of local chapter meetings, both in person and virtually, every month.

At these events, you can meet other members, network, share information, share opportunities, and establish friendships and relationships with positive, motivated, successful people who will support you and help you achieve your goals and dreams in life.

And when you go to live events, either in person or virtually, you will have the luxury of meeting other successful people and creating *Masterminds*, which are so, so powerful and helpful in the manifesting of your goals and desires.

I briefly touched on the power of the "Mastermind."

It is one of the most incredibly strong and powerful ingredients in the manifesting formula. Andrew Carnegie talked about it as a vital key to success. So did Aristotle Onassis. Both of these men were the ultra-rich.

Napoleon Hill discussed the power of the "Mastermind" in his books, *Think and Grow Rich* and *The Law of Success.*

The "Mastermind" makes everything work exponentially faster. When you put two horses together to pull a cart, they don't pull twice as much weight; they pull over three times as much weight. Synergy.

A true Mastermind is when several people get together who are like-minded, have the same purpose and mission, and work together in harmony.

So when you are working with other people, who have the same goal, who are like-minded, and work in harmony with each other, the power of each member of the Mastermind increases.

The ability of each member of the Mastermind to broadcast, or transmit, goes up dramatically because the Mastermind tied all your brains together and created a NEW mind, the *Mastermind.*

So being part of the Global Information Network (GIN) can be a major advantage in that respect. You can meet the *right* people to establish Masterminds with.

GIN also provides free to its members other key skill trainings and courses, such as "How to Keep Score" and "Managing by Statistics".

Successful people manage their life and business by statistics. They keep score. This is a very specific skill and art. This is an interesting concept because in business and in their lives, most average people don't know the score. In their life, most average people don't know the score.

When you are making money, one technique that you can use, which will help you focus on what you want so that you are thinking about it all the time, is to use physical graphs of key scores and statistics that compare week to week, or month to month. *You need to know where you are in relation to where you have been.*

These are physically put on the walls so that you can see them all the time. This helps you focus on your key objectives and goals. It shows you how close you are getting to the target.

I teach the difference between a *score* and a *stat*. Sometimes stats are called analytics or metrics. There are also *substats.*

In business the main score is always profit. How that is defined takes time to explain. Another score is sales or income. Again, how that is defined takes time to explain in detail.

Stats or statistics, or metrics or analytics, are the certain variables of your business. The idea is if you increase the stats, you will increase your score.

Stats will vary greatly based on the type of business you are in. The score is generally the same.

Every business should have the basic score graphs.

If you have a business, or a moneymaking situation, or if your goal is to make money, then you need to chart how much money you are making. *You need to chart your progress.*

You need to know how much money you are bringing in and how much money is going *into* your bank account, and how much money is going *out* of your bank account, each week and each month.

So the first score graph you have is called gross income or sales. It is actually deposits. If the money does not go into your bank account, it does not count.

The definition of gross income or sales is money deposited into your accounts. If you make a sale and you won't get the money for three months, it is not gross income.

Have a weekly and monthly graph for gross income/sales using this definition.

There are three graphs you should have for gross income/sales.

Have a weekly and monthly graph, and a cumulative graph, which is year-to-date.

Use your weekly graph to focus on increasing sales each week, trying to get gross income higher each week compared to the previous week. This keeps you focused. You are charting your progress. Do this for your monthly gross income graph as well. You want to have each month higher than the previous month.

The simple action of putting those score graphs on the wall, where you can see them often, causes you to create an increase with your vibration. You want the graph to go up. You want the income to go up. You want more money being deposited into your bank every single week.

By looking at the graphs every day, it causes you to focus on making it go up.

Remember, you get what you think about most of the time.

You can't have this graph only in a computer, because you won't look at it as often. You have to have it on the wall so you can see it most of the time.

This is why pictures of your goals and dreams, when plastered on the wall, are so powerful. Your vision or dream board is a powerful ingredient in the manifesting recipe.

Your dream or vision board will get you to look at your goals and dreams throughout the day and think about them consciously and subconsciously. They remind you to think about what you want. And you then will get what you want.

You get what you think about most of the time.

So where do you go from here?

This is the beginning, not the end, of the teaching process and the learning process. You now have the starting point. You virtually have everything you need right now to manifest all your goals and dreams. You need nothing more.

I would encourage you, however, to, as I mentioned early in this book, to tap into the system so that you really *know* this material.

There are two ways for you to truly learn and know this data. One is by doing it by applying it in real life. Don't become a professional student. Get out there and use it. Every time you do it, every time you apply it, you experience a result, and you get to fine-tune it. You will either win or learn.

The second way is this. You really need to learn this material well enough to teach it, and you learn it well enough to teach it by *teaching* it. Not to others just yet. If you try that now, it will be like the blind leading the blind. You teach it to yourself. Increase your awareness of what you are doing and getting better at doing it.

As you do it, as you read this book and the others on my suggested reading list, as you listen to the Success Mastery Course audios and do the Lessons in the Science of Personal Mastery Course, as you go through the various GIN success training materials, you begin to see how to apply this properly. You have cognitions and "aha" moments where you get clarity. You understand the subtleties, the distinctions, and the nuances of how this works in real life.

You start fine-tuning. It is like when you are learning anything for the first time, like golf. You find a great golfer who is also a great teacher and you get lessons on the driving range.

Then you go golfing for the first time on the golf course, your first full round of golf. You are not going to hit five under par. The first time you play an 18-hole round on the golf course, you are going to hit a couple of great shots and a couple of bad shots. When you hit a bad shot you ask what you did wrong so you can correct it next time. You either win (hit a great shot) or learn (hit a bad shot and figure out what you did wrong so you can correct it next time).

The first time you start applying this material, you are going to manifest a few goals that are in your sweet spot. Things will seem to work perfectly.

And a couple of other times you try to manifest your goals, things won't seem to work out so well. And when what you want does not manifest, it means you haven't done something 100 percent right. Learn what you did wrong and correct it next time. Just like you would do on the golf course.

You may slice the ball: "Oops, I did something wrong. What did I do incorrectly?" You figure it out by *teaching yourself*, through your awareness.

But unlike golf, which can take years, and years, and years of practice, and practice, and practice, to perfect—here, with the manifesting method—you are going to get to a level of proficiency and expertise incredibly fast, where you manifest your goals and desires on a regular basis.

This is why so many people who learn this material, by reading this book, never go any further with their training. They use this material and get great results. They become so happy and ecstatic with the results they are getting.

I am, however, going to provide and offer to you more advanced, in-depth training for those who want more. We know that within the societies, most members get a little bit of the knowledge, apply it, experience great results, and become blissfully happy. They don't want more training.

They are not at the point where they want to learn more, or fine-tune and get better at the manifesting method.

Some of you will start applying this material and fine-tune it through your own awareness. You will be getting such great results that you will be happy with where you are. You will go no further in the training. You will never get your MBA or PhD. There is nothing wrong with that.

And some of you reading this will be thinking right now, "I want *more*. I want to be better on this particular subject or that particular area. I want to know *all* the secrets."

You will read the books, listen to the audios, go to the events, engage in more of the training, and join GIN. You will get better and better and better. You will get your "black belt" in success, your PhD in manifesting. You will release your own superpower.

Some of you will want to know everything about everything, at the highest levels. You will want to be one of the highest-ranking Members of GIN and be in the "inner circle."

In five, ten, or twenty years from now, you are going to be at such a level of mastery that you will be walking through life like a magician. Like a wizard. Like a Jedi Knight.

And that is not for everyone, but it is available if you so choose.

That is what we are doing. Offering to you a gift of total freedom and liberation on all levels. I hope you appreciate and understand that what we are doing is something that we don't have to do. We are doing it out of love. We are doing it out of a knowingness that we are bettering society and adding value to society by offering GIN Membership to you.

There are two types of groups of people at the highest levels in the societies. Those that add value to society and those that are parasites that live off the value production of others.

That is what we saw. For us, we noticed that the desire that we had to be blissfully happy was really the most important desire. We found that adding value to society gave us the highest level of bliss. The secret to living is giving.

That is what we are doing. We know that you will be able to use these techniques to not only manifest your desires and improve the conditions and standard of living in your lives, but to add value to society as well.

You will add value to your own life and become someone that people want to emulate, that people admire and respect.

I heard something early on in my life. I decided I wanted riches, and I manifested that. I wanted the private planes, and I got them. I wanted the luxury yachts, and I got them. I wanted the mansions around the world, and I got them. I wanted the Rolls-Royces, the Ferraris, the Mercedes, the Porsches, and I got them. I wanted the $15,000 custom bespoke suits, and I got them. I wanted the millions of dollars worth of jewelry, and I got them. I wanted to fly in the Concorde, and I did that many times. I wanted to travel all over the world first class. I wanted to drink the finest wine and the finest cognac, and smoke the finest cigars. I wanted to eat the most expensive caviar and food and have private chefs, butlers, and drivers. And I DID!

I manifested all that stuff and more.

There were many people around me in the Brotherhood that just wanted money, money, money, money, money, and they manifested it in the billions.

I remember sitting with some of these guys very early on when we were all manifesting money and the things that money could buy. One of the senior members in the Brotherhood told us a secret.

He said, "Remember, it is okay to manifest money and riches, but you will find out at a certain point, it is not what you have acquired, but it is who you become, that is truly important."

And for many people, they never figure that out.

My colleagues and I know that it is who you become that is most important. Not being attached to things will keep you free.

Integrity, honesty, character, love, forgiveness, compassion, giving, appreciation, gratefulness, and understanding is what it is really all about. Work on becoming a better you.

We know that life is about feeling good right now. This moment, feel good. Feel good *now*. Every step, every moment, regardless of what you are looking at, regardless of your situation, try to feel better.

If you can live life feeling really, really good, you will have the most thrilling, exciting, blissful, happy, joyous experience you can imagine.

You can have it all.

It has been an honor and privilege to share this with you.

I deeply want to thank all of my special guests and colleagues for coming to the live recorded event. They came from all over the world at their own expense. They revealed themselves as members of various societies and their powerful positions in government and international business affairs. It was a huge commitment of time for them to be there. They invested their most valuable asset, their time, so that you could reap the benefits of their knowledge. They felt they had an obligation to do it and did it because I asked them.

They know, as I do, you can be, do, and have anything and everything you want.

May you never be the same.

LESSON 16

⟨⟨⟨⟨❦⟩⟩⟩⟩

The Manifesting Formula of the Brotherhood

Here are the ingredients of the manifesting formula. If you skipped reading the book and jumped to this Lesson, you will get nothing out of reading this summation. You must read the book in order to be both deprogrammed from your subconscious failure thinking and programmed with success patterns via the hypnotic language patterns and embedded commands that are in the text, activated by reading them.

The Manifesting Formula of the Brotherhood

- You were born to win, but programmed to fail. You have in your DNA and energetic field such things as counter-intentions, energetic imprints, postulates, decisions, agreements, and contracts that prevent you from manifesting your goals. You must "clear" these and transmute their energy, replacing them with positive programs and new success patterns and habits. You achieve this by reading this book over and over, as well as listening to the Success Mastery Course audios, reading the Science of Personal Mastery Course, and doing the "Processes" that I deliver, which neutralizes and "clears" out all these counter-intentions.

— Who Do You Listen To? Listen to people who have what you want and have been where you are. You learn from everyone but, listen to and follow those who know success, not just those who know about success. The rich man learns from the fool, but the fool does not learn from the rich man.

— Have a high Teachability Index. Have a high willingness to learn and a high willingness to accept change. Be coachable. Be humble. Know that you don't know what you don't know.

— Understand the Training Balance Scale. Success is 90 percent thinking, broadcasting the right vibration and frequency. Don't worry about the "how" in the beginning of the manifesting process. The "how" will present itself. Work on your attitude and "thinking".

— Understand the Four Magic Steps: unconscious incompetence; conscious incompetence; conscious competence; unconscious competence. Work on getting to unconscious competence by doing the right things at the conscious competence level with deliberate intent until they become a part of you, until they become a habit, and until you do them automatically.

— The brain is a transmitter and receiver of frequency and vibration. Your brain broadcasts vibration and frequency. If it is broadcasting on the Beta wave, you will not manifest what you desire. Beta is the slave wave, the poverty wave. The wealth wave, the billionaire brain wave, and the manifesting wave is right in between Alpha and Theta. When you broadcast on this brain wave, it affects other brains and all matter in the universe instantaneously.

— You can increase the intensity and power of your broadcast. Doing so for an extended duration creates the fastest results.

— Everything in the universe vibrates and has a frequency. Everything in the universe actually is vibration or frequency and thus is affected by your thinking and what your brain broadcasts.

— Your number one goal is always to feel as good as you can right now. Your feelings are your indicator. Trust your feelings.

— Find your pain. Find what you will not tolerate anymore. This is the why behind the why. You are more motivated to avoid or eliminate pain than you are to want pleasure. Use these negative emotions to contract your energy so that you can increase the power and intensity of your broadcasting of what you want. Use thinking about what you don't want to help you clarify and clearly define exactly what you do want and must have. Use it to create a need.

— Make a decision that you are going to get the thing you desire; that's it, period! Success is a decision away. The entire universe will conspire to manifest the dream of a person who knows exactly what he wants and is committed and determined to get it, no matter what.

— Clearly define what you do want.

— Write down what you do want on white paper with a pen with blue ink.

— Make sure what you do want is your goal, not someone else's. It has to be something you want. Not something you feel obligated to want.

— Don't set a deadline on your dreams. Do set a deadline on your activities or on a short-term goal you know you can attain if you simply put in the effort.

— Know the difference between a dream and a goal. Have a dream, but don't live in a dream world. Focus on attaining your goals, which will bring you closer to your dream.

— Get pictures of what you do want and put them on your dream/vision board. Include yourself in the picture if you can.

- You can have many dreams, but you should have one chief aim—a goal, an objective, an objective.
- That goal should be in the sweet spot. Big enough to excite you and small enough so that you are 100 percent confident that you can and will attain it.
- Develop a burning desire to attain your chief aim. Be obsessed with attaining your chief aim.
- See yourself in your mind's eye in possession of your chief aim. See this picture as clearly as you can and with as much detail as possible. Include what you see, hear, feel, taste, and touch.
- As you picture yourself in possession of what you do want, FEEL NOW AS IF you would feel if you were already in possession of what you do want to manifest. Enjoy those feelings. Maintain those feelings for at least sixty-eight seconds. When you do this, you are broadcasting the frequency of what you do want on the manifesting Alpha/Theta wealth-creating wave.
- Then release any attachment to the outcome. Think that it is 100 percent Okay if you never attain that which you desire to have. While doing this, maintain the feeling you have, imagining that you do actually have what you desire.
- Know that the Law of Attraction says that whatever frequency or vibration you broadcast on the Alpha/Theta brain wave will attract first like-minded thoughts, and then attract into your life and manifest the "thing" that matches the frequency of your broadcast.
- Go dream-building and engage in all the dream-building exercises and processes described in this book.
- Read positive books on a daily basis, even if it is just one paragraph a day. Reading for one minute a day is better than not reading something at all. The more you read each day,

obviously the better, but the key is to read something every day. Get this success habit. Leaders are always readers.

— Chart your progress by keeping score and having stats, using graphs that you can see often. Know where you have been and where you are. Know that you are getting closer to your goal in a quantifiable, measurable way. Life is a game; you need to keep score and keep your eye on the score.

— Associate with successful people. Your income will be the average of your five best friends'. Establish friendships with successful people. You should be spending time with, talking to, and socializing with successful people. Success rubs off. The people you spend the most time with positively or negatively affect your vibration, thus your ability to manifest your desires. You need to have relationships with people that will pull for you.

— Your network is your net worth. Your friends should be successful people. Having connections and a strong network of people is key to success.

— Establish a Mastermind. You should have other people as part of your Mastermind. and you can be part of theirs. This is a group (two to ten people) that have the same objective and chief aim, are like-minded, and work together in harmony as a team to manifest that goal.

— Go to motivational, inspirational events on a regular basis. Ideally one per month. This is where you recharge your batteries, hear success stories, get motivated and inspired, and bathe in the Mastermind that is created where the energy changes you from the inside.

— Watch your words. You are hung by the tongue. You are snared by the words of your mouth. What you say is what you get. Watch the words you say and how you say them.

— Activate and illuminate words. When reading, never go past a word you don't fully know the definition of. This will cause you to go into confusion, get sleepy, and stop activity. Look up the meaning of words, the history of the word, the word's original language and definition, then use the word in several sentences until you feel good about the word.

— Be a "Fly on The Wall" to successful people. You learn by observation, IF you are aware and conscious, and if you pay attention. Take advantage of any opportunity to be in the presence of successful people and observe. Watch. Pay attention. Then mimic and model their behavior, the way they speak, their mannerisms, and their thinking.

— Take responsibility for everything in your life. Don't blame anything or anyone other than yourself for your circumstances. Anytime you point your finger, there are three fingers pointed directly at you. As within, so without.

— When something does not work out and you "lose," remember, in every situation you either win or LEARN. You never "lose." Within all adversity are the seeds of a greater benefit. Take "losses" as learning opportunities. You don't fail. You successfully find a way it does not work. You LEARN.

— It's your attitude, not your aptitude, that will determine your altitude in life. Focus on being a better you. Invest in yourself and your attitude by investing time and money in personal development.

— If you want to feel enthusiastic, ACT enthusiastic. Change your physiology to mimic and model successful, positive, motivated, confident people. Act AS IF you would act if you were actually that person. Feelings affect the way you act, but the way you act affects feelings as well. Take control of your feelings with your willpower by acting "AS IF."

— The secret to living is giving. Be a giver. You reap what you sow. What you give, you will get. If you want something, you have to give it away first. Give, and it will be given back to you a thousand-fold. Get into the habit of J.D. Rockefeller and all wealthy people. They gave money away to charity when they were broke and first starting off. The wealthy all say that it was their charitable giving early in their careers that set themselves to reap the rewards of wealth.

— Find opportunity to give recognition to others. When you give praise, encouragement, and accolades to others, the universe will bless you by putting into your life a thousand times more of what you gave. This is the expanded golden rule. Think about others as you want them to think about you. Talk about others as you wish they would talk about you. Talk to others as you wish they would talk to you. Do to others as you wish they would do to you. Whatever you put out will come back to you.

— Find an opportunity to be recognized and receive recognition. When others praise you publicly, your energy changes in major, positive ways. Both giving and receiving recognition is something all super-successful people do on a regular basis. It supercharges them and helps transform their energy and make them a magnet for success. GIN is the ideal place to give and receive recognition. It is a critical ingredient in the "System."

— Use a Priority Manager system to get more done in less time. Using a paper-based "to-do list" system, which includes appointments and communication planners for all the people you deal with—combined with technology—will help you focus on getting done your priorities, thus manifesting your goals faster, all with less stress and no feelings of overwhelm.

— Improve your self-image. You must see yourself as a winner. The image you have of yourself determines how much confidence you have in yourself. Do the "Self-Image" Lessons in the Science of Personal Mastery course. When you change your self-image, you are changing your insides. When your insides change, your outside reality will change. As within, so without.

— Invest time and money in yourself. You will get the highest returns when you invest in yourself by spending time and money on personal development. Work on becoming a better you. GIN offers the best personal development and success training in the world, most of which is exclusive and for "Members Only." GIN training comes directly from the Brotherhood and is not available anywhere else. Warren Buffett, one of the richest men in the world, said that the difference between successful people and the average person is successful people invested huge amounts of time and money on personal development when they were first starting in life. Think, talk, and act like successful people and you will be successful too. Do what successful people did when they were where you are now, and you can achieve similar success. Follow a pattern for success and you will get the results you seek.

— Learn all this material well enough to teach it. You learn it so well you can teach it by doing it, by applying it in your life, and teaching yourself, making yourself better and learning from your mistakes. Everything you will know at the top, you will learn at the bottom. You need to fully know this material, not just know about the material. It has to become a part of you. It is not when you got this book that matters, it is when this book got inside of you that will determine if you manifest your goals and dreams. If you think you know this material but are not doing it and seeing results, you don't know it. To know and not to do is not to know.

Key Axioms

- Where your attention goes, energy flows.
- Energy follows thought.
- Thoughts are things.
- Thoughts have magnetic, attractive, creative power.
- Don't confuse activity with accomplishment.
- Keep score, and always know what the score is.
- Keep your focus on your objective and always work on getting closer to reaching your goal.
- Knowledge is power but only if it is used.
- It is not what you eat, but what you digest that makes you strong; it is not what you earn, but what you save that brings you wealth; and it is not what you learn, but rather what you remember and use that makes you wise.
- If it is to be, it is up to me.
- A good plan executed with enthusiasm today is better than a perfect plan implemented tomorrow. Get in the "Do it Now" habit.
- Analysis leads to paralysis.
- Failures are always good at one thing: making excuses.
- Cure yourself of excusitis, the failure disease.
- A failure in life is always a SNIOP: Susceptible to the Negative Influence of Other People.
- Don't let people put rats in your head.
- You cannot do anything with a positive attitude. But you can do everything BETTER with a positive attitude than a negative attitude.
- You either make things happen, watch things happen, or wonder what happened.
- Whatever you see in others is only a projection of what you really see in yourself.
- Believe and you receive; doubt and go without.

- Success creates confidence. Confidence creates activity. Activity creates habits. Success habits create success, which creates more confidence.
- Successful people are always willing to do what the other guys are not willing to do.
- Successful people are not people without problems; they are people who have overcome their problems.
- The mistake is not that you fall, but rather that you don't get up.
- Your ship will never come in if you don't put it out first.
- Inch by inch, anything is a cinch. But yard by yard, it's hard.
- Five years from now, the person you will be, will be based on the books you read and the people you associate with.
- Never let anyone steal your dreams.
- A man without a dream is dead.
- Fear is False Evidence Appearing Real.
- Success is not what you have done compared to what others have done. It is what you have done compared to what you could have done.
- Victory is always worth the struggle.
- The journey is the reward.
- Everything is possible for those who believe.
- You don't pay a price for success; you pay a price for failure.
- What you resist, persists.
- What you want, wants you.
- Don't let anyone steal your dreams.
- It is never over until you win.
- You are never defeated until you quit.
- Winners never quit and quitters never win.
- Don't confuse temporary failures with total defeat.
- Obstacles are just stepping stones along the way.
- Riches do not respond to wishes.
- You can get everything in life you want if you just help enough other people get in life what they want.

- You can only build as high up as your foundation is deep.
- A Master is the person who has mastered the basics.
- Believe it and then you will see it.
- Faith is the substance of things hoped for, the evidence of things not seen. Walk by faith, not by sight.
- Deny what your senses tell you. Hold firm to your conviction and believe that what you hold clearly in your mind as a desire will become your reality. Then your dream will manifest in your life.
- Yesterday is history, tomorrow is a mystery, but today is a gift. That is why it is called the present.
- Live your life with passion.
- You can if you think you can.
- Whatever the mind of man can conceive and bring itself to believe, it can achieve.
- Whatever you measure, will get done.
- Focus on what you want, not what you don't want.
- Success is a journey, not a destination.
- Pray to understand others, not to be understood; to hear others, not to be heard; to respect others, not to be respected.
- Success is the progressive realization of a dream.
- Be happy now.
- People don't care how much you know until they first know how much you care.
- Worry is negative goal-setting. It is thinking about what you don't want to happen.
- The secret of living is giving.
- What you sow, you will reap.
- You are the pure expression of God's love. Just as God is love, so are you. You are love.
- Life is for laughing, loving, and living.
- Lead, follow, or get out of the way.

- A living is made 9 to 5, but a fortune is made working nights and weekends.
- You have to put in before you can take out.
- Practice delayed gratification.
- When faced with a mountain, do not quit. Build a tunnel through it, climb over it, go around it, fly over it, or just stay and turn that mountain into a gold mine.
- It's not just what you know. It is what you do with what you know.
- Success is a decision away.
- It's not what happens to you; it is how you respond to what happens to you.
- It's not your aptitude but your attitude that will determine your altitude in life.
- When life gives you lemons, make lemonade.
- In every adversity are the seeds of a greater benefit.
- Pressure turns coal into diamonds. When under pressure, know you are being turned into a diamond.
- When you mine gold, you move tons of dirt to find just a few ounces of gold. But you are not looking for the dirt, you are looking for the gold. In your life, don't look for the dirt; look for the gold in every situation.
- You can if you think you can; it is the thinking that makes it so.
- You will never hit a goal you can't see, and you will never hit a goal you don't have.
- The way you do anything is the way you do everything. Always do your best, even when no one is watching.
- Your mind is like a parachute; it only works when it is open.
- When you must, you can, and you will.
- The rich man said, "Do as I did, say as I said, and most importantly, think as I thought when I was where you are, and you will have what I have."

- Put all your eggs in one basket, then watch that basket. Focus on ONE chief aim.
- The theory of throwing a lot of stuff against the wall and seeing what will stick is a lie. You have to have singleness of purpose, focusing on one goal if you want to attain it.
- Successful people are always too busy doing what the other guys are still talking about.
- Successful people are always doing what the other guys are too good to do.
- If you want things in your life to change, you have to change things in your life.
- Stop trying to change others or make others better. Change yourself and make yourself better. Be the change you want to see in the world.
- You are either growing or dying, going up or down, getting better or worse. You are never static.
- Things that get measured get attention and results. Chart your progress. Manage everything in your life and business with measurable, quantifiable statistics using graphs.
- If you don't love yourself, no one else will.
- Only people in pain do painful things to others. Those who are suffering create suffering. Those who are confused do confusing things.
- Things that get scheduled get done.
- Plan your work and work your plan.
- Attaining things will not bring you happiness. But being happy will bring you things.
- Nothing will ever be attempted if all possible objections must first be overcome.
- Never, never, never quit.

Do these things, follow the pattern for success, and if you do, I know I will see you all on the beaches of the world.

Much love,
Kevin Trudeau

———•———

"First they ignore you, then they laugh at you, then they fight you, then you win."   — GANDHI

———•———

"Great spirits have always encountered violent opposition from mediocre minds."   —ALBERT EINSTEIN

———•———

My Personal Declaration

"I now declare that I am the creator of my reality.
These are the wishes I command into being:"

My Commitments

"I commit to living in alignment with my highest vision
and to commanding into reality the life I desire."

481

Who Is Kevin Trudeau?

Kevin Trudeau is not just a man. He is a phenomenon, a movement, and a revolutionary force in the evolution of human potential. He is called the #1 Success Coach in the world and the World's Greatest Mentor. Kevin is one of the most unique, controversial, and impressive success stories in history. He's been called many things: a marketing genius, a spiritually enlightened guru and master, a whistleblower, a modern-day Nostradamus, a multibillion-dollar international business tycoon—and even "The Most Interesting Man in the World." After nearly fifteen years away from the spotlight, Kevin Trudeau has returned with a single mission: to reveal hidden truths, empower the masses, and spark a global transformation of health, wealth, and consciousness.

Kevin's mission is to empower the powerless and help increase the quality of life and standard of living for people all around the world. Kevin wants to take you out of your "trance" and help release the power and greatness that lives within every person.

For those who seek more out of life, and liberation from conventional thinking and systemic control, Kevin Trudeau is not merely an option—he is a necessity.

A LEGENDARY RISE

Kevin Trudeau's life reads like a mythic journey. Born into a working-class family—his father a union welder, his mother a homemaker—Kevin overcame significant childhood hurdles: a speech impediment, a learning disability, no higher formal education, and growing up on the "wrong side of the tracks." But these early struggles could not suppress his visionary drive.

483

Kevin was born with unique abilities and gifts, including the ability to "see energy" and "move energy with his mind." He entered into higher dimensions and experienced "oneness" and spiritual SELF realization. Kevin was "awakened", enlightened, and SELF aware.

His life changed forever, however, when he met a mysterious mentor he called his "Uncle," a high-ranking member of an elite global organization known only to a select few: *The Brotherhood*. Under this mentor's and other high-ranking members' guidance in that "secret society," Kevin received a secret education in esoteric wisdom, influence, and the hidden levers of global power. Kevin was taught how to expand his abilities and control them. Kevin would work with people in the highest power positions in the world: royalty, presidents, prime ministers, and other members of the global elite. Kevin spent time in presidential and royal palaces, and would be a regular attendee at Bilderberg, Bohemian Grove, and other elite meetings, where the most powerful and influential people in the world would gather.

BUSINESS MASTERMIND

Kevin Trudeau became a self-made business magnate, having launched over a hundred companies spanning health, publishing, media, and personal development—with cumulative revenues exceeding an estimated $25 billion in today's dollars. Kevin became one of the greatest copywriters and mass communicators of all time as well as a fearless free speech, natural health freedoms, and consumer advocate. In the 1990s he transformed the infomercial industry, becoming its most iconic figure.

Dubbed "the Infomercial King" and "the greatest mass communicator of all time," Kevin's media impact has been acknowledged by leading publications:

- "America's Marketing Guru" – *Wall Street Journal*
- "The Master of Modern-Day Marketing" – *New York Times*
- "A Marketing and Business Genius" – *Chicago Tribune*

Beyond commerce, Kevin created cutting-edge educational platforms, founded international media outlets and TV networks, and launched the first-ever, $3 million prize International Pool Tour, revolutionizing the sport of billiards.

BEST-SELLING AUTHOR AND LIFE COACH

Kevin Trudeau is the author of multiple international #1 *New York Times* bestsellers, including the record-breaking *Natural Cures "They" Don't Want You to Know About*, which remained #1 on *The New York Times* bestseller list for 26 weeks in a row and sold over 50 million copies. It was the best-selling book in America the year it was first published. His body of work—spanning over 100 million books and audio programs sold—has positively changed lives worldwide.

His teachings include:

- Mastering the Law of Attraction
- Achieving lasting financial freedom
- Revealing the secrets of direct marketing
- Mastering the art of communication
- Restoring health through natural, suppressed cures
- Living in bliss, abundance, and spiritual harmony

His flagship Success Mastery Course and the Your Wish Is Your Command program are regarded as some of the most impactful personal development programs in modern history.

His Science of Personal Mastery Course contains some of the secret training Kevin received in the Brotherhood, revealing for the first time in history, the lessons and methods taught within that ultra-secret society.

SPIRITUAL LEADER AND HUMANITARIAN

Kevin's journey of transformation extended beyond the material. He has trained with mystics, gurus, monks, and yogis, exploring ancient wisdom and spiritual science across the globe—from sacred caves in the Himalayas to ashrams.

His spiritual training includes:

- Shaolin kung fu with Master Shi Yan Ming
- Advanced yoga and meditation disciplines
- Tai chi and qigong training with Grand Master Tsai
- Intensive studies in the Vedas, Zohar, Kabbalah, and Hermetic teachings

Kevin is also a philanthropist, having anonymously donated hundreds of millions of dollars to educational, health, and humanitarian causes. His true impact lies not in material wealth, but in lives elevated through self-empowerment and enlightenment.

As Kevin often says:

"I am nothing special. I am a humble servant. The Divine Light that shines in me, shines in you."

THE PERSECUTED PROPHET

Trudeau's rise triggered fierce resistance from entrenched interests. For challenging the pharmaceutical-industrial complex, exposing government overreach, and speaking inconvenient truths, he faced relentless persecution.

His crime? Being a whistleblower who exposed corporate, media, and government corruption at the highest levels, publishing contro-versial books, and defying a system threatened by transparency. He was sentenced to nearly a decade in prison for the "non-crime" of contempt of court—without a victim, without fraud, without a single harmed customer.

Meanwhile, tech giants shadow-banned him, media outlets launched smear campaigns, and federal agencies sought to silence him. But the people stood by him. Over 100 million supporters around the world continue to share his work, protect his legacy, and amplify his message.

A Voice for the Voiceless

Kevin Trudeau has always spoken truth to power. He teaches that every individual holds within them vast, untapped potential—suppressed by conditioning, fear, and disinformation. As Kevin states, "You were born to win, but programmed to lose."

His core teachings empower people to:

- Cultivate joy, peace, and fulfillment
- Turn their dreams into reality
- Reclaim their health from mainstream suppression
- Master the laws of energy, karma, and spiritual growth
- Achieve financial independence
- Attain spiritual awakening, liberation, and freedom

He is being called the World's Greatest Mentor and the #1 Success Coach in the World.

The Return of a Master

Kevin Trudeau is back. And this time, he's revealing what was once considered too powerful, too sacred, or too dangerous to share. Kevin *knows* this information, instead of just *knowing about* this information. Kevin has gained never-before-revealed knowledge and wisdom from his thirty-year membership in the Brotherhood, reaching its highest level and being on its Inner Circle Council, as well as through his unique international personal experience and tapping into the "universal field," or "Akash."

Through live events, exclusive trainings, private coaching, and books, Kevin is unveiling the most potent tools and teachings ever offered to the public to improve conditions in every area of life. Kevin helps the able be more able.

His renewed mission includes:

– Teaching you how to be Happy, Healthy, and Wealthy
– Exposing the lies "they" don't want you to know
– Awakening you and taking you out of your "trance"
– Bringing you spiritual liberation and freedom
– Giving you inner peace, joy, and bliss
– Helping you be, do, and have anything and everything you desire

A GLOBAL IMPACT

Kevin has personally addressed over five million people in live events across 60+ countries. He's appeared on virtually every major media platform—CNN, FOX, ABC, CBS, NBC, CNBC, *The Howard Stern Show*, *Rush Limbaugh*, *Mancow*, and more.

Front-page headlines and magazine covers have documented his influence:

– *Wall Street Journal, New York Times, London Times, Sydney Times, Los Angeles Times*
– *Time, Newsweek, U.S. News and World Report*, and dozens more

He was a distinguished member of the World Masters of Business—alongside figures like Mikhail Gorbachev and General Norman Schwarzkopf. He has shared the stage with legends like Zig Ziglar, Brian Tracy and Charlie "Tremendous" Jones. Kevin was also one of the founding speakers on the Masters of Success program.

The Man Behind the Legend

Despite the headlines and history-making milestones, Kevin Trudeau remains grounded. He meditates, maintains a fitness routine, and maintains an unwavering dedication to lifelong learning. At 60, he competed and triumphed in physical fitness competitions against athletes half his age.

He has lived in over a dozen countries, traveled to every U.S. state, and holds stamps from over 100 nations. He bridges cultures, classes, and paradigms with ease.

But his greatest legacy is not what he has achieved—it is what he enables others to achieve.

As Kevin states, "It is not what you attain in life, it is who you become that is important."

Kevin is dedicated to selfless service of others and humanitarian causes. Increasing social and financial equality through opportunity, increasing love and compassion, as well as understanding and acceptance, are forefront in Kevin's goals. Ending racism, prejudice, hate, misinformation, censorship, and "Fake News" are some of Kevin's passions.

Why You Should Listen

Kevin Trudeau does not deal in theory. He teaches what he has mastered. From building billion-dollar companies to decoding ancient spiritual wisdom, from overcoming persecution and adversity, to igniting global movements—he has lived it all. Due to his extraordinary ongoing spiritual development and exhibited "mental and energetic powers," he has been called by people that know him well such things as: Guru; Enlightened; SELF Realized; A Perfected Spiritual Master; Sage; Seer; Psychic; Channel; Clairvoyant; Medium.

Kevin states:

"I am nothing special. I am a humble servant and student of my spiritual "Master." I am what you know that I am. I am what you see. I am the same as you. The only difference is I am awake, and you are still asleep."

Kevin also states:

"God (or Source, Consciousness, The Universe, or whatever term you choose to use) dwells within everyone equally. God is in us, AS us. The same Divine light that is within me dwells within everyone. I am simply aware of it. We are all an expression and extension of the same ONE consciousness/energy that is all things."

A partial list of Kevin Trudeau's many past accomplishments includes:

- Founder of the American Memory Institute, which became the largest memory training school in the world with over five million students worldwide, and author of the book and home study course *Mega Memory*
- Founder of the TruStar Global Media group, which included Golf TV UK, Shop America (a TV home shopping channel in the UK), and YOU TV (an inspirational TV channel in the UK)
- Host of *The Kevin Trudeau Radio Show* (estimated over 100 million listeners worldwide)
- Co-host of The Debbie and Kevin Show (both on radio and TV)
- Builder of a multibillion-dollar global business in over 150 countries
- Consumer, natural health, and free speech advocate
- Whistleblower and exposer of corporate and government corruption
- Philanthropist who has given away much of his fortune over the last thirty years

— Author of over a hundred courses, including the Success Mastery Course, The Science of Personal Mastery Course, Your Wish Is Your Command, How Anyone Can Make Millions, and The Money Making Secrets They Don't Want You to Know About

— A motivational/inspirational speaker with over five million attendees worldwide

— Dubbed Mr. Enthusiasm, Mr. Motivation, and Mr. Positivity

Kevin Trudeau was taught "The Secrets of Success" in his Brotherhood training, which included how to:

— Release the power of the mind

— "Move" energy

— See the future

— Influence other people

— Mass communication techniques

— Manifest and create what you want in life

— Make millions and get rich

— Develop dynamic physical health

— Control emotions and rid the mind and body of negativity

— The cause of uncontrollable and irrational emotions and how to eliminate them

— The secrets of karma and the Law of Attraction

— How the world really is run and controlled

— And much more

Kevin would go on to read over five thousand books and attend hundreds of seminars, workshops, and training programs on these subjects. He also studied, in depth, quantum and atomic physics; the mechanics of how the mind works; yoga; tai chi; qigong; and many other ancient methods and systems that produce health, wealth, and happiness.

"The difference between you and I is: I am awake, and you are still asleep. My goal is to awaken you—to take you out of your trance, to have you become aware of who you truly are."

—KEVIN TRUDEAU

"TO BE THE BEST, YOU MUST LEARN FROM THE BEST."

If you seek:

- Financial freedom
- Vibrant health
- Deep joy
- True awakening

Then your time has come. Kevin Trudeau is back—and the knowledge he brings may be the catalyst your life has been waiting for.

LISTEN. LEARN. AWAKEN.

He is Kevin Trudeau. The most interesting man in the world.

"You are the pure expression and extension of God's love. Just as God is love, so are you. You are love. God dwells within you, as you."

—KEVIN TRUDEAU

"First they ignore you, then they laugh at you, then they fight you, then you win."

—GANDHI

"Great spirits have always encountered violent opposition from mediocre minds."

—ALBERT EINSTEIN

Read What People Are Saying About Kevin Trudeau:

I've done the Money Processes and Relationship Processes. And had one-on-ones with Kevin. I see lights and feel energy moving up my spine during the training. I feel expanded and I feel like all these things have cleared. Negative energy and emotions are out of my field. People notice the difference. **Everything in my life is going better.** *I smile all day and things in life simply don't bother me anymore. I feel better than ever.*

Joining GIN and being a partner with Kevin has been the best thing I've ever done. **I feel free and liberated from worry, stress, and anxiety. I'm making more money than ever before.** *My health has improved. My relationships have improved. Most of my debts have almost miraculously been paid off, and I'm earning more money than ever before. Every aspect of my life is better. Thank you, Kevin. You are amazing!*

Since joining GIN and being a partner with Kevin, my life now is magical. **I've lost 30 pounds,** *got multiple job offers paying much more than my current job, and even got an offer to go into business with a local multimillionaire. How this all works I don't fully understand, but the power that Kevin gives, in addition to the specific techniques, create the perfect scenario for prosperity, abundance, and success. Blessings are now coming into my life without any effort. This is amazing and awesome!*

When I came into contact with Kevin, I was suffering from depression and bouts of anger. Everything in my life was hard. I was behind in my bills. Within three months, my whole life has changed and most importantly, I have changed. I am happy and full of joy every day. I smile and love life. All my bills are now paid. Being a partner with Kevin and a member of GIN is **like tapping into Kevin's power and energy and getting his blessings by being connected to him.** *This man is special.*

---

*After doing the Relationship Processes, a few weeks later, **I met my soulmate in an unrealistic way**. We've been together now for over a year, in the best relationship I've ever had. The best decision I've ever made is associating with Kevin and listening to his teachings.*

———————

*I sent a question to Kevin as a partner in the Kevin Trudeau Fan Club. That night before I went to sleep, **Kevin came to me like in a dream**, but I wasn't sleeping. It was like he was in the room. He told me to get some paper and a pen and write down the answer. I did. Then I felt like I came out of this dream and I was sitting on the bed. I looked at the paper and read what I wrote. It was the perfect answer. Two days later, on the partner call, Kevin read my question and gave the answer. It was almost word for word what I wrote down. Who do you listen to? Kevin Trudeau.*

———————

*Kevin is a magician. **I was blown away by his sense of compassion and caring**. He always desires the best for me and everyone around him. Since following the **Your Wish is Your Command** techniques, miracles are happening in my life on a regular basis.*

———————

*Within a week after doing the Money Processes, **I unexpectedly received a $90,000 check in the mail**. Awesome. It is now six months later and my business income and **profits have almost doubled without any more effort**.*

———————

*I've been looking at my business numbers every day for a year, and they're always the same. I did the Money Processes. The day after, **magically, the numbers went up 50%**. Nobody in the company could believe it. They've maintained that increase ever since, and now are going up even more. The Money Processes are magical, miraculous, and more powerful than anyone could imagine.*

———————

During my session with Kevin, I felt tingling over my entire body. **I'm now feeling lighter, brighter, energized.** *I'm taking action, and my posture has improved.*

———————

The Money Processes changed everything for me. I'm a sales consultant for Honda, and **I just manifested $5,000 in a few hours on one deal!**

———————

I think the Money Processes will go down someday as one of **the most profound three-day courses in history.**

———————

Kevin, in three days have given me **more than I received in two years at Yale University's MBA program** *and for a lot less money. Plus the results are infinitely better!*

———————

Since I completed the Money Processes, I realize I've already **made back 10 times the price of the course.**

———————

I've gone through all success training from Tony Robbins, Joe Dispenza, Joe Batali, Bob Proctor, and many more. I've read many of the books on the Law of Attraction. Kevin's training is by far the best I have ever taken or even thought about. **I feel like I'm walking on the moon.** *He and his teachings are truly life-changing. They are one of a kind and totally unique. They create better and faster results and give you a sense of complete knowingness and understanding.*

———————

I did **Three Keys to Internet Millions** *course and was blown away. I am an internet marketing expert and copywriting expert — so I thought. What Kevin teaches us no one knows. Since applying his techniques (that I've never heard before)* **every aspect of my business is more profitable** *and* **I'm spending a lot less time working** *the business. Kevin is amazing.*

———————

Resources

Book Recommendations

The Secret by Rhonda Byrne

It Works! The Famous Little Red Book That Makes Your Dreams Come True! by R.H. Jarrett

Think and Grow Rich by Napoleon Hill

See You at The Top by Zig Ziglar

How to Win Friends and Influence People by Dale Carnegie

The Magic of Thinking Big by David J. Schwartz

Psycho-Cybernetics by Maxwell Maltz (Use 1960 version)

The Magic of Believing by Claude M. Bristol

Ask and It Is Given by Esther and Jerry Hicks (The Teachings of Abraham)

The Go Getter by Peter B. Kyne

The Law of Success in 16 Lessons by Napoleon Hill – There are two versions, one published in 1925 by Vieux and one published in 1927. We suggest you read both versions.

How to Have Confidence and Power in Dealing With People by Les Giblin

What to Say When You Talk to Yourself by Shad Helmstetter

Success Through a Positive Mental Attitude by Napoleon Hill and W. Clement Stone

How to Solve All Your Money Problems Forever by Victor Boe

Skill with People by Les Giblin

The Go-Giver by Bob Burg

The Art of Dealing with People by Les Giblin

Karmic Management by Geshe Michael Roach,
Lama Christie McNally, Michael Gordon

Richard Hittleman's Yoga: 28 Day Exercise Plan
by Richard Hittleman

The Science of Getting Rich by Wallace D. Wattles

The Sedona Method by Hale Dwoskin

Becoming Rich by Doug Wead and Dexter Yager

The Diamond Cutter by Geshe Michael Roach and
Lama Christie McNally

Natural Cures "They" Don't Want You to Know About
by Kevin Trudeau

Dress for Success by John T. Molloy

The Power of the Subconscious Mind by Joseph Murphy

The Greatest Salesman in the World by Og Mandino

The Game of Work by Charles Coonradt

The 7 Habits of Highly Effective People by Stephen R. Covey

The Alchemist by Paulo Coelho

The Richest Man in Babylon by George S. Clason

A Happy Pocket Full of Money by David Cameron Gikandi

The Obstacle Is the Way by Ryan Holiday

Nuggets of Gold for Happiness, Joy & Bliss by Kevin Trudeau

Nuggets of Gold for Total Success in Life by Kevin Trudeau

Also by Kevin Trudeau:

**Natural Cures
"They" Don't Want You
to Know About**

**More
Natural Cures
Revealed**

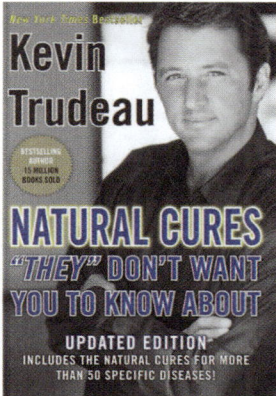

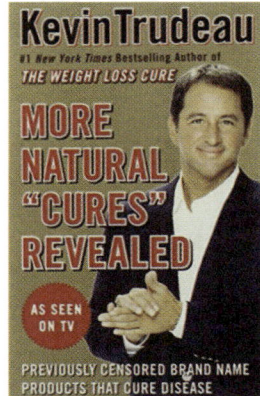

The Weight Loss Cure

Debt Cures

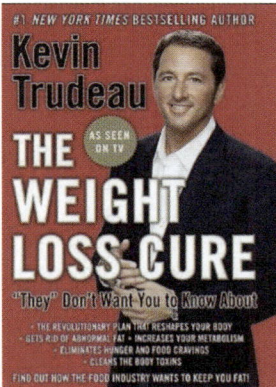

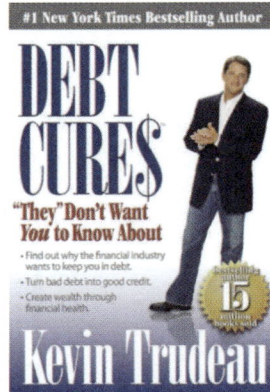

KevinTrudeau.com

Scan Here:

Get the AUDIO version

of this book

read by Kevin Trudeau himself AND the original audios of the live event that this book is based on!

For more information visit:
YourWishAudioBook.com

Or Scan This QR Code:

Get

One-on-One LIVE virtual
Personal Coaching
with Kevin Trudeau

The #1 Success Coach in the world
and the **World's Greatest Mentor**

*"I just had one on one Zoom session with Kevin.
All I can say: wow!!!"*

*"After I did a one-on-one session it was incredible.
Everything in my life has changed for the better.
I paid off debt. I tripled my income."*

Book a Session at:
1on1withkevin.com

Or Scan This QR Code:

Hire Kevin Trudeau to speak at your event and **Learn more** about all that Kevin Trudeau has to offer at:

KevinTrudeau.com

Join the
#1 Success Club
IN THE WORLD...

The
Global Information Network!

Get more information about Kevin Trudeau's
International Success Club.

Get access to his *Success Mastery Course* and his
100 Lesson *Science of Personal Mastery Course*.

<u>Meet Kevin Trudeau in person!</u>

Watch an interview with Kevin Trudeau at:
GlobalInformationNetwork.com

Become a "Partner" with **Kevin Trudeau!**

MAKE MORE MONEY

Learn from the World's #1 Marketing Expert.

Be tutored by the
#1 Success Coach in the World and
the World's Greatest Mentor.

Get a LIVE ZOOM call with Kevin every month where Kevin answers Partner's questions for just $25 a month.

By being a "Partner" you can learn directly from Kevin Trudeau. To be the best you must learn from the best.

"When I decided to become a Partner I was skeptical. But miraculously, a week after I joined, my income DOUBLED!"
Mohammad R.

"Since becoming a Partner... I got a job that TRIPLED my income! I now have a Mercedes 100% paid for, and I am happier and more at peace than ever before. And all this happened in just a few months after becoming a Partner."
Stephen M.

YOU could get FREE gifts valued over $65,000 when you become a Partner with Kevin Trudeau right away! This offer could expire any day!

Watch a RARE interview with Kevin Trudeau discussing the Partner program

KevinTrudeauPartners.com

Or Scan This QR Code:

You can make money while you sleep!

There are 3 Keys to Internet Millions:
- Communication Secrets
- Copywriting Secrets
- Internet Marketing Secrets

Learn from the Master of Modern-Day Marketing, **Kevin Trudeau**

With the Internet today, it's easier than ever to make money

Kevin Trudeau has generated billions in sales across multiple marketing platforms. People always wondered how he can virtually PRINT MONEY in ANY marketing platform.

That's because they don't know the secrets that Kevin Trudeau will share with YOU in his "3 Keys to Internet Millions" online course!

People want you to think it's hard to make money online. The OPPOSITE is true when you know the real secrets of sales and marketing. Plus, you don't need ANY experience at all!

You can make money while you sleep when you know the "3 Keys to Internet Millions"!

"Using Kevin's communication methods allowed me to modify my advertising in my company, increasing sales over 60% in just 3 months! Awesome!"   *– JS*

"Wow, Kevin, you have been giving this course away. This course should and could be sold for $10,000 or more. I've taken multiple courses and what I've learned here I've never seen before. This was 1000x my investment. Thank you!"   *– JD*

"Using Kevin's methods, our newest marketing campaign has generated 10X more profit than ever before!"

Get more information at:
ThreeKeystoMillions.com

Or Scan This QR Code:

Instant Love!
Attract the love of your life!
You CAN have the relationship of your dreams!

There are 33 COUNTER INTENTIONS in your subconscious mind STOPPING you from having the passionate loving relationship you want and crave.

Kevin Trudeau can ELIMINATE those counter intentions so you can manifest the romantic relationship you deserve, faster and easier than ever before. Do the "Relationship Processes" and all your relationships will get better than you ever imagined.

"I did just ONE Process. When I went home, my wife was nicer to me than ever before and seduced me into having passionate sex!"

"I did 10 Processes. I have not been on a date in 2 years. But in the last month, I have been asked out by beautiful sexy women! THEY come up to me. This is awesome!"

"Men are just walking up to me...AND they are all AMAZING, HIGH QUALITY MEN!"

Your dream relationship could be closer than you think!

Watch the video with Kevin Trudeau answering questions about relationships:
Relationship-Processes.com

Or Scan This QR Code:

Awaken your **_dormant_**

"SUPERPOWERS"

If a prisoner has been shackled their whole life, then is released, are they weak? YES! They have forgotten how to do the most basic things that everyone takes for granted. They are timid.

Think about your own life. What if **you are powerful beyond measure**—but have simply forgotten this truth? Are you powerful enough to break free from the "shackles"? It may feel like you are not, but this is a lie.

You are a sleeping giant. There is awesome power within you, but it is asleep. It is dormant.

You can awaken to your true potential sooner than you may think. You don't do it by "breathing fire" or "walking on hot coals". Therapy or "psychedelics" won't do it. Affirmations and motivational speeches won't either.

Learn more about what can PERMANENTLY awaken the giant within at:
TheSuperpowerProcesses.com

Or Scan This QR Code:

ELIMINATE
YOUR Failure habits
NOW!

Kevin Trudeau has a powerful "Process" that **STOPS your failure habits** in its tracks. These Processes **stop your self-sabotage HABITS**, makes you aware of them, allowing you to ***replace them with SUCCESS habits***. This is a critical key element for your success.

We all live by habit. Most of you live by failure habits. Winners live by success habits.

The ACCELERATOR Processes make everything Kevin Trudeau teaches work FASTER and EASIER because they energetically blow out your failure habits and increase your self-awareness. You will feel more powerful and in control.

Get more information at:
AcceleratorProcesses.com

Or Scan This QR Code:

Watch Kevin for **FREE** every week on his Podcast

The Kevin Trudeau Show: LIMITLESS

Available on:

FOLLOW KEVIN ON SOCIAL MEDIA

Instagram   @thekevintrudeau

TikTok   @thekevintrudeau

X   @thekevintrudeau

facebook   @theofficialkevintrudeau

LinkedIn   @thekevintrudeau

Get free training from Kevin Trudeau on Telegram:

@TheKevinTrudeauFanClubChannel

Get the **WORLD'S BEST** Vitamins,
Minerals, and Supplements
recommended AND
used by Kevin Trudeau himself!

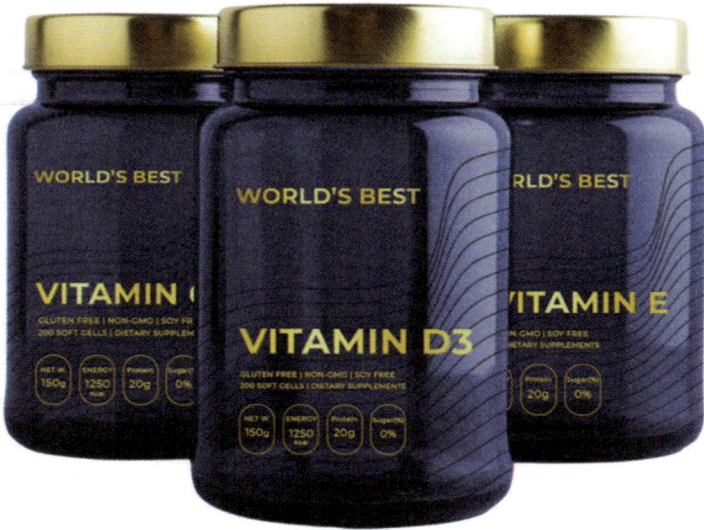